THREE WISE MONKEYS

THREE WISE MONKEYS

Iwazaru — 'Speak No Evil'

III

The Quest for Wealth without Work:
The Lourenço Marques Lottery, Protestant
Panics and the South African White
Working Classes, circa 1890–1965

Charles van Onselen

Jonathan Ball Publishers
Johannesburg · Cape Town

Published in South Africa in 2023 by
JONATHAN BALL PUBLISHERS
A division of Media24 (Pty) Ltd
PO Box 33977
Jeppestown
2043

ISBN 978-1-77619-248-9
ebook ISBN 978-1-77619-249-6

*Every effort has been made to trace the copyright
holders and to obtain their permission for the use of
copyright material. The publishers apologise for any
errors or omissions and would be grateful to be notified
of any corrections that should be incorporated in future
editions of this book.*

jonathanball.co.za
twitter.com/JonathanBallPub
facebook.com/JonathanBallPublishers

Cover and slipcase design by MR Design
Design and typesetting by MR Design Proofreading
by Paul Wise
Index by George Claassen
Set in Garamond

CONTENTS

The Three Wise Monkeys in Imperial and
Colonial Southern Africa .... **IX**

Preface **3**

Introduction **11**

IWAZARU – 'SPEAK NO EVIL'

I | Infection **19**

II | Headaches **55**

III | Sweating **99**

IV | Fever **135**

V | Nausea **201**

VI | Relapse **247**

Postscript **261**

Select Bibliography **270**

Acknowledgements **274**

Notes **277**

Index **306**

After some hesitation, indeed, something more than
hesitation, he confessed that, though he had never received
any injury of the sort named, yet, about the time in question,
he had in fact been taken with a brain fever, losing his mind
completely for a considerable interval.
HERMAN MELVILLE, *THE CONFIDENCE MAN* (1857)

'Tis surprising to see how rapidly a panic will sometimes
run through a country. All nations and ages have been
subject to them ... Yet panics, in some cases, have their uses;
they produce as much good as hurt. Their duration is always
short; the mind soon grows through them, and acquires
a firmer habit than before. But their peculiar advantage
is, that they are the touchstones of sincerity and hypocrisy,
and bring things and men to light, which might otherwise
have lain forever undiscovered ... They sift out the hidden
thoughts of man, and hold them up in public to the world.
TOM PAINE, *THE AMERICAN CRISIS*,
23 DECEMBER 1776

THE THREE WISE MONKEYS IN IMPERIAL AND COLONIAL SOUTHERN AFRICA

The origins of the three wise monkeys, some speculate, lie in Hinduism, and the maxims surrounding them made their way into the wider world via the Silk Road. Confronted with the choice of going east or west, the monkeys went east, where, they believed, they were more likely to find succour than in the west. Their wisdom was readily adopted, perhaps adapted, by Confucius, making an early appearance in his *Analects* hundreds of years before the Christian era. In the 16th century, Buddhist monks, valuing their lessons, ferried them silently across the South China Sea to take up residence in Japan.

By then seasoned travellers, the monkeys moved easily through the forest of ancient religions abounding on Honshū Island. It was with Koshin, God of the Roads, a friend to Buddhist, Shinto and Taoist wanderers alike, that they felt most at home. Fittingly, they are honoured on a carved wooden panel at the Toshogu Shrine, at Nikkō, in the region where they were widely respected.

How, why or by whom the three were smuggled into the Anglophone world is unclear, but it took some time. Only in the 20th century did they put in an appearance in Western popular culture. An air of mystery clung to them and, perhaps incongruously, they were occasionally reported as having been seen in military arenas where notions of discipline and obedience are always de rigueur. By then, however, their wisdom may already have undergone a rather subtle cultural twist.

In their earliest Eastern setting, the messages of the primates may have come across as a positive proactive injunction to those seeking to live the good life and cultivate a sense of tranquillity. Evil in its many forms existed; it was rooted in place, totem-like. Those in search of wisdom should be pre-emptive and *do something* to avoid it by averting their eyes, not listening to it or speaking of it. Evil was fixed, but intelligent people could navigate their way around it. By acknowledging its existence and acting, the potential for evil could be minimised.

But something had been lost in translation by the time that *Mizaru*, *Kikazaru* and *Iwazaru* got to whisper to English speakers in their customary hushed tones. Wickedness still existed, as it did, always, everywhere, but it was no longer static; it was mobile and on the move towards people. And so, instead of being proactive and doing something, as back in the East, folk needed to sit tight and *do nothing* – see no evil, hear no evil and speak no evil. It was as if people were urged to recognise the presence of evil, and then promptly to deny its existence.

The wisdom of the Three Wise Monkeys came to southern Africa via English, from the West, replete with a cultural coding that encouraged settler ideologies of denial, rootedness and silence when confronted by moral ambiguities. In a setting where colonialism and imperialism posed questions of profound ethical importance about issues of conquest, occupation and gross dispossession, the willingness to see no evil, hear no evil and speak no evil held some appeal. How those ancient directives – in both their old active and new passive form – helped shape the deeply entangled social history of 20th-century South Africa and Mozambique is the subject of these three volumes. Only by seeing, hearing and speaking honestly about the past can we hope to understand a troubled present.

THREE WISE MONKEYS

PREFACE

GAMBLING VIEWED THROUGH
A WIDE-ANGLE LENS

When as a young and unknown man I started
to be successful I was referred to as a gambler.
My operations increased in scope. Then I was a
speculator. The sphere of my activities continued
to expand and presently I was known as a banker.
Actually, I had been doing the same thing all the time.
ATTRIBUTED TO SIR ERNEST CASSEL (1852–1921),
MERCHANT BANKER

The nature of markets and the 'animal spirits' that are said to drive them are impossible to determine with certainty. If we follow John Maynard Keynes, the desire 'to do something positive', to risk or to speculate – either individually or collectively – is part of the DNA of human beings. Capitalism is portrayed as being part of the 'natural' order of things, a sometimes reluctantly accepted truth that helps shape the world we live in. This widely accepted secular wisdom, oftentimes conceded with a sigh, is seldom checked against religious prescripts.

The parable of the talents (Matthew 25:14–30) prioritises investment and speculation, along with the hidden elements of gambling and risk-taking, over the mere retention of capital. Money, if not the people who are lucky enough to possess it, must *work*. Elsewhere, the Bible provides little explicit guidance as to how to reconcile the elements of gambling and investment, and a lottery, or 'drawing of lots', was not unheard of among Jesus' disciples. Somewhere between the 'animal spirits' and the productive deployment of capital, then, lies a zone of ethical uncertainty, a space that post-Reformation Calvinists somehow occupied successfully, giving rise to Max Weber's 'Protestant ethic', which helped promote Western capitalism.

In this shadowy cognitive world, capitalism and Protestantism grow up, side by side, in an uneasy relationship – at times complementary, at others contested – as they compete to reach the sunlight of material prosperity. Capitalism thrives on 'booms', a non-pejorative term that hints, only in passing, at human irrationality or mental instability. Periodic surges in risk-taking and investment are generally welcomed because they provide the fuel for commercial or industrial expansion in the never-ending pursuit of profit. Protestant churches might regard these surges sceptically, but they are seldom condemned outright as mere manifestations of greed centred on speculative gain, and thus tend not to gain mainstream party-political traction. Calvinism avoids a head-on collision with capitalist excesses, choosing instead to attack it from the rear, insisting that wealth can only be legitimately acquired through 'work', undefined.

Investment bankers work. But so, too, do those who dig ditches, even though a Grand Canyon separates the nature and ultimate outcomes of mental and manual labour. When bankers use their huge disposable incomes, amassed through speculation and mediated via the investment market, to acquire luxury cars, they are cast as clients, as rational, albeit slightly self-indulgent consumers, folk who contribute ultimately to the social well-being by helping to underwrite the viability of the commercial sector of the economy. But when manual labourers invest their modest, unmediated disposable incomes on horse races or lotteries, curtailing the amount that can be spent in retail outlets or other sectors of the economy, they are cast as wholly irrational spendthrifts. They are, it is suggested, undermining the wider economy, leaching household budgets of essential items such as food and threatening the reproduction of the working-class family as a source of cheap labour. Investment bankers, gambling with funds raised in the marketplace, are economically engaged, responsible citizens; ditchdiggers spending their wages are seen as caught up in parasitic, socially questionable practices. One of Calvinism's core commandments is that, for the well-off, the link between wealth and work must remain indirect, mediated and invisible, but for workers, the link must be direct, unmediated and visible. In the eyes of the church, class and notions of social responsibility differ; lottery tickets and fancy sports cars bear almost no similarity.

For ministers of religion and those sheepish capitalists bent on downplaying the speculative element in choices and lifestyles during 'booms', working-class gambling of all sorts, especially during 'slumps', is then often portrayed as being irrational. It is said to threaten the social order and to constitute a gross violation of a basic Calvinist tenet – the visible uncoupling of the acquisition of wealth from work. Notable surges in underclass gambling during recessions, unlike the mirror image of investment booms or horse racing among the rich, during economic upturns, are framed as being fever-like, as a form of mass insanity, requiring intervention from the elite and representatives of the governing classes.

It is now conveniently forgotten that the late-19th-century South African mining revolution, which seeded the development of secondary industry during the interwar years, was strongly influenced by Calvinist thinking. That thinking, which rested on its own distorted versions of predestination and a chosen people, helped give rise to a state structured along political lines that was deeply racist. And, just as capitalism and religion overlapped when it came to the silent notions that informed business investment and speculation, so race became a determining, overlapping and vocal consideration when addressing – and dividing – the black and white components of an emerging proletariat over the issue of gambling. Economically privileged white workers had to be disciplined into a more responsible approach to gambling and thereby set an example for black workers.

The marked increase in white working-class gambling along the Witwatersrand during the depression of 1906–1908 – a phenomenon that was to be repeated several times in the recessions that followed between the two world wars – beat all the basic ideological ingredients into a froth that dripped from contemporary newspaper accounts. The miners, it was said, had lost their individual and collective minds and were no longer in control of their destiny. They were suffering from a gambling and racing 'craze' that, because it could not readily be reconciled with rational, underlying Calvinist reasoning, constituted a 'social evil'. The miners were their own worst enemies: 'Many a wife and family have to go without proper food or clothing because a foolish husband has lost practically his whole month's wages in betting.' 'Eternal race meetings' undermined the work ethic and the much-prized, supposedly quintessentially Victorian 'habits of thrift and steadiness' that had underwritten the first industrial revolution. Who, then, would be surprised as to 'where the houseboy's wages go'? 'Why, we even had a coloured bookmaker here, an American Negro', a Johannesburg detective complained in 1908.

But just beneath this supposedly overriding concern for the fate of irresponsible black, and more especially white, workers lay a strong layer of commercial and financial self-interest presided over by shop-keepers and stockbrokers. Money that 'rightly belongs to creditors' was being wasted at the racecourse. 'This paper believes that a great many of the unpaid bills which are the curse of shopkeepers on the Rand remain unpaid simply because the money is gambled away at race meetings.' 'This wild gambling', the editorial continued, 'is not a healthy sign. It is unsettling to the public and very bad for legitimate business.'

White workers, who apparently formed no part of 'the public' during recessions, were undermining 'legitimate' businesses owned by the middle classes. But, it was claimed, the problem went deeper than that, making it marginally more difficult to raise capital for the mining industry from those with more disposable income than the white miners. Stockbrokers – bookmakers to the bourgeoisie and therefore of superior social standing – were also suffering. 'It is probably a fact', opined a leading Sunday newspaper, 'that the increase in betting is due to a great extent to the stagnation in the share market having driven those who once frequented the stock exchange on to the racecourse.' The results were shocking. 'There are literally hundreds of men here today [26 April 1908] who simply live by betting and there are hundreds more who lose on the course the money which rightly belongs to creditors.' The fever, as with an outbreak of cholera, was worse among the lower classes but could never be fully confined to them.

If the origin of gambling fever derived from the unleashing of 'animal spirits' during the secular cycles intrinsic to capitalist development, then the moral panics that almost invariably accompanied them were driven by religious radicals, clergymen based in Protestant churches, ranging from Baptists and Congregationalists to the three Dutch Reformed churches and their counterparts in the Presbyterian and, more especially, Methodist churches.

Capitalist investment in the stock market, driven by the rich and influential and largely uncontested by the church, made for tolerably 'good' gambling during booms, but horse racing and lotteries, more intently resorted to by social marginals and white workers during the slumps that followed, made for 'bad' gambling condemned by clergymen and editors, both groups with easy access to public platforms.

The problem for politicians intent on building, or governing, a secular democratic order amid competing religious noise is that 'good' and 'bad' gamblers alike are enfranchised, and both compete for their attention and have votes in a zone of ethical uncertainty. 'Good' gamblers have influence and money but relatively few votes, while the 'bad' gamblers frequently have more substantial electoral clout. It has all the makings of an acute political predicament – how to reconcile capitalist and working-class forms of speculation without, too obviously, resorting to ethical double standards that are class-based. Moral confusion and uncertainty around gambling in the electoral marketplace makes for party-political policies characterised by expediency at very best, and by hypocrisy at worst. It was never going to be easy. As Edward Bulwer-Lytton once observed: 'No task is more difficult than systematic hypocrisy.'

And when ethically compromised policies are translated into laws designed more for ideological gratification than effective implementation, they can give rise to discretionary legal dispensations characterised by hesitation and uncertainty. Prosecutors become reluctant to issue summonses, and magistrates and judges, sensing that a divided society sensitive to double standards around gambling is watching closely, are less inclined to impose prison sentences, and instead hand down only modest fines. This logic swiftly descends to street level, making it increasingly difficult to distinguish between arbitrary and discretionary power, thereby contributing to an environment more conducive to police bribery. But, all that said, it remains difficult to foretell how the changing balance of historical forces around games of chance will play out in a polity or economy; each case is *sui generis*. In 1994, Albania, England and South Africa, each for its own set of historically distinctive reasons, were all without national lotteries.

The United States, born of immigrant settlers seeking a transatlantic refuge from 17th-century European religious persecution, has a lengthy tradition of powerful, albeit constantly fragmenting, often mobile, Protestant militancy. The Amish may have moved into Pennsylvania and the Mormons to Utah as they sought to fine-tune their religious freedoms in regional strongholds, but, at its core, the United States remained solidly Protestant and therefore disapproving of gambling – though always welcoming of speculative capitalist investment. By the turn of the 20th century, most forms of gambling were illegal across the US, and the 1920s saw the adoption of a nationwide policy of prohibition, largely for the ideological gratification of those religious and political zealots intent on bringing church and state closer together in what nominally, and constitutionally, was a secular state.

Several American presidents were acutely aware that they were trapped in an ethical minefield that required careful navigation when formulating policies around either gambling or speculation in a capitalist universe. In January 1908, in the wake of a banking panic that precipitated a sharp recession, which had a ripple effect across the globe, Theodore Roosevelt told Congress: 'There is no moral difference between gambling at cards or in lotteries or on the racetrack and gambling in the stock market. One method is just as pernicious to the body politic as the other.' Animal spirits were as dangerous as were gambling fevers.

Although the American constitution expressly prohibited the adoption of an established church that enjoyed the protection of civil authority, the US administration found – and still finds – the dominant Protestant tradition impossible to ignore. Twentieth-century South Africa, too, did not have an established church, yet it, too, was in the thrall of militant Protestants from the turn of the century. Indeed, so strong were the voices of the three Dutch Reformed churches in the decades leading up to the electoral triumph of Afrikaner nationalists in 1948 that they might as well have constituted an established church. The National Party was led by a dominee, DF Malan, and according to him, it was the church that led the way to the party's adopting apartheid as a policy. In South Africa, it was not a party of modernising secular capitalists but a religiously inclined party of aspirant capitalists that enjoyed its strongest support in the countryside and shaped the charge against gambling. The party strongly disapproved of the uncoupling of work from wealth while simultaneously encouraging those animal spirits capable of underwriting the growth of an economy that fed into white prosperity as it sought to build political solidarity.

In their attempts to eliminate gambling fevers while encouraging investment booms, the Dutch Reformed and English Protestant churches won a significant battle when dog racing was abolished a few months before the National Party assumed office in 1948. But, after that, the pickings became thinner. As with virtually all their pre-decessors, nationalist governments virtually ignored the sport domi-nated by the financial elite of the ruling classes – horse racing – but repeatedly passed laws and regulations designed for ideological grati-fication rather than the effective elimination of football pools, pinball machines and lotteries among the under- and working classes. The deliberately orchestrated moral confusion that informed and inflated apartheid policies – the big lie – made many smaller lies around gam-bling easier to swallow. As that great historian of fashion, James Laver, once noted, 'Nothing is more revealing of an age than its hypocrisies.'

Hypocrisy is, however, a human condition as adaptable as it is enduring, and in South Africa, as elsewhere, its shelf life is indetermi-nate. The coming of a new democratic order in 1994, and the hurried passing of the Lotteries Act 57 of 1997, just 36 months later, saw the inauguration of a national lottery meant to provide significant, sustained support to charities and non-governmental organisations devoted to social upliftment in a country racked by gross inequalities.

The age-old double standard was abolished at the stroke of a pen, the lottery provided with a collar and tie and allowed to take its rightful place beside investment bankers and stockbrokers. The ethical playing field had, seemingly, been levelled, a 'new South Africa' born. But in the absence of African Protestant churches and voices that are as will-ing to challenge the ethics of gambling as they are open to question-ing the redistributive powers of capitalism in alleviating poverty, the awkward debates of the 20th century have lapsed and been replaced by fake, silent moral certainties. As already noted, every country must find its own way of balancing the speculative forces within it that help build 'a better life for all'. That journey is always *sui generis*, but a painful passage is lightened by much laughter along the way and filled with delicious ironies. Today, the National Lotteries Commission lies buried beneath a veritable avalanche of allegations of bribery, corruption, theft and nepotism, itself possessed by strange animal spirits bent only on consumption, without investment or work.

> *The gambling known as business looks with austere disfavor upon the business known as gambling.*
> AMBROSE BIERCE, *THE DEVIL'S DICTIONARY* (1906)

INTRODUCTION

L ike the frontier settlements portrayed in some American westerns, many gold-mining camps around the world metamorphosed into relatively short-lived 'towns' whose earliest days were characterised by irredeemably 'wild' behaviour. Young or middle-aged men, without access to 'respectable' young women in meaningful numbers and isolated from 'normal' family life, reverted swiftly to feral lifestyles marked by excessive drinking, gambling and whoring. Indeed, some of the charm of such films lay in the muted, optimistic, hints of 'the camp' overcoming its primitive male roots and metamorphosing into a 'civilised', gender-balanced, family 'town' with its first home-grown, blue-eyed children.

The midwife of this change from cultural chaos to a semblance of civic order – something longed for by a God-fearing majority but not by the few bad men – was often extreme violence, culminating in a sense of collective relief but at the cost of personal trauma. A good man, or a band of good men, had to clean up the camp by ridding it of a bad man, or a gang of bad hombres. That necessitated the honourable few having to examine their ethical choices and make difficult decisions about how best to exercise their individually arrived-at positions, or the collective briefing by 'good' people to expel or, if necessary, kill the purveyors of anti-social exploits whose ill-gotten gains were in danger of becoming entrenched in a community keen to establish an authentic, harmonious identity.

The key agents in bringing about the painful transition to peace and progress, the forerunners to commercial stability and more ordered profit-taking, came in many forms – the lone gunslinger with a troubled past undergoing a belated revolution in his own attitudes and values, a minister of religion hoping for a Christian moral order to manifest itself in an outpost of hell, or a tough sheriff who may or may not himself be part of the problem through bribery, corruption or manifest greed.

So much, then, for the fictionalised, romanticised image of the gold-mining camp becoming an urban embryo as portrayed on stage and screen. But when it comes to towns sprouting from mining camps, real-world changes from free-for-all frontier economics to ordered commerce or industry can sometimes be as troublesome as those portrayed in fiction. A good number of, if not most, discoveries of gold arise near alluvial deposits, the hope being that glitter in a pan of gravel taken from a pristine stream will point to the more bountiful reef origins of the precious metal. Sometimes it does – but not always. When not, it often translates into another much-loved film trope – the abandoned mining town, with its deserted dusty streets and saloon doors creaking ominously in the wind, and the hired gunslinger, the minister of religion and the honourable sheriff all long gone.

Male-dominated frontier mining economies generate excitement. Hope and promise, it would seem, then give rise to recognisable patterns of social behaviour that deviate from other, more mature urban forms lasting until such time as the underlying source of wealth either disappoints or disappears.[1] If, however, the underlying economic promise does not falter, or is exceptionally slow in its decline, mining camps can make a successful transition from camp to town, from town to industrial city and, very rarely, from industrial city to regional metropolis.

Successive sequential transitions, including the shift from commerce to primary industry supported by a sound financial infrastructure, compel changes in the comportment of most of the citizens to bring them into alignment with the demands and needs of a changing economy. The alteration in their demeanour, and the changing composition and consolidation of classes, is overseen by law-enforcement agencies of the state to ensure the collective well-being of society. But mass-based, 'anti-social' male behaviour in a mining camp cannot simply be eradicated by the brandishing of a gun or the stroke of a pen and, depending on a host of factors, can take a longer or shorter period to manage more effectively.

Situated on the most continuous and richest gold reefs the world has known, Johannesburg underwent an extraordinary sequence of changes, sprinting from a mining camp in 1886 to a town, an industrial city and then a regional metropolis in a matter of decades. Moreover, these changes took place in the context of a colonial setting, with a European minority enforcing its authority over an African majority, which it sought to tap into as an endless supply of cheap, servile, unskilled labour. Extreme violence formed an integral part of the backdrop, as well as the content, of this continual urban metamorphosis. By 1925 the city had seen an attempted armed invasion (1896), an imperial war (1899–1902), strikes calling for armed military intervention (1907 and 1913), a rebellion in the surrounding Highveld (1914) and a full-scale revolt by white miners (1922). In the same socially revolutionary era, Johannesburg was subjected to three different governments wanting the policies of city and province to come into greater alignment with a national dispensation.

Given such eye-catching conflict, it is understandable why violent clashes between mining capital and organised labour in the opening decades of the 20th century came to occupy a pivotal position in South African historiography. Historians point to the strikes and the failed revolution of 1922 as increasingly militant efforts by white miners to defend their standard of living by protecting wages and securing for themselves a structured, racially privileged position in the labour market at the expense of African workers. The same struggles helped pave the way for the coming together of Afrikaner nationalists and the Labour Party in JBM Hertzog's 'Pact' government (1924–1933), which helped entrench the position of white workers in a political economy increasingly predicated on race.

But foregrounding only the most dramatic moment of conflict comes at a price. Sharply focused, stand-alone economic and political histories cast a long shadow over other questions equally worthy of examination by those interested in what Eric Hobsbawm termed 'the history of society' rather than 'social history'. By adopting the former rather than the latter approach, we can cast additional light on the hidden continuities in class cultures and deepen our understanding of the pivotal moments in an epoch as the city moved from mining camp to regional metropolis. In Johannesburg, the creation of a racially distinctive and industrially disciplined proletariat took place not only on the factory floor, or in the mines, but downtown where an excessive number of outlets for the legal and illegal sale of alcohol, along with widespread organised prostitution, militated against social tranquillity. And, since the history of society in southern Africa remains relatively unexplored, because racial and nationalist contestations tend to take precedence over almost all other issues when setting historiographical agendas, we are free to approach a more integrated analysis from some apparently unlikely angles.

In most historical settings colonial or metropolitan – other than southern Africa – gambling in its myriad forms has emerged as a prominent feature in works exploring the making of the underclasses. Industrialisation, religion and urbanisation, along with dreams or nightmares of escaping from the strictures of hardship and poverty, if not from the working class itself, constitute central themes for those studying the evolving consciousness in different social formations. That, in and of itself, should prompt the historically curious to delve more deeply into the history of gambling in South Africa in general, and in the industrial heartland of the Witwatersrand in particular. But we lack a broad-based, dedicated study of the place that games of chance or skill – or both – occupied in the thinking of white workers or, for that matter, an overview of the success or failure of the state to keep various forms of gambling within generally acceptable, economically aligned parameters as Johannesburg assumed new forms over many decades. The early-21st-century fiasco that enveloped a South African lottery presided over by corrupt, incompetent African nationalists makes this lacuna more lamentable.

The lack of such studies is puzzling.[2] Even a casual glance at the statute books reveals how, almost without exception, legislative attempts at controlling gambling came after the discovery of precious minerals in the interior in the 1860s, and were co-terminous with the social transformations that accompanied an industrial revolution centred on Johannesburg and the Witwatersrand between the world wars. Nor will it come as a surprise to note that the bulk of the restrictive laws were passed by Afrikaner nationalist governments as demanded, for more than 70 years, by their devout Calvinist minders in the shape of the three Dutch Reformed churches from the late 19th century and well into the 20th.[3]

Laws aimed at curbing or outlawing gambling in southern Africa may, in good measure, have been cumulative in the way that they shaped the functioning of society and the underworld over the long term, but they were never implemented or enforced in linear fashion. The search for unearned income or wealth – from sources other than the sale of labour or skills as demanded by the Protestant faithful – pulsed largely to the beat of the economy and the underlying religious-ideological predilections of its ruling classes at critical junctures. But that broad generalisation does not take us very far and requires some additional refinement.

No class is born fully formed; it is continuously in the making and remaking. On the Witwatersrand, a white working class capable of, and willing to, reproduce itself in situ was assembled only gradually over more than two decades. Fortune seekers and migrant miners, unconvinced of the long-term prospects of the gold-mining industry and living in boarding houses on the frontier of empire in the 1890s, were slow to take up residence in the white working-class suburbs of Johannesburg before World War I. It was this first and second generation of workers, without the benefit of a reliable safety net supported by employers, and with a state that was slow to meaningfully underwrite the cost of education, health and housing for families, who were financially relatively more vulnerable than their successors in the years between the two world wars.[4] It was during those same formative decades, as dreams of wealth acquired instantly through chance or circumstance made way for the grinding day-to-day economic realities of family life, that the foundations of working-class gambling culture were laid on the Witwatersrand, at a time when church and state were still comparatively weak.

But that caveat, too, calls for amplification before being translated into persuasive historical explanation. In practice, the two, perhaps three, foundational generations of the white working class – from, say, 1902 to 1922 – were more prone to financial hardship and therefore also more likely to engage in gambling as a way of addressing either occasional fantasies or ongoing needs. This was especially notable during periods of sharp economic decline, such as 1890–1892, 1906–1908 and, of course, 1929–1933, or when other marked challenges emerged, such as when the cost of living increased by 50 per cent over the period 1916–1920. Much to the annoyance of the largely uncomprehending charities, churches, governments and middle classes, then, it was precisely when workers were facing their most serious economic challenges that they were also most likely to invest in the rafts of chance to ferry them across the rivers of distress. Seen in that way, the propensity of white workers to gamble excessively was – understandably – countercyclical.

The flip side of that logic followed. As sharp economic downturns became both less frequent and pronounced – with the notable exception of the Great Depression of 1929–1933 – the white working class became comparatively financially secure and more socially established between the world wars. As the economic climate changed, the dangers of financial flash flooding receded and white workers, in growing numbers, forded previously menacing streams to take up safer positions on the racially privileged higher ground of the lower middle classes. In prolonged periods of much greater financial buoyancy, in the mid-1930s, the late 1950s and much of the 1960s, new generations of the white working class, declining in number as cheap black labour became more prevalent in industry, were less inclined to gamble. Whereas many whites in the formative decades of the Witwatersrand often gambled out of weakness as they looked around for an escape from hardship, their successors, in reduced numbers, took their chances out of relative strength. Hope relates to need and security in very different ways.

Broad brushstrokes daubed onto the canvas of economic history can, however, overwhelm the detail that needs to be focused on if we are to develop a fuller appreciation of the emerging picture. Three counterstrokes stand out. First, we need to note how the electoral influence of the unions and white workers on the Witwatersrand bridged the era between the founding generations of the working classes – those in the making – and those that followed and were more firmly rooted in the economy. The voting power of trade unions and the influence they exercised over the policies of the South African Labour Party in the Johannesburg City Council, Transvaal Provincial Council and House of Assembly was most evident between circa 1910 and the demise of Hertzog's Pact government in 1933. That political reality fed into a second salient consideration.

Gambling was most strongly embedded in white working-class culture before the Great Depression, that is, at a time when the Labour Party was most influential in the structures of governance. That, in turn, gave rise to other noteworthy but contradictory forces. The Labour Party was increasing in political strength and growing in stature during a period when the Calvinist and other churches, often in partnership with the state, were starting to extend their influence and power of enforcement over the working classes. The two groupings were on course for a collision, from which, in the short run, the

Labour Party and white workers might emerge relatively unscathed. But, over the longer run, church and state – almost always working in ideological tandem – would claim victories that turned out to be pyrrhic. The successes of the Labour Party at the polls rendered it vulnerable in other ways, however. A political party enjoying electoral success on a scale that provided it with substantial political power, such as the Labour Party had in the Johannesburg municipal and Transvaal Provincial councils, was unlikely to be easily overturned at the polls, and that opened the door to serious malpractice.

Something like an iron law governs the evolution of political parties, the refinement of legislation and the enforcement of the rule of law. Whenever and wherever there is a serious imbalance between political power and wealth that is distributed grossly unevenly across society, politicians-turned-criminals, or criminals-turned-politicians (the most successful practitioners being virtually indistinguishable), will attempt to short-circuit the checks and balances of democratic systems through acts of bribery and corruption with or without the cooperation of the police. Moreover, the greater the unwritten constitutional and legislative linkages between church and state, and the wider the disjuncture between party-political power, as with the Labour Party between 1910 and 1934, and the prospect of money-making by taking control of games of chance – including lotteries and sweepstakes – the greater the likelihood of criminal acts.

Unsurprisingly, lotteries and sweepstakes were taken up as an electoral issue by the Labour Party at the height of its political power and came to play an important part in the public policies and private lives of many of its leading politicians, as well as several prominent figures in the Witwatersrand underworld. In Johannesburg, the two-way flow between crime-as-politics and politics-as-crime was especially noticeable between 1910 and the violence of the white miners' strike in 1922.

Perhaps crucially, from the first law prohibiting lotteries, in 1890, until the moment that all the intervening legislation was repealed and a national lottery established under a freely elected democratic government, in 2000, the most important lotteries within Protestant South Africa were based beyond the country's borders in central and southern Africa – in Catholic Mozambique, in Northern and Southern

Rhodesia – and in Europe, in Ireland and in Malta. These international dimensions to the problem, evident from World War I and becoming increasingly important after World War II, did much to leave the South African Police hamstrung as they struggled to implement anti-gambling legislation that was constantly in danger of becoming a dead letter. The resulting gap between the law on lotteries and its implementation, and the opportunities it created along the Witwatersrand, were first exploited, brilliantly, by an Australian adventurer who hailed from the Kalgoorlie goldfields and who teamed up with an undomesticated Portuguese-Mozambican Catholic priest – effectively defrocked but well-connected – who acquired the concession to run the Lourenço Marques Lottery (LML).

In short, gambling, a phenomenon glimpsed only through the monocle of 'social history', is probably better viewed through the bifocal of 'history of society'. Johannesburg and the Witwatersrand's white working-class culture bent beneath gambling legislation that outlawed lotteries for 75 years, and it took the country a hundred years to establish a state lottery. Yet, during the intervening decades there was never a moment when the oppressive views of a Calvinist minority, working in tandem with the government of the day to suppress gambling, whether it be dog racing, football pools, pinball machines or lotteries, were not challenged, circumvented or ignored by a white working class that effectively defeated Calvin's police. This, then, is the story of a religious war lost.

PART I

INFECTION

[There is a] gold mining madness in the City [of London] ... In short, we are in the midst of one of those eras of feverish speculative activity which, as all students of finance and economics know, are constantly alternating with periods of stagnation and depression.
THE NINETEENTH CENTURY: A MONTHLY REVIEW, VOL 38, JULY–DECEMBER 1895

The Imperial Umbrella and Emergence of a 'Gambling Problem' on the Witwatersrand, circa 1886–1899

Modern South Africa was the offspring of a mining revolution fathered politically by the British Empire, mothered by mutating settler nationalisms and suckled into a robust infancy on the racist profits of capitalist industry. When Britain re-annexed the Cape Colony in 1806, English laws on gambling were in the midst of a long-term swing in policy over lotteries. With roots in the biblical practice of drawing lots in which 'God has chosen you', lotteries had been around since the time of the Romans and had been popular in England before they were first banned in 1699. The roots of the stubborn perennial were, however, never fully lifted. The ashes of the industrial revolution only encouraged new growth, and a surge in urban gambling saw the flowering of fully secular lotteries. With an ability to instantly transform the economic and social status of an individual without their first having to undergo the sacrifices of biblically sanctioned toil, and in an era marked by radical changes in class structure, lotteries were incompatible with the views of the church, the rich and merchants and shopkeepers who wanted workers to settle their debts on payday. The last legal draw for a lottery in

England was in 1826, after which they were again banned, this time successfully.[1]

The pall of anti-gambling legislation, of a sort more expected in port cities, thus settled over southern Africa before the formation of the landlocked Boer republics, or the mineral discoveries in the remote interior. By the mid-19th century, the shadow of English class legislation complemented, rather than conflicted with, the Calvinist thinking of the theologically conservative Dutch Reformed Church. In a colonial, racially divided country, Calvin and class not only overlapped but could, where necessary, provide the ideological grammar and weaponry that might conveniently be extended when it came to exercising moral authority and control over the indigenous majority destined to become a distinctive black labouring underclass. However, our concern here is how the Calvin-and-class, and class-and-Calvin, combinations played out among white workers.

Gold was discovered on the Witwatersrand, in 1886, in low-paying ores drawn from reefs that dipped sharply beneath the surface, but the saving grace was that they were continuous and, once crushed and the mineral content refined, yielded quantities that soon invited capital inflows of global proportions. Within a matter of only a few years the original adventurers, diggers and prospectors in the frontier camps – fortune seekers high on hope but low on cash – were bought out and replaced by mining companies, which, in turn, were eventually devoured by the even larger mining finance houses, the repositories of 'deep-level' corporate giants that formed a cartel in the shape of the Chamber of Mines. Johannesburg, the city at the centre of it all, was born of individual and collective gambling and speculation, and investment in industrial capitalism that, as ever, swiftly ensured the economic marginalisation of most of the vulnerable – black and white alike.

These financial fireworks erupted amid the stillness of an unlikely setting. The Witwatersrand, an urban excrescence where people pursued profit with greater zeal than bookmakers pursued punters, mushroomed in a sparsely populated agrarian republic. The Zuid-Afrikaansche Republiek (ZAR), underpinned by a weak economy, was loosely controlled by farmers of Dutch and European extraction in the throes of becoming Afrikaners – people with a distinctive culture, history, language and religion. Many of them, conservatives

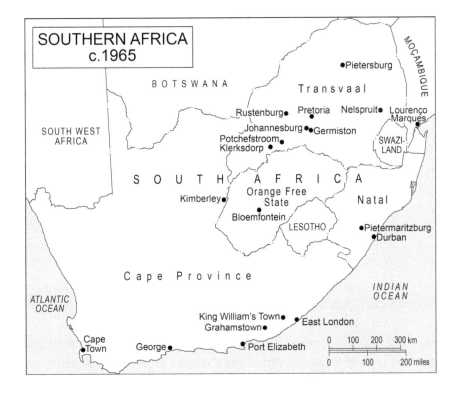

resentful of British imperialism and the emancipation of slaves, as well as being semi-literate, were descendants of Cape settlers who had moved north in a search for independence on the Highveld. The ZAR also lacked significant internal markets and towns, or a solid infrastructure of established roads or railways connected to the coast.

Drawing on the same sturdy outlook and independence of spirit, these northern Afrikaners approached God and his word from an angle the origins of which could be traced easily enough, but which deviated from that of two of the establishment's churches – the Nederduitse Gereformeerde Kerk and the Hervormde Kerk. The Gereformeerde Kerk and its followers, known as Doppers, although part of the broader family of Dutch Reformed churches, were drawn together in President SJP Kruger's backyard constituency, in Rustenburg, in 1859.[2] Although constituting only roughly ten per cent of Afrikaners, Kruger and the Dopper community, which believed strongly in the notions of the elect and predestination, played a disproportionately important role in the formulation of social policies designed to control urban immigrant cultures amid an industrial revolution – laws destined to last for more than half a century. The Doppers were pitted against the Enlightenment, the evangelism of the Methodists and others, liberalism, racial equality and integration in church or state – ideas that later informed many apartheid policies. The faithful saw no inherent evil in the moderate consumption of alcohol or tobacco – both commodities produced by its farming faithful and destined for urban markets. But, by then, its tolerance had reached its outer limits. Doppers objected to boxing, cinema, circuses, clubs and dancing, as well as to men and women bathing together in municipal facilities.[3] It was a world view wholly at odds with what was happening in what they called *Duiwelsdorp* (Satan's City) – Johannesburg – or along the rest of the Witwatersrand.

The new gold-devil worm eventually burrowed its way from Krugersdorp and Roodepoort in the west, through Johannesburg at the centre and then proceeded to hollow out the earth beneath the railway junction at Germiston and on as far as Boksburg, Benoni and Brakpan and Springs at the far eastern end of the Reef. As it delved in the darkness below, the helminth fed off the roots of 'social evils' on the Dopper checklist. Brothels, seedy clubs devoted to games of chance and a seemingly endless string of noisy bars and canteens lubricated the workings of the evil eye as it searched for victims who were, all too often, within easy reach.

In Duiwelsdorp, a man could bet on anything, from a downmarket contest as to how many rats a dog in a pit could bite to death in five minutes to the outcome of a fancy horse race. When, in 1889–1892, technical problems in the gold recovery process triggered an economic downturn, it nudged some of the most vulnerable sections of the population into a betting frenzy. That was enough to direct President Kruger's Dopper-dominated Volksraad (legislature) in Pretoria to pass a clutch of seminal laws designed to curb the excesses of the recalcitrant godless.

The first ambitious tug on the reins of what became a runaway horse came in 1889 with the passing of Law No. 6. But, as with the Dopper omission of drinking and smoking, Law No. 6, aimed at curbing games of chance, was born with a troubling hole in its heart, and Johannesburg, along with much of southern Africa, promptly descended into an

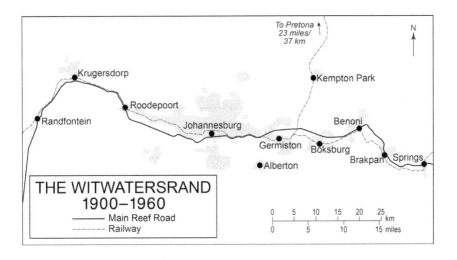

To Pretoria
23 miles/
37 km

N

Krugersdorp

Kempton Park

Roodepoort

Randfontein

Benoni

Johannesburg

Germiston
Boksburg
Brakpan Springs
Alberton

THE WITWATERSRAND
1900–1960
———— Main Reef Road
------- Railway

0   5   10   15   20   25 km
0   5   10   15 miles

exempted 'sweepstake craze'.[4] The following year, with the economy in the doldrums, it was followed by more desperate pulling in the form of the long-lived Law No. 7 of 1890 outlawing the operation of lotteries, though, perversely, 'sweepstakes' remained legal.[5] But the animal never faltered, charging on and on, dragging the unhappy lawmakers along behind it. Twelve months later, in 1891, the Dopper faithful were tossed a frayed lasso by way of a law that sought to ban Sunday betting and horse racing.[6]

There was, however, no turning back. By the time that renewed enthusiasm heralded the start of the 'Kaffir Boom', which stretched from 1893 to the biggest gamble yet on the continent, the Jameson Raid, in 1895–1896, there was no stopping either the beast or the trailing populace. The betting shops were 'crowded from morn to night'. WA Phillips organised the sale of sweepstake tickets with a first prize of £5 000, and things only got better. So extensive was Phillips's clientele that he soon attracted a competitor, JB Legate, who, shortly thereafter and in a sign of things to come, shifted his operation first to Durban and then, after the Anglo-Boer War (1899–1902), to Lourenço Marques. In 1892, the Portuguese administration in Mozambique, hoping to siphon off a share of the working-class spoils on offer, sold a concession for a short-lived provincial lottery of its own. By the time the 'craze' reached its high point, in 1895, a rival, David Moss, was selling sweepstakes to the value of more than

£30 000 (about £4 million today) – at weekly race meetings in dusty Satan's City.[7]

Frenetic gold rushes, followed by bouts of wild speculation and then periods of consolidation of capital-intensive industries by financial entrepreneurs, were nothing new.[8] It was, after all, the story of California (1848), Australia (1851) and Venezuela (1871). But the diamond (1867) and gold (1880s) rushes in southern Africa were attractive for a few additional reasons. The rapid development of steamships and a drop in the price of intercontinental travel in the late Victorian era had helped shrink distance. Ease of travel and increased speed placed the new fields within easier reach of prospectors and diggers, and the mechanics and miners who followed them as labour markets became more specialised. Indeed, by the 1890s and for a decade thereafter, something akin to an internationally mobile proletariat had emerged.[9] Not only were Kimberley and Johannesburg within easy reach of each other by coach or rail, for the better-paid and more skilled white miners, but the most dangerous and physically demanding of tasks fell to thousands of low-paid black workers.

The mail ship and the telegraph, integral parts of a globalising world, meant that there was no keeping the good news from Cornish and Lancastrian miners, who were among the first to entrench themselves on the Rand in significant numbers. But once the inflow of the northerners steadied, a new stream of Anglophone immigrants, attracted by the market-manipulated profits of the 'Kaffir Boom', began debouching from the southeast. The Australians arrived in more significant, albeit still modest, numbers from 1891 to 1895.[10]

The Australasians were, as always, comprised of a number of loosely woven strands that put to rest any simple-minded notions of 'national' identity, even though they were all drawn from a country reputed to host the world's most lucrative gambling culture. The majority – mechanics and mineworkers – reconciled to the new reality unfolding on the Rand, made their way directly to the mining companies to seek employment. But some who had missed the earlier boat to southern Africa had expectations that harked back more to frontier fortune-seeking days than to deep-level mining. Among the latter grouping were several bookmakers and a few younger Irish Australians, professional sportsmen who made their living from anything ranging from baccarat and billiards to boxing. And, hidden among the whole lot, as had happened previously in the shifts between Australia and California, in mid-century, were some criminals.[11]

From its earliest days until World War II, the white working class's love of horse racing and lotteries on the Witwatersrand was serviced by a coterie of Australian immigrants and their offspring. Years later, church and state sometimes cast them as anti-social predators at best or, at worst, as gangsters. In the eyes of most white and some black workers, however, the same bookies and lottery salesmen came across as honest and reputable entrepreneurs, and one or two went on to become minor folk heroes as trusted guides who repeatedly proved they could lead a man through the forests of fortune or misfortune and on to hidden treasure.

But Australians did not figure as the most menacing, numerous or prominent underworld figures in the years leading up to the Anglo-Boer War. Between 1895 and 1899, law-enforcement agencies in the ZAR were at full stretch dealing with problems other than lotteries and sweepstakes. East European gangsters, the core of whom had come from New York City, dominated the trade in organised prostitution, underwritten in good measure by a traffic in 'white slaves' drawn from ports all around the Atlantic. Calvinists and others found the situation intolerable, and Dopper legislators responded, in 1898, by passing a new comprehensive Immorality Act. The Volksraad was, however, far less keen on enacting legislation to curb excessive drinking by black miners. When it eventually did so, Law No. 7 of 1896 gave rise to an extensive illegal trade in cheap spirits dominated by marginalised East European immigrants.[12]

Excessive drinking, gambling and whoring by solitary males, in the absence of long-term partners or wives, are quintessential markers of frontier settings in which the class destinations and future of the initial adventurers, entrepreneurs and fortune seekers are open-ended. But the dreams of unearned wealth and ways of gaining access to it shift over time in response to deep-seated political, economic and social forces. The church and an industrialising state set about gaining greater control of a populace that – half-approving, half-resentful – was being moulded for settled family life and directed into increasingly controlled and policed working-class communities.

In South Africa, that transition was facilitated by the triumph of British imperialism in the Anglo-Boer War. In the aftermath of the British victory, the extent and nature of gambling along the Rand gradually metamorphosed, but in confusing and hesitant fashion. Proclamation 33 of 1901 repealed Kruger's Law No. 7 of 1890 on lotteries and horse racing, but it, in turn, was repealed by Act 37 of 1909 shortly before Union.[13] The problem was that, while Act 37 was explicit about horse racing, there was a puzzling silence around lotteries and sweepstakes. The ensuing bewilderment lasted for decades.

The Coming of the White Working Class and the Foundations of Family-Centred Popular Culture, circa 1902–1914

Not all professional gamblers attracted to South Africa were sucked into the slipstream of an increasingly mobile English-speaking international proletariat or drawn from a trickle of hopeful traders from the Mediterranean littoral. As we will note, some immigrants, including a few Australians, had joined the British imperial forces during the Anglo-Boer War and chose to stay on once demobilised. But, as in the early 1890s, when an unsuccessful attempt was made to launch a brotherhood of Australians along the lines constituted by Cumbrians, Cornishmen and Lancastrians, they again proved too few to cohere properly.

The few Australians, along with thousands of returning wartime refugees, soon realised that the Witwatersrand's frontier days were a thing of the past. First, the British military administration and then Alfred Milner's post-war reconstruction regime – backed by a police force recruited largely from demobilised ex-servicemen – set about creating a new dispensation for the Witwatersrand. A sustained, largely successful drive against organised crime, particularly the illicit sale of alcohol and prostitution, helped dispel many of the larger pockets of stale air lingering in Johannesburg. The underlying objective was to create a climate more conducive to sustaining the family life and values of an increasingly socially rooted white working class. To that end, Milner ensured that new suburbs were laid out within the boundaries of a greatly expanded municipality and linked to the inner city by a rail and tram network.

But the overall success of the transition from frontier setting to urban formation depended ultimately on the ability of the mining industry, local government and state to provide accommodation for their racially divided working classes at an enhanced clip. Unlike single black migrant workers, herded en masse into barracks-like compounds on mine properties without choice, white working-class families looked to modest cottages or small houses to support their changing lifestyle. But the authorities struggled to keep up with the demand for housing on the part of white miners and workers, thereby prolonging the much hoped-for transition.

In 1897, barely 12 per cent of the European mine employees along the Witwatersrand were married and had their families living with them. Five years later, by 1902, the figure had increased to 20 per cent. But progress thereafter remained painfully slow. By 1912, a decade later, still less than half the white miners – 42 per cent – were leading recognisably more socially rounded working-class lives. The high price of machine-made bricks, largely under the control of a few of the leading mining houses, did not help. Faced with the prospect of housing funded by local government or the state, a development likely to encourage the emergence of radical political ideologies along the same lines, some leading companies set about erecting additional married quarters between 1902 and 1905. That spurt, however, ended promptly when the industry collided, head-on, with the recession that followed.[14] As late as 1923, local architects were still actively pursuing designs for low-cost cottages that might appeal to white working-class families in search of a home.[15]

Caught between a rapid falling-off in the grade of ore being mined, on the one hand, and rising labour costs, on the other, the mining industry, further unsettled by a strike of white workers in 1907, languished from 1906 to 1908. The downturn resulted in significant hardship for white miners, including a score or more stranded families repatriated to Australia at the Chamber of Mines' expense. The sharp recession did nothing to ease the shortage of accommodation for many married workers, who sank further into debt despite a temporary reduction in rents. In Johannesburg, some 60 professional moneylenders competed via press advertisements and clearly had little difficulty in drawing in white workers, who were forced to pay extortionate interest rates on most short-term loans.[16]

In dire straits and surrounded by loan sharks, white workers were forced to look around for other ways of obtaining relief, and, through the gloom, it was the beacons of the merchants of luck and salesmen of chance that stood out along the shoreline. But getting a clear view was difficult. How was one to distinguish between legitimate professionals approved by the state to make a living from taking risks – bookies, moneylenders or pawnbrokers – and the more numerous underworld characters peddling get-rich-quick schemes? The fog of recession and the urgency of the housing crisis only further impaired visibility, and some men moved freely along the murky borders separating the categories.

William Thorne Seccombe, born in Paterson, New South Wales, in 1873, was the son of George Seccombe and Amy Naylor and died, aged 70, in Durban, in 1943. Little is known about his childhood other than that he was raised in a farming community that bred and raced horses and exported them to India. Like others in his extended family, Seccombe developed a taste for adventure, gambling and travel. Moving north, he bred horses and served as a steward at an unknown racecourse.

In 1899, he volunteered for the 2nd Queensland Mounted Infantry and attained the rank of lieutenant during the Anglo-Boer War. Upon demobilisation, in 1902, he married Mary Lynch in Bloemfontein and secured a position with the Orange River Colony Cold Storage Company. His primary interest, however, remained horse racing, and he was warned off the Bloemfontein Sporting Club's course without the right of appeal.[17]

When the company sent Seccombe to open a branch office in Johannesburg, around 1904, he became a founder member of the Auckland Park Racing Club (APRC). Shortly thereafter, he went to Cape Town, either of his own accord or on behalf of the APRC, to assist enthusiasts hoping to establish a racecourse at Goodwood or Milnerton. The visit did not end well. In 1905, he was given the option of a fine for running a meeting that did not comply with the rules of the Jockey Club of South Africa. He returned to Johannesburg, where he became editor of the *Sporting Times* and, always convivial, energetic and often genuinely civic-minded, secretary to the Transvaal Horse Owners' Association.[18]

The end of the Anglo-Boer War had brought home to Seccombe

how difficult it was to find suitable accommodation to raise a growing family on a modest income. Acquiring the deposit that would enable one to raise a mortgage loan was hardly a novel problem, and as he scrabbled about in his tucker bag of ideas, Seccombe was reminded how, in Australia, the difficulty had been addressed, if not solved.

Starr-Bowkett societies, rudimentary forms of non-profit building societies, rested on monthly subscriptions for shares that entitled contributors to qualify for interest-free housing loans repayable over a predetermined period. Societies would be dissolved once all members had received loans and made their repayments. In their original form, Starr-Bowketts did not make provision for the raising of, or provision of, loans to third parties, for the employment of the promoters or for remuneration other than through the payment of modest honoraria. There was, however, the ever-present potential for serious abuse, if not outright theft.[19]

Pioneered in England in the 19th century as cooperative schemes until they were outlawed there in the 1890s, Starr-Bowketts had been a feature of Australian urban life for a few decades and remained both legal and popular well into the 20th century. But they were building societies with a twist insofar as, once sufficient contributors had paid their subscriptions, the names of those eligible for a loan would be drawn by ballot – a feature English law had deemed to be akin to a lottery and therefore relegated to a form of gambling. The legality or otherwise of Starr-Bowketts had never been tested in the South African courts.

In 1904, with Leslie Leo as partner, Seccombe launched the First South African Starr-Bowkett Building Society, focused on the mining industry, tradesmen with sufficient capital to afford slightly higher subscription rates and other house-hunters lower down in the socio-economic pecking order. The scheme attracted attention from various mechanics (skilled artisans) and a working-class public that did not always read the fine print. But the police did. In January 1908, both men were in court charged under Law No. 7 of 1890. Presenting his evidence in a way designed to appeal to middle-class sensitivities, Seccombe claimed that he was intent on forming a company and that the scheme was designed primarily to help independent skilled craftsmen wishing to 'enlarge their businesses'.

The magistrate, taking his cue from English law, could not, or would not, be fooled. He found both guilty, saying, 'it was a lottery pure and simple' and 'a dangerous scheme [that] would defraud the public'. Seccombe was sentenced to a £50 fine or four months' hard labour, and Leo to £30 or two months. Not everyone agreed. Sensing that the Anglophone public's sympathy no longer lay squarely behind what they saw as antiquated Dopper legislation, Seccombe took the matter on appeal and had his sentence reduced to £15 – or one month's hard labour.[20]

The latter judgment, by nodding in the direction of public opinion, acknowledged some of the social changes that had come in the wake of the Anglo-Boer War and pointed to a certain hesitancy on the part of the state when it came to dealing with lotteries, and thus constituted a minor legal landmark. It was read with approval by dream merchants and lawyers but did little to encourage those charged with applying the law – the magistrates and police. Moreover, it came at a time when the Lourenço Marques Lottery – which had got off to a bad start through poor organisation by failing to penetrate the Johannesburg market and meet fully its obligations to local church charities – was in complete disarray, if not moribund. The result was that, from time to time, new and better organised lotteries continued to surface along the Witwatersrand, despite that fact that they remained illegal.[21]

Undaunted by a reduced sentence, Seccombe continued to peddle Starr-Bowkett shares but encountered growing resistance from the existing membership as the recession deepened their financial plight.[22] Hard-pressed contributors discovered that, should they wish to withdraw from the scheme, they could recover only ten per cent of their monthly subscriptions over a period of several years. Investing in the Starr-Bowkett scheme was, for some, a bit like the man trapped in a 20-foot-deep pit who chances upon a ladder, only to find that it is only ten feet long. By May 1909, there were streams of complaints to employers and lawyers about the society, including 'hundreds from the working class'. By then, however, the society had more than 450 members and assets said to be worth more than £80 000, and it was reported as still in a healthy financial position when it was finally wound down in 1919.[23]

After 1909, Seccombe had little if anything to do with Starr-Bowkett, as the society continued to function, while the magistrate's ruling that it constituted a lottery appears to have fallen into desuetude.[24] Indeed, over the three years that followed, the original scheme was slowly but successfully transformed into the 'Premier Starr-Bowkett Building Society'.[25] Seccombe's withdrawal is easily explained. Ever since November 1908, he, along with some black and countless white workers, had been in awe of, in the thrall of, probably the most extraordinarily sharp adventurer ever to have traversed southern Africa, where he achieved legendary status, as he did back in his homeland. A quarter of a century later, Johannesburg newspapers were still reporting on his exploits to interested if not spellbound readers. A creative, energised, impatient, peripatetic force of nature, the newcomer's reading and understanding of the needs and hopes of working-class families drew on experience derived from travel through a dozen countries on four continents. His mind had never shown much respect for rest, space or time. On the Rand he combined business ventures, entertainment and gambling in breathtakingly innovative ways. Australian by birth, he was almost certainly distantly related to, and some years younger than, Seccombe, who was probably a cousin on his mother's side.

Christened Rupert Theodore Naylor (1882–1939) in Chippendale, a suburb of Sydney, he was raised, along with five brothers and two sisters, by his mother and a restless fortune-seeking labourer-turned-hotelier father. In 1894, when he was 12, his parents moved to the West Wyalong goldfields in New South Wales where he worked on a mine property that gave him a liking for adrenalin-charged settings. Disliking his given name, he changed it to Rufus or Rufe and then displayed the first signs of a turbo-charged mind and metabolism when, at 14, he became a partner in a bicycle repair business. Two years later, he returned to Sydney where, aged 17, he became the youngest registered bookmaker in Australia.[26]

But turn-of-the-century Sydney was too old and too sedate for Naylor's need for excitement. Heading north, he looped through Queensland, taking in Brisbane and moving on to the wide-open mining towns of Charters Towers and Gympie, refining a speciality that combined two great Australian passions – sport and gambling. He promoted races between professional athletes – 'world champions' – with track records and identities that ethnic communities within a nation in the making could readily identify with.[27]

By the early 1900s Naylor and his wife, Catherine, had crossed the continent and set up shop in the Western Australian mining centre of Kalgoorlie. He registered as a bookmaker, became a committee member of the athletics club and blew away any residual notions of isolation and provincialism by helping to stage the famed 'Kalgoorlie Hundreds' – novel programmes featuring amateur and professional events. In 1906, the Hundreds featured a race between the Australian champion and hero, Arthur Postle, and the reigning Irish world sprint champion athlete, BR Day.[28]

The paroxysms of excitement and patriotic delight that accompanied a Postle victory underscored Naylor's marketing genius. The carnival-like event, spread over several days, was said to have attracted between five and ten thousand spectators, many of whom had trundled in from the outback aboard chartered trains. Using the modern miracle of the steam engine to breathe additional life and profits into productions was part of a formula that would serve him for many decades.

But, hidden away within the numbers flocking to the 'Sixth Hundred' lay another element of Naylor's success – his ability to read social change and reach beyond the often exclusive, masculine culture of mining towns to expand the market potential and enhance self-control within potentially unruly crowds. He wanted everyone, including women and their children, present at his events, and the 1906 meeting included female athletes – the weirdly named Loyal Forward was crowned Western Australia's first woman state champion. In short, it was a triumph. 'Rufe Naylor', the press reported, 'cleared an enormous profit over the Day-Postle match, as admission charges were high, ranging from two to six shillings.'[29]

But in Naylor's businesses it was frequently a matter of feast or famine. As with the circus, there was a limit to the number of spectacles that could be staged for low-income earners in a particular town or city before he was forced to move on to the next location. In that sense, his enterprise was part of a robber economy, one in which, once local resources were exhausted, he *had* to explore new horizons. It was this, coupled to a chronic itch in the distal parts of his legs, that turned him into a worldwide traveller. Sadly, however, his problems did not always end there. Since financial famines tended to last longer than feasts, there were often difficulties either in covering the costs of the next round of travels, or in raising the capital necessary to develop some new global enterprise – sometimes both. And, when short of funds to bridge the gap between the current famine and impending feast, it was tempting to resort to short-term 'solutions' that were not always legal, and a criminal record only added impetus to the need to get out of town or country.

Just months before the Sixth Hundreds, where winning professional athletes were rewarded with gold medals and prize money, Naylor was arrested for fraud at the Perth racecourse.[30] His abrupt departure appears not to have resulted in a serious denouement since he was quickly back in Kalgoorlie planning his next, more ambitious move. In May 1907, he and Day undertook a whirlwind tour of New Zealand before boarding a steamer for Vancouver. From there they worked their way across Canada, down into the northeastern United States, and then on from New York City to Liverpool and a well-advertised athletics event with the equally peripatetic Arthur Postle at Salford.[31]

With Catherine and the two children in England, Seccombe in place on the Rand and the wind of Australian experiences at his back, 27-year-old Naylor turned southward to conjure with the entertainment needs and gambling propensities of the richest gold-mining city in the world. He surged through Johannesburg like a tsunami, casting aside obstacles and forcing his way through existing structures until it seemed as though there was not a square inch of any avenue, street or alley that did not bear traces of his presence. For four years, from 1908 to 1912, and then again some years later, his footprints and sometimes even his fingerprints were found everywhere. Everyone knew when Rufe was in town.

To start with, bookmaking provided Naylor with his bread and butter, the jam coming from inside information provided by Seccombe, a committee member at the booming Auckland Park Racing Club. But, for some time, there had been worrying signs that horse-racing meetings, considered to be excessive in their frequency, were falling into official disfavour, and so Rufe spread his bets by diversifying the existing opportunities available to bookmakers and the public.

Building on a long-standing English pastime, racing dogs of various breeds was an almost natural extension to horse racing, and it was not long before Naylor was correctly suspected of trying to gain control of all whippet racing.[32] Drawing on the template developed

'Rufe' T Naylor, international entrepreneur extraordinaire and Lourenço Marques Lottery concessionaire.

at Kalgoorlie, he brought in, from Australia and far beyond, a steady stream of 'world champions', including the indefatigable Arthur Postle and BR Day, and staged not only professional athletics meetings and cycle races but an international sculling event, held on the muddied waters of the Germiston Lake.[33]

None of the venues were ever large enough for Rufe, and the events never frequent or profitable enough, to douse the fire that always raged within him. Constantly driven, Naylor's watchwords were 'bigger', 'better', 'more'. There was no time for 'joy or sweet contemplation'; he liked working under 'high pressure'. 'He was one of those men', an Australian who clearly knew him well later wrote, 'who really cared little for actual money. He revelled in the chase after it, the scheming, the work, the planning, and the tense excitement of the game as he saw and played it, and perhaps he had a streak of vanity which was flattered by possession.'[34]

Within weeks of his arrival, Naylor, managing director of the 'Johannesburg Athletics Club Ltd', persuaded 20 to 30 investors to back his latest grand – some would have thought grandiose – scheme.[35] Located in the inner city, on the corner of End and Main streets, the 'Stadium Sports Ground' housed an athletics track and saucer-shaped cycle track, supported by an electronic judging device and sufficient lighting for up to 10 000 spectators, who paid between one and three shillings for places in separate enclosures.[36] After a shaky start, average attendance rose to more than 2 000, but on an evening in April 1909, a crowd of 6 000 spectators attracted 12 registered bookmakers to the betting shops and reserved sections, the larger public enclosure being strictly for viewing only.[37]

Beyond all the advertising, hoopla and press publicity that accompanied Stadium events up to their dying days in 1912, Naylor's pioneering social philosophy – never restricted by venue – was clear for all who wished to see. He was hoping to benefit from the transition from the wild, all-male mining-camp entertainment and recreation of the 1890s to something recognisably modern that would resonate with settled working-class communities in developed countries around the world. As he put it to sceptical members of the Transvaal gambling commission, in 1909: 'We use every endeavour, and I venture to say with success, to keep out all undesirable elements, whether male or female, from the Stadium and for this purpose we have a special private detective at the gates. We are particular in this respect for the reason that we have hundreds of ladies who visit the Stadium regularly, besides which, many of these ladies bring with them their younger children for we have found here, as I found both in Australia and America, that a very considerable section of the population, prefer this kind of entertainment to a theatre, music hall or any other kind of entertainment.'[38]

Nearly always abreast of demographic trends, Naylor was intent on growing the market as far as possible by drawing in recently urbanised Afrikaners to the Stadium. Afrikaner men and women with strong ethnic identities, driven off the land by the British, had more than a passing resemblance to the Irish he had courted in Australia. But they had no recent history of involvement in often venerable English sporting codes, so who was to assume the role that Day had played for the urbanising Irish back in Kalgoorlie?

The answer lay in finding cyclists that Afrikaners could identify with, and who, when pitted against the resented '*Engelse*' usurpers or

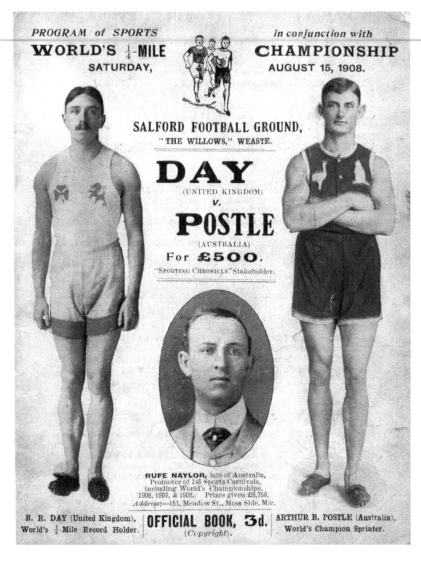

Twenty-six-year-old Rufe Naylor's professional athletics promotion, 1908, prior to his departure for South Africa.

their proxies, might help settle a few scores – albeit only in symbolic terms. On chilly winter evenings over two seasons, the champion South African cyclist FD Venter, of Pietersburg, and others were pitted against visiting Australians or New Zealanders, such as PB Quinlan, in contests such as the one billed 'Kangaroo Comet vs Springbok'.[39]

But, even as the company set about refining the Stadium's infrastructure, Naylor was becoming increasingly aware that they were rowing against a strong-flowing, outgoing tide – one reversing incoming forces he had helped trigger and set firmly against new betting practices and a perceived excess of horse-racing meetings. The tempest was being driven not only by the winds of the old conservative Dopper legislation spawned in the countryside but by gusts from a new urban alliance. At its core lay intertwined strands of quasi-Calvinist ideologies serving the interests of the mine owners and middle-class retailers burnt by unpaid debts incurred during the downturn of 1906–1908. And championing the need for a commission of inquiry into gambling, to encourage the virtues of restraint and thrift in the unsettled white working class, was the *Sunday Times*.

The Chamber of Mines, not all that distant from the sections of society that sashayed into the turf clubs, did not make its objections to working-class gambling or racecourses known formally. Why would it, at a time when white workers were becoming noticeably more militant, organised and unionised in the shape of the emerging Labour Party and the older Transvaal Miners' Association?[40] But some mine owners were more frank when corresponding privately with the police. The directors of West Rand Consolidated Mines, for example, were of the view that '[i]t is notorious that race meetings attract, amongst others, the undesirable elements of the population and that much drinking is associated with them', and that they caused 'periodical dislocation of mining operations'. Clearly, horses and horse owners needed one set of rules, horses and white workers another.[41]

This class-and-culture 'problem', starkly outlined in the depressed economy, predated Naylor's arrival in the city. In April 1908, the *Sunday Times*, frustrated by the Jockey Club's unwillingness to curb the number of racing days along the Reef, ran an editorial feeling its way to what it branded as a local 'evil'. 'Desperation and bad times' had made people 'reckless' and shifted the attention of some from 'the Stock Exchange [to] the racecourse'. Which white workers frequented the stock market it could not, or would not, specify. Thirty days of racing since the start of the year, the newspaper argued, had seen £300 000 pass through the hands of the bookies, and 'this paper believes that a great many of the unpaid bills which are the curse of the shopkeepers on the Rand remain unpaid simply because the money is gambled away at race meetings'. Government intervention would invite widespread resentment but, at the same time, only a return by the public to more 'sober ways' could ensure the 'revival of ordinary, legitimate commerce'.[42]

Taking to its role as a stern father of the wayward, if not the backward – at a time when the white working class was showing growing signs of wanting to leave the capitalist fold and set out on a socialist path – the *Sunday Times* clung to the issue like a fox terrier with a large woollen stocking. The stridency of the campaign makes one wonder what, if any, personal as well as professional issues were at stake.

The answer, it seems, was none, directly. The editor, LR MacLeod (1875–1941), was born in New Zealand, the son of Scottish parents, and pursued a career in journalism in Australia before emigrating to South Africa. A conservative of cultivated literary taste, MacLeod lived through the 1906–1908 recession, editing the *Sunday Times* from 1907 to 1910. From his vantage point as journalist, he saw the structural damage wrought by the downturn, but it was only much later, after he had become the literary editor of the *Daily Mail*, in London, that he became aware of a member of his extended South African family who was said to be a 'feckless spendthrift' and who had 'lost the housekeeping money at the races'. By then he was corresponding with, and publishing essays by, Joseph Conrad before returning to South Africa to edit the *Rand Daily Mail* from 1924 until 1941.[43]

MacLeod's editorials about gambling in the recession became increasingly interventionist, moralistic and paternalistic in tone, and one or two Protestant churches could not resist joining in and fighting the good fight. The paper never singled out Naylor by name, but by January 1909, just as the Stadium project was taking off, the Sunday weekly's tone had become much more strident. Too many racing days 'had a bad effect on the business life of the community' and the 'habits of thrift and steadiness' that characterise a more mature and responsible working class 'suffer'. 'The Transvaal Government' – increasingly toothless and destined for the scrap heap of history with the rapid approach of Union – needed to step in and take its cue from Australia, a colonial cousin, where state legislation restricting the number of racing days allowed each year had long since been enacted.[44]

But one had to be careful what one wished for, and Louis Botha's government, sensing its muscle wasting away, was keen to demonstrate its residual strength before it disbanded and MPs were called upon to compete for their places on a larger stage. The Attorney General was one of the first to sip the *Times*'s printer's ink, and by April 1909 a commission of inquiry into gambling was gathering evidence, including from Naylor and Seccombe, who did their best to open the commission's eyes to more tolerant legislation across the wider Anglophone world.[45]

The Attorney General, Jacob de Villiers, insisted on passing the chalice around, and members of the commission, more accustomed to drinking than sipping, partook freely – some thought too freely – of a press potion said to cure the public, if not politicians. By June, the *Sunday Times*, having got a glimpse of what by then was thundering down the track towards the cowering public, was, along with others, having second thoughts. The government, the Oracle of Outrage argued, had been right in framing new legislation to control gambling 'but it might have kept in mind the fact this isn't a nursery or yet a colony of hopeless imbeciles'.[46]

By then the genie was out the bottle and the Holy Ghost afoot in a church or two. The short reference to Act 37 was the 'Horse Racing and Betting Restriction Act 1909'. But it was the long title that revealed how ambitious in scope it was. The Act 'to regulate and control Horse, Pony, and Galloway Racing, to restrict Betting and Wagering, and to prevent the dissemination of information as to Betting' might as well have borne another subtitle: 'The Abolition of the Stadium Act'. The Act was so comprehensive that Attorney HD Bernberg, a man said to have 'capitalist principles' but who went on to become the Honorary Secretary of the South African Labour Party until messy financial transactions prompted his suicide, in 1913, published a guide for those bewildered by its provisions.[47]

The licensing of new racecourses would be for the approval of the Attorney General and, if necessary, the Minister of Mines. There, then, was the 'hidden hand' linking the mine owners to white working-class recreation laid bare for all interested enough to read. The minister could determine if, where and when horse races might be conducted. In addition to restricting the number of racing days and taxing the turnover on the tote, the sale of race cards and betting was to be confined strictly to racecourses – that is, away from town. All these provisions outlawed existing bookmaking practices, but the Act also made it an offence to bet 'at any time or place upon the result of any foot race, cycle race, or any shooting, running or boxing contest or prize fight'. The Act, which came into force on 1 October 1909, sought to fell Naylor and the Stadium with one blow.

It failed to do so. Well, not with a single swipe and certainly not instantly, although a decade later, Naylor claimed to have been 'ruined by legislation in the Transvaal in 1909' and by 1911 was advertising in the press, hoping to attract a partner with capital for one of his new ventures.[48] Even without the benefit of legal on-site betting, the Stadium continued to provide locals with a venue for professional athletic, cycle and dog-racing spectacles until 1912.[49] The truth of the matter was that Naylor had seen what was coming and, fleet of foot, by the closing weeks of 1909 was taking evasive action with a few unexpected moves.

The latest thing in the UK and the US was the showing of moving pictures – silent films – interspersed with live vaudeville acts performed by leading international artistes of the day while the reels were changed. Naylor owned a number of downtown properties, and a friend, Marks Prechner, had ready cash. By February 1910, the New Tivoli and Picture Palace were up and running, feeding a 'bioscope' (cinema) craze, while Naylor took over the Orpheum Music Hall, soon converting it into a 'theatre'. As with the Stadium, it was the emerging mass market rather than the old miners that Naylor courted, and so the Tivoli was sold as a 'select family theatre'. The formula worked so well that, within months, the partners opened additional bioscopes in Boksburg, Germiston and Pretoria.[50]

Manic energy alone, however, could not ensure lasting business success. Managerial muscle had to match the reach of the managerial arm or cash could evanesce from unsecured tills. Seccombe, loyal to a fault, was already undergoing a metamorphosis from factotum/timekeeper at the Stadium to part-time impresario.[51] He also assisted Naylor in keeping on good terms with the likes of Isaac Friedman, who had a gaming house frequented by Sam Kahn and a few other Jewish radicals.[52] Legitimate and illegitimate businesses functioned best when trust was interwoven with family ties, and Naylor had brothers to spare.

First to be drawn into his new orbit was the low-profile Peter Charles Naylor, who, based in London from 1910, served as an agent contracting vaudeville acts and procuring films.[53] Peter went on to play an important role in producing the 'African Mirror' newsreel. In 1912, slippery George Sylvester Naylor, who held power of attorney when Rufe was out of town, appeared in Johannesburg, sliding easily between his roles as now bookmaker, now horse breeder, now horse importer.[54] Later they were joined by the youngest, Henry John 'Harry' Naylor.

Believing the door was swinging open on a post-Union dispensation in which it might be easier to harness personal to political success – a circuit that had eluded him when the Horse Racing and Betting Restriction Act was passed – Rufe neatened up his image and worked harder on presenting a stronger, more pleasing profile to men of influence and the public. Part confidence man, part trickster, Naylor had courted fixers and trade unionists right from the moment the Stadium was launched.[55] But what was needed now was for him and Seccombe to move in behind the politicians and capture the hearts of those who voted them into power – the public.

The American titans of the age, unlike almost all the Randlord millionaires, who had their eyes set on Europe or their retirement, combined conspicuous success with notable acts of generosity, signalling that a hard head was compatible with a tender heart. Citizens on the Reef, some of whom knew Naylor from Kalgoorlie days, claimed he was 'a kindly individual', and there is no doubt of his popularity among many of their compatriots. Naylor's caring nature for those experiencing personal hardship was there for anyone willing to look. In 1911, he staged a concert to assist a lady, broken in health, in need of the funds to cover her passage back home to Australia. Not long thereafter, when the *Titanic* went down, he donated the proceeds of yet another concert to the Empire-wide disaster fund.[56]

The positive publicity, in a press mesmerised by Naylor's exploits, along with his reputation as an honest bookmaker and an informed tipster, if not an always reliable partner in business, went down well in domiciled working-class communities. But not all his employees – from athletes to artistes – were either resident or full-time workers in a city built partly on the strengths of organised labour. There was a darker side to Naylor, who drew a distinction between the wages of the working class and the wishes of contracted employees.

Like many an American mogul, Naylor was publicly sympathetic to the working class, and, in his case, he had a direct interest in seeing a rise in disposable incomes. But in private he was bitterly opposed to unionism in risky enterprises that frequently described an arc of profitability as they sped from novelty to norm. There were good reasons for his and Seccombe's willingness to risk prosecution – repeatedly – either by overcrowding their cinemas and theatres, or by staging shows on Sundays.[57] When professional athletes, including a few who doubled as shop assistants downtown, attempted to form an athletes' union, in 1909, Naylor's response was uncompromising: 'he would not recognise any union or club in any shape or form' and 'the meeting broke up in disorder'. Individual objections or protest actions were met with summary suspensions.[58]

His objection to collective action did not, however, stretch to employers. Later that year, Naylor was a moving force behind a 'Bioscope Proprietors' Association' whose objective appears to have been twofold: to hold, reverse or slow the rate at which wages for variety artistes had been rising after the depression, and to establish a 'combine' that would reduce overheads through the creation of a 'central booking office'. Rumours about wage cuts led to a strike and, perhaps unsurprisingly, the heat of artistes' anger was directed outside the Tivoli Theatre, where three of the most militant were arrested, one of whom later sued Naylor.[59]

Once significant financial support had been garnered from seven of the theatre proprietors who had not joined the Bioscope Proprietors' Association, and the dispute had been taken to the Witwatersrand Trades and Labour Council, a compromise was eventually reached.[60] But not with Naylor. For some time thereafter, the Tivoli Theatre showed films without the benefit of any vaudeville performances. While the conflict did little damage to Naylor's public reputation, and none to Seccombe's, it could not have gone down well with the emerging leadership of the Labour Party. It is noteworthy that, while Naylor remained publicly committed to the interests of working men and women, he did not join the party, but Seccombe did, and with some success.

These straws in the wind, hinting at a periodic if not chronic shortage of cash over several months, predated the big push that came when Naylor and Prechner extended their chain of cinemas at the height of the 'bioscope craze'. But the 'craze' was levelling off and box office receipts were not what they once had been.[61] The Naylor-Prechner twin rocket, low on fuel, was floating in the outer reaches of the financial universe. Naylor's orders from the flight deck were all too familiar and predictable – go faster, push further. With additional capital supplied by yet more partners, the business was consolidated and expanded, and registered as African Amalgamated Theatres Ltd (AAT), on 31 October 1911.

For Naylor, suffering from lean-wallet syndrome as the Stadium business wound down, it was not a happy experience. Appointed and then unseated as managing director, Naylor struggled to raise the £2 000 needed to take up his allocation of shares, and the AAT board became nervous. Things got increasingly fractious, and the office door was soon girded with lock and chain. By mid-1912, the dispute was playing out in the Supreme Court, which handed down a judgment that offered only partial solutions to Naylor's problems. The directors then suggested that he join his brother Peter in London as a second agent representing the company.

A farewell dinner in Naylor's honour – of the type customarily reserved for those departing permanently – was held at the Grand National Hotel, in July 1912, and attended by the Friedmans and members of the racing fraternity but not, it would seem, by too many AAT directors. Naylor used the occasion to butter up the press and send a clear message to the company's shareholders. Monty Friedman proposed a toast 'to the health of the Press' – who, none too fortuitously, were represented by reporters – while Naylor turned the ideological tables on the doubters and scoffers. He already owned, he said, one-third of the shares in AAT, and was set on acquiring even more. He had every confidence in the future of the city and, he was pleased to announce, would only be away for about six months.[62]

But who knows what Naylor's intentions really were? Shortly after his arrival in London, he signed a 21-year lease on 'Rokeby Villa', in Upper Richmond Road, Putney. He worked for AAT out of ideally located offices, first in Charing Cross Road and later Gerrard Street, off Shaftesbury Avenue. Things went reasonably smoothly, and Naylor showed no sign of wanting to return to a city where the sun never stopped shining. The adage about the mice being able to play while the cat was away appeared not to extend to Johannesburg, and the company's affairs seemed fairly settled. The problem for the mice, of course, was that things became more fraught when there was another cat in town.[63]

There was, and his name was Isidore. An American millionaire, the Rand-based IW Schlesinger was every bit as restless and hungry for success as Naylor, the difference being that he had secured a fortune by focusing on one business – insurance – before branching out into other fields. As the biggest cat in town, outside of the mining industry, IW enjoyed many things, including acquiring enterprises that had the potential to become monopolies and the company of showgirls. In early 1913, he started taking as much interest in the commercial as the social side of theatre and vaudeville and, intent on dominating the industry locally, set his eyes on acquiring AAT. But Cat Two, who had unfinished business of his own with the AAT mice, was also on the move, and bounded into Johannesburg on 22 May.[64]

Naylor was in trouble, deep trouble, which, in his and partner Prechner's opinion, stemmed from AAT's inability to liquidate the massive debt that it had agreed to settle when it took over Tivoli Theatres Ltd, as well as to 'indemnify them against their creditors'. The bank was pressing Naylor to stump up £13 000, and he wanted AAT to take on his debts as it wound down the company and reached a reduced settlement with creditors. Within hours of his return the matter was before the Supreme Court, and Naylor appears to have not only lost the case but been ordered to pay the costs.[65] The AAT directors then pressed, or persuaded, Naylor to agree to the company's being sold to Schlesinger, which, within days, it was. AAT was folded into IW's African Theatres Trust (ATT) and African Films Trust (AFT), which dominated the southern African film industry for many decades.[66]

But, in the wake of a recession and a general strike, Naylor's creditors foreclosed on his remaining assets. By August 1913 he was penniless. He lacked the funds for the passage home and was unable to meet the rent for Rokeby Villa or support his wife, who, responsible for their two children, had reason to view the Thames in the way that Edwardian females were often driven to. Somehow he secured a

American-born IW Schlesinger, the most successful commercial millionaire north of the Vaal River, c. 1913.

position as a clerk at the Robinson Deep Mine and, with the help of an exceedingly modest loan from a nervous HJ Retief, moved into the mine's single quarters. The feast-to-famine cycle had taken barely 36 months to complete.

Humiliation piled upon humiliation. Unable to repay the loan swiftly, it was not long before Retief dragged Naylor to court. When the messenger of the court arrived at the single quarters to attach his assets, on 8 August, Naylor told him that he had 'no money, property or assets' with which to satisfy the writ. Retief then pursued his quarry via a garnishee order, hoping to get the mine to enforce a monthly deduction from Naylor's salary – but to little if any avail.[67]

But could so charismatic, enterprising, determined and innovative a man ever be 'bankrupt'? Naylor had abilities, contacts, energy and skills that could not be captured on a balance sheet but were worth a fortune if harnessed imaginatively. In terms of social capital, he remained well-off indeed. The long road back to solvency lay in his ability to convert his contacts into cash.

As a man who cared for and delivered excitement and value for money to white working-class families, Naylor's reputation was firmly established. A small army of barmen, barbers, clerks, cab drivers, shop assistants and waiters who distributed, or sold, everything from handbills to race cards knew him. Just above them, overseeing operations, was the family, in the shape of his brothers and Seccombe. Editors and reporters craved the heady cocktail of ideas, schemes and projects that he slipped them in coupes brimming with sensationalism. In an age of paper and ink, he was well connected to the local printing industry. Moreover, the racecourse had helped put him on nodding terms with several rich investors and influential politicians in the city, as well as the occasional fixer.

In short, Naylor – even at a low point in his career – presided over a network that, if linked to some new professionally run enterprise, such as a lottery, had the potential to haul him out of a canyon of failure. He needed two things if he was to reconquer Johannesburg – the funds to get back to Rokeby Villa and the seeds of a new scheme. Without his realising it at the time, both slipped into reach while he lay on the bed contemplating the ceiling at the Robinson Deep Mine. And, as often happened, the most direct route to success lay through the right connections.

It was Cat One that got him to London. Schlesinger took him on in the same role that he had forfeited when ATT and then AFT had gobbled up the ailing AAT. Back in Gerrard Street, Naylor once again fed artistes and films into the pipeline that led to Schlesinger's steadily expanding business empire.[68] But it was another man, whom Naylor first met at the mine during that miserable August, who was to exercise greater influence over his fate and that of two generations of Naylors.

The fellow introduced himself to Naylor as Padre José Vicente do Sacramento, the 'Assistant Curator of Natives', a resident official, in Johannesburg, looking after the interests of black miners for the Mozambique administration. The Padre, who had 14 years' service in the colony, appeared in Johannesburg in 1909, and was always in awe of Naylor's business acumen, connections and initiative.

But there was no instant meeting of minds or outpouring of love and trust. It was wise Seneca who reportedly first suggested that 'luck is what happens when preparation meets opportunity'. Wisely, the Roman never ventured to say what the time lapse between preparation and opportunity might be. How could he? Preparation lies partly within one's control, in plain view, while opportunity sneaks up on one from behind. It took three years for the Bookmaker and the Priest to get lucky.

Courting the Rand's White Working Class in a Season of Global Storms, circa 1914–1916

It is difficult now to imagine the contrast between the savagery of the Great War of 1914–1918, in blood-soaked Europe, and the relative tranquillity of the southern part of the African continent. While the war saw about 20 million men, women and children lose their lives in the northern hemisphere – split more or less equally between civilian and military lives – South Africa, involved briefly in campaigns in South West Africa and east Africa, lost about 7 000 soldiers. While a million African soldiers from elsewhere on the continent contributed actively to the successes of the Allied war effort, the closest that South Africa got to the war was in relatively marginal theatres. Empire took South Africa to war, including in Europe, where black South Africans, too, lost their lives, but left it largely at 'peace' in the remote south.

Seccombe spent most of World War I acting as Naylor's informal agent in Johannesburg while the latter was away in England, burrowing his way sideways into society and working-class politics. Seccombe remained in the public eye with an ongoing interest in the APRC and was involved in whippet racing at the Simmer & Jack Mine. Being embedded in the local gambling culture helped keep his hand in as assistant editor and 'General Sporting Editor' of the *Evening Chronicle*. A father, and one apparently in good standing, he was elected chairman of the board at the Spes Bona School. He was, if not wholly 'respectable', then a gentleman of sorts who straddled two worlds.[69]

His interest in party politics predated the war and later lit the way for Naylor by introducing him to prominent politicians. The war was barely under way when Seccombe and a friend, Ralph H Tatham, a speculator, appeared at an inner-city meeting of the Labour Party agitating for the resignation of an executive member of the party who held a seat on the corrupt Transvaal Provincial Council. In mid-1917, Seccombe was the Labour Party's unsuccessful candidate for a seat on the Johannesburg Town Council, an entity not renowned for clean administration.[70]

Tatham, later also Naylor's friend, was another eccentric, flamboyant opportunist addicted to roller-coaster rides during the extremes of economic booms and slumps. Like Naylor, Tatham was always on the lookout for some new way of getting rich quickly, but whereas for Naylor a surge of adrenalin usually triggered a search for the next money-making enterprise, for Tatham it induced a political epiphany. Naylor wanted the thrill of chasing cash, but Tatham wanted both political power and money, and had had so many bad driving experiences on the road to Damascus that his professional licence, his accreditation to practise as an attorney, had been revoked by the bar association.

The son of an impetuous County Durham immigrant, Tatham was born and raised in Natal and attended Bishop's College, in Pietermaritzburg, before being admitted as an advocate, in Durban, in the mid-1890s. The outbreak of the Anglo-Boer War allowed him to make a small fortune through land speculation and he was soon elected a city councillor. But, deeply upset at how the Boers were treated by the British invaders, he said, he left for England to turn a small fortune into a larger one. He bought the slightly misleadingly named Starborough Castle, in Surrey, invested heavily in the London stock market and lost even more heavily.

His debut as a budding capitalist may have helped Tatham see the world in a slightly different light, but it failed to dampen his enthusiasm for speculative ventures. On his return to South Africa, in 1906, he pegged several gold claims on the East Rand before returning to Natal, where, championing the cause of the working man, he was elected to parliament. He borrowed heavily from the banks and invested in a printing company and later that same year resigned from his seat in the House of Assembly when he went bankrupt, only to be rehabilitated in 1907.[71]

Shortly after Union, in 1910, Tatham sidled back to the Witwatersrand, where, in August 1912, without much fanfare, he joined Louis

Botha's South African Party (SAP), claiming a few months later that it was his intention only to try and encourage republicanism from within that party's ranks.[72] A few months later still, practising as an advocate but not making financial progress, he met Seccombe and told him how he, Tatham, would make his fortune from the East Rand gold claims.

Until such time as he was rich, however, all that was left was for Tatham to cash in as much of his dwindling social capital as possible, and he began trading heavily on his former status as an MP. As an urban insider with the gift of the gab, his pro-Boer sympathies went down well with disillusioned rural Afrikaners who remained suspicious about Botha and the republican credentials of the ruling SAP. In January 1913, Tatham was billed to appear on the same platform, in Pretoria, as General JBM Hertzog, newly departed from the SAP, and Tielman Roos, an advocate and loyal friend who, like Tatham, entertained presidential ambitions and strong white working-class sympathies.[73]

Increasingly trusted in some elite Afrikaner circles, in April 1913 Tatham accompanied the war hero General Christiaan de Wet on a sweep through the countryside, focusing on pockets of political discontent.[74] He came back from the tour convinced that the future of the country lay with republicans, and that he probably had an important role to play in the coming struggle for votes. But tracing the footsteps of a great man can be dangerous, and can lead a dwarf to believe that he, too, might become a giant. Tatham, sensing that he had grown in stature, ceased looking up, choosing to look around at men he now considered as his peers.

But no sooner had this train of nationalist thought picked up steam in Tatham's undulating mind than it was derailed by a blast of reality from an East Rand mining community that reverberated across the Witwatersrand, reminding him of his credentials as a champion of the white working class. The general strike of mid-1913, in which troops were used to help crush the miners' resistance, demanded his attention. In May he sent letters to all the members of the House of Assembly hinting at his ability to solve the problem – an initiative that triggered a satirical speech from a cabinet minister. A few weeks later, at a public meeting, in Pretoria, Tatham appeared as the main speaker, demanding that the Governor General, Lord Gladstone, be recalled for sanctioning the use of imperial troops during the strike. Cheered by the approval of Pretoria, Tatham headed to Cape Town where he attempted, unsuccessfully, to convince rival Botha and Hertzog supporters to adopt a more unified approach to the country's problems.[75]

Disillusioned by the narrow ethnic exclusivity of Afrikaner nationalism, and still suffering from the after-effects of dwarf–giantism and the general strike, Tatham returned to Johannesburg set on a new political adventure. Reading Rosa Luxemburg – 'a woman of remarkable ability', he said – convinced him of the perniciousness of imperial economics and the importance of class struggle.[76] The South African problem, he concluded, was that Marxism and nationalism had been left isolated, on opposite sides of a great ravine. What was needed was a bridge between class and political culture, and who better to tender for its construction than Ralph Heathcote Tatham? In August 1913, almost a year before Hertzog got around to forming his Afrikaner-centred party in July 1914, Tatham launched a 'National Party'. The new party, he said, would embrace English and Afrikaans speakers, advance the cause of industrial protectionism, encourage the membership of both sexes and 'obtain the suffrage of women'.[77]

But the dwarf had run too far, too fast. His National Party failed to gain traction and his legs collapsed beneath the weight of avant-garde policies. The failure of the body, however, did nothing to encourage the realignment of the mind. Tatham clung firmly to the idea that, given the right circumstances, he might yet become the first president of a republic – to the point that some thought hinted at derangement. It was, however, not all bad news. In summing up a court case, in 1919, a judge was of the slightly more reassuring opinion that, while Tatham was 'not a good character', he 'did not think that he was a lunatic'.[78] A few of Tatham's ex-wives – he was much married – might later have agreed with half of the judge's observations, although which half will forever be unclear.

Either way, politics without the benefit of political office – and in some cases even when in office, as Tatham well knew – was a costly business.[79] After the stillbirth of his National Party, Tatham sought to keep his working-class credentials on display by joining the badly divided Labour Party, where he became a leading advocate for its pro-war faction.[80] But too much talk, too much travel and too little legal work did nothing for the bank balance and encouraged him to probe the outer limits of a profession never known for its modesty when it came to money matters. In 1915, he was struck off the roll of advocates for 'discharging the function of an attorney, accepting money, and appropriating it towards his own fees, improperly retaining bail money in his possession, and by insinuating himself into a family dispute obtaining exorbitant fees and himself employing an attorney so that he might obtain instructions from him'.[81] So egregious were these transgressions of the 'Order of Advocates' that twice thereafter, in 1917 and 1923, his pleas for readmission were swiftly dispatched.[82]

As the war rumbled on and the cost of living skyrocketed, all that Tatham had left to cling to were his dreams of becoming president and the East Rand gold claims. But, as the cliché would have it, it is always darkest just before dawn, and something was happening high in the night sky, even though the first movements were so faint that not even Tatham and Seccombe, in Johannesburg, or Naylor, in London, could detect them. What was happening was that inexorably, the twin planets of influence and wealth, imagined by two gentlemen-hustlers at opposite ends of the earth, were slowly being drawn into a new alignment. An unknown force was sucking Tatham, with all his political connections, and Naylor, with his exceptional ability to raise capital at short notice, out of remote orbits into new pathways. But where precisely was the gravitational pull coming from, and what would happen when the two bodies met? Would they explode upon impact, or merge to form some new, gigantic stellar object? Or what if some mysterious, even larger, third force, an uncharted menacing black hole, swallowed them both?

Rufe Naylor had left Johannesburg late in 1913 and, by his own telling – and therefore perhaps not entirely truthfully – was without assets, an employee of IW Schlesinger's ATT and AFT. In London, Naylor's rickety raft, last sighted on the Rand, righted itself and despite, or perhaps because of, the wartime gloom, found shelter in familiar waters. Schlesinger approved of Naylor's choices, and he directed a stream of successful artistes and films to the trusts for distribution across southern Africa. Naylor's interest in athletics and the human body remained with him, and in 1915 he cast two world champion sprinters in 'The Sports Girl', a revue reported as having done 'big business in the English provinces'. His brother Peter Charles was put on AFT's payroll, and after a tour of duty in India he, too, returned to England.[83]

But as their older brother, George, was constantly being reminded, Rufe's primary passion remained bookmaking, horses and the turf club. From his base in London, Rufe, already planning his return to Johannesburg once the war ended, bought horses and exported them to South Africa. The racing industry in a mining town was easier to penetrate than in class-ridden England. It all suited George, who had become confident enough to revert to the name he had been baptised with, and added the hold-all term 'speculator' to his own occupation of bookmaking.[84]

Seccombe, Mr Faithful, provided Rufe with information about where the richer hogs along the Rand were sniffing out wartime truffles. Not all of it was comforting, although Seccombe assured him that it was. There had been a shift in the locus of most wealth, and 'eleven mines on the Far East Rand were generating more than twice as much profit as the forty-odd mines along the rest of the Witwatersrand'.[85] Tatham had sold his claims, more 'east' than 'far east', to the Modder West Gold Mining Company (MWGM), in which he had also taken up a large parcel of shares. So, too, had Seccombe – now styling himself a 'director' and 'financier' of the same company – and through him some shares had also gone Rufe's way.[86] Anxious to retain the value of their MWGM holdings, Seccombe had, in 1916, presided at a public meeting to oppose the government's selling or leasing of its East Rand holdings to 'private capitalists'. The state would be better advised, he argued, to retain the land for the benefit of poor whites.[87]

At the time, Rufe was concerned, although not unduly so, about the fate of the East Rand mines. He was more of an inner-city man, and it was the racing industry, focused on the profitable Auckland Park racecourse, where Seccombe served on several committees, that interested him most. What Naylor, as bookmaker and owner of racehorses, aspired to was access to the racing industry right across the Witwatersrand. But he knew that those in control of Auckland Park were suspicious about his ambitions and motives. To succeed, he would first have to gain control of a racecourse or two in his own right. By early 1916, Seccombe, company director, financier and Labour Party member, along with a few friendly town councillors, was testing the waters to see if they could obtain a licence and buy the property necessary for a new non-proprietorial racecourse within the Johannesburg municipality that might compete with, and throw off, the Auckland Park stranglehold.[88] They lacked financial backing, but they also knew the one man who could raise capital out of nowhere.

By mid-1916, his 'big business' in London and the county circuits behind him, Naylor was back on his feet but no longer in the employ of IW Schlesinger. The two had parted on friendly terms since they had long since ceased to be business rivals – competition being a thing both men disliked intensely. Towards the end of that year, Rufe applied for, and was granted, a passport 'to travel to Africa stating he was coming here [to South Africa] to settle up certain business and then returning home to Australia'. And, after the disaster at Gallipoli the previous year, Naylor had also given 'an undertaking to join the Australian Forces, if required'.[89]

Ever the optimist, Naylor set out for the Rand knowing not only that he had the Modderfontein investment against which to raise funds, but also that he could rely on his two brothers and Seccombe, along with the family's new friend and supporter, Tatham, for assistance. The situation was promising since, unlike when he had been caught unprepared by the gambling commission, back in 1909, he would have access to considerable political leverage to help him raise additional capital.

The effects of the first Naylor tsunami to strike Johannesburg lasted for about five years, from 1908 to 1913. The immediate force behind the second, larger tsunami was felt for half as long, from 1917 to 1919, but the long-term effects cut deeper and spread much wider, right across the region. It was not long before everyone along the Witwatersrand and beyond knew that Rufe was back in town.

Believers afflicted with ill health travel to Lourdes in the hope of curing their ailments; those suffering from want of capital come to Johannesburg. The Naylor financial fountain began to flow again late in 1916. One of the first to arrive in the city, hoping for a miracle, was a short, sunburnt, bearded pilgrim from Lourenço Marques wearing a hat at so jaunty an angle that he seemed like a most unlikely supplicant.[90] And he was. Naylor recognised him and recalled their first meeting, at the Robinson Deep Mine, three years earlier.

PART II

HEADACHES

If you want to lose your faith, make friends with a priest. GEORGE GURDJIEFF, *MEETINGS WITH REMARKABLE MEN* (1963)

Padre José Vicente do Sacramento – The Bookmaker's Friend, 1893–1916

P adre José Vicente do Sacramento (1868–1933) was an even more liminal being than the mercurial Naylor and, like him, a man difficult to classify, constantly shifting in and out of mental and geographical terrains.[1] Charitable folk might have cast both as being slightly eccentric, their critics judging them a touch insane, though never dangerously so. In physics, like charges repel one another, but, in the universe of personalities, love of money can draw men much closer.

Castelo-Sertã, where Vicente was born into a Catholic family of modest means, was a smallish town, lying inland from the Atlantic coast, about halfway between Lisbon and Porto. An intelligent child, Vicente was educated in a period after Portugal's 'long anti-clerical century' (1759–1850s), a period when church and state were groping their way towards a new accommodation. At a time when imperial rivalries in sub-Saharan Africa were accelerating – and more especially after the Berlin Conference of 1884–1885 – the state was hoping to underscore its authority in the colonies, while the Roman Catholic Church was, as ever, keen on expanding its influence.[2] An era of tentative rapprochement saw the rise of a novel – slightly hybrid – institution.

The Royal College of Missions at Cernache do Bonjardim, from which Vicente graduated in 1893, aged 25, was the offspring of the testy relationship between church and state rather than a marriage. The college produced hundreds of 'secular missionaries', men with loyalties to both Lisbon and the Vatican, some of whom, like Vicente, could be as fiercely nationalist as they were religious.[3] Most men of integrity experienced little difficulty in finding the sweet spot where the demands of church and state intersected – but not all. For the few who suffered the misfortune of having been being born and/or raised with bifurcated, manipulative personalities, the church-state divide presented a convenient fault line across which one authority or institution could be played against the other.

For a man serving more than one master, the integration of attitudes, beliefs and values in a coherent way could be difficult and give rise to tensions manifesting in erratic and occasionally defiant behaviour. And when the resulting dissonance became marked or exacerbated by problematic personal traits, notions of chastity, obedience and poverty – whether cemented into place by vows formally taken in the church or not – could be among the earliest casualties in the priestly life.

In 1893, Padre Vicente was deployed to Mozambique, commencing an eight-year tour of duty in the then capital of the colony, Ilha de Moçambique (Mozambique Island). In retrospect, it may or may not have been a propitious moment for his arrival. It coincided with the first great boom in the gold-mining revolution on the Witwatersrand, which changed the entire economic orientation of the elongated coastal colony, from gazing northeast into the Indian Ocean – the source of its past trading fortunes – to looking southwest, inland, towards the new industrialising Eldorado.

The Padre served the Church in various capacities in and around the Island for six years, during which time he did important lexicographical research in association with the ultra-patriotic Lisbon Geographical Society, which helped raise his profile within the all-important ministry of the Secretary of State of the Navy and Overseas Affairs.[4] During his tour the importance of the Island declined noticeably, and in 1898 it lost its status as capital of the colony to the economically more buoyant Lourenço Marques, in the far south. The following year, Vicente contracted malaria and returned to Portugal to regain his health and extend his influence and networks in Lisbon, where he was becoming much better known.

The Padre recovered from the bouts of fever relatively quickly, but within weeks of his return he underwent what now seems like a momentous change of heart and mind. His attitude towards the Church

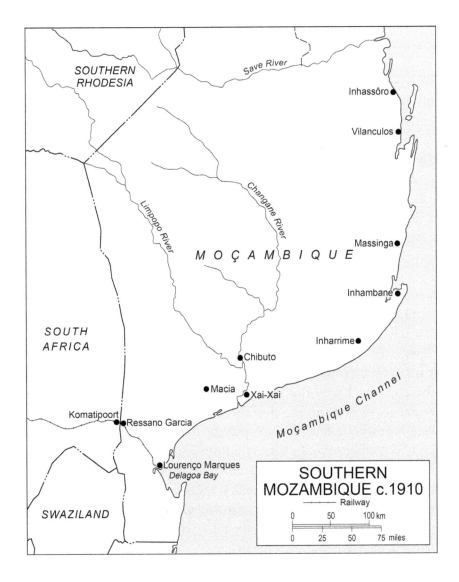

Map showing Southern Mozambique c.1910 with labels: SOUTHERN RHODESIA, Save River, Inhassôro, Vilanculos, Limpopo River, Changane River, MOÇAMBIQUE, Massinga, Inhambane, SOUTH AFRICA, Inharrime, Chibuto, Macia, Xai-Xai, Moçambique Channel, Komatipoort, Ressano Garcia, Lourenço Marques, Delagoa Bay, SWAZILAND, SOUTHERN MOZAMBIQUE c.1910, Railway, 0 50 100 km, 0 25 50 75 miles

underwent a shift but in ways that were confusing and could neither be reconciled easily nor resolved satisfactorily. On the one hand, his faith appeared to have deepened because, in April 1899, he underwent an official, state-approved change of name from José Vicente to José Vicente do Sacramento.[5] On the other hand, however, having nearly completed his mandatory tour of duty, the Padre seems to have decided never again to accept blindly the dictates of church or state and to plot the course of his career on terms only of his own making. As part of that decision, and perhaps as importantly, the Padre was now of the view that all good works, including those undertaken by a missionary, went hand in hand with making progress in material life. It was simply not possible to live off the stipend he was paid by the state. His future, as he now saw it, lay in the developing south rather than in northern Mozambique.

But the Catholic hierarchy had a mind of its own. Upon his return Padre Vicente was sent back to the Ilha de Moçambique and placed in charge of an arts and crafts school. With increasing insistence, he asked to be reassigned as a parish priest and was eventually sent to Lourenço Marques, where went on to develop a few business sidelines between 1901 and 1904. As a partial beneficiary of the short, post-Anglo-Boer War speculative boom in the new capital, he was convinced by a visit from the bishop in Johannesburg that the true source of wealth lay on the Rand.

Of the seven virtues, the one that the Catholic Church and the Portuguese state perhaps set most store by in fragile colonies was 'obedience', and a discontented Vicente was redeployed to Chinde, a small port halfway up the Mozambican coastline at the mouth of the Zambezi River. But shortly after his arrival there, in 1905, he found a way of returning south when he persuaded a doctor to provide him with a certificate to present himself in the capital on the grounds of ill health. Granted a month's sick leave, he nipped off to Johannesburg for more discussions with the bishop there. Upon his return to Lourenço Marques, he first tried to be appointed as chaplain to the local hospital, and when that failed, 'impertinently' demanded to be redeployed to the Witwatersrand. The Bishop of Mozambique refused, ordering him back north.[6]

The rising waters of resentment now began testing the strength of the Church's dam wall. With an interest in property in the south, Vicente returned to Chinde only with great reluctance. He took to it in the same spirit that a transported French citizen might take on arrival at Devil's Island and behaved like a recalcitrant convict. During 1907–1909 he was consistently choleric, combative and vexatious as he tried, unsuccessfully, to get transferred to the Witwatersrand. Vicente was, the bishop said, a priest who 'disturbed more than he served'.[7] Vicente, however, was not only disrupting but actively redistributing some church and state funds. During a depression and at a

Padre José Vicente do Sacramento, turbulent entrepreneur, priest and Lourenço Marques Lottery concessionaire.

time when wax, used for candles and other purposes, was one of the colony's main exports, he and an unnamed parish priest in Lourenço Marques set up a scheme to defraud their employers.

Vicente applied to, and was granted funds by, the colonial treasury for the purchase of a quantity of wax for use in his northern parish. As usual, he ordered wax from his business partner, a friendly priest in Lourenço Marques. The friend dispatched, and invoiced Vicente for, a much larger quantity of wax than was needed in Chinde, which Padre Vicente acknowledged by issuing a 'false receipt'. The difference in value between goods supposedly sent and received was pocketed by the priestly pair, leaving both church and state poorer. The scheme was not discovered until three years later when the former Lourenço Marques priest, but not Sacramento, confessed to the wrongdoing. The Church then did its very best to cover up his role in the business, but not that of Vicente.[8]

That Vicente's small stipend was already being fraudulently supplemented did nothing to dampen his desire for money; it primed it further. Nor did it ease his desire either to get reassigned to Johannesburg or, if it proved necessary, to abandon his state-funded post.[9] Benefiting from the fall in prices during the recession, he used the little capital he had accumulated, and borrowed more, to purchase some farming land from a widow on the outskirts of Lourenço Marques, at Infuleni.[10] At Chinde, his already obnoxious behaviour reached a new low.

To help meet his new commitments, Vicente wrote a letter to the district governor asking for his stipend to be augmented, but the missive revealed so 'undisciplined and choleric [a] mind' and was so 'disrespectful and irreverent' in tone that it was returned to him.[11] He and a coadjutor argued so aggressively and consistently that it was feared they would come to blows, and the Church arrived at the conclusion that Vicente would have to be transferred. During what might have been an ecclesiastically engineered cooling-off period, Vicente undertook a trip to Portugal. When he got back to Lourenço Marques, sensing that he lacked sufficient funds to go into farming, he renewed his pleas to be sent to Johannesburg.[12]

But if Vicente thought he was at last bound inland for the Witwatersrand, he was mistaken. In church chess, a pawn is no match for a bishop. He pleaded to be reinstated as a parish priest, in Lourenço Marques, but was instructed to pack up and ship out to Sena, further up the Zambezi.[13] In order to linger at his property outside the capital and plead his cause anew, he took leave, and when that failed too he spent two months giving all sorts of excuses for not having boarded the steamer heading north.

In Sena, in December 1908, the Padre's resentment reached flood level and the prelate's dam wall was breached within weeks, if not days. Unable to win support within the Church hierarchy, Vicente abandoned his post, and for some months was the administrator-manager at the nearby Anguaze and Andone *prazos*. The estates, near-autonomous relics of medieval Portuguese law, opened multiple possibilities for fraud and corruption by way of tax collection, allocation of black labour, manipulation of market prices and diversion of African workers' wages.[14] He then abandoned those posts, too, for reasons the bishop did not wish to explore, but the prelate provided Vicente with the funds to get back to Lourenço Marques.

Back in the capital by early 1909, the Padre, still partly in the grip of the church-state crab, resolved to free himself from the claw he always felt the more offensive of the two – the poorly paying state. Having completed the mandatory minimum period of service stipulated in his state contract, this was easily achieved. On 8 January, he officially left the service of the Ministry of Overseas Affairs but remained a member of a church always reluctant to excommunicate him.[15] At Infuleni he renewed his friendship with Velha Carlota – the rich, elderly African widow who had ceded him a portion of her land for farming some months earlier.

Although not a member of an order bound by vows, Vicente was shedding his core priestly values. Notions of honesty, obedience and poverty were buckling beneath the weight placed upon them. More slippage and weight transference were on the cards. He and the widow might have started out dancing the then-popular Hesitation Waltz, but they were unwilling to take the cautionary part of it seriously.[16] The Church, befuddled by age, bad eyesight and poor hearing about priestly transgressions when it suited it, retreated into a familiar pose of indifference.

The Church kept its silence: Vicente's weaknesses were partly offset by the priest's numerous public displays of patriotism and piety. Indeed, as with crustaceans, the darker the shell, the tastier the white flesh became to those intent only on salvation.[17] On the Witwatersrand, where the Catholics had long suffered a shortage of priests in their battle with increasingly aggressive Protestant missionaries for the souls of African workers, including a black Mozambican majority in the mine compounds, the Padre's imperfections were less visible and more tolerable than on the east coast. Within weeks of his arrival in Lourenço Marques, Vicente, free from church-state restrictions, took up Bishop William Miller's invitation to join the Fordsburg parish in inner Johannesburg.[18]

In missionary mode, but still carrying the debt of Infuleni, Vicente could feel the shackles of poverty chafe at his wrists throughout 1909. The church was in dire straits and Fordsburg was a poor, racially mixed working-class community. He nevertheless founded several new schools on mine properties to counteract the influence of the resentful Anglican and other Protestant churches. The absence of his former state stipend reduced Vicente to living in 'a shack', and he was chastened to discover the even poorer lot of the black miners whose care he was charged with.[19]

For some time, Vicente supplemented his income by selling to African workers, on a commission basis, hundreds of copies of O *Africano*, a biweekly newspaper founded by João Albisini, forwarded to him from Lourenço Marques. He wrote articles, brimming with customary patriotic fervour and highlighting the plight of African miners, for the new paper.[20] It was the Protestants, he later suggested, who saw to it that he was eventually prevented from circulating or selling the newspaper in the sealed-off mining compounds. By then, he was also having difficulty recruiting black teaching assistants for the mine schools.[21]

Vicente clashed swords with poverty for some months, but when it became apparent who was winning, he looked around for ways of reconnecting with Portugal's state armoury. It was a propitious moment. Friends got him in through the back door and he was appointed part-time clerk in the office of the Curator of Indigenous Labour – the overseer of African miners on the Rand, and the same office that was notorious for intercepting the bulk of the workers' remittances to Mozambique.[22] But the Padre apparently resisted the obvious temptation and then secured an appointment as Portugal's acting vice-consul in Johannesburg.[23]

History was on his side – well, for a while at least. Having regained the trust of the administration and no longer directly involved in a struggle with the church hierarchy, he was back on the front foot. In June 1910, he was appointed as consul and duly recognised by the new South African government.[24] Cashing in on his new position and old nationalist sympathies, he approached the Ministry of Overseas Affairs to supplement his income by re-instating his monthly stipend. In August 1910, his application was approved by the Governor General, Freire de Andrade, in Lourenço Marques. In October, a coup orchestrated by the Republican Party in Lisbon, and supported by parts of the armed forces, dispensed with the power of the monarchy.[25] The new, profoundly anti-clerical Portuguese government then proceeded to unscramble – as best possible – the mixed church-state omelette that it had snatched, and the knives soon came out.

In 1911, the Republicans, going back on the Concordat of the 1850s, passed a 'law of separation' and launched their attack on ecclesiastical power by setting the hours at which mass might be held, curtailing some of the civil rights of the priests and decreeing that 'the clergy was to be paid by the state administration and not by the church'.[26] As a graduate of Cernache do Bonjardim and a 'secular missionary', Vicente was better placed to survive the onslaught than priests who were directly affiliated to the Vatican. Nor would the Padre's cantankerous relationship with the Bishop of Mozambique have worked to his disadvantage as the worst of the anti-clerical storm burst around him. As before, whatever his personal limitations, he remained a practising Catholic.

Vicente hunkered down, maintaining a low profile, but it was insufficient to retain his position as consul under a new administration.[27] He stoutly defended his de Andrade-approved stipend, but in mid-1912 it was withdrawn.[28] After that he experienced the same deprivation he had encountered three years earlier when he first arrived in Johannesburg. But friends in the Curator's office again came to his rescue with another short-term appointment that ended in May of the following year. But no sooner was he back in the fields of Infuleni than he received an invitation to return and take up an interim position as amanuensis in the Curator's office. In late 1913, he was back on the Rand during a recession.[29] It was then that he met Rufe Naylor for the first time, at the Robinson Deep Mine – the one an Australian bankrupt, the other a Portuguese pauper. Not long thereafter Naylor left for London, and in January 1914 Vicente returned to Lourenço Marques.[30]

The three years that followed were among the most physically demanding that Vicente had faced. Men *in extremis* sometimes reach for the economic template and skills of their youth to survive. The Padre's love of agriculture, evidenced by his candle-wax-funded investment in a plot of land, may have harked back to his childhood in Sertã. At Infuleni, in his mid-forties, he sought farming success, manifesting formidable bodily strength while simultaneously advancing his nationalist, not excluding black African nationalist, ideas with contributions to O *Africano*. A contemporary recalled seeing him 'blackened by the sun', undernourished and mounted on a donkey on his way to the city market to sell the only crops that could be harvested from the hopelessly sandy soils.[31]

But, as ever, Vicente's venture was not without public costs or private comforts, sometimes at the expense of others. He managed both his own fields and the more extensive ones belonging to the widow, but the hardest work of all – hoeing, planting and ploughing – was often undertaken by *shibalo* (forced labour) supplied, at sub-subsistence wages, by a colonial administration well-disposed to him.[32] Moreover, as manager, the costs of most of the farming operations were under-written by Carlota – a woman with some experience when it came to taking in notable white lovers – who drew comfort from his skills and work ethic. Indeed, between 1914 and 1917, the couple had become so open about their domestic arrangements that most people considered them to be 'married'.[33]

The Church, however, did not. It nevertheless chose not to do, or say, anything directly about Vicente flaunting its injunction to chas-tity either in its formal correspondence with the local administration or, for some years, in its exchanges with office holders in the Vatican. There were good reasons for not doing so. It would only have fed into the prevailing hostile anti-clerical climate. As importantly, it would have puzzled one of the Church's three wise monkeys, more particu-larly the one that *saw* no evil, because there were thousands of other such arrangements in a colony significantly short of European women and where Portuguese men routinely took African lovers or wives. Instead, the Church, rightly fearing Vicente's potential for causing disruption, chose not to excommunicate him but rather to shun him as far as was officially possible. It was a difficult decision and one that the Church came to regret. In effect, then, if not in black and white or in law, Vicente, a secular missionary, was much like a defrocked priest.

Vicente was a padre in name only, kept from complete financial failure by the grace of the good widow of Infuleni. Unwilling to sup-plicate before his former church and state masters, he was in a pre-carious and extremely stressful situation, without office or a regular income, despite the title and name he clung to. But fate was about to intervene in his life.

In the first week of November 1916, Rufe Naylor returned to Johannesburg after a successful stay in London. He was reported as being 'interested in a certain sporting venture'.[34] The war had contrived to keep him and the Padre half a world apart, but they were about to meet again under circumstances very different from those under which they had parted three years earlier. Vicente had heard of a 'mine' of sorts that, while admittedly dependent on other, all too real gold mines for its viability, lay beyond the control of the Chamber of Mines, one that would continue paying 'dividends' until the last of the Reef was exhausted. He wanted to mine the pockets of the white miners rather than ore bodies. Both men knew, from recent painful personal experience, the point where poverty and human nature intersected, and, more importantly, they appeared to trust one another.

The Racecourse Wars and the Dividend Cigarette Company, circa 1916–1917

The coming of war unleashed a series of political, economic and social storms that ravaged southern Africa for a decade, and which, on the Witwatersrand, culminated in the white miners' strike of 1922. The unsuccessful Rand Revolt saw white workers lose the battle, only for them to go on to win the decade-long political war that followed. The Pact government (1924–1933) entrenched the privileged position of white – especially white male – labour in the economy.[35]

For skilled English-speaking white miners, pacesetters for the wages of half a million people on the Witwatersrand, this enhanced state-driven job security was long overdue. Among the less skilled, unemployed Afrikaners drawn in from the countryside, a third of whom lived in cities by 1921, the protection that came with the jobs colour bar on the mines and the railways was more welcome still.[36]

Unlike the sharp upturn experienced in the mid-1890s, economic growth in the years following Union was sluggish when not stagnant. The 1910s and 1920s were not 'a period of growth either for the gold mining industry in particular or the economy as a whole'.[37] The early and late 1920s saw 'sharp recessions' while the intervening periods presented problems of their own: 'The post-war years saw an astronomical increase in the cost of living with prices rising by almost 50% between 1917 and 1920.'[38] As had happened during the 1906–1908 recession, the white working class again found itself in a state of financial siege manifesting in familiar ways, including the issues of affordable rents or home ownership.[39]

For those whose inspiration was drawn from the church, government or industry, the answer to unemployment and white working-class hardship was largely self-evident – working harder, more disciplined spending by the profligate poor and the need for increased savings. It was a message that chimed well with Calvinists, who already had a biblical formula to hand linking sacrifice to charity, with economists not yet burdened by Keynes's *The General Theory of Employment, Interest and Money* (1936), and with employers. The conventional wisdom, built on a cue taken from the US, was made practical through the launch of a national thrift movement, in 1916, that is, at the very moment that the cost of living was rising most rapidly.[40] The already yawning gap between the departing SS *Thrift* and those marooned on the wharf of financial reality widened so dramatically and so suddenly that it was impossible for the majority to clamber aboard.

As in the 1906–1908 recession, those with ideological influence and political power wanted to inculcate restraint and self-discipline in the less well-off, who appeared all too ready to indulge in gambling. Back then, it was the *Sunday Times* that had blown on the embers of ruling-class resentment until they flared up as the Horse Racing and Betting Restriction Act of 1909. But white workers, confronted by many of the same problems in 1917–1920, responded as before. They dreamed of hearing the thud of a newspaper arriving at the front door informing them that they had become wealthy overnight rather than the sound of the mine hooter. For the nervous among the ruling class, however, the presence of Seccombe, and a bit later Rufe Naylor, only underscored their sense of déjà vu.

Naylor's lifelong passion – no, his obsession – was how to secure a personally elevated standard of living from horse racing and gambling by gaining control of the entire chain of value, from owning and controlling thoroughbred horses and racecourses to managing betting outlets and manipulating the odds offered to punters. Almost everything else was of secondary interest. Throughout his stay in England he remained in close contact with brothers George and Peter, as well as with Seccombe, the latter acting not only as manager of his few remaining holdings in Johannesburg but also as chief informant about the prospects of the horse-racing industry and ongoing changes in society.

Naylor's original intention had been to loop back through the Witwatersrand, wind up his business interests and proceed to Australia. But Seccombe's stories about the rude health of the horse-racing industry and Tatham's tales about a fortune just waiting to be made on the East Rand, where Ernest Oppenheimer was about to float the Anglo American Corporation, tripped all his travel switches. Rufe's future clearly lay in Johannesburg, but if he were to avoid the errors of 1908–1909, he would need a far more considered approach to attain his objective.

Naylor's 'plan', in truth more a pragmatic adjustment to changing circumstances than a premeditated strategy, had several parts to it. Foremost was the need for the political cover that had eluded him at the time when the passage of the Horse Racing and Betting Restriction Act of 1909 had caught him largely unprepared. This time, things would be different. He would have to craft an independent political identity for himself, and his locksmiths, Seccombe and Tatham, would help. They had spent the war fashioning keys to the back doors of the local houses of corruption, even if parliament's portals remained sealed. Seccombe, friend of the white 'working man', had no need of back doors. As an activist who had already stood, though unsuccessfully, for a seat on the Johannesburg Town Council, he was well in with some of the leading lounge lizards of the popular Labour Party.

Among Seccombe's friends were Dan Dingwall, president of the hefty Boilermakers' Union, and Mrs NE Dingwall – both prominent Labour Party members. Dingwall served on the executive of the Transvaal Provincial Council, while he and his wife both occupied seats on the Johannesburg Town Council, where the Labour Party often dominated the formal proceedings. A militant trade unionist, Dan Dingwall was open to the idea that the redistribution of wealth in society did not always have to come via ponderous social-democratic routes.[41]

Tatham, once from the other end of the political spectrum, now a disciple of Rosa Luxemburg, was busy seeking a new home among the organised white working class. His credentials as the urban mouthpiece of the failed 1914 Afrikaner rural rebellion and a hankering for a republic led by a president – preferably himself – ensured him an audience with some diehard nationalist politicians in the countryside. One was the gloriously named Christian Tiberius Zwanepoel van Veyeren, who sat on the Provincial Council as the representative for the constituency of Rustenburg.[42] Like Dingwall, van Veyeren felt that the wheels of democracy turned best when greased with oil of palm. Moreover, even though Tatham had been struck off the advocates' roll, Naylor felt that his legal training might prove useful when speeding up or slowing down the grit-filled wheels of justice.[43]

Working individually, Seccombe and Tatham could open doors for Naylor, but working together they offered more. Their dreams for Tatham's Modderfontein West claims were by then so vivid that they lit up barrooms by day as easily as they did bedrooms at night. Indeed, Seccombe, feeding off his rise into the ranks of the newly respectable, began to see his future as a 'director' of a mine manned exclusively by white labour – a quintessentially Australian idea – and began a short, deliberately leaked correspondence with former Cape premier John X Merriman.[44]

Real mining directors and investors did not take Seccombe seriously, but his pronouncements may have packed a bigger punch when it came to potential investors drawn from other sectors of the economy, and he was already in discussions with the emerging movie mogul IW Schlesinger. Already a millionaire, IW had no need of mining investments and was deaf to many shady deals put to him. He was perfectly capable of doing his own. He was, however, intrigued by Naylor's entrepreneurial genius and the potential it held for competition, and so remained curious about the horse-racing business. If necessary, IW was as capable as the next man of oiling a squeaky wheel.[45]

But, as Naylor and his partners in the gambling and entertainment industries knew, grey-going-on-black projects could not be sealed off entirely from the mainstream economy or the law and its enforcement agencies. Many of the shadows that fell across underworld economies came from reputable institutions with sunlit front entrances for legitimate clients cashing crisp cheques, and side entrances for irregulars bearing creased banknotes. The ground floor, overseen by bespectacled bank managers, separated men by class, but in the vaults clerks stuffed money in bags without questioning its pedigree. And, whenever the manager did come down to check, he said nothing and just winked at the clerks.

Wartime Johannesburg had more than one winking bank. Rufe found it reassuring and chose a bank that served two generations of Naylors.[46] In similar fashion, Naylor and those who assisted in the lottery business sought out friendly faces in the South African Police.

A few poorly paid constables, although less greedy than businessmen and politicians who worked openly in the economy, were unwilling to wait for 25 December to receive 'gifts' from shady friends.[47]

Naylor, Seccombe and Tatham were like so much charcoal, salt-petre and sulphur. As with the three base chemicals, they needed to be stored separately at cool temperatures and mixed in the correct proportion to achieve the optimum explosive effect. Warehouses of that sort were at a premium in wartime Johannesburg, heightening the attendant danger. But Naylor, mixer-in-chief, looked out of the warehouse window rather than into the chemicals, and fixed on a tar-get – the registered name of which was the Auckland Park Racing Club Limited.

APRC shareholders and the club's sluggish affiliate, the Springs Racing Club, which relied on mid-week East Rand punters, had a good war as the slaughter in Europe continued unabated. In fact, 'the Park', as it was commonly referred to, had an excellent war. Registered in 1904 and loosely overseen by the Jockey Club of South Africa, the Park was controlled by Colonel JJ Furze. Taken at face value, Furze was an old-school officer and gentleman whose reputation had been made in the 1906 Bambatha Rebellion. Disliked by the Labour Party and the trade union movement for his reactionary role during the 1911 tramway workers' strike, Furze was nevertheless at various times a member of the Johannesburg Town Council and the Transvaal Provincial Council.[48]

In 1916, the APRC was re-registered and floated as a company with a share capital of £85 000 and a board of seven directors.[49] Furze was made a permanent lifetime director at the Park and he and four others constituted what critics claimed to be an 'autocracy', a group of five within the board whose word, it was said, was 'law'. These directors allegedly '[waxed] fat at the expense of the ... owners and trainers' since they did not reinvest any of the profits by way of stakes for races, instead 'amassing ... reserve funds and dividends' that, 'in comparison to the ... capital originally put into the club', were 'simply colossal'.[50] It was quite a prospect.

Questionable financial motives were the least of the APRC board's sins. Furze, like Naylor and company, commanded more political colours than a chameleon. He was a man well versed in the ways of a frontier mining town undergoing the transition to an industrial city.

As he stated publicly in 1918, even though 'the old atmosphere of bribery was gradually clearing', he 'had lived in Johannesburg for 30 years and bribery had always been rife'. It was, he said, necessary to 'have friends in favour at court'.[51] A waxed moustache was all well and good for appearances, but when it came to making things happen, oil of palm was needed.

In effect, by 1916, even before Naylor came back to town, the Park was effectively under the control of the Furze acolytes, who at best might be seen as ethically compromised and at worst as plain crooked. Throughout the Great War, the war of the racecourse on the Witwatersrand was contested by two sets of gentlemen-hustlers – led, respectively, by Naylor and Furze. The relationship between the two groups was, however, never solely, or even entirely, opposi-tional. Like rival packs of hyenas coming across a carcass, sometimes there was enough for all to partake. Problems arose when the more entrenched of the packs refused to share.

As adverse economic conditions made the going tougher along the Witwatersrand, so did white workers flock in growing numbers to one of eight racecourses each Saturday, in the belief that chance and a horse's hooves might drag them free of wartime hardship, even if their employers would not. Thousands more found it unnecessary to go as far as Auckland Park. Hundreds of illegal betting outlets – so-called bucket shops – sprung up all along the Reef, bound them-selves into an association and openly operated a current account with the winking bank.[52]

Given its dominant position and a site accessible from Park Station – via horse-drawn cab, whose owners earned £7 on each of the 60 days that the club was entitled to race in each year – the Park had a licence to print money. By 1915, the APRC was the largest and most success-ful racing body in the country, and its totalisator – effectively a lottery in a city without legal access to a lottery – made huge profits. Indeed, so well did the company do financially that, after 1916, it made con-sistent efforts, often linked to allegations of bribery, to persuade the town council to share the cost of extending the tramway from the city centre to nearby Auckland Park.[53]

But successful racecourses, unless they fall unambiguously within the exclusive domain of the rich and privileged, can occupy an awkward position in the minds of the better-off. Racecourses dominated by the hoi polloi, without any of the veneer of class, fashion and snobbery that characterises upper-crust society, can all too easily lay bare the highs and lows of human emotion that accompany the frequently vulgar spectacle of grubbing for money. The rich few like money. What they do *not* like is being seen transacting large sums in front of the many or mixing too readily with those who do most to create wealth. Someone had to take responsibility for keeping the grandstand grand, a task less easily accomplished in a mining town than in the Home Counties, and more especially so in hard times.

In Johannesburg, the upper crust mostly frequented the oldest racecourse in the city, Turffontein, opened in 1887, a year after the mining camp was established. It was, asserted JA Clark, a part-time employee there and socialist organiser of the Boilermakers' Union, in 1919, 'the home of the snobocracy' and socially very well segregated: 'They have a series of fences dividing off the different classes', he explained, 'until you come to the very elite – "the whitest of the white".'[54]

Fortunately for those who governed, they were seldom on their own when it came to policing society's underclasses. The monthly cheque-cashing middle classes, sometimes only just freed from weekly brown-paper wage packets, were often willing to keep the less fortunate in line. Precisely because of its wartime success, the Park never wanted for critics. Some muttered about army recruitment being inhibited by horse racing; the Chamber of Mines was silently resentful; the Dutch Reformed churches were opposed to any form of gambling; and the thrift movement was unhappy about its seedy mirror image. Between them, they formed the kindling for outrage, and all that was needed for another moral panic, such as that of 1906–1908, to catch fire was for some institution or individual to put an ideological match to the underlying, enfranchised middle-class discontent.

Yet, despite the warning signs, Rufe Naylor wanted to be part of the club, to be inside rather than outside the Auckland Park marquee. In early January 1917, he twice attempted to buy his way into the company by offering to purchase it outright, or to lease the grounds at £6000 per annum (about half a million pounds sterling today). 'I am instructed to inform you', the club secretary chided him, 'that the Auckland Park racecourse is neither to let nor for sale.'[55]

Furze and friends had reason to be wary of the innovative Rufe and his family. As chairman of the Auckland Park Owners' and Trainers' Association, Seccombe had, in 1915, led the attack on the APRC for not redirecting sufficient of its profits back into stakes. Poor rewards did little to encourage better breeding and contributed to threadbare nags being raced too frequently. Naylor, who had few qualms about racing horses under the names of fictitious owners, was, via brother George, already importing the odd mare of quality. Moreover, Rufe had always been a formidable force in professional betting circles, and the APRC board feared the influence he wielded over owners, trainers and jockeys. His application for a bookmaker's licence at the Park, too, was refused. In short, the board wanted nothing to do with him and barred him from the racecourse.[56]

How and where exactly Naylor was going to raise the capital for his Auckland Park ambitions was unclear because he lacked the funds to purchase the racecourse outright. But then, just as the flame on his financial wick began flickering dangerously low, there was a knock on his door and a man of God entered. He was carrying an Aladdin's lamp that had, he claimed, an everlasting flame.

Padre Vicente had endured three miserable years on the land at Infuleni, but on a brief excursion into Lourenço Marques he had heard what, for all the world, sounded like an angel singing. The concession for the national lottery, first granted during the financial crisis of 1892 and thereafter forever struggling because of poor management and a chronic inability to meet its statutory commitments to charity, was up for renewal. Who better to tender for the contract than a patriot and man of the cloth who knew how the administration operated and how the Church and charity reached out to the poorest?

It was, Vicente explained to Carlota and friends, the chance of a lifetime. In his view, if the lottery were imaginatively marketed and properly managed, it could be a 'huge and never-ending source of wealth for the colony'. Moreover, during a war-triggered financial crisis few local capitalists had sufficiently deep pockets or the experience necessary to put together a competitive package capable of winning the concession. He, on the other hand, had worked on the gold mines, and if his friends agreed to fund an exploratory trip or two, he could probably raise the necessary capital and find men capable of administering the scheme. The capitalists agreed and funded several speculative visits to Johannesburg. But no sooner did the Padre have something promising in place than one or other administrative problem in Lourenço Marques caused a delay, or 'the capitalists fled' because he was unable to convince men who lacked either the energy or imagination to see the potential. Then, just as the delays in awarding the concession seemed never-ending and he was about to give up, he heard of Rufe's return to the Rand, and the merry widow came up with the money for a visit to the Last Chance Saloon.[57]

The door to Naylor's office was as open as his mind. He might have wanted for ready cash, but he had all the other attributes necessary to make a success of the business and asked only for a week or so to mobilise the capital for a strong bid. Naylor spent a day or two putting in place part of a developing strategy for dealing with the APRC and then easily got the financial backing of a half dozen largely undistinguished acquaintances, to the tune of around £5000. By 15 February 1917 he was on a 'business visit' to Lourenço Marques, a port that already had strong connections to Western Australia via the timber trade.[58] It was, Vicente maintained, Naylor's crisp notes and smooth tongue that ensured their success in jointly obtaining a concession to run the lottery and a sweepstake.

The train journey back to Johannesburg, in a way reminiscent of his experience in organising rail links to the 'Kalgoorlie Hundreds' 20 years earlier, allowed Naylor ample time for reflection. Maybe he could, as before, provide eager gamblers with a convenient way of connecting their dreamworlds to the more exciting spectacle of a live lottery draw at a popular seaside resort? It was a thought worth bearing in mind. The Lourenço Marques Lottery promised to be a source of steady funding, and he was committed to making it work by blanketing the Witwatersrand with tickets, if necessary, but it would never match his desire to dominate the horse-racing business, which had sustained him for most of his life.

He had failed to gain access to Fortress Auckland Park through financial inducements by trying to lure Colonel Furze and his lieutenants out of their stronghold with a Trojan Horse stuffed with cash that he did not have – but soon would. The wisdom of the forefathers – join them if you cannot beat them – seemed not to have worked, but the conditional 'if' was just another call to arms. It underscored the need for yet more vigorous attempts at beating the Furzian forces of privilege rather than backing away from a fight or supplicating yet again.

What was needed, Naylor believed, was an agile, cunning and sustained campaign, a full-scale war, not a battle, and the elements of his master plan were already beginning to fall into place. As Tatham confessed a few years later, 'We wanted Auckland Park smashed.'[59] There was, Naylor reasoned, little point in fighting the middle-class voters and newspapers that shaped 'public opinion' – the unseen forces that had cheered the state on to its triumph in 1906–1908. The low mutterings of the churches and other conservatives about grossly excessive gambling by the underclasses had to be orchestrated into a unified battle cry that rejected 60 racing days a year at Auckland Park and helped open the space in a crowded market for the other less popular racecourses on Wednesday and Saturday afternoons. It called for a great deal of messy, undercover political lobbying, and the lead would have to be taken by himself and trusted agents.

Some of the groundwork for Naylor's evolving plan to 'smash' the APRC had been undertaken the previous year by half a dozen not particularly well-off men, racing enthusiasts with long-standing links to various smaller clubs. Building on Seccombe and others' deep-seated objections to the low stakes at the APRC, the Rand Sporting Club (RSC) was awarded a licence to operate a non-proprietorial course in the Krugersdorp municipality. But, given the founders' lack of finance, their initiative was not activated for more than 18 months. Another site for a new racecourse, at Newclare, was not far from the Johannesburg municipal boundary and, being a non-proprietorial entity, held out the promise of offering rather better stakes and attracting more owners and trainers than did the APRC.[60]

The east-coat train smoke was barely out of Rufe's nostrils when he saw the impecunious directors of the RSC, who had not yet got round to registering their enterprise in Pretoria. The RSC was, in truth, a shell company, just waiting to be upended and have its insides stuffed with funding by anyone intent on a takeover. Naylor was ruthless. In return for taking up £3 000 worth of debentures, he would get a seat on the board, be made managing director of the company and receive the enormous salary of £150 a month. And then, in case anyone did not get the message, existing directors' fees were to be slashed to two guineas per meeting. And so the starving rather reluctantly agreed to feast on crumbs only.[61]

By then, Naylor had further strengthened his position in the racing industry by founding the 'South African Non-Proprietary Trainers and Owners' Association'. It was designed and launched precisely to undermine the authority and standing of the dominant Auckland Park Trainers and Owners' Association and succeeded in attracting many, if not most, of the APRC's better-off existing members.

But within weeks of the meeting with Naylor, the RSC directors had second thoughts when their financial appetites returned. They called a meeting – to which Rufe was not invited – to reconsider their own positions and that of the company, their hope being that the overall situation might improve if they could get racing going on their West Rand property. Intrigue, however, can seldom resist the temptation of humming before the choir bursts into song. Naylor got to hear of the meeting and called in his counsellor, Tatham. On 8 March 1917, the Supreme Court confirmed Naylor's standing as board member and granted him an interdict preventing any meeting from taking place without his presence. A protracted legal standoff ensued because, by then, Naylor had more urgent matters on his mind.[62]

On almost the same day the RSC was interdicted, Naylor's offices were raided. Detectives seized various documents, including a prospectus for 'Rufe Naylor Lotteries Ltd' that advertised for 'reliable agents ... in all towns throughout the Union of South Africa'. The LML, it seems, had got off to a flying start. Naylor, Seccombe and two others were arrested and charged under Kruger's lottery law – No. 7 of 1890.[63] Just days later, John A Coetzee, acting as 'Chairman of the Board of Management' of the RSC, hurriedly placed a notice in a newspaper distancing the company from Naylor: 'Mr Rufe Naylor does not hold any interest in the Club whatsoever.'[64] The British-inspired modernisation of southern Africa was proceeding apace in much of the economy and society, but when it came to gambling and waged men and women, it remained mired in the marshland of Protestant churches, English law, the electorate and politics. On the Rand the gap between the state and the white working class was only widening.

It took the prosecution a month to prepare its case against the principal movers behind Rufe Naylor Lotteries Ltd – also known as the Delagoa Bay Trading Company – with notable professionalism. The state, struggling to cope with the betting craze and the rash of bucket shops spreading across the Rand, was intent on one thing only. It wanted the infant lottery strangled before it was fully weaned, and to that end sought exemplary sentences for the moving force behind it – Naylor and his trusted chief lieutenant, the omnipresent Seccombe. The case was eventually heard, in the small Johannesburg Police Court, on 16 May 1917.

The *corpus delicti* seized during the raid was so damning that the accused had no option but to plead guilty. The defence, building on Naylor's record of supporting good causes, such as at the time of the sinking of the *Titanic*, portrayed him as 'a kindly individual', a man motivated largely by philanthropic concerns. His 'business visit' to Lourenço Marques that February was downplayed. 'Naylor happened to be in Delagoa Bay when he heard of a lottery run there for the benefit of the poor known as the Central Board of Charities', it was claimed. It was 'under the supervision of a religious gentleman and the government', and because it was in dire straits, Naylor 'came to the rescue of this body' and then sold tickets in the Transvaal. Building on the popular perception of Mozambique as little more than an informal South African colony – a view reinforced during the war – Naylor's attorney explained that the accused 'simply thought he was within the law in assisting, through the Union, a charitable organization in another part of South Africa'. It was, apparently, an example of charity beginning at home.[65]

AC Hadfield, the presiding officer in the Police Court – focus fixed – refused to be sidetracked by such flights of fancy. The defence had offered an implausible tale. 'Money had been deposited in a bank', Hadfield noted, and the lottery and sweepstakes had been conducted both openly and extensively by the accused and his agents. 'Now, no one can conceive that Naylor is doing this for nothing.' It was 'not a trifling matter' and the 'concession was set to run for some time'. He therefore fined Naylor £150, 'or five months' imprisonment with hard labour', while Seccombe was fined £15, or two months' imprisonment with hard labour. The fines were paid, and that night Naylor clambered aboard the train for Lourenço Marques.[66]

Rufe's second visit to Delagoa Bay heralded a remarkable top-to-bottom reorganisation of the lottery over a three-month period. The reconstruction of the company and subsequent expansion bore testimony to his ability as an exceptionally creative, determined and talented grey-market operator. And, through another stroke of genius, it simultaneously presented him with an opportunity to refine and renew the increasingly subtle attack on his detested Auckland Park adversaries by confronting them with yet another Trojan Horse.

With the assistance of Padre Vicente – that 'religious gentleman' – and the enthusiastic silent support of the Lourenço Marques administration, the holding company was reconfigured. The formal legal division between the lottery and the sweepstake dimensions of the business was nominally extended. Naylor then withdrew his original sterling investment in the holding company, which the Padre made good by raising a loan in devalued escudos from the Banco Nacional Ultramarino (BNU). As the colony's de facto central bank, the BNU invariably moved in unison with the administration.[67] Aided by the original coastal manager of the lottery, WM Southward, a man formerly connected to the Park racing establishment, Naylor redirected his sterling investment into a new venture that he already had in mind.

The Delagoa Bay Cigarette Company (DBCC), 'Incorporated in the Transvaal', was a work of legal art.[68] Naylor splashed colours onto a canvas that, in another world, might have adorned a boardroom in Commissioner Street. The finer legal detail was the brushwork of 'Advocate' Tatham. Profiting from a customs agreement that exempted raw tobacco imported from Mozambique from duty, the DBCC marketed only one brand, which became enormously popular right across the Witwatersrand.[69] A pack of ten Dividend cigarettes selling for ten shillings, it was reliably reported, was, in truth, probably worth about sixpence.[70]

The addiction to Dividends had little to do with tobacco and everything to do with the lottery; the kick came from adrenalin, not nicotine. The DBCC, it was later argued, was part of an elaborate 'co-operative' investment scheme. If so, it resonated with Seccombe's Starr-Bowkett project, then approaching the end of its life, and the ascendant policies of the Labour Party that he and Tatham were members of. Each pack of Dividends contained a unique number, effectively turning it into a coupon. The holder qualified for a monthly 'dividend' draw, as well as for the possibility of sharing in post-war windfall profits when the Mozambican currency regained a value last seen in 1914. It was laid out on the coupon:

> Receipt _____. Received from _____the sum of 10 shillings for investment in Portuguese Government currency at present rate of exchange, which will be held for realisation after the war, when the rate of exchange reaches pre-war values. Should any profit accrue from this investment this receipt must be produced when demand is made for payment. Such profits to be subject to 5 per cent commission. Delagoa Bay Money Agency.[71]

The Delagoa Bay Money Agency, authorised by the BNU – a winking bank if ever there was one – was fully owned by Padre Vicente and Rufe Naylor.

With the end of the war nowhere in sight, the high cost of living and death from miner's phthisis omnipresent, white miners on the Witwatersrand were less interested in a long-term 'investment' than in the possibility of an immediate return from the lottery. At the directors' discretion, two-thirds of the DBCC's gross profits was channelled into dividends each month to the potential benefit of subscribers. The remaining third remained within the company to cover the costs of administration, directors' fees and their share of the company dividends.[72]

The police and prosecutors knew that Naylor was the moving force behind the DBCC, but all that they could make out through the legal fog was a registered cigarette company offering the possibility of a monthly 'dividend' and the promise of a post-war payout based on currency speculation.[73] White miners, however, pierced the gloom with ease. All *they* saw was a lottery orchestrated by a flamboyant bookmaker with a reputation for prompt payment and straight dealing. Listing himself as the 'manager of Rufe Naylor Lotteries Ltd', Southward's lamp lit the way. As the head of the CID put it, 'the fact remains that Naylor, through his agents, is still selling monthly in the Union, tickets in his lottery to the extent of several thousand pounds, and in defiance of the law'.[74]

The Dividend Company was another Naylor masterstroke. It provided foreign-based concession owners, which included a Catholic priest, with considerable protection against the criticism of the churches, charities or thrift movement. But it was not the company's legal shell but the innards – the composition of its new board of directors – that did most to reveal the range of Naylor's business ingenuity.

Naylor suspended the lottery for July 1917 and set about providing himself with increased protection against prosecution, while simultaneously gaining some traction in the cabal running the Auckland Park racecourse.[75] Using Southward, 'Managing Director of DBCC', as intermediary, Naylor offered the three leading office bearers in the APRC shares in, as well as seats on the board of, the Dividend Company. The cagey Colonel Furze, GJ Plunkett (managing director of the APRC) and R Powell (board member) sensed an illegal operation. It took a personal intervention from Naylor to encourage Furze take greater interest in the proposal. But Furze then insisted on further reassurance by getting his advocate's opinion as to the legality of the scheme. It was only after Edward Nathan, Furze's counsel, assured him that the DBCC was a registered company, running a legally watertight business, that the Auckland Park three eventually took up the offer.[76]

Getting the Trojan Horse into Auckland Park was a minor triumph. The Colonel was a pillar of civil society, and as a director his name added lustre and respectability to a lottery already popular among white workers. Furze provided the DBCC with significant political and social insurance. Public prosecutors would think twice before dragging the Colonel to court. The new DBCC directors diluted some of the hostility that had been directed at Naylor but never enough for him to gain unrestricted access to the inner circle.

The Colonel grew to trust Naylor a little more, even though the cigarette business proved to be a bit of a distraction, leaving the APRC board members a little less vigilant than they might otherwise have been. Naylor drew the Furzians further into the operational realities of his scheme when they agreed to have agents sell Dividends directly to punters at the track. Indeed, Auckland Park, already a home from home for gamblers, became an important outlet for Naylor's lottery tickets.

When it came to strictly horse-racing matters, however, Naylor and the rest of the APRC management remained at loggerheads. The APRC zealously guarded its 60 race days a year, while Naylor remained equally intent on getting them reduced via a covert campaign to advance his own interest in Rand racecourses. Already at full stretch with the relaunching of the lottery in Lourenço Marques, Naylor was willing to play a waiting game. So, through much of 1917 he continued to develop and expand his transnational network for the sale of lottery tickets. It was the increasingly profitable lottery concession that funded Rufe Naylor's focused – no, near-obsessional – desire to control Johannesburg's inner-city racecourses.

In early June 1917, Naylor left for Natal on what the press presented as 'an extended holiday in Durban'.[77] This was nonsense; the man did not know the meaning of the word 'holiday'. The venue had been chosen because it offered a subsidiary base for the lottery, a sea link to Delagoa Bay and a cross-country route to Lourenço Marques via Swaziland. For the same reason, Vicente purchased a farm at Mailana, on the Umbeluzi, upriver from Delagoa Bay, situated on the useful rail link between Lourenço Marques and Goba on the Swaziland border. And if there was any doubt as to the source of the funding for the new venture, or its secondary function – to facilitate the onward movement of lottery tickets to the Witwatersrand – then Padre Vicente left no one in doubt. The farm was renamed Quinta da Boa Sorte, the Property of Good Fortune.[78]

But it was Naylor who led the way in opening a new, alternative route linking Mozambique to South Africa and developing an important secondary market for the sale of lottery tickets in the Union. In Natal, that June, 'Naylor Investments Ltd' purchased a property within easy reach of Durban, at Winkelspruit, on the province's south coast.[79] English-speaking Natal, with fewer Dutch Reformed churches, and less dominee-dominated than the Highveld, offered him a route to the Witwatersrand that circumvented the Lourenço Marques–Johannesburg rail corridor, where customs officers and the police were more vigilant than in Natal.

Naylor and Seccombe now effectively directed and controlled the northern route for lottery tickets from Delagoa Bay into the Transvaal and a hinterland that stretched as far as the diamond-mining centre of Kimberley and across much of the Free State. The task of managing the slightly more expensive southern route into Natal fell to brother George, who had been moved to Durban some weeks earlier. Keeping business – including shady business – within the family is a maxim not always easily effected. The new and growing Natal operation demanded an additional lieutenant and Rufe had run out of brothers.

The Naylor brothers' choice was vindicated over several decades. The fellow's credentials were sound, and he was married to his work. He loved gambling and travel to the point that his wife eventually divorced him. He had a passion for horses and was so comfortable with animal bloodlines that he went on to become a breeder in his own right. Raised, one suspects, in a country district, he, like Tatham, enjoyed important connections to a few leading rural-based nationalist politicians. Although himself an Afrikaner, he was comfortable among English speakers and mixed easily with racegoers and breeders of the Union Jack type. He was Paulus Johannes van der Linden but was far better known as just 'Paul'.[80]

Back in Johannesburg, and with the enhanced logistics for importing Dividend Cigarettes in place, Naylor tightened security at the company's Eloff Street offices. His efforts would have got a nod of approval from Alphonse Capone, whose smuggling operation in Chicago he predated by three years. Rufe commissioned a large desk with hard-to-detect secret compartments for stashing cash or coupons. The office walls sported hidden recesses behind wood panels.[81]

Naylor had been fascinated by the potential of the telephone for rapid communication ever since he had fixed the odds on a race in Sydney while based in Perth. He perfected an early-warning system for any unexpected developments among business rivals or imminent police raids. He bribed police officers to phone him with advance notice of any moves by detectives, and hired operators at the central telephone exchange to pass on any information that might be of interest or use to him. Police communications, too, it seems were scrutinised by the exchange operators.[82]

The improved systems, ineffectively challenged by state law enforcement agencies, underwrote the success of Dividend Cigarettes for eighteen months, from August 1917 to December 1918. Van der Linden, on a retainer and earning 12 per cent commission, as opposed to the ten per cent that regular agents earned, managed the Natal operation so well that George Naylor was recalled to assist on the Rand. Seccombe, who controlled Transvaal and Free State sales, moved constantly within the

Hidden compartment in Rufe Naylor's desk, Johannesburg c. 1920.

Johannesburg–Kimberley–Bloemfontein triangle. There were agents, it was said, 'everywhere' across the Witwatersrand, some attempting to make a living on a full-time basis, but many others – barmen, café proprietors, Chinese storekeepers, clerks and waiters – doing so as a sideline, earning extra income.[83]

The exact financial return from the lottery is difficult ascertain, but it would seem that Rufe and Vicente drank freely and frequently from the cooling waters of a Lourenço Marques fountain that flowed ever more strongly. The Commissioner of Inland Revenue estimated that in ten weeks, between July and mid-September 1918, the Dividend Company grossed £11 000 (a quarter of a million pounds today).

Over the same period, the company announced the payment of its first 'dividend' from its currency 'investments'.[84]

In the Witwatersrand heartland, the public success of the lottery left the police and public prosecutors privately frustrated. They were reduced to using the Post Office Act to intercept incoming copies of the Lourenço Marques-based *Guardian* newspaper, which carried advertisements and notices about the lottery. It was a tactic that the state was forced to use repeatedly for decades thereafter. An attempt at prosecuting a lottery agent, in July 1917, ended badly for the state.[85]

When an undercover policeman, Constable Larden, approached William Scott and asked after a ten-shilling ticket 'investment' in 'Portuguese currency', the agent, suspecting a trap, said that he did not have any. It was only when Larden said he had been directed to Scott by 'Mr X of Auckland Park' that the agent relented and referred the policeman to a Chinese storekeeper, Stephen Luk (Luck). Larden gave Luk ten shillings and received a 'ticket', but the policeman questioned whether it was valid for the lottery because the only identification on it was the Delagoa Bay Money Agency. Luk reassured him that the ticket was valid for both the lottery and the sweepstake.

The police followed up by sending Detective Lane, also undercover. Lane bought an entire book of tickets from Luk, who said that he was Scott's sub-agent and part of Naylor's outfit. Lane proceeded to the Eloff Street offices where, rather conveniently, he allegedly 'saw' a letter from Naylor to some unknown correspondent claiming that he had nothing do with lotteries. When questioned directly by the detective, Naylor replied that he would have nothing to do with lotteries 'after the decision of the courts', and Lane believed him. The policeman may not have been entirely dependent on his monthly salary as a source of income.[86]

When Scott and Luk appeared in court, charged under the lottery law, the prosecution received short shrift from the magistrate. As reported in the press:

> The Magistrate said there was no evidence of what Rufe Naylor's sweep was or that a lottery existed.
>
> The Public Prosecutor: But they could only run a lottery by means of a subterfuge.

The Magistrate added that he could not convict on suspicion.

The Prosecutor argued that it would be obviously impossible for it to be stated on the tickets that they were for Rufe Naylor's lottery.

'What is Rufe Naylor's lottery?' queried the Magistrate blandly.

'Nobody knows!' confessed the Prosecutor. The Court smiled.[87]

The smile mirrored those on the faces of ordinary folk. Ever since the gambling spectacles staged at the Stadium, in pre-Union days, white workers considered Naylor more folk hero than villain. Successful prosecutions were harder to come by and magistrates, caught between a Calvinist law and public opinion, preferred street-corner wisdom to antiquated religious teachings.

By the same token, Dutch Reformed churches on the Rand, attempting to shepherd their flocks of newly urbanised Afrikaner workers away from the leisure and recreational preferences of their more secularised English-speaking counterparts, consistently under-scored the 'evil' of gambling. Back in Kruger's day, Volksraad candidates had been made to take a vow to try and abolish lotteries, but initiatives of that type were increasingly difficult to secure after Union. Instead, the Dutch Reformed Church set aside certain Sundays for sermons highlighting the evils of horse racing, lotteries and sweepstakes. But if Afrikaners were less visible than others at race meetings and elsewhere, it was more likely to have been a by-product of poverty and worklessness than the exhortations of their clergymen.[88] For his part, Naylor was openly contemptuous of Kruger's Dopper church and the influence it still wielded over what he branded the 'Priest-Ridden Rand'.[89]

But by the time Naylor returned to Johannesburg from Natal that June, his energy was focused elsewhere; he was more interested in chaps than chapels. He was set on undermining the Auckland Park establishment and gaining control of an inner-city racecourse that would attract most white workers. His hopes lay with the Rand Sporting Club, in which he held a controlling interest, and a board that he had packed with accomplices – Seccombe, Tatham and a lottery agent, Fred Fraser. The RSC had two licences: one for the West Rand Racing Club (WRRC), at Krugersdorp, and another for a racecourse at Newclare, a racially segregated freehold township for coloureds (people of mixed race) that dated back to 1905. With a railway station of its own just six miles west of central Johannesburg, Newclare was well placed to compete with uppity Auckland Park.

It required a herculean effort to get the two clubs up and functioning. Moribund for two or more years, they would need a capital injection of several thousands of pounds if they were to be refurbished and put in running order. This was at a time when the full financial benefit of the lottery was not yet coursing through Naylor's many bank accounts. The licences for the clubs were also up for renewal, and, in a climate of corruption, that was an uncertain business.

As in 1906–1908, a few ominous gusts were already swirling around the layered outer garments of public opinion. The mitres, suits and top hats – pack hunters – were unhappy about the time and money that white workers devoted to wartime gambling.[90] The efforts of the Rand recruitment committee to enlist cloth caps to die a faraway death for King and Country, it was claimed, were hampered by too many racecourses and too many racing days.[91] The organised Anglophone working class was divided, with the Labour Party splitting into anti- and pro-war factions, leaving it ideologically rent.[92] Only police helmets remained easily in place as a storm began whistling across the 'evil' plains of goldfields gambling.[93]

For all winter's bite, June and July were not a write-off. It is true that Naylor sensed the danger. He had 'been ruined by legislation in 1909', could see more laws coming and 'knew something of the power of legislators'.[94] He was given a smart reminder when an application to renew the licence for the WRRC at Krugersdorp was turned down by the legislators in Pretoria.[95] But the odds were changing, albeit slightly. The Transvaal Provincial Council, which was not well respected, had seen a strong performance by Labour Party candidates, who held a majority among the newly elected, while the National Party had secured a few seats in conservative rural strongholds such as Rustenburg.[96]

More pertinently, Dingwall of the Boilermakers' Union and van Veyeren of the National Party had both secured seats on the all-important Provincial Council executive, through a system of proportional representation.[97] Both were within easy political reach of the Naylor syndicate. Rufe had taken the precaution of contributing to Dingwall's campaign expenses, and both Dingwall and van Veyeren had been carefully cultivated by Seccombe and Tatham for some time.[98]

Still more promising was the fact that both Dingwall and van Veyeren suffered from PSS – public service sickness – a condition that left its victims high on status but low on cash – more precisely, about thirty silver pieces short. 'Provincial Councillors', Dingwall later willingly conceded, 'were always [financially] hard pressed'.[99] Liberal infusions of cash in return for political favours helped to ease the pain. The problem was that the palliative medicines were highly addictive; once partially dependent, the victim wanted ever more without caring too much where the dose was coming from.

Seen another way, corruption was a bridge so shaky that it offered only a one-way crossing. Once across, there was no way back. Dingwall, a thick-skinned man of the world, at home in town and with union politics, was robust enough to risk a crossing, knowing where he was headed. But van Veyeren, off the farming flats, was of a nervous disposition and temperamentally unsuited to negotiating heights. Naylor saw him as 'a coward, always in tears and crying', and Tatham had witnessed the man from Rustenburg in 'great distress' whenever involved in risky business.[100]

There was another more impressive string to Naylor's bow – Harry W Sampson. Naylor's relationship with 'Sammy' – almost certainly corrupt – dated back to pre-Union days when he had given Sampson, president of the powerful South African Typographical Union and Member of the Transvaal Legislative Assembly, a seat on the board of the Stadium. Predictably, Sampson was one the few MLAs who had voted against the 1909 Horse Racing and Betting Restriction Act.[101] Sampson went on to become chairman of the Labour Party and an MP, and in 1918 was awarded the Order of the British Empire. He and Naylor remained very tight and shared a friendship with LS Schmulian and his lovely wife, Chase, another Johannesburg town councillor and, happily, a director of Dividend Cigarettes.

Even by the prevailing low standards, Lazar Schmulian, proprietor of the United Printing and Publishing Company, was special. He was perfectly ambidextrous – left in politics and a right crook. A favourite with the Labour Party, Schmulian held the exclusive publishing and distribution rights to the workers' anthem, 'The Internationale', the lyrics of which spoke powerfully to the times:

Behold them seated in their glory
The kings of mine and rail and soil!
What have you read in all their story,
But how they plundered toil?
Fruits of the workers' toil are buried
In strongholds of the idle few
In working for their restitution
The men will only claim their due.

United Printing figured prominently among the select few authorised suppliers to the Town Council approved by the Typographical Union, leaving the firm well placed to compete for tenders right across the country. Schmulian was also known for an ability to iron wrinkles out of business propositions by applying liberal pressings of hot cash. Who was it that said that power tends to corrupt?

The mainspring of Schmulian's infamy was bolted firmly to Johannesburg's otherwise socially turbulent wartime history. As the official report of a government commission into bribery and corruption later recorded:

> [Schmulian] was of considerable notoriety, firstly, generally, on account of his business methods, and secondly, particularly, on account of his association with the robbery by the Foster Gang of some 2000 postal orders from Roodepoort Post Office in 1914, and subsequent trafficking therein in 1917, resulting in Schmulian's conviction on a charge of 'Receiving' and a sentence of 18 months' imprisonment with hard labour.[102]

The Typographical Union had little trouble in reconciling corruption, monopolies and tenders even as it 'struggled' to build a better white society. Conservatives and radicals may offer voters different ideological visions, but, once in power, many find the cash register more appealing than the conscience.

Print dominated mass communication and, on the Rand and in Natal, Rufe cultivated bevies of ink men. Printers produced the illegal lottery coupons and sweepstakes tickets that the business depended on, and journalists were a source of intelligence and occasional muted positive publicity. For Naylor, already entertaining the idea of putting out a publication of his own to advance gambling propaganda, access to a friendly printer was of great importance.

Lazar was Naylor's kind of guy, but his public indiscretions meant that he could not be courted too openly. To consolidate his hold over Mrs Chase Schmulian and raise additional capital for his war chest, Naylor made Lazar a partner in the Newclare club by persuading him to take up £3000 worth of debentures.[103]

Naylor, aware that the Newclare licence was set to expire, was in a hurry to demonstrate that the club, unlike its Krugersdorp sibling, was alive and active. The grand 'inaugural meeting', scheduled for 6 August 1917, carried the hallmarks of a Naylor initiative, combining public philanthropy with private gain in indeterminate proportions. The 'net profits', announced a press notice signed by Naylor and the chairman of the club, John Coetzee, would be devoted to charity – the 'Soldiers' Hostel Fund'. 'Special trains' and taxi cabs, operating at affordable rates, would convey punters to and from Park Station, only six miles from Newclare.[104] The inaugural was a great success, but subsequent events failed consistently to yield a profit, largely because owners and trainers feared that if they continued supporting Newclare, they risked being denied access to Auckland Park.[105] But Naylor's temperament had no room for despondency. He remained confident that he could turn things round.

Looking back, by the third quarter of 1917, Naylor had access to a network of political contacts stretching from street-level operators like the Schmulians, into the Provincial Council executive via Dingwall and van Veyeren, and into parliament via Sampson. For a consideration, all were willing to facilitate an attack on the number of racing days at Auckland Park to benefit the WRRC at Krugersdorp or the Newclare racecourse. It looked to be a safe bet since the hirelings knew that aiming extinguishers at the fires of working-class gambling would be supported by the churches, employers and government. It was an unusual combination of circumstances that provided good cover to all, making it nearly impossible tell the sincere social forces from the anti-social ones.

In theory, Naylor's men were set to advance unannounced and strike Colonel Furze's force at Auckland Park under cover of a barrage of bribery. The Furzians, some in the thrall of Dividend, the Trojan Horse, were slow to appreciate the danger and Naylor stole a march on them. When the Park people did eventually realise what was happening, Furze was quick to spot the weakest link in the enemy ranks – the mercenaries. Dingwall and van Veyeren, men of pounds rather than principle, were up for hire, open to a better deal. Indeed, so corrupt were they that they saw no reason to disclose to Naylor, or to Furze, that they were taking bribes from both. Naylor and the Colonel were going into battle backed by treacherous, thoroughly duplicitous opportunists.

Mixed motives, public versus private agendas and elected officials paid to advance or retard lawmaking depending on shifting interests became hopelessly intertwined. It was a spectacular mess, a contest in which sumo wrestlers randomly engaged one another in thick mud. The only way of knowing who was 'winning' or 'losing' was to focus on the big boys and try to follow the moves as best glimpsed through the muck.

In early July 1917, middle-class muttering about excessive gambling among the lower classes was becoming so loud that the Administrator of the Transvaal, Alfred Robertson, could no longer ignore it. The gist of his proposed ordinance, which envisaged an across-the-board reduction in the number of racing days at all eight racecourses throughout the Witwatersrand, surfaced in the press within days. He invited club representatives, one of whom was Naylor, to attend a meeting of his executive to reach an agreement on a new, reduced allocation of racing days. But horse number one, 'Reasonableness', refused to go into the stalls. Unsurprisingly, club representatives were unable to settle on a formula capable of satisfying the entire industry. It was not all bad news, though; it gave Naylor, Tatham, Dingwall and van Veyeren more space to work in.[106]

Tatham, at Naylor's prompting, had invested in the Newclare racecourse, and it was he who introduced Naylor to van Veyeren. In the first week of August, they twice visited van Veyeren in his rooms at the Victoria Hotel, in Johannesburg. Tatham's republican political credentials and his vouching for Naylor opened the door for business. Naylor offered van Veyeren £1 000 (about £750 000 today) in return for his supporting the Administrator's bill to reduce the number of racing days, and for ensuring that the licences for Krugersdorp and Newclare were renewed. A day later, Tatham and Naylor intercepted Dingwall at the City Hall. Naylor offered the trade unionist £500 for his support of the bill. But Dingwall, who was well accustomed to bargaining, and may already have spoken to his friend van Veyeren, would not do it for less than £1 000, claiming the risk was too great. Naylor recoiled at the amount and he and Tatham both left, puzzling over what their next move might be.

The success of the inaugural meeting at Newclare forced Naylor back to the bargaining table. A week later, Dingwall was on his way back from Pretoria when Tatham intercepted him on the inbound platform at Jeppe station. After Tatham had risked the second approach and not been dismissed, he escorted Dingwall to a secluded part of the station, where they joined Naylor.

Naylor was businesslike. He repeated his offer of £500 if Dingwall were to abandon his role as a champion of the working man and instead support the Administrator's initiative to reduce the number of racing days and get the licences at Krugersdorp and, especially, Newclare renewed. Naylor said that he would brook 'no opposition from Auckland Park races', whose racing days could only be curtailed if the draft ordinance was passed as it stood. But Dingwall again balked at the risk. But Naylor could tell a sprinter from a stayer. He upped his bet from £500 to £1 000 and horse number two, 'Risk', drew up lame. The deal was done, and Naylor handed Dingwall £50. Seven days later, as he disembarked at Jeppe, Dingwall was again intercepted by Tatham and escorted to a car, where Rufe handed him another £50.[107]

Dingwall may have believed that he had reduced the risk, but Naylor had doubled both his chance of being exposed and his expenditure. His returns from the lottery were increasingly tied up in bribes, racecourse licences that were about to lapse, administrative and office expenditure, salaries and investments in Tatham's shaky Modderfontein gold-mining venture – all criminal and/or highly speculative ventures. Naylor Inc. was expanding too rapidly, in too many directions, with insufficient cash and no strong credit line. As Tatham later put it, Rufe had no paying businesses and was 'impulsive'.[108]

In a world where religious and political ideologies were poorly synchronised, Naylor wanted his criminal and legal enterprises to operate side by side in the gap, and to have a freer flow of finance between the two. As an entrepreneur, he sensed how white working-class culture was shifting and how he could facilitate flows of cash by employing people at above-market-rate salaries and risk investing in joint enterprises that purchased goods and services in the grey economy. It might arguably have been a sleazy role but, in strictly economic terms, it was never entirely self-centred. Dingwall and van Veyeren, however, were concerned exclusively with self-enrichment and consumption.

For those like them, already bent, or bending fast, the logic of 'in for a penny, in for a pound' was irresistible. Van Veyeren, keen to increase the take from the Administrator's bill, sought out Furze and told him that Naylor was set on destroying Auckland Park and that he had bribed him to ensure the passage of the Administrator's bill. The Park faced the prospect of having its racing days cut from 60 to 30, and to perhaps as little as 15. Furze, an old hand at bribery, knew what van Veyeren was after and wanted to protect the club and his totalisator from losses amid growing middle-class hostility to horse racing.

The Colonel found Naylor's duplicity almost impossible to understand, having been pulled into the Dividend Company, and was understandably furious.[109] In effect, he and two other directors who served on the boards of both the APRC and the Dividend Cigarette Company were being asked to choose between the ownership of a long established, successful but threatened racecourse and the promise of more money, yet to materialise, from the lottery.

Plunkett and Powell, Furze's co-directors, refused to choose. They wanted returns from both enterprises, reasoning that as the profits from the one fell, so the other might rise. Patience, it seemed, was the order of the day. Furze, who was largely dependent on the income from the tote that he operated at Auckland Park, was less sanguine. His co-directors irritated him. They were, he later alleged, too slow in appreciating the financial dangers that the APRC was facing and, by the time they did come round to Furze's view, were insufficiently 'generous' when dealing with Dingwall's and van Veyeren's demands. Furze's initial response was to ignore them and use his own money to deal with the problem.

He did so but without precaution or subtlety. In the latter part of August, he began paying off van Veyeren and Dingwall, knowing that they were working in tandem and simultaneously milking Naylor. He gave Dingwall £100 and van Veyeren £200, but the attitude and demands of the two diverged as the crucial debate in the Provincial Council executive crept ever closer.[110]

It was van Veyeren, accustomed to life in the Victoria Hotel, who was the hungrier of the two. And, while in the driving seat, van Veyeren was both more avaricious and more arrogant than was his more financially stressed trade-unionist partner. He 'practically demanded', Furze later complained, £1 000.[111] Dingwall, bringing up the rear, fell into line, and Furze, pleading poverty and waiting on the support of the equivocating Plunkett and Powell, eventually managed to beat the politician twins down to £500 each.

These meetings, if not the details of the transactions, had not gone unnoticed. The growing number of people involved in the conspiracy did nothing to guarantee secrecy and, in a way that is now lost, loose talk about corruption reached the ears of the newly re-elected Member of the Provincial Council (MPC) for Springs, George Hills.[112] Hills, president of the Printers' Union – a circuit in which Naylor was well known – was a smart, old-school, straight-as-a-die member of the Labour Party and a social activist with a nose for the truth. Hills recalled how, when the Newclare course had first been granted a licence, in 1916, van Veyeren was an MPC, and it was said at the time that 'the rustle of money' could be heard around Pretoria.[113]

As part of his preparation for the coming debate on licence renewals, Hills spent the closing weeks of August in the Council questioning van Veyeren and others about why they had agreed to grant the licence for the Newclare course in 1916. No one could come up with a clear answer, most taking refuge behind procedural issues or the oath of secrecy taken by members of the executive. Van Veyeren simply said that the record did not reveal the reasons behind the 1916 decision. Hills's questioning sent up a flare into the night sky, but those fixated on the moon and the prospect of easy money failed to heed the warning.[114]

The Administrator's draft 'Horse Racing and Betting Restriction Amendment Ordinance', debated over three days in late September 1917, followed the customary stages, although the environment in and around the chamber was anything but normal. It was like a diggers' camp on the frontier, on payday, with half-trousered miners lining up outside a shack sporting a red lantern.

Hotels in the vicinity were fully booked. Everyone in the racing fraternity knew what was happening and, even when not directly involved, was keen to follow the action and establish how their interests might best be accommodated. The gallery in the Council chamber was packed with breeders, bookmakers, bucket shop owners, racecourse owners and trainers. Some, including Naylor and Tatham, had long since put down their deposits and were only waiting to witness the outcome.[115] Others, less proactive, had got into town late, hoping that their wallets might yet secure them a place in a long queue.

Among the stragglers, high on desire but low on cash, was the bucket shop owners' association, which, wishing to see the cuts to the number of racing days kept to a minimum, gave Dingwall £200 to keep him onside. Colonel Furze, a former provincial councillor, had persuaded Plunkett and Powell to back his initiative and arrived in town carrying wads of notes. He was desperate to protect his and the APRC's interests but, for a man familiar with a culture of bribery, remained puzzlingly uncertain as what exactly to do with the £3 000 in his pocket. Could he get into the red-lantern tent without Dingwall and van Veyeren, whom he remained suspicious of, and what might they now demand if he had already been outbid by Naylor, the queue's chief steward?

In the end Furze, an old fox, might have read the commotion in the coop correctly and decided not to enter. In Naylor's case, most of the money had changed hands remotely and secretly, via Tatham, in cars, at railway stations or in hotels and tea rooms. Granted that the presence of the racing fraternity provided additional cover, but flitting about the Council chamber and lobbying, even if no additional cash changed hands, was probably not the wisest move. Naylor's hovering, and that of van Veyeren, although not noted by the police, who appeared to have little or no interest in the proceedings, was observed by George Hills.

After a third reading, Ordinance No. 11 was approved, on 28 September, and became law on 10 October 1917.[116] Dingwall and van Veyeren, having double-crossed Furze, felt that they had achieved most of what Naylor wanted and were content with the outcome.

Naylor, however, noticed that Dingwall had gone a touch soft in that, while the Administrator wanted the maximum number of racing days reduced from 60 to 15, Dingwall was willing to settle for 25. In the end, the ordinance reduced the number of racing days to 15 a year. A snip of the lawmakers' scissors and the APRC was transformed from stallion to gelding. The 15 days suited Naylor, but the renewal of the two licences for his racecourses remained a pressing problem.

Still grappling with the red tape that slowed down the registration of the Dividend Company, Naylor sensed the ongoing danger of a seasonal outbreak of Mother Grundyism bedevilling the renewal of the licences. The Park had been knee-haltered, but he was in danger of not getting to the races at all. Ownership of the Krugersdorp and Newclare tracks was folded into the WRRC, which in turn belonged to the RSC. An application for renewal of licences could emanate from one of several sources.

Within hours of the ordinance's promulgation, Naylor set up a meeting with Dingwall and van Veyeren in the latter's room at the Victoria. Naylor was up against the clock. He was spending far more on stakes at various race meetings running at a loss than he was earning from the lottery, even though that was growing. He wanted more legislative action from them; they wanted more of the £1 000 they had agreed on. Rufe felt the job was half done, as did they, but they were looking at different halves, which only heightened distrust. Naylor gave van Veyeren another £200 towards the original fee, and the following day, at the Parisian Tea Rooms, he handed Dingwall £400 in an envelope, on the back of which he had taken the precaution of writing 'Ichnos at £200 to 1'. Once they had been fed, the dogs were less given to growling, and Naylor again emphasised the need for their active lobbying in support of the licence renewals.[117]

The following morning, the WRRC secretary wrote to the Administrator requesting the renewal of the licences at Newclare and Krugersdorp. Given that the licences were about to lapse, Robertson had little choice, but the timing was unfortunate. How could the Provincial Council renew licences when, just days before, it had passed legislation aimed at curtailing racing? Four days later, on 15 October, the WRRC's application was refused, despite the best efforts – one can only assume – of Dingwall and van Veyeren. Naylor later attributed the refusal as being motivated by 'pure malice' but did not name the person responsible.[118] Whatever the reason, after the refusal and with his personal liquidity problems escalating rapidly, Naylor became far more circumspect in his dealings with the two councillors that he had bought.

The turning-down of the WRRC licences started a sequence of events that had serious repercussions for Naylor and took two years to unfold fully. The immediate problem lay at Newclare, where, Naylor claimed, he had invested £11 000. More importantly, the application, in the wake of the lobbying circus that led to the passing of Ordinance No. 11, along with Dingwall's and van Veyeren's unwillingness to help, prompted Hills to share his suspicions with Robertson.

A day after the refusal of the licences, the Administrator asked the police for a 'confidential report' on the RSC and the financial forces behind it. A week later he had a comprehensive reply. The report, compiled by Deputy Commissioner Vachell, CID, correctly identified the underlying causes of the friction between the APRC and the RSC and outlined Naylor's chequered career in South Africa, as well as his interest in the burgeoning lottery. Vachell also fingered Seccombe as Naylor's chief lieutenant, along with Coetzee of the RSC and Tatham, who were all connected to the West Rand clubs. Remarkably, Vachell's report somehow remained 'confidential', which meant that neither Dingwall nor van Veyeren, nor Naylor, knew of it.[119]

Naylor's name had, however, moved up a few places on the police agenda. It is possible, but by no means certain, that had Naylor and the Victoria Hotel conspirators known about the Vachell report, they might have been more circumspect about the timing of their next move. Instead, Naylor misjudged the seriousness of his cash-flow problems over the closing months of 1917. Focused on the racing industry and taking financial strain from his compulsion to grow the WRRC at the expense of the APRC, Naylor also did not fully appreciate how rapidly the lottery was taking root along the Reef. Had he only waited a few more weeks, he would have been rewarded with an enhanced income stream that dwarfed any leakages from the dam out at Newclare. Instead, he pushed hardest where the wall was weakest – the corrupt MPCs.

On Wednesday 14 November, a month after the WRRC's request for renewal had been turned down, another application for the renewal of a licence – this time from a different angle – appeared on the Administrator's desk.[120] Three unknown members of the board at Newclare, all with seemingly squeaky-clean police records, applied for the renewal of the course licence. Robertson must have tipped off Hills about the new application because that same day, in an open council meeting, Hills put a sweetheart question to the Administrator: '[had] a licence for the Newclare Racecourse been renewed for another year?' Robertson, playing the straight man, said it was 'still under consideration'. For most light-footed dancers, the question might have come across as an offbeat note from Hills's band. But Dingwall and van Veyeren, compromised and seemingly politically tone-deaf, danced on regardless.[121]

The following morning, Hills again asked the Administrator, in open council, about the Newclare renewal and got the same response. Bound by law to place the matter before the executive, Robertson did so that afternoon. Dingwall and van Veyeren, depending on your point of view, never put a foot wrong or a foot right. To the amazement of outsiders, the Newclare licence was renewed not only in the wake of Ordinance No. 11 but after a point-blank refusal to do so four weeks earlier. The decision to renew, but not the reasoning, was recorded in the council minutes. That resolution was followed by executive resolution No. 106, of 28 November, sanctioning race meetings at both West Rand clubs despite earlier strong objections from the Commissioner of Police.[122]

By then, punters were totally bewildered. So, too, were some in the press and most of the public. With Risk and Revenge fighting it out for a win over the last furlong, very few other than bookmakers and insiders knew where most bets had been placed. But one man kept his head, preparing to lodge an objection regardless of which of the two ringers won. Five days after the renewal by the executive, Hills was back at it, in open council, asking a half-dozen pointed questions about the WRRC, including wanting to know whether the approval for racing had been given over the objections of the Commissioner of Police.[123]

The answers to Hills's probing left the executive, other than those who had been bought, and ordinary members of the council feeling uncomfortable as he outlined the strange history of decisions relating to horse racing on the Rand. The music was about to stop and Dingwall and van Veyeren sensed that they might be left without chairs. From that point on, and for five months thereafter, Hills explored a variety of allegations about corruption in the Provincial Council. The trial led back to Dingwall, the Schmulians and other Labour Party members in and around the largely corrupt Johannesburg Town Council.

Dingwall, who was exceptionally hard up, was desperate to get the balance of the money he had been promised by Naylor. On Christmas Eve he and Tatham went to Naylor's rooms, in Blinman's Buildings, but the atmosphere was noticeably subdued. When Dingwall asked for the outstanding £500, Naylor said 'he was losing money at every [Newclare race] meeting and asked [Dingwall] to give him a chance to recoup himself'. Van Veyeren, so emotionally distraught that he had failed to make contact at all, was left in the role of ghost of Christmas past.[124]

By March 1918, rumours about corruption along the Witwatersrand had become so widespread that in Cape Town, Hugh Wyndham, a member of the Unionist opposition in the House of Assembly, began to press the Botha government for a commission of inquiry. But a basic law of politics is that no government should be seen to be responding, let alone quickly, to the demands of the opposition. The prime minister, moving behind the cover of war, was not about to flout that rule and George Hills was running low on patience.[125]

Back in Pretoria, on 8 May 1918, Hills rose and requested that 'The Governor-General-in-Council appoint a Judicial Commission to inquire into the circumstances under which the Administrator and Executive Committee of the Province of Transvaal granted a licence to the West Rand Racing Club' in the light of six facts he laid out before members.[126] The match was in the tinder. The government, usually able to get away by only sniffing oppositional smoke, was forced to contend with the heat of the fire. On 12 July 1918, a commission of inquiry into allegations of bribery and corruption in the Johannesburg Town Council and Transvaal Provincial Council, led by Inspecting Magistrate OW Staten of the Department of Justice, was announced in the *Union Gazette*.[127]

PART III

SWEATING

Gambling is a principle inherent in human nature.
EDMUND BURKE, 1780

A Standoff: The Law, Lotteries, and White Workers, circa 1917–1918

The unsuccessful prosecution of Dividend Cigarettes/Lourenço Marques Lottery agents, in July 1917 – the case in which the magistrate was reduced to smiling at Naylor's ingenuity – effectively left public prosecutors unemployed when it came to lotteries. The police stumbled about in the fog of legal uncertainty that had settled over the town, but a few enterprising underworld types were already hard at work in printers' workshops, turning out fake lottery and sweepstake tickets by the thousands.

The least gifted of these Johnny-come-lately types met Wilde's dictum that 'imitation is the sincerest form of flattery that mediocrity can pay to greatness'. Aping Naylor, one or two 'syndicates' explored the possibility of gaining lottery concessions in Angola or the Congo.[1] Other tyros, taking their cue from Dividend Cigarettes, inserted coupons in boxes of matches that were sold at grossly inflated prices. The problem was that, unlike cigarettes, matches were subject to wartime price regulation, and the scheme was soon snuffed out.[2]

Still others, aware of how the cash from Dividend Cigarettes was channelled through Naylor's Delagoa Bay Money Agency, which had a questionable currency speculation component to it, sold tickets that fell under the auspices of the fictitious 'Lourenço Marques Money Discount Agency'. Some cleverly worded lotteries, including a few claiming to benefit local charities, did offer cash prizes, but the police, found it impossible to distinguish between 'genuine' and 'fake' lotteries when all lotteries were supposedly illegal.[3]

In Protestant South Africa, the idea of acquiring instant wealth other than through the sweat of one's brow became coupled ever more tightly to notions of the exotic, of the foreign, as the 20th century wore on. It helped underwrite the notion of an enlightened Afrikaner nationalist racial elect with a pure and special destiny to govern on a troubled 'dark' continent. Gambling was seen not only as sinful but as being sent by the godless, an unwelcome intrusion into the fatherland that took root within the faithless among the chosen. Eschewing gambling helped lend shape to a purer, enhanced form of good governance in a frequently troublesome universe populated by 'other' people. The geography of sin reinforced the need for national integrity.

But belief in ethnic or racial exceptionalism degrades the occipital lobe, leading to Cyclops-like vision incapable of taking in wider social horizons. Afrikaner nationalists and Protestant churches of both language groupings along the Reef found it hard to accept that many English-speaking gamblers on the Witwatersrand, the very workers they wanted to coax into racially exclusive zones, not only were *buitelanders* – people drawn from 'outside the land' – but were from a wider, sprawling Anglophone universe. Worse still, they were part of an internationally mobile proletariat that cheap rail and steamship fares had exposed to gambling and working-class cultures in several different, often more tolerant, settings across the globe. English-speaking miners could see and embrace racism as readily and as well as the next man, but when it came to their dreams, their families and lotteries, they were never nationalists.

Experiences gained elsewhere, and knowledge about more flexible gambling dispensations, disrupted the thinking of those Afrikaner nationalists set on forging a 'white' nation from disparate parts. The Empire was a cognitive as well as a geographical reality that nationalists had to overcome. As a widely read Sunday weekly put it in 1917: 'British ideas differ widely in various parts of the British Empire. (With apologies to General Hertzog.) In Johannesburg lotteries of all kinds are prohibited – even for war funds.'[4] The editorial went on to laud how, in Bombay, the West India Turf Club ran a lottery, offering £10 000 in prizes, without hindrance from any local or national authority.

On the Rand, the organisers of illegal wartime lotteries and those who bought tickets were all too aware of how gambling ventures hinging on domestic-exotic and legal-illegal considerations made prosecutions difficult. The LML, legally based in Mozambique, which in the rudimentary cognitive maps of many whites somehow formed part of 'South Africa', paled into insignificance when it came to law enforcement issues. The proliferation of exotics complicated policing and prosecutions, and bedevilled the drafting of new legislation, determining the provenance of tickets and the role that the Post Office might play in intercepting mail and money.

Ideas of empire and state hesitancy when it came to prosecuting offenders only encouraged lottery and sweepstakes sales. In wartime Johannesburg, and for several decades thereafter, the words 'lottery' and 'sweepstake' were used interchangeably as gambling increased its footprint across the Witwatersrand. Authentic and fraudulent tickets could be purchased for the Australian, Tasmanian or Bombay lotteries, while the venerable Calcutta Sweepstake, based on the outcome of an English race, evolved from a uniquely Anglo-Indian combination of ticket-buying, ticket-drawing and ticket-auctioning.[5]

Despite growing competition from the exotics, Dividend Cigarettes dominated the market for lottery tickets. Towards the end of the war, the police claimed that, on the Witwatersrand, Naylor's agents were selling seven tickets for every one disposed of by lesser operations. To compensate, one new entrant, drawing on the 'dividend' model, sent agents to 'all parts of the Union and Rhodesia', as well as to the newly proclaimed South West Protectorate. It was reported that 'Germans in the conquered territory were big supporters of Union lottery schemes'. The police estimated that over six months, in 1918, smaller lotteries collectively brought in about £50 000 for their secretive principals.[6]

With the market in danger of becoming over-supplied, lottery owners took the fight out of the bars and streets and into the commercial bush. By the winter of 1918, there were tell-tale signs of a guerrilla war being waged behind the lines. It was pot-and-kettle season. The 'illegal lotteries', one newspaper reported, 'are beginning to call each other nasty names'. The bigger the target, the more enemy fire it attracted. A pamphlet branding the operators of the LML as 'swindlers' circulated widely enough for the Dividend Cigarettes Company to offer a £50 reward for information about the authors.[7]

Sniping alone was insufficient to halt the march of Naylor's army across the Union. As Paul van der Linden reported from Natal: 'There was a big demand for these tickets because the public quickly realized that all prizes were paid out without demur. I sold several thousands of these tickets monthly.' He bought lottery tickets at source, in devalued Portuguese currency, thereby ensuring a profit, and earned a further 12.5 per cent commission on all his sales.[8]

Using the same trade winds, Seccombe sailed across the Highveld, ferrying tens of thousands of tickets between Johannesburg, Kimberley and Bloemfontein on countless round trips, while a few Cape Town-based agents trawled the coastal flats.[9] He and van der Linden were in and out of Lourenço Marques constantly. Problems with customs officials at the border crossings, or with the police at Park Station, were obviated using duplicate tickets printed by the Schmulians in Johannesburg or by shady characters and firms in Durban.[10]

These peripheral extensions were dwarfed by the success Naylor achieved with his core business on the Witwatersrand. There, as always, many in the inflation-wracked white working class had a recurring dream about owning a freehold home, a house beyond the reach or control of a landlord or the mining companies. Leading figures in the LML and their agents, vision-peddlers in a capitalist world character-ised by economic inequality, were aware of the conscious or unstated connections between white workers' hopes and home ownership.

Seccombe had pioneered the Starr-Bowkett scheme, appealing to miners and the lower middle class, and the project was eventually folded into a regular building society. Naylor himself owned and let out several houses to white workers, while JA Coetzee, Naylor's part-ner in the WRRC, was said to be a 'house agent' in Germiston.[11] In late 1918, Seccombe, reporting on the success of the LML over the past 24 months, recorded that no less than 80 first prizes worth £2000 each had been distributed and that, of those, 74 had gone to South African residents. More pertinently, he went on to note:

> Seventy-four people – including six women – have been eased
> of all the usual daily worries of life. The real estate agents of
> Johannesburg will tell you that fully half these people purchased
> house property with their winnings and are comfortably established

for life, whilst playing no small part in the Johannesburg property boom of the past year.[12]

Dan Dingwall spent most of the money he got from Naylor paying off a mortgage.[13]

With the global influenza pandemic lifting and the end of the Great War, which had seen thousands flock to the racecourse in the earliest years, LML agents spread out to every corner of the Witwatersrand. In roller-coaster times, a mindset reminiscent of a cargo cult took hold of many in the populace, not excluding African workers and white women. 'In Johannesburg', it was reported, 'it is quite common for customers in down-town stores to be asked by lady shop assistants if they would like to buy a ticket for the Delagoa Bay Lottery.'[14] In demure middle-class settings that was no doubt true, but the general mood was perhaps better captured in another observation: 'Not a section of the community – even the native mine workers – but is more or less affected by the gambling spirit and will continue to be affected until the long-anticipated millennium arrives.'[15]

The influenza pandemic was abating but the fever raged on. As another chronicler of wishful thinking noted: 'Nine-tenths of the people on the Rand are going to win a big lottery one of these days and live happily ever afterwards watching other folks work.'[16] Capitalism and industrialisation might have expelled diggers dreaming of wealth from their mining camps and pushed them into a city coming of age, but the spirit of the mining camps remained locked within the inner man.

Much of the fun that comes with such magical thinking lies in an elevated state of anticipation rather than in any verifiable reward going to an individual.[17] Everyone knew of someone who knew someone who knew someone who had won the lottery, even if they personally had been left only clutching a faded ticket or an empty purse. But, whatever the outcome, while optimism trumped pessimism, action bent the knee to expectation, and the result was palpable. Throughout 1918, the illegal trade was reported to be 'booming', the city buried beneath an 'avalanche of lottery tickets', or, perhaps more predictably given the recent deaths, 'an epidemic of lotteries is gripping Johannesburg and the Reef'.[18]

Boom or bust, an adrenalin-addicted Naylor clung to the lottery for the ride of his lifetime. In December 1917, when the crowds began

cheering the lottery more openly, he responded, heightening the excitement. The Delagoa Bay lottery 'is now offering three series of prizes a
month instead of the one with which it started about six months ago'.
'This thing has got such a hold', it was reported in the press, 'that it
will be an extremely difficult matter to put a stop to the sale of tickets.'
Any attempt at prosecution, it was said, would be 'most unpopular'.[19]

The unimpeachably legal status of the business in Mozambique
– as opposed to that of the exotic fraudulent schemes – fuelled confidence in the lottery. The prizes were drawn, in Lourenço Marques,
in public, by the Delagoa Bay Money Agency 'after fair-and-square
manipulation of barrels and coloured marbles under the supervision
of government representatives'.[20] Yet, as we shall note in due course,
for decades thereafter the South African Police sent undercover
detectives into the neighbouring country to verify the unfailing honesty of LML draws.

For Naylor and his partners in the parent company, the lottery
was, for a time, a veritable magic money machine. It is difficult to
determine just how much cash was generated in 1918, its best year by
far, since the miffed authorities had as much reason to inflate the figures as the secretive owners had to deflate them. The figure probably
lay somewhere between the manufactured extremes conjured up by
the two contesting parties.

In August that year, the *Sunday Times*, claiming to be in possession
of 'reliable information' – probably fed to it by police or Post Office
sources – stated that, during that month, LML tickets to the value
of £135 000 had been sold on the Rand. A few weeks later, frustrated
police authorities claimed that 'in recent months' approximately
£350 000 in total (£24 million in today's terms) had 'been sent across
into Portuguese territory'.[21] The number '35' clearly had something
of a ring to it; only a few months later, a few well-connected Labour
Party activists, who, as active lottery agents themselves, had more
reason than most to take a keen interest in Rufe Naylor Lottery Ltd,
claimed that each month saw £35 000 slipping across the border and
on to Delagoa Bay.[22]

The disputed and probably deliberately poorly kept accounts of the
Johannesburg affiliate, the 'Delagoa Bay Cigarette Company', 'sole
sellers of Dividend Cigarettes', told a modest tale that the police never

Public drawing of the lottery, Lourenço Marques, c. 1940.

disputed. In the same year, 1918, Walter Southward, Naylor's one-time lottery manager in Lourenço Marques, claimed that the company was running at a loss but not in imminent danger of going bankrupt. The state authorities in Pretoria, without a proper paper trail to follow, relied on guesswork.

In the absence of proper returns, the Commissioner of Inland Revenue estimated the total sales of cigarettes by the company under its scheme, from 1 July 1918 to 11 September 1918, at £11000.[23] The Commissioner convinced a court that the state was owed £2000 in taxes in a case that had less to do with taxes than with the lottery scheme.

Naylor's estimates of his net worth in that pivotal year appear to have been in an orbit closer to the sun than the moon. He had reason to lay out only shining assets and conceal the extent of his liabilities as he sought to renew racecourse licences or stave off other creditors as things started going financially sour. He may also have been projecting the prospective value of his share in the lottery company after an exceptional year's trading; it is difficult to know, because there were moments when Naylor appeared to be sharing an office with Walter Mitty.

Pressed by his *consigliere*, Tatham, to reveal the true extent of his wealth, in January 1918 Naylor said that he was a 'rich man', worth a quarter of a million pounds. Tatham, himself once a very rich man, correctly suspecting that there were other assets hidden in Mozambique, considered this an underestimate, and told him so. In what may have been a slightly more carefully thought-through statement a few months later, Naylor came to roughly the same conclusion. He was, he then estimated, worth £242000, and owned racehorses valued at around £25000.[24]

Naylor's liabilities at the time are even more difficult to determine than his assets. They were, however, substantial and growing.[25] Money and impulsivity can be fine propellants in any short-term drive for wealth but, used in tandem, they soon run out of energy and are invariably overtaken by patience and prudence. Cavalier bookkeeping, a by-product of running a business of questionable legal status in what was an economic grey zone, exacerbated the underlying problems.

With lottery banknotes floating down like leaves on an autumn day, Naylor swept into several costly new ventures. The 'Rufe Naylor Building', heavily mortgaged, occupied a prime site on the corner of Eloff and Commissioner streets. He launched, but did not register, two new companies employing full-time managers and staff. One, the South African Prudential Company, had an office in Regent Street, London.[26] The Dividend Cigarette Company and the Lourenço Marques Lottery, each served by a manager and clerical staff, occupied yet more offices in the inner city, as did the spluttering Rand Sporting Club. On the West Rand, the Newclare racecourse bled losses of £700 per month and Naylor was spending a small fortune on legal fees. Overseeing all of this, at several more handsome salaries, was Rufe himself.

Like most folk heroes, Naylor was capable of acts of spontaneous generosity and often willing to donate to charities. When not work-ing – which was seldom – he apparently led a modest private life. He supported his family at home and abroad financially and provided his kinsman Seccombe with a good living. Seccombe, in turn, was loyal to a fault. Other personal expenses included outlays on bribes and the occa-sional, more indulgent, entertainment of members of the press corps.

In 1918, many months before Charles Ponzi bought postal 'reply' coupons abroad and redeemed them back in the US in a classic arbitrage scam, no one questioned Naylor's countless cross-border transactions. But everyone in Johannesburg saw his agents, building, employees, horses, houses, offices, advertisements, prospectuses, racetracks, stables and, of course, the ubiquitous LML tickets. The lighthouse of his success could be seen from miles away. But the foun-dations, cast on sand, had to be inspected from close up to understand how interconnected they were below the surface. Newspapers took their bearings from a lighthouse that flashed only 'gambling fever' and 'obsolete legislation'.

The Labour Party and working men suggested that lotteries be made legal. But the press, hoping to refine public opinion and influ-ence policy-making at the national level, saw itself as occupying a higher moral plane. So, noisy as a Highveld summer storm, it spewed lightning and thunder. Lighting came in the form of goading the government into action by mocking police and prosecutors for their manifest quiescence in the face of the Scott-Luk ruling. The lightning made for an instant, vivid picture but was cast briefly, and only in black and white.

The Kruger-era legislation, nearly 30 years old, was 'badly drafted'; the situation called for 'definite action'; and 'all these lucrative little illegalities would be knocked on the head were the Provincial Council to repeal the existing act'. But until a better dispensation could be set-tled upon, the existing 'law should be used to the full extent to stop the lottery transactions'. The problem was, however, that, as it stood, the law was so poorly structured that 'the lottery-runners can drive the proverbial coach and four through it, and that it is practically useless'.[27]

The thunder came as growls of embarrassment from deep within the Witwatersrand, rolling outward. The situation was intolerable. Naylor, a 'hustler', and his working-class associates were giving the state the run-around: 'Precisely how many lotteries are today in existence on the Rand even the CID does not know.'[28] The currency speculation built into the Delagoa Bay Money/Lottery Agency, 'has given our best legal and magisterial persons bad headaches'.[29] The impasse had made of 'the Government and the Police a laughing-stock'.[30]

In Pretoria, the civil service became the subject of scandal. On 18 September 1918, the Secretary for the Interior sent out a circular letter, warning government employees of the need to set an example if they were not to lose caste in the eyes of the populace at large:

> I am directed to inform you that the attention of Ministers has been drawn to the growing practice amongst members of the Public Service of taking part in raffles and lotteries despite the fact that, by so doing, they are committing an offence against the law and encouraging a spirit of gambling in the service.
>
> It is therefore desired to issue a definite warning that any public servant who is found to have contravened the law will be proceeded against and dealt with under Chapter 11 of the Public Service and Pensions Act, No. 29 of 1912, apart from any steps taken against him by those responsible for the prosecution of criminal offences.[31]

In a youthful colonial civil service, the habits of a disciplined middle class had to be seen to be different from those of the unruly lower classes, even at the cost of exposing public servants to the possibility of double jeopardy.[32]

A decade earlier, the *Sunday Times* had deplored working-class indiscipline in an economic downturn and championed a reduction in the number of racing days. That campaign had culminated in a commission of inquiry and new legislation. But, since then, the newspaper had undergone a change of heart. A violent strike in 1913 and the Bolshevik Revolution in October 1917 saw newfound respect for, and understanding of, the culture of the common man amid rampant inflation. Perhaps those with sensitive feet and formerly hard hearts had somehow sensed the first tremors of what was coming, in 1922?

Among the paper's new allies were leading figures in the Labour Party and some members of the Transvaal Provincial Council. An ultra-sensitive weathervane when it came to gambling, the Council moved when two sparrows chirped in unison. The *Sunday Times* and the Labour Party, up against the churches and nationalists, had to fight their way out from between the veld fires they had helped set. Upwind was the larger of the two blazes, the popularity of the LML among enfranchised male voters. The other fire, burning towards their backsides, was the need for control over an increasingly restless white proletariat.

Seemingly trapped, the hope was for rain and for the wind to drop. Genuflecting before the 'nature of man' and acknowledging gambling as an integral part of working-class culture might take some of the heat out of resentment expressed through the ballot box. Taking gambling out of private hands and placing it in those of the state would not placate the churches or the nationalists, but it would do something to reassure those intent on state-making and strengthening at a time when 'socialism' seemed to be on an upward ideological trajectory. In short, the way out of the gambling maze, if not the 'craze', was a new state lottery.[33] As Cicero exclaimed, '*O tempora! O mores!*' Or, as one analyst noted, 'our morals change with our development'.[34]

New lenses in press spectacles suddenly allowed wide-eyed journalists to see things that had apparently entirely eluded them when advocating betting restrictions some years earlier. It was time, they averred, to 'drop the hypocrisy', find an outlet for 'the speculative element in human nature' and acknowledge that 'the ordinary man likes to take a dip in a lottery'.[35] While too much state regulation might be bad, and the free market the best servant of economic and social development, when it came to private enterprise, lotteries were different.

First, there was a need to stop funds flowing into a neighbouring country. Somerset Maugham once referred to Monaco as 'a sunny place for shady people', and this was a description well suited to Lourenço Marques. Mozambique was a territory that could not realistically be seen as a 'country', and one that South Africans were anyhow thinking of annexing. Then there was the importance of nation-building

and scent-marking for a political pup – the Union, not yet ten years
old. The economy was suffering because 'In South Africa a very large
amount of money is put not into productive enterprise but into speculation or extravagance.'[36]

Second, state lottery funds – presumably quite unlike those from
racecourse totalisators, which were already taxed – could be channelled
into 'the good of the community as a whole'. As ever, a hidden and
far more holistic 'community' could be forged through the magic of
money. After the flu pandemic, hospitals were potential beneficiaries,
as were schools. But there was something in it for all whites, urban and
rural alike. Imagine: 'if lottery-obtained grain elevators were built all
over South Africa, will anyone assert that the community would be
worse off than if the money went into private pockets?'[37] Certainly not.

The *Sunday Times* had hoisted the 'state lottery' flag. It remained
to be seen which way the wind was blowing and who took notice
of it. In truth, compared to the gusts emanating from Mozambique,
the *Times*'s breezes were erratic and weak. Most days were perfectly
windless, and the churches and the nationalists could be forgiven for
seeing in that God's work.[38] For all that, even the Minister of Justice,
NJ de Wet, was tempted into putting up a kite when he floated the
idea that a state lottery might stem the flow of funds to Delagoa Bay.[39]
Most white workers had more faith in Naylor's lottery than some
shaggy-dog story. When the flag did flap once or twice, it caught the
eye of Labour Party politicians, but given the problems around the
issuing of racecourse licences, they, too, remained skittish. It took
the populist Provincial Council two years to come around to the idea
of backing a provincial lottery.[40]

Naylor was anything but complacent. A press campaign around
gambling, let alone one explicitly focused on lotteries, was a painful
reminder of how the *Sunday Times* had choked the life out of off-
course betting at the Stadium, in 1909. True, this time he had a few
more politicians on his payroll, but what was needed, he felt, was a
weekly magazine to counteract the venom from the *Times*. Tatham,
fearing the libel suits that might follow from poorly disciplined journalism, counselled against it. But Naylor would have none of it, and
on 16 March 1918 the first issue of *Life, Sport and Drama* appeared on
newsvendors' stands. The dependable, shapeshifting Seccombe was,

for a time, the editor of the journal, and the secretary to the eponymous company that steered it, until it eventually expired two years
later, on Christmas Day 1919.

Set against Calvinist ideology and the killjoys who propagated it,
the new journal took direct aim at the churches and the 'wowsers' –
puritans intent on denying others pleasures they deemed immoral.
Life, Sport and Drama complained about 'The Priest-Ridden Rand',
pointed out ways in which 'pagan' celebrations underlay class and
Christian hypocrisy at upper-crust weddings, and ran a cartoon
mocking pious wowsers gathered in a cemetery contemplating grave-
stones commemorating the sad passing of card games, Sunday con-
certs, 'glorious woman' and 'sweet wines'.[41] Predictably, even more
column inches were devoted to defending the lottery in general, and
to Rufe Naylor in particular.[42]

Tatham's misgivings had a point. *Life, Sport and Drama* looked
and read a bit like a 'satirical shadow' of *Stage & Cinema*, the trade
magazine launched by IW Schlesinger in 1915, when Naylor was still
his employee.[43] The underlying problem was that, for a decade or
so, Naylor's entrepreneurial skill had, on more than one occasion,
served as Schlesinger's tracer when it came to the early identification of business opportunities. Schlesinger was forever being publicly
acclaimed as an 'American' tycoon with access to limitless funding,
but sometimes the little cash-consuming Australian was first on the
scene. Moreover, Naylor, with 5 000 shares – worth about £60 000 – in
Schlesinger's African Theatres Trust Limited, had a direct interest in
how ATT was run.[44]

It was Naylor who had lit the path to the real stage and cinema,
and possibly to the idea of the eponymous magazine as well. It was
Naylor who served as Schlesinger's icebreaker when it came to the
possibility of a non-proprietary racecourse, to the point where the
police saw IW as a possible front for Naylor and suspected 'some
trickery' behind a licence application.[45] In turn, Naylor had probably
taken a leaf out of Schlesinger's mighty African Realty Trust when he
started taking a serious interest not only in housing and rental properties in Johannesburg, but, through his new Prudential Company,
in the development of a large commercial fruit-farming estate in the
northeastern Transvaal, just off the main route to Lourenço Marques.

This rivalry came to a head between late 1917 and early 1918 when the lottery was booming and Lady Lakshmi tending to favour Naylor. In retrospect, it is difficult to know who was leading and who was following. Perhaps they initially moved in tandem, but the resulting animus may have stemmed from citrus farming. In 1918, Schlesinger started the colossal Zebediela Citrus Estate, and around the same time Naylor started Crocodile Valley Estates, which combined a plot-selling and settlement venture with fruit farming. Valley Estates primed a long-standing Naylor family interest in the region. But, while Zebediela went on to become the largest citrus estate in the world between the wars, Valley Estates spluttered into bankruptcy in 1925.[46]

Whatever the underlying cause, there can be no doubt that, in 1918, *Life, Sport and Drama* was the vehicle that Naylor used for a sustained attack on Schlesinger's financing companies and the latter's interests in the film industry.[47] As Tatham feared, it led to a libel suit, leaving Naylor increasingly friendless and without access to a natural financial lifeline at a time when the *Sunday Times* was attacking the police and prosecutors for their unwillingness to deal with the lottery.[48]

By mid-1918, Naylor was in the best and worst of times. On the one hand, his quasi-legal lottery business was booming, even if the West Rand racecourses and other ventures were not. But, on the other hand, it was becoming clear that the authorities were lining up their principal – no, perhaps their only – target when it came to lotteries and the Provincial Council scandals of the previous year. In Pretoria, the long-suffering Attorney General, Charles W de Villiers, was becoming ever more intent on enforcing antiquated laws, and Naylor was in increasing danger of being caught in a state-directed pincer movement.

Beneath the Blindfold: Lady Justice's Squint, circa 1918–1919

Clues about a counterattack by the state went back to the opening weeks of 1918. It was reported that, at Marshall Square, the Johannesburg police headquarters, authorities were 'actively engaged in enquiring into a scheme which is advertised as operating outside the Union'.[49] But, as noted, pursuing lottery operators presented formidable legal obstacles and, in the short term, 'activity' did not translate into action. For its part, the weekly press continued to poke fun at an ineffectual government. Naylor, with his own channels of communication – in and out of Marshall Square – heard little that alarmed him.

But, as the evenings grew chillier and the grass browner, there was talk of a cold winter coming from an unusual direction – Pretoria. On 28 June, a national commission of inquiry into allegations of bribery and corruption in the Provincial Council and Transvaal town councillors was announced, with instructions to 'proceed with all expedition and diligence'. Naylor found it disquieting. He had ceased dealing too directly with Dingwall and van Veyeren, but it was only months before his racecourse licences would be up for renewal; a commission of inquiry did not augur well. The bribed councillors were both weak men.

The evidence presented to the commission was damning. When Part I of its report was eventually published, in October 1918, the very first page of the document contained an 'explanatory note' for readers penned by WE Bok, the Secretary for Justice:

> As regards Mr. Naylor, the Attorney-General has intimated that he is satisfied that there is sufficient evidence to justify a prosecution. In accordance with the recommendation of the Commissioner Annexures 'D' and 'E' to the report being the affidavits by Messrs. Dingwall and van Veyeren respectively are therefore not published. [50]

The commission confirmed what Naylor had been expecting, but his concerns went back deeper and further afield. Weeks before the publication of the report, sources within the police informed him that the bribery proceedings were only the opening move in a state attack. Attorney General de Villiers, sensing a shortage of political birds, wanted to kill the goose that laid the golden egg. Naylor was confident that, suitably defended, he had a chance of getting off on the bribery charges due to a lack of documented evidence. But the lottery left him vulnerable because of an abundance of documents.

Criminal charges called for legal counsel; politically motivated initiatives demanded political responses. In early August, weeks before the commission reported, Administrator Alfred Robertson received a request for a meeting he could not refuse. It came from the Labour

Party MP Harry Sampson. Sampson, it will be recalled, was president of the South African Typographical Union and enjoyed excellent connections in the printing trade in Johannesburg. He was also a former member of the board of directors at the Stadium who had opposed the draconian Horse Racing and Betting Restriction Act of 1909.

What precisely Sampson wanted from his meeting with the Administrator, on 10 August 1918, is not clear; he may only have been clearing the way for the renewal of the racecourse licences. But, more likely, he was also engaging in a little political 'log-rolling', hoping to protect Naylor and a few printing firms from the coming turbulence. Some idea of what transpired can be gleaned from an incomplete handwritten note, penned either by Robertson himself or, more probably, by his secretary, that survives in a police file: 'Mr. Sampson for ½ an hour spun a long yarn as to what a good chap Naylor was – great man in the racing world – wanted the Admin. to know what an honest fellow Rufe was ...'[51]

Naylor was taking as much forward political cover as he could afford. At the same time, he looked round for ways of diverting his lottery income and diversifying his portfolio as best and credibly possible. Either that or, like what was shortly to become notorious as a 'Ponzi scheme' in the United States, he was searching for additional funding to prop up linked projects that were faltering: Crocodile Valley, *Life Sport and Drama* and the Newclare racecourse.

Adept at reading the public mood, Naylor now sought to link market sentiment to Tatham's belief that his East Rand mining claims could be converted into millions. Ernest Oppenheimer's 1917 flotation of Anglo American Corporation – backed by English investors and JP Morgan & Co, in New York – had prepared the way for renewed speculation in East Rand mining enterprises. At Naylor's prompting, Tatham agreed to allow his mining claims in the Boksburg district to form the basis for the flotation of the Modder West Gold Mining Company, which Naylor would help finance. It was an ill-fated venture that proved fatal to their on-off relationship and subsequently complicated Naylor's life as it began to unravel in late 1918.

Early in October, a prospectus 'filed with the Register of Companies' invited investors to take up £97 000 in ordinary shares, with another £125 000 being reserved for the 'vendor' – Tatham – and the principal 'financiers' – RT Naylor and WT Seccombe. Of five other principal subscribers to the shares, four were minor partners in the LML and had been prosecuted as such the year before.[52] Naylor's name and cult-hero status was the bait. But for professional investors approaching the traffic lights at the intersection of caution and opportunity, the signal was amber, and about to turn red. The company's head office was in Rufe Naylor's Building. The banker was the notorious Standard Bank, which had been reprimanded by the bribery commission for conducting business with the illegal Bucketshop Owners' Association. The names of the company's 'secretaries', too, raised an eyebrow or two. The South African Prudential Company, housed in Rufe Naylor's Building, was managed by AH Meyers, a Labour Party stalwart who in 1917 had been a candidate for the Provincial Council in an election that Naylor had had more than just a political interest in.[53]

In Johannesburg, commerce, crime and corruption shared a bed. For the ruling classes, the governing political party and the state – the wheels that kept the economy turning – the trick was as it had been since time immemorial: how best to maintain the illusion of ethical central control, coherence and justice without prosecuting too many of the leading lights in public life once their transgressions could no longer be concealed. Justice had to be seen to be done, but Lady Justice wore a blindfold, not to guarantee impartiality – a rigged game was often past that – but to ensure that her squint was not visible.

By the latter half of 1918, the government and the 'responsible' classes, as opposed to the 'unruly' white underclasses in South Africa's industrial heartland, ensured that the blindfold was firmly in place before sending the Lady out to do battle and underscore the time-honoured mantra about the need for control, for law and order, for 'justice'. There was a flurry of coordinated activity, focused overwhelmingly on Rufe Naylor.

The first round of the ensuing contest did not go easily or well for the powers that be. Naylor and van Veyeren were in the former's office on 14 September, around 10 pm, when the phone rang. It was the police tip-off that the offices of Dividend Cigarettes were about to be raided, and 'shortly afterwards a telephone message came through' (from someone in the telephone exchange) confirming 'that the company's offices had been raided'.[54] Naylor did not seem unduly perturbed about the news of the raid since many if not most of the incriminating books and documents had long since been relocated. What he was not prepared for was to be arrested for something that had nothing to do with the lottery, but everything to do with events at the Provincial Council.

The police took some joy in taking Naylor to the station and charging him with the bribery of Dingwall and van Veyeren, under Section 6 of Law No. 10 of 1894, another law dating back to the old Kruger republic. The Attorney General, likewise, took pleasure from the fact that bail was set at a staggering £5000 (about £200000 today) and that Naylor had to provide the names of two additional sureties for £2500 each. Naylor's attorney got the preparatory examination postponed to the end of the month.[55]

Less joy was forthcoming from the raid on the Dividend offices. Ostensibly searching for evidence of tax evasion, at the behest of the Commissioner of Inland Revenue, the state's primary objective was to try and demonstrate that Dividend Cigarettes was a front for the illegal operation of the Lourenço Marques Lottery. The allegation of tax evasion was easily established, and the holding company, the Delagoa Bay Cigarette Company – the board of which included Furze and two Auckland Park notables – was ordered to pay £8000 in back taxes, a figure that may have been a serious underestimate.[56]

The state's ambition, however, went further. It wanted the court to empower it to tax the 'dividends' – the lottery's cash prizes. If granted, the request would have crippled Dividend Cigarettes and the local dimension of the LML at a time when the company had already given notice of its intention to appeal the £8000 tax liability ruling. The Commissioner therefore sought an interdict to prevent the cigarette company from distributing any 'dividends' until such time as its tax liabilities had been properly assessed and fully met.

The granting of an interdict was opposed by Dividend Cigarettes. Judge Bristowe was aware of what was at stake. Most law officers knew that the Lottery Act was deficient, and the judge refused to be drawn into a ruling that would impact directly on the functioning, or legality of, the lottery. As Bristowe put it, 'I do not think it material to this case whether the business carried on by the company is legal or illegal', and the 'crucial question' was 'whether the prize distributions are part of the taxable income' of the income.[57] He decided that it was not. He found for the respondent, dismissing the state's application with costs. With the Attorney General whispering in his ear, the Commissioner gave notice of intention to appeal against the ruling.

The appeal – heard on the second-last day of October – was dismissed, with costs, by Judge Gregorowski, and the state was deflected for a second time.[58] The Gregorowski ruling gave Naylor, fending off a swarm of stinging legal initiatives coming at him from several directions, some momentary respite. To his relief, no more was publicly heard about the Dividend Company.

Perhaps that was because, by then, Attorney General de Villiers's beekeepers at Marshall Square had released a second swarm of raiders that, it was believed, would lead them to the source of the sweetness behind the Naylor lottery. Nine days before the Gregorowski ruling, on 21 October, the police conducted simultaneous raids at Life, Sport and Drama Ltd in Naylor's Building, and at Schmulian's United Printing & Publishing Co Ltd at 45 Simmonds Street.[59]

This time there was no covering feint about 'tax evasions' but a direct attempt to come up with evidence pointing to the contravention of the Lottery Law of 1890 – that hoary old Calvinist survivor from a bygone theocratic dispensation. At the offices of *Life, Sport and Drama*, from where Seccombe was managing the lottery, many books and documents were confiscated. At United Printing, whose owner, Lazar Schmulian, had been heavily implicated in municipal bribery scandals, and there was a need for still more proof, a larger number of items were seized.

It is likely that Naylor received prior warning about the raids and that most incriminating material had been removed from both premises before the police arrived. What is certain is that it was a centralised, coordinated effort by the long-satirised state officials to strike at Naylor and the lottery, and that the Attorney General, Johannesburg magistrates and police all knew about – and feared – Naylor's reach into the heart of police corruption at Marshall Square.

As the seized material was unloaded at police headquarters, the Assistant Resident Magistrate, Archibald Cramer, appeared as if out of nowhere. Cramer, one of three commissioners on the bribery commission, instructed the acting station sergeant, Robert Binnie, to ensure that none of the documentation went missing. Binnie's entry, No. 157 in the station's 'Occurrence Book', bears evidence to what the authorities feared most, and the lengths to which they were willing to go to avoid having corrupt white police officers in Naylor's thrall:

> Mr. A. Cramer, A.R.M. requests that a guard be placed on the storeroom upstairs till tomorrow morning when he will make arrangements with the District Commander Police for safe custody of articles (Rufe Naylor's Lotteries). Arranged for Native Constable to be on guard tonight, Native Constable preferred by Mr. Cramer.[60]

Beneath her blindfold, Lady Justice had got a glimpse of the widespread rot.

From mid-September to early October 1918, Naylor was put under insurmountable financial, legal and personal pressure by the state. The Dividend Company was in abeyance, money was spewing out of the Newclare racecourse faster than from a torn nosebag, and legal fees were spiking dangerously. At this juncture, Naylor's relationship with his *consigliere* began to unravel, and out of cynicism or desperation – probably both – he proceeded to reel Tatham in.

For almost six months the two of them had toyed with the idea of unlocking the value of Tatham's East Rand mining claims, but little had come of it. In late August, Naylor suggested they revisit their plans and float a limited-liability company with a market capitalisation of £200 000. Tatham was unconvinced. Naylor had already put up a few thousand pounds for the machinery that worked the claims in desultory fashion, and there was no need for massive new capital investment. Moreover, given other developments along the East Rand, Tatham felt that there was little chance of getting the public to subscribe to a larger number of shares in an unknown property.

Naylor was having none of it. He was, he said, a 'rich man' and would personally guarantee £75 000 as part of the mine's working capital. When that did not persuade Tatham, Naylor surrounded his *consigliere* with enthusiasts drawn exclusively from lottery loyalists and the Prudential Company. All agreed that shares in the MWGM would be snapped up faster than a Rand barman could slip an unclaimed florin into his waistcoat pocket.

Seccombe told Tatham that 'he, alone, could sell thirty thousand of the shares; but he did not sell one share'. Meyers of the Prudential, destined to become one of the company's 'secretaries', suggested that 'he could sell twenty thousand shares'. In the end 'he sold thirty'.[61] Naylor, as the principal financial underwriter of the venture, would receive ten per cent commission on his £75 000 and any other shares sold, while Tatham himself, as the 'Managing Director', would earn £1 200 per annum for such services as he rendered.[62]

The deal agreed in principle, they all went back to Naylor's flat where, in Tatham's presence, he hastily drew up a prospectus. But, since it was 'not in accordance with law', it was rewritten a day later by Naylor's attorney. Naylor was in a hurry and distracted. On 4 October, just days after the preliminary examination in the Dividend Cigarette Company matter, and ten days before his scheduled appearance for the preliminary examination on the charges of bribery, he, Tatham, Seccombe and others signed the necessary documents to turn the MWGM idea into a reality with legal standing.

In the eight years he spent in southern Africa, the month of October 1918 was the most difficult Naylor experienced. Funds coming in from the lottery, although growing, were insufficient to meet his collective commitments, bail conditions, bribes and legal expenses. He remortgaged Rufe Naylor's Building on the corner of Commissioner and Eloff streets at the obliging Standard Bank.[63] But his relationship with Tatham, whom he had once written letters to that were said to be 'almost affectionate', reached breaking point and Dividend Cigarettes was lost as a front for the LML.[64]

It is not clear what happened next. Naylor, 36 years old, staged a temporary withdrawal, allowing him to regain his composure and plan exit strategies from his many predicaments. Mystery surrounds the events, but it was strange that neither *Life, Sport and Drama* nor the dailies carried any report of the newsworthy Naylor having had an 'accident', been assaulted or been taken ill. Months later his advocate, FET Krause, dropped a hint when he claimed that Naylor had been 'nearly killed' by some unnamed person or persons.[65]

Whatever the truth, shortly before he was due to appear in court for the preliminary examination arising from the charges of bribery, Naylor checked into the upmarket Park Lane Clinic. There, he chose to be treated by Dr Hermann Graf – a 'very German, German' – who had been successfully prosecuted for dismissing his English nurse and replacing her with a fellow countrywoman. It was a shabby case, reeking of ethnic prejudice of a predictable wartime type.[66] The unhappy Graf had no reason to be well disposed to a 'British' court, and was clearly of the opinion that Naylor was in a bad way, although he never recorded what exactly his patient's ailment was.

On October 13, Graf wrote to magistrate JC Juta,[67] testifying that Naylor was 'progressing fairly well but will not be able to attend Court for three weeks yet'. But Naylor was clearly not progressing well, because by 3 November he was again said to 'progressing well' after an unspecified 'operation' but would not be 'able to appear in court for four weeks'. A further setback followed: on 17 November, Dr Graf told Juta that Naylor would be unable to appear in court 'for another four weeks'.[68] Doctors, as is well known, are even closer to God than judges or magistrates when it comes to matters of life or death, and the case was remanded on 3, 9 and 12 December.

Fortunately, Naylor's condition was never sufficiently serious to inhibit the conduct of important business throughout the three months that he was indisposed. During a month-long stay at the Park Lane, he received visits from a stream of associates, including Seccombe, Tatham and van Veyeren. Almost all these visits occasioned pains in the head rather than the heart – which was to trouble him in later life – since they invariably revolved around bribes paid or unpaid, the need to find yet more capital and several ongoing police investigations.

The cash-strapped Naylor relied on his *consigliere* for legal advice and practical assistance throughout his Park Lane stay. Some of his actions were 'impulsive', and Tatham, already off the roll of advocates, was being pushed hard. Tatham was given £15 and instructed to approach an unnamed magistrate – presumably dealing with a lottery case – and tell him that they were the winnings of a bet placed with Naylor. But 'the magistrate said that he had no bet and Naylor had no power to bet for him'. Tatham left, 'rather ashamed'.[69]

Fearing that he was becoming deeply involved in manifestly criminal activity, Tatham grew wary of Naylor's increasingly cavalier approach, and when pushed to agree to provide perjured evidence in certain unspecified proceedings – almost certainly the upcoming bribery case – he refused.[70] Naylor felt that it was a defining moment in a deteriorating relationship, and Tatham suspected that he may have been suckered into the MWGM flotation, and that it was simply another, more elaborate, part of Naylor's financial juggling act.

The more Tatham delved into the matter, the more unsettled he became. And the more unsettled he became, the more suspicious Naylor became, believing that his *consigliere* was about to sabotage his hope of raising capital through the sale of shares. All that was left was to decide who would strike first – the mongoose or the snake. But which was which? In early October, Tatham checked to see if, as claimed in the prospectus, the company had been registered. It had not. A week went by, and he checked again, to no avail. 'This went on for weeks.' He told Naylor and Seccombe that the company had, as suggested in the prospectus, to be registered by 25 November – the day that share applications closed – or they would certainly be in breach of the law.[71]

The company remained unregistered. Naylor and Seccombe had insufficient funds to pay for its registration, and Tatham set a deadline that they failed to meet. A flurry of letters followed as 25 November came and went. Three days later, Naylor eventually admitted that he had no funds and, in another sign of impending financial disaster, placed a notice in *Life, Sport and Drama* informing readers that 'neither the new company [Modder West] nor myself will be responsible for any orders that do not bear my signature'. On 1 December, he told Tatham that he had insufficient funds to underwrite the ongoing operations at the mining claims and could not pay the salaries of the manager or workers. After that exchange, Naylor feared that Tatham, then still residing in the elite Carlton Hotel, would respond by selling the claims to a third party before the company was registered.[72] The critical moment was fast approaching. The mongoose raised its head, and at the same instant the snake reared and bared its fangs. There followed a bewildering set of court cases that did much to shape the remainder of Naylor's South African career but that ended in a stalemate.

On Monday morning, 30 December 1918, Mr Justice Mason granted

Naylor an interdict ordering Tatham to show why, by 7 January, he should not transfer the ownership of the claims to the MWGM forthwith, and preventing him 'from dealing with, disposing of, alienating or encumbering the said claims or any of them'.[73] The Great War was over, but in South Africa the struggle between the state and Rufe Naylor was just starting.

Pyrrhic Victories: The State versus a Folk Hero and White Workers, 1919

It is at the lowest point in the valley that the ascent to the pass above commences. What lies beyond the pass is not always known, and the ascent draws heavily on the individual's reserves of courage and energy. At some point after his release from the Park Lane Clinic, in the closing quarter of 1918, Naylor, walking straight into the extreme variations in financial temperature that characterised his life, adjusted his backpack of tricks of the trade, and set out not on the road leading to the pass but along a short sidetrack.

Lateral thinking and the ability to read the public mood had long been Naylor's forte, but, when it was compromised by the 'impulsiveness' that Tatham complained of, it could be a weakness. But this time Naylor got it right. His priority was to breathe new life into, and protect his investments in – and returns from – the Lourenço Marques Lottery following the collapse of Dividend Cigarettes.

Dividends had been the primary, but not the exclusive, means of distributing lottery tickets on the Highveld, and the disruption was devastating. One solution to this logistical impasse, Naylor reasoned, was startlingly obvious. Francis Bacon, drawing on a Turkish proverb, had laid it out in an essay in the early 17th century: if the mountain would not come to Mohammed, then Mohammed would have to go to the mountain. If the lottery tickets could not come to the workers, then the workers would have to go to the lottery tickets. It was inspired, radical Rufe Naylor thinking at its best.

The twice-weekly, narrow-gauge rail journey from Johannesburg to Lourenço Marques cut across the Lebombo Mountains. With numerous halts at small stations along the way and a time-consuming border stop at Komatipoort, it was not for the faint-hearted. Bachelors and other white males, hoping to enjoy the relatively free access to alcohol and prostitutes in Catholic Mozambique at a time when Protestants were intent on pushing the demi-monde out of the reach of white working classes on the Rand, were willing to endure a journey that could take up to 18 hours.[74] That ordeal had to change.

Naylor persuaded the management of South African Railways not only to lay on a third service, early on Friday mornings, but to reduce the travel time to Delagoa Bay by several hours by providing a non-stop train that paused at Komatipoort only for the necessary border checks, with a return journey early on Sundays. The new service did little for the economic and social stability of families on the Rand, still undergoing the change from mining town to industrial city, but worked well for thousands of male demi-monde dwellers and lottery aficionados. White workers could explore the delights of Lourenço Marques by night, witness the lottery draw by day and be back at work on Monday.

The service further boosted Naylor's reputation as a friend of gamblers and the white working class. The return journey became the vehicle for the importation of thousands more lottery tickets. The train became popularly known as the 'Naylor Express', a name that stuck like soot to a carriage window for almost a decade after it was first used, in 1918.[75] It was an honorific title without precedent in popular culture, then or subsequently, one that eluded all Labour Party politicians, railway administrators and statesmen.

It took a slightly crazy Australian to provide South Africa with an unlikely folk hero, one capable of challenging the suffocating hold of the churches and employers, and of a government intent on creating a state served by the socially disciplined white working class. The seeds of the brutally suppressed Rand Revolt of 1922 lay not only in class struggles waged by trade unions in the workplace – between white miners seeking to entrench their position of structured privilege over cheap black labour – but in the largely unexplored social fabric of white working-class culture. More evidence of Naylor's growing social stature along the Rand was about to come down the line.

Largely for business reasons, Naylor cultivated the public image of himself as a brave and honest man reluctantly entangled in a struggle with benighted Protestants calling the tune for a mindlessly vindictive state. It was a necessary part of running successful bookmaking and lottery operations. But there were other, indirect, benefits that came with being known as a man capable of spontaneous acts of generosity, of supporting worthy causes, of being a champion of the common man with a respect for working-class culture. In a criminal justice system that relied in part on juries, it did no harm to be respected as a folk hero, as a little man struggling against the odds in hard times.

In purely civil matters such things counted for little. So when Naylor's and Tatham's attorneys confronted one another about the ownership of the East Rand mining claims and the need for them to be handed to the Modderfontein Company, over seven days, in early January 1919, there could be no playing to the gallery. The case had to be decided on its merits as laid out before the court. Justice Mason found for Naylor, with costs, and Tatham, who risked losing his only substantial remaining asset, gave notice of intent to appeal.[76]

For the remainder of 1919, there was scarcely a month in which Naylor was not in a Johannesburg or Pretoria court for periods ranging from a day to more than a week. On 6 February, Transvaal Attorney General Charles de Villiers led the case for the prosecution in the Supreme Court, in Pretoria, before Justice Mason and a jury. Dr FET Krause, arguably the best and most expensive criminal lawyer north of the Vaal, led Naylor's defence against the charges of having bribed Dingwall and van Veyeren.[77] Neither of the provincial councillors was prosecuted, nor was Colonel JJ Furze, himself a former provincial and town councillor, who appeared as a witness for the defence, and who admitted freely to having bribed Dingwall and van Veyeren.

When the Attorney General reminded the Colonel that he was 'liable to prosecution', Furze replied: 'I have been very severely punished for any crime I have committed.' De Villiers did not demur.[78] The lesson was clear: state office bearers were not readily prosecuted. Lady Justice readjusted her blindfold so that very few noticed her unattractive squint, though Naylor did.

In a trial lasting eight days, a long-winded Krause argued that, while money had changed hands between Naylor and the councillors, as testified to by Tatham, these did not constitute bribes. They were, he argued, acts of extortion directed at a successful businessman by

Dingwall and van Veyeren, who now enjoyed the protection of the prosecution. Naylor suggested that the two councillors' versions may have been supported by Tatham because the latter had an overriding political ambition to become a republican president – an aspiration so divorced from reality that it pointed to him possibly being of unsound mind. In effect, to reach a verdict, the hard-pressed jury was being asked to decide which of the two versions it heard was true: was it a case of bribery or extortion?

Aware of how Naylor's popular image might sway members of the jury, Mason used his summing-up to hack away at the reputational undergrowth and open a pathway to clearer thinking. He condemned the 'atmosphere of bribery' around the Provincial Council and was unimpressed by Dingwall and van Veyeren, 'who had saved their own skins by turning King's evidence'; 'Tatham's evidence was on a lower plane [than] even that of Dingwall or van Veyeren'; Tatham 'was not a good character', and there 'was no doubt that he was aggressive and hostile to Naylor', and that he had 'exploited Naylor', but the judge 'did not think that he was a lunatic'.[79] So, then, what of the accused?

'Naylor', Mason opined, 'was a very capable man and gave his evidence frankly and, on the whole, in a manly way.' But the jury should be warned that 'demeanour was not an infallible test'; 'it was often a matter of temperament or experience'. In terms of court appearances, only veteran attorneys and magistrates had more 'experience' than Naylor. Upon retiring to consider their verdict, the members of the jury spent nearly three hours swinging a sword at the two-headed question, trying to decide which head of the monster – bribery or extortion – should be lopped off.

But, as in the case of Humpty Dumpty, all the King's horses and all the King's men could not put something together. When the jurors returned, 'the foreman indicated that they could not agree'. 'The Judge discharged the jury, bail being reduced on the application of Dr Krause, from £5 000 to £2 000. The Attorney General did not indicate what steps he proposed to take.'[80] Members of the public left no doubt as to where their sympathies lay: 'Mr Naylor on leaving the Court was loudly cheered.'[81] But Naylor sensed that de Villiers would be back, sooner rather than later, and the opposing advocates smiled.

With the bribery case seemingly on hold, Naylor and Tatham were left circling one another about other matters. Tatham left the court an embittered and wounded man, intent on salvaging what little was left of his reputation after the mauling from Judge Mason. He was financially stretched and had moved out of the upmarket Carlton, in central Johannesburg, and into the Cecil Hotel, in Benoni. Naylor, on the other hand, felt reasonably buoyed by proceedings. His reputation as an independent-minded maverick was intact, if not slightly enhanced. When asked whether the Lourenço Marques Lottery was illegal in South Africa, he had shot back that it was, 'at present', but that 'when people here become more enlightened it will become legal'.[82] Being commended by a judge for being 'frank' and 'manly' did a fellow no harm in a mining town.

But there was something about Naylor's masculinity that seemed puzzling, despite his being married with two children. He had a life-long interest in the human body, health issues and male athletic prowess.[83] During the ten years (on and off) he spent in Johannesburg, his wife never spent any time with him. His closest associates, Seccombe, Tatham and van der Linden, were all married men and, in Lourenço Marques, even Padre Vicente had a common-law wife.

Naylor, well-dressed and wealthy, owned three motor vehicles and a private apartment. He had a personal and shareholding interest in the 'International Variety and Theatrical Agency Limited', which put him in contact with females, but he was never reported as being seen in the company of women. He inhabited a male universe, surrounded by cronies or, at the office, younger male lottery clerks, who, despite picking up criminal records because of being employed in an illegal business, remained totally loyal to him. In Johannesburg it was unusual – a manly gangster who appeared to be asexual. It may, however, have been an appearance that he chose to cultivate in 1919.[84]

Away from the manly haunts that Naylor frequented, the one-time impresario developed a growing interest in Phyllis Penberthy, a young lady working in the offices of *Life, Sport and Drama*. Miss Penberthy, a talented young musician and singer, came from a Cornish mining family in Roodepoort, a Labour Party stronghold. Shortly after the outbreak of the war, the good-looking lady began promoting worthy causes and the drive to recruit men for the army. She rose to become a minor socialite, gracing the social columns of the local press.[85]

Phyllis's interests and social profile appealed to Naylor, and she encouraged his commitment to the war effort. He may have needed a bit of prompting since, upon returning to South Africa in 1916, he had given the police 'an undertaking to join the Australian Forces if necessary'. But apparently it was not necessary. He later claimed to have donated a thousand pounds to the Governor General's Fund and said that he had sent 'three substitutes to the front while maintaining their dependants during their absences abroad'. Miss Penberthy found much to admire in him, and her approval of Rufe as a patron of the arts loomed large in their developing relationship.[86] But Naylor's mind was not always focused exclusively on Miss Penberthy. Tatham haunted him.

The depth of the Naylor-Tatham feud was reminiscent of a contested divorce. On 4 March, Naylor was arrested on a charge of perjury. Back in court for a preliminary examination, he was closely watched by Tatham, who somehow knew about the impending proceedings. The prosecution alleged – correctly, as it later transpired – that Naylor had lied during the MWGM case when he claimed that he had invested £7 500 in the company. But there may have been other issues at play. The Attorney General had not taken kindly to his failure to get a conviction in the bribery case, and Tatham was still smarting over the loss of the claims case. De Villiers may have sensed there was no closed season in mongoose-and-snake country and hoped to add fuel to a feud that had long since assumed a life of its own.

Anyhow, that was how Naylor saw it. *Life, Sport and Drama* made certain that his view – that the state was out to harass and victimise him – was widely known. 'The Crown', Naylor asserted, 'was being used in order to assist a private prosecution.' He, as the accused, was not being prosecuted by Tatham but by the state, and he then reeled off a series of facts that might have given rise to a little awkwardness in the prosecutor's office.[87]

The bribery commission, Naylor argued at the preliminary examination on the charge of perjury, had granted indemnities 'to at least a half-dozen self-confessed bribers and bribees' but had refused to take evidence from him. Naylor alone had been charged. His room at the Park Lane Clinic had been searched, and he had been arrested at 5 pm and ordered to come up with £5 000 in bail money – at a time when it was known that the banks had been closed for two hours. He and Seccombe had also been subjected to yet another court appearance, for an alleged breach of company law, but the state's case was so palpably thin that a magistrate had thrown it out 'without calling the defence'. And Naylor's bribery charges 'were heard in Pretoria, although he [resided] in Johannesburg and the alleged offences were committed on the Rand'. The magistrate and prosecutor Archibald Cramer took exception to that line of argument and, backfooted, made a point of emphasising their fairness and impartiality, but some damage had been done to the state's case. It did not matter; Naylor was again committed for trial.[88]

The Attorney General and Tatham appeared to be moving in unison, which, if true, cramped the space available for Naylor's response.[89] The Attorney General may have been out of reach, but Tatham was not. Forty-eight hours later, on 12 March, Naylor struck back, seeking an interdict to force Tatham to pay the legal costs in the claims case or face imprisonment for contempt of court. But, realising that the argument about contempt of court was not particularly compelling, Naylor withdrew it. He was thus not in court eight days later when the judge told Tatham that the application had been withdrawn. Tatham's counsel submitted that 'His Lordship [was] treating these people with a lot of latitude'. Justice Ward replied, 'I don't suppose any harm will arise', but then, to Tatham's immense relief, awarded him costs.[90]

Three weeks later, from 12 to 17 April 1919, Naylor, assisted by advocates Krause and Morris, was back in the Supreme Court in Pretoria, for a second time, before Justice Curlewis and nine jurors, for allegedly having bribed Dingwall and van Veyeren. Charles de Villiers again acted as prosecutor for the state. With nothing new of substance to offer, both prosecution and defence rubbed away at magic lamps, trying to conjure up the same old genies, and hoping that one – bribery or extortion – might imprint itself on the minds of the jury. Naylor, seemingly as 'manly' as ever, added a gloss to the case for the defence, admitting to having had a 'bad record' in Australia, and adding that it rendered him vulnerable to Dingwall's and van Veyeren's threats of blackmail and extortion.[91]

The prosecutorial genie, looming large, was the first to appear. He reminded the jurors that as charming and persuasive as Naylor could be, there was a darker side to him that was seldom on display in public, and that he was perfectly capable of threats of blackmail or other threats. Tatham, himself never above bullying, said he had been 'trapped' by Naylor and ended up being 'enslaved'. Van Veyeren, quizzed as to why he had been party to granting the Newclare licence, explained: 'I was so in the claws of these people that I was compelled to vote for the renewal because I had accepted the money.'

In another instance, reported only days after the case was concluded, a lottery runner named HS Foster had more to offer along similar lines. He recalled how, seeing bundles of banknotes on his boss's desk, he had jokingly said that he would take it all; Naylor then 'pulled out a revolver'. Naylor, a good shot, was also an excellent clay pigeon shooter. An aura of hidden menace around Naylor and his associates may explain why he had been 'nearly killed' and ended up in the Park Lane Clinic. The judge, Curlewis, was wary of jury members being suborned, and sure enough Seccombe visited one of the jurors after hours.[92]

The genie for the defence, smoother of tongue and nimbler of foot, wove a web even stickier than that of his counterpart. Tatham, granted indemnity as a witness for the prosecution, was cast as having been so down and out when Naylor first met him that he had to be 'dragged out of the gutter'. Disbarred and dishonest, Tatham was a deeply treacherous man, and Naylor had a right to expect 'a certain amount of honesty even amongst people of his class'.

When cross-examined, Tatham admitted that there had once been 'complete confidence' between him and the accused. Naylor, he said, had been almost 'affectionate', and had his 'good points', but his 'bottlewasher' sidekick, Seccombe, was 'a convict'. He – Tatham – had only rounded on Naylor when the latter, too, proved to be 'disloyal' and capable of entrapment. This, then, was no ordinary conflict arising from business failures; it was deeply personal warfare.[93]

There was a puff of smoke and the defence genie disappeared, to be replaced by a man who never had need of a lamp to hide, a person comfortable on any stage, one singing his own song. Naylor presented himself as a man of honour, a man of his word, a loyal person, one who would never 'squeal'. He was, he said, responsible for the financial well-being of a hundred employees. He was a man of the people, for the people, who benefited working men and women. But, as 'a lottery man' he unfortunately 'was not in good standing with the government'. Like the trade unionists whom the government had deported in 1914 – leading to a massive surge in support for the Labour Party – he, too, was being treated as an 'agitator', as someone vulnerable to deportation.[94] Indeed, the presence of Attorney General de Villiers proved that he was being targeted by a vindictive government, and that, in his own way, he was a political martyr.

It was brilliant presentation, homing in on the political sympathies of nine white men good and true drawn from the ranks of an aggrieved mining town that, 36 months later, would rise in armed revolt against the policies of the government of the day. The result of the de Villiers vs Naylor contest, fought over 12 months for the political championship of Johannesburg, was never in doubt. The foreman of the jury delivered to the judge a unanimous verdict – 'not guilty' – and the folk hero acquired another title.[95]

Naylor understood the importance of his victory perfectly. Politics and economics were inseparable. Profits could, and should, be derived from both sources whenever possible. For those aspiring to become major players, city bosses, the trick lay in arbitrage, in turning the currency of politics into economics, and economics into politics. Within two weeks of his acquittal, on 27 April, Naylor set about converting his popularity into slightly more durable form by standing for public office as a town councillor. Ward 11, which incorporated the Turffontein racecourse, was a suburb in which he owned property and the location of the famous Robinson Deep Mine, where he had once worked.[96]

In 1907, shortly before coming to South Africa, Naylor had had a close-up view of how the Democratic Party ran New York City, becoming acquainted with Tammany Hall-style politics. In Johannesburg, fathered by greed and mothered by money, crime-as-politics and politics-as-crime formed an intrinsic part of the city's genetic make-up, and one destined to last well into the 21st century. In the 1890s, the city's underworld was dominated by the powerful 'American Club', dominated by Polish pimps. The Jameson Raid, in 1895–1896, offered a further example of how, with a little American tutoring, politics could metamorphose into criminality by drawing on a transatlantic tradition of filibustering.[97]

What Naylor lacked was the political space in which to operate successfully. The Labour Party machine in the city, along with those of other persuasions – nationalists, reformers and SAP men – carved up the wards between them. The answer therefore lay in turning perceived weakness into a strength. Naylor's exclusion from the dominant parties, some of whose members he was known to have bribed, played to his advantage. He was the courageous champion of the common man, the self-made business tycoon, the political underdog up against the might of the establishment and self-serving politicians. He was 'Rufe Naylor: The Independent and Fearless Democrat', willing and able to pursue every avenue of populist politics.[98]

He claimed that 700 people 'of all classes' had 'requisitioned' him to stand as a candidate. He took the issue of corruption head-on. The existing system of municipal government, he argued, provided 'opportunists' with the chance to see 'how much money and graft they could get'. It should be replaced by five well-paid councillors who would be beyond temptation. He advocated a municipal bank to lower the level of city debt and sought a 40-hour working week for municipal workers and returning soldiers. He pushed for lower tram fares and free municipal transport for schoolchildren, and, drawing on his Lourenço Marques experience, a municipal orchestra and band. Three hundred people attended his main event, and only two attendees dissented from a vote of confidence.[99]

With an election manifesto far more imaginative than most Labour Party candidates could muster, Naylor won the election by a record majority, the largest ever secured in a municipal contest. Shortly thereafter, his sidekick, Seccombe, also stood – albeit unsuccessfully – as the Labour Party candidate for Ward 4 in a town council by-election.[100] The lottery men had set their sights on acquiring greater direct influence within the municipal power structure.

Morris Kentridge of the Labour Party, who had to court Naylor's support on certain progressive issues, had a generally low opinion of the wartime council. He told the bribery commission how he had seen 'baneful influences introduced when, professional politicians and place seekers, by log rolling and illegal methods, usurped the control of municipal affairs'. He knew that there were some in Naylor's thrall, and yet others who, independently, used their positions to expand a network of clandestine agents selling lottery tickets. Kentridge told the commission about 'gentlemen who apparently as soon as they get in [to the council] run sweeps or lottery tickets. I will not mention names ...'. Both Schmulians must have breathed a sigh of relief.[101] LML agents might have facilitated the rot in local government, but when it came to the cost of municipal transport and working hours, Naylor achieved several of the objectives that he had earlier set out in his manifesto.

Naylor's election was impressive for another reason. Even as towns-men were coming to terms with the election, he was again arrested for contravening the lottery law. The charges arose from a raid on Seccombe's office, on 10 April. The government had pushed the Attorney General, wearing no more than the old Kruger-era gloves, into yet another exhausting contest in the hope of wearing down and discrediting the local champion.[102]

The fight for control of the white working class dragged on. De Villiers was set on curbing, incrementally if necessary, Naylor's influence and eliminating the lottery. Naylor's subsequent appearance in yet another preliminary examination, before JC Juta, and committal for the trial that was to follow were hardly decisive. But they did come at a cost to de Villiers' quarry. It unsettled Naylor supporters, who feared that the persistence of the state might eventually triumph, and there was a falling-off in the sale of lottery tickets.

In the cradle of corruption – the Provincial Council – opportunists in the Labour Party saw in this public hesitancy the chance to push for a provincial or state lottery of their own, while in the seedier parts of Johannesburg, underworld types attempted to fill the vacuum by printing and selling more – but fake – lottery tickets.[103] Sugared water attracts bees and wasps alike. Biding his time, Naylor responded by switching the core LML operations from the front line of the battle, on the Rand, to Natal, where van der Linden successfully pushed the business in the larger urban centres and on into the countryside.[104]

In Johannesburg, the hurricane of court appearances in relation to lottery offences, driven by the Attorney General, showed no sign of letting up. The magistrate's court was subjected to more vigorous buffeting, on 17 June, when Naylor, Seccombe, Mrs Chase Schmulian and four others were committed for trial based on evidence secured during the raid some months earlier. But Councillor Naylor, aware that in a legal storm public opinion and the jury system offered better protection than a sou'wester, was suitably dressed. The accused demanded to be tried in a higher court before a judge and a jury. The magistrate forwarded the papers to de Villiers for the state to consider its next move. It took months. It did not help that a rumour began to do the rounds that Rufe was going to stand for parliament as an Independent Democrat.[105]

The gale howled on into July. The ramifications of the Dingwall and van Veyeren bribery case continued to spill over into the Naylor-Tatham vendetta until they eventually enveloped Seccombe. Seccombe took his standing as chairman of the school board, 'Director' of a mining company and Labour Party candidate more seriously than it merited. Incensed at having been labelled a 'convict', he sued Tatham for 'reputational damages' set at £1 000.

Going to law at a time when lottery sales had slumped and he was cash-strapped was a risky business, but Seccombe may have wanted to show where his loyalties lay in the Naylor-Tatham matter. Whatever the truth, the judge was not convinced that any damage had been done to Seccombe's social standing and dismissed the case, awarding costs to Tatham, who by then was also feeling the pinch of legal fees and was almost as impecunious as Seccombe.[106]

The Naylor Express carried news of the legal and political storms in and around the lottery operations on the Rand down to the coast. In Mozambique, Padre Vicente was facing his own problems relating to the lottery. The political fallout of war-induced economic hardship included a prolonged bout of labour unrest among white settlers in Lourenço Marques.[107] Rampant inflation, strikes and job losses occasioned destitution, and the administration looked to the lottery to dispense charity. The public, resentful about rumours of Smuts's imperialist design to take over the labour-rich Sul do Save, saw only a hugely successful lottery awarding large monthly cash prizes to well-off white miners on the Witwatersrand while needy locals were all suffering.

Upcountry, Naylor was being squeezed ideologically and politically by Protestant churches and the government. The lottery was said to encourage idleness and lower the productivity of white workers, and to export valuable sterling from an industrialising economy. On the coast, the administration, the Catholic Church and Padre Vicente felt that the lottery was directing too much cash inland and devoting insufficient funds to the unemployed in a notoriously sluggish commercial economy. The principal lottery concessionaires found themselves caught between what seemed like an irresistible force bearing down on an immovable object. Something was bound to give way. And it did.

PART IV

FEVER

Show me a hero and I will write you a tragedy.
F SCOTT FITZGERALD, *THE CRACK-UP* (1945)

The Disappearance of One Folk Hero and Emergence of Another, Lourenço Marques 1919

Who knows where the tipping point lies in a battle, let alone a transfrontier battle? By mid-1919, Attorney General Charles de Villiers had reason to be despondent. He had lost his principal legal encounter with Rufe Naylor and was awaiting the outcome of other, relatively minor, cases yet to appear on the rolls. The nature of his fight with Naylor had shifted, from face-to-face encounters across a Pretoria courtroom to legal guerrilla warfare, with lots of fighting behind the lines and liberal use of sniper fire. The outcomes of guerrilla wars, often determined by the lapse of time and by exhaustion, are difficult to predict. Often they are decided by underlying mindsets as much as by physical resourcefulness.

By late May 1919, Naylor was back in Lourenço Marques, deeply involved in discussions with Padre Vicente about the future of the lottery. One was a relatively unimportant priest of questionable standing in the church, but an ultra-nationalist who enjoyed the trust of the administration, the other a dynamic, self-made gambling magnate helping to prop up the faltering Mozambique economy. Both were mavericks with growing reputations for being able to weave straw into gold, but neither had reason to be too sanguine.

Naylor, who had already publicly mused about the possibility of being deported from South Africa, was coming round to the view that, if forced to choose, he would jump rather than be pushed. As Witwatersrand gangsters had known for decades, hurried exits into the wider world were relatively easily effected via Lourenço Marques, where money could buy just about anything. He had £20 000 on fixed deposit with the BNU and an 80 per cent interest in the lottery, and there was a fleet of ships constantly ferrying mine timber from Western Australia to Lourenço Marques.[1] If anything, he felt he had too much money tied up in Mozambique. His faith in the lottery remained intact, but he wanted to conceal his share in the business and reduce his investment so that, should he have to flee, he would have sufficient funds.

For Vicente and the Mozambican administration, the news that one of its most lucrative sources of foreign exchange was about to dry up could not have come at a worse moment. Without access to the Naylor name, the principal market, in Johannesburg, along with a nationwide network of agents, would be lost. Mozambique needed access to Naylor's capital as well as to his organisation in South Africa. But, because the lottery was technically illegal there, the Lourenço Marques administration could not be seen to be directly involved in a rescue operation at a time of palpable hostility from the Smuts government. The Mozambican administration needed the troublesome priest as its front.

No baby can be delivered without waiting for the dilation to take place or blood on the midwife's hands. For the parents of the new-born, it is the waiting that is more painful and memorable than the scrubbing down that follows. The lottery was suspended for June and July while Vicente looked around for partners willing to take up a half share of Naylor's 80 per cent holding in the concessionary company in which the priest owned the other 20 per cent.[2] He called on wealthy Portuguese friends in the city but was given short shrift. No one could see a long-term future for the lottery without Naylor, 'but shortly afterwards they deeply regretted not having entered into the business'. In desperation and at the last possible moment, Vicente obtained a loan, in his own name, from the BNU. In effect, it was a loan from the fiscus, since the BNU was as close to a being a state bank as was possible.[3]

For Vicente, it proved to be a life-changing but perhaps not soul-saving risk, though one worth taking. The church remained unwilling to overlook his ongoing secular-based interference in religious mat-ters, or his earthly transgressions. To him it mattered greatly, and he later attempted, unsuccessfully, to buy his way back into the grace and favour of the Pope.[4] To others it mattered not.

The loan was repaid within 24 months, and a decade later Vicente was a philanthropic millionaire and a man of some importance in the governance of the city. As the lights dimmed and one folk hero threatened to leave centre stage of the lottery, so another was born in the wings, ready to play his part as a champion of *às pessoas* (the citizenry), including black Mozambicans. More importantly, the BNU loan presented him with the tools necessary for negotiating with Naylor, for recapitalising and reconstructing the concession.

The Padre offered the Lourenço Marques administration two incentives as the terms of the concession were renegotiated over eight weeks – that being a blink of an eye for the notoriously sleepy coastal bureaucracy. First, the managing company would retain the name 'Rufe Naylor Lotteries Ltd', even though it no longer had a controlling share in the business. The lottery would continue to operate in South Africa and remain a cash cow for the Lourenço Marques administration. Second, the share of profits destined for local charities would be increased substantially, which would help ease pressure coming from the deeply discontented local Portuguese settler population.[5]

In June, while negotiations in Lourenço Marques were still unfolding, the Johannesburg press reported that Rufe Naylor had sold his share in the company holding the lottery concession.[6] For a man still facing charges of contravening the Lotteries Act and of perjury, it was a useful half-truth that became even more useful in the months that followed. But it was a half-truth. Naylor had indeed sold most of his shares to Father Vicente, but ownership of his remaining shares had been disguised, or reallocated to trusted lieutenants.

In legal and illegal businesses alike, the routinised concealment of assets, and issues of control and succession planning, are matters of genuine concern for entrepreneurs. In family businesses, where a balance must be maintained between insiders who are kin and talented outsiders, such matters have the potential to become ever more problematic. Up to 1918, Rufe had kept his three brothers largely at arm's length from his biggest money-spinner – the lottery.

The youngest Naylor brother, the last to arrive on the Witwatersrand, Henry John – 'Harry' – was furthest from the mainstream businesses and the sibling that Rufe had least to do with. The second youngest, George, the first to arrive in Johannesburg and at various times a bookmaker, horse breeder and speculator, was more of a risk-taker, in the mould of Rufe himself. He and Rufe, along with Seccombe, were involved in various deals, including with Tatham in the Modder West venture, a northeastern Transvaal mining venture at Gravelotte and gold claims in the Magaliesberg. When lottery sales in Natal spiked during the war, and the police closed in on the Rand operation, Rufe sent George to manage the region with the help of Paul van der Linden. Van der Linden's loyalty to the family was total and, once Tatham withdrew, he inherited the informal role of *consigliere* during the interwar years. But it was the oldest brother, Peter Charles, that Rufe trusted most. He was an experienced, level-headed businessman, best suited to assessing and balancing opportunity and risk. Later in life, however, Peter Charles, too, developed an appetite for serious gambling and, like Rufe, had his share of financial ups and downs.[7]

Rufe had been assisting and promoting Peter Charles's career in various fields of legitimate enterprise for more than a decade. In 1910, when Rufe's interests in cinemas, film and theatre were expanding most rapidly, Peter had served as his 'agent' in London. When Rufe's African Amalgamated Theatres was folded into the Schlesinger conglomerate a few years later and war broke out, Peter Charles was in India, representing the new company in which his brother was a shareholder.[8] After the war, Peter and wife returned to England, and in 1921, after a visit to India, the couple eventually settled in Johannesburg.

By mid-1919, at the time of reconstructing the lottery, Rufe knew that if he was to avoid imprisonment, he would have to abandon South Africa, and that Peter Charles's future, like that of the other brothers, lay on the Witwatersrand. So he transferred, and split, the 20 per cent of the shares he still held in the company between Peter Charles, van der Linden and two partners who had helped raise the capital for the original venture in 1917 – Albert Adamson and William Harvey. The split had the added advantage that Adamson and van der Linden were based just down the coast, in Durban, serving the Natal market, while the two other brothers remained at the centre, in Johannesburg. If Peter Charles ever needed encouragement to move south, he now had it.[9]

When the sale of lottery tickets resumed in Natal and the Transvaal in August 1919, there were few signs of diminished public interest in the redesigned business. Rand agents took the precaution of selling tickets only to new clients who came to them with personal recommendations from existing, long-standing clients. Elsewhere, there were signs that the lottery had expanded further down the east coast to larger centres, including East London, where an unnamed female 'general agent for the Union' was sentenced to £100, or three months, for selling tickets. Some idea of the public's willingness to defy the state was evident when two others in that port city were committed for trial: 'Practically all the witnesses expressed regret that the lottery had been stopped [in July] and added that, if it were resumed, they would again take tickets.'[10]

The reconstructed company regained momentum faster than the Naylor Express, but the mid-year suspension of sales proved costly for Naylor and Seccombe. The worst of Johannesburg's winter legal season was barely past when they received warnings about more inclement weather approaching from Pretoria, driven by de Villiers, and revolving around criminal cases. But the first squall came from a different direction. In August, a civil suit in an illiquid case between Rufe Naylor and a certain Charlie Henwood, who appears to have been a punter fallen upon hard times, was hastily settled out of court.[11]

The Attorney General was still hoping for early trials in two cases: Naylor's perjured evidence in the Modder West mining dispute with Tatham, and lottery infringements arising from the raid on Seccombe's office. But the Crown Prosecutor in Johannesburg lacked de Villiers's zeal. When, on 19 August, the Crown Prosecutor asked for trial dates to be set, he was poorly prepared. Krause, appearing for Naylor, objected to an early date and the judge agreed, ordering that both cases be heard only in October.[12] Naylor, busy realigning his interests, was intent on stalling any criminal court appearance.

Trouble multiplied. Seccombe, strangely overlooked in the redistribution of shares in Lourenço Marques, was in deep financial trouble, having unsuccessfully sued Tatham for libel. He had not only over-committed himself in the launching of the ill-fated Modder West mess but had then got independently involved in another venture, at Olifants Geraamte, near Sabie, where he was mining gold on tribute with a large estates company. Lacking assets and cash to meet his commitments, in mid-October he was declared bankrupt by the court.[13]

Given that only hours separated their appearances before the judges and magistrates, Seccombe and Naylor might as well have exchanged greetings on the courthouse steps. Later that same month, Naylor spent three days in court defending a case brought against him by one John Krige on a matter dating back to the previous year at the Krugersdorp racecourse. The plaintiff had been inadvertently caught up in a scam when a horse had been run in a race under a different name. Krige had been arrested at the instigation of Naylor, who had retained a private detective – a practice dating back to his days at the Stadium – who was on good enough terms with a police constable to be able to have personal exchanges with him. The plaintiff wanted £750 compensation for 'wrongful arrest, imprisonment and malicious prosecution'.

It was a complex matter, and Justice Leonard Bristowe, who had presided over the Dividend Cigarettes case and knew a good deal about Naylor, was respectful of the plaintiff's rights.[14] After three days of argument, he granted Krige the right to reformulate his plea and ordered Naylor to pay any costs arising from the delayed proceedings. The case was remanded until November. Naylor's pending lottery case was, by then, in danger of being bookended by Bristowe, who was becoming even more familiar with Rufe's doings.[15]

Naylor now faced the daunting prospect of appearing before Bristowe on two or three more occasions before the year's end, for both civil and criminal infringements. The state had already indicated how seriously it was taking the criminal matters when, a few months earlier, it had taken Councillor Naylor's fingerprints – a sign that it was aware of the danger of a sudden departure.[16]

For his part, Naylor would have been aware that, in 1909, the year of his arrival on the Rand, the Transvaal government had succeeded in getting 'One-armed Jack' McLoughlin, once of Johannesburg, extradited from Australia on a charge of murder and executing him.[17] Ever since the 1880s, British colonies had shown a willingness to cooperate when dealing with crimes ranging from fraud to murder. The world had grown smaller as railways, steamships and the telegraph shrank the distances between continents.

Naylor, a man of his times, was always quick to pick up on changing social trends or developments in audio technology, and then to bend them to his own ends. His South African experiences in the grey economy put him in the forefront of contemporary practices elsewhere, such as those described in Walter Serner's *Last Loosening: A Handbook for the Con Artist and Those Aspiring to Become One*, published in 1919, and Charles Ponzi's financial fraud that same year.

Naylor had little need of lessons from Ponzi or Serner. Indeed, his exploits were, arguably, better concealed, more ingenious and more imaginative that theirs. They, nevertheless, offered lessons that Naylor would have been in full agreement with. 'If you are wrong', Serner wrote, 'you still have a chance to win litigation.' It was a maxim that Naylor had followed since his adolescence in New South Wales. More pertinently, Serner wisely counselled that when all else fails, 'go to ground, disappear and never return'.

On 3 December 1919, Judge Bristowe handed down his judgment in the Krugersdorp racecourse case and awarded Krige, the plaintiff, costs and damages of £75.[18] Of Naylor himself there was no sign, and, at the other end of town, Phyllis Penberthy failed to appear for work as usual at the offices of *Life, Sport and Drama*. The daily press, which tended to record Naylor's every move of significance, made no mention of him, nor of Miss Penberthy.

They could have gone anywhere other than within the British Empire. Delagoa Bay looked out over half the world. Naylor knew that he could not outsprint cablegrams but sensed that ponderous state bureaucracies moved so slowly that he had a small window of opportunity. In late November, he and Phyllis boarded a timber vessel in ballast at Lourenço Marques, bound for Fremantle. Then, around 8 December, they surfaced in Perth as Mr and Mrs RT Naylor, staying at the Ocean Beach Hotel. For all the world they must have looked like a pair of newlyweds, a couple possibly on honeymoon.

But the underwater cable, a sea serpent, could move faster than any coal-fired steamer when it came to devouring time and distance between continents. Within days of their arrival, two telegrams took some of the gloss off Cottesloe Beach. The first and 'most disconcerting' came from Cape Town. The press had latched on to Rufe's failure to appear in court not only for the Krige case but also to answer long-standing charges of perjury and contravening the Lotteries Act. A warrant had been issued for his arrest, but it was known that he was in Perth and that he was 'in a nursing home'.[19] It was the news Naylor feared most.

The second – from Johannesburg – also made for unpleasant reading but was reassuring in the sense that it vindicated Naylor's decision to estreat bail of £2 000. Bristowe had been surprisingly lenient in handing down sentences in the lottery case. The judge had disagreed with Advocate Krause's view that 'public opinion had altered since the passing of the thirty-year-old law' and 'that the legislature did not always keep pace with public opinion'. Nor was Bristowe impressed by the fact that lotteries were legal in so many countries.

Nevertheless, Rufe's clerk, Hyman Miller, and Mrs Chase Schmulian were given suspended sentences only. Even Seccombe, with several previous convictions, got off lightly with a fine of £150 or six months. They were given lenient sentences, the judge said, since they 'were not the main instruments in carrying on lotteries. He took it that the person who was most responsible was Rufe Naylor himself and he was not going to inflict a larger sentence on people who were employees'.[20] In Australia, Bristowe's thoughts on lotteries would have carried little weight, but news of a warrant for Naylor's arrest set the cat among the Perth pigeons. The cat had to be removed, the pigeons calmed.

Naylor walked directly towards the backyard disturbance and fought back as vigorously as possible through the local newspapers. For the next ten days the Ocean Beach Hotel mimicked a World War I propaganda office when it came to dissembling, red herrings, fraudulent documents, false trails and the telling of a mess of half-truths or outright lies that were impossible to disentangle at short notice. It was a master class on how to organise an obfuscating retreat between continents. Serner and Ponzi, in the north, could learn from the south.

'Councillor Naylor' called in at the offices of a weekly newspaper and granted interviews to any other journalists interested in his well-being at Ocean Beach. Rufe had long-standing concerns about his health – indeed, some considered him to be a 'crank'. He readily conceded that he had not been confined to a nursing home – an echo of his stay at the Park Lane – but had come to Perth to 'recover his health'.[21] The Johannesburg Town Council had been most understanding and he produced a document purporting to grant him indefinite leave 'until recovery from an [unspecified] illness'. His absence would not, however, interfere with his political career. He had already achieved much, and he and Mrs Naylor, his wife, were intent on returning to South Africa in February. He was thinking seriously about standing for the Union parliament as an Independent Democrat in his Turffontein constituency the following April.

Naylor's pronouncement about a political future in South Africa was a lie – a consciously contrived bit of dissembling. The primary print medium for advancing his career had long been the fittingly named *Life, Sport and Drama*. If he had been intent on returning to Johannesburg within a matter of weeks to prepare for an election campaign, then he would have wanted easy access to the magazine. But the decision to close the journal had been taken even before he fled. The final edition of *Life, Sport and Drama* hit the streets on Christmas Day 1919.

Health issues dealt with, Naylor turned his attention to other matters that interested the Australian press far more. The lottery business, he explained, was legally based in 'Portuguese East Africa' but not tolerated in South Africa, where it had had been 'persecuted'. As result he had 'left in disgust' – implying a permanent departure. But, oops, that did not fit readily with the story about an imminent return, so, for those who had clapped eyes on the new Mrs Naylor, he embroidered another version. Yes, he would shortly be going to Sydney (where he did not resurface for some years) but was currently 'engaged on a leisurely tour' of 'the East' or, more ambitiously, 'the world'. It would, presumably, be a whistle-stop world tour and one completed in less than 80 days, one that would have left even the adventurous Phileas Fogg astounded.[22]

What happened next is difficult to know. The four years that followed Mr and Mrs Naylor's arrival in Western Australia is a mystery awaiting its historian. It seems that Rufe may have spent a year or more in and around the old mining town of Gympie, in Queensland. It was terrain abounding with Naylor kin and a horse-breeding centre. It was also well known as a region supplying horses to chronically equine-deprived India. Naylor was a big-city man, but it made sense for him to avoid both Brisbane and Sydney as much as possible.

In early November 1920, the Naylors boarded the Orient Line's luxurious, refitted RMS *Ormonde* on its maiden commercial voyage from Brisbane to Colombo, where they stayed for a week. From there they took the Talaimannar train to Mannar Island, on Ceylon's northwest coast, which offered the easiest and most convenient passage to India. They may have been on their way to link up with Peter

Charles and his wife. In 1921, Peter Charles was in India, on his way to Johannesburg to manage the lottery.

If Rufe's visit to India was to brief Peter Charles about the lottery, which, in his absence, was being run by George Naylor, Seccombe and van der Linden, then it was probably not of long duration. The largest cities in India, like those in Australia, were best avoided by a man on the run, and so nothing is known about Mr and Mrs Naylor's seemingly lost days in India. But Rufe, always impatient and by then a denizen of five continents, was unwilling to wait on a move by imperial law enforcement agencies, and two years later was back in Sydney.

Naylor was, as ever, capital-hungry – a chronic condition for someone always ready to construct castles in the air without sufficiently robust financial foundations. By late 1923, he was so unhappy with Peter Charles's custodianship of his business interests in Johannesburg that he retained attorneys Currie & Wood of Sydney, to write directly to the Manager of 'Rufe Naylor's Lotteries Ltd', José dos Santos Rufino, in Lourenço Marques:

> [We are instructed] to inform you that he [Rufe Naylor] is still the rightful owner of the shares representing one-fifth interest in Rufe Naylor's Lottery Limited. That these shares were simply transferred to Peter Naylor in order to enable the said Peter Naylor to have a guarantee with the lottery company and establish his credit therewith for the purchase of tickets ... We understand that the dividends on these shares have been regularly paid to the said Peter Naylor but have not been remitted by him to our client, the rightful owner of the shares ... It is our client's intention to proceed to Africa in the near future with a view to establishing his claim to all past dividends paid, in the Court.[23]

It was a familiar Rufe ruse – part bluff, part legal reflex, part sibling niggle. After this intervention, Peter Charles, replaced by George, became less directly involved in the formal, legal and public arrangements of the lottery. The High Commissioner of Mozambique, Brito Camacho, perfectly capturing the prejudice of the day and the important position that Natal occupied in the lottery after Rufe's wartime troubles with the law, cast George Naylor as a 'Durban Jew' who had sold the lottery concession to an ethically deficient Catholic priest.[24]

In Sydney, Rufe came across like a runaway express train moving along tracks very much like those he had torn up during his wild ride through southern Africa. For certain reasons, some not difficult to understand, the Pretoria government showed no desire to pursue him legally. Of Phyllis, once the belle of the Roodepoort Ball and maybe of India too, there was no sign in the Australian press. Like dark matter pulled into a black hole, her career and personality had been obliterated.

As before, Naylor revelled in the hurly-burly of litigation, male company and professional sport. He constructed a sports arena and invested in theatres and cinemas. But it was the adrenalin rush that came with bookmaking, gambling and horse racing and the appeal of dodgy grey-market schemes during economic downturns that got his strained heart beating fastest. He became a minor 'folk hero' for a second time and, on the Witwatersrand, his every step – along with all the old familiar moves – was reported for fascinated readers.[25]

Naylor's revitalised career included running for political office and a Great Depression scheme selling 'shares' in lottery tickets, a scam for which he was criminally prosecuted. But, in the long run, an excess of chemicals eats away at the body, and when Rufe died of 'heart disease' in September 1939, aged 57, his corpse was moved across town to the Sydney Hospital for research.[26] As ever with the folk hero of two continents, however, there was a poignant twist at the end of the Rufe Naylor tale. His ashes were forwarded to his first wife, Catherine, in London.[27] Whether intentionally or unintentionally, it was a symbolically fitting end. The two neglected wives appear to have got little out of marriage to the big man.

The Lourenço Marques Lottery and Regional Economic Divergences, 1919–1928

After World War I and the suppression of the white mineworkers' revolt of 1922, southern Africa was characterised by linked regional economic disparities and consciously cultivated financial divergences. South Africa busied itself with constructing the infrastructure of a modern state built around a gold-mining industry that, by 1930 – with the aid of increasingly cheap indentured black labour from Mozambique – produced half the world's output. A central reserve bank and a stable economy buoyed the value of South African sterling. By contrast, Mozambique, a coastal strip with an abutting southern enclave dependent on South Africa and hoping to acquire the rudiments of statehood, had to settle for political and economic survival for half a decade. A relatively powerful neighbour with imperialist ambitions and policies did nothing to assist the financially inept economic management of the Mozambican economy by the BNU – a quasi-reserve bank – leading the country into rampant inflation. By 1926, and approaching its low point, the local escudo had lost between 50 and 75 per cent of its value against British and South African sterling.[28]

The South African economy, although growing slowly, did not want for foreign exchange for developmental purposes, but Mozambique, teetering on the edge of collapse, remained chronically deprived of a matching resource. In South Africa, governments were never happy to see the drainage of lottery earnings into a neighbouring 'territory' but, depending on the urgency of the prevailing circumstances, were frequently willing to tolerate what they saw as a net loss to their 'country'. The Mozambican administration, although never able to openly endorse the illegal operations of the lottery concessionaires across its western border, was, for obvious reasons, keen to grow the lucrative business.

In theory, structured inequality might have resulted in inter-governmental exchanges hoping to monitor the unwritten modus vivendi that developed around the lottery after 1919. It is true that, west of Komatipoort, there were a few flailing attempts by the South Africans to deal with the mass importation of lottery tickets in the early 1920s. It helped that gambling was supposedly a provincial rather than a national matter. But those moves were not matched by the Mozambican administration, which made no effort to check the ceaseless movement of lottery agents across the border. Instead of the lottery increasing the risk of conflict, both governments were content to send to the border rail crossing corrupt, sensorily-deprived officials who saw, heard and spoke no evil. Such orchestrated insensitivity, part of the larger traffic of black bodies sent west, in sealed railway carriages, and the eastward flow of foreign exchange on the Naylor Express and in the pockets of returning migrant workers, were left underreported.

Passivity on the part of the Mozambican administration was understandable, the low-key response from South Africa, at first glance, less so. It was, after all, a new 'state' that, from Kruger's day until the Naylor show trials of 1917–1919, had set itself against gambling, horse racing, lotteries and sweepstakes. This lazy, semi-official tolerance of the lottery by the South African government arose from a unique alignment of domestic political forces that encouraged significant trade-offs in inaction in the mid-1920s.

Part of the answer to South Africa's unwillingness to become too involved in the suppression of the LML lay in its over-reaction to the 1913 strikes, its determined response in crushing the 1922 mineworkers' strike, the resulting growth in support for the Labour Party and the subsequent unseating of the SAP. The 1924 election saw a meeting at the political crossroads of the Labour and National parties, and the formation of the Pact government, which lasted for 11 years, through the Great Depression, until 1933.

The Faustian decade that followed the signing of the Pact gave rise to the structured protection and privilege of the white working class in the labour market at the expense of proletarianised Africans. But dealing with the white devils came at a cost to both parties. For nationalists, sensitive to the strains of Calvinist choristers in the countryside and wary of noise from the Labour Party's trade unionist allies in the cities, it pointed to a compromise. In practice, it meant having to largely ignore the 'excesses' in working-class culture, much of it derived from British immigrants with lingering imperial loyalties.

For the Labour Party, which supported the idea of a state-sponsored lottery, it led to a studied silence about lotteries on the part of its leader in the cabinet, Walter Madeley. Successful coalitions, however, are made up not only of what is explicitly agreed upon but also of what is tacitly ignored, or, as William James once put it, 'The art of being wise is knowing the art of what to overlook.' The exception came in 1927. The nationalists, hoping to shut the east coast backdoor to the lottery, passed a Natal Gambling Law Amendment Act, which had the benefit of reassuring the Calvinists that their partner in government had some muscle, even when dealing with gambling in that venerable English-speaking stronghold.[29]

The economic stability of the Faustian decade contributed to the Pact's ability to steer largely clear of direct, or prolonged, confrontation with lottery-loving English speakers and a growing number of poor urbanised Afrikaners. Even the Great Depression, whose impact in gold-producing South Africa was muted, did little to unsettle the government's willingness to overlook the white working class's love of gambling. This comparatively subdued response from the state contrasted with the stridency of the churches, the press and the politicians during the financial degradations of 1906–1908 and 1914–1917 – both periods that saw the introduction of new gambling laws on the unruly Witwatersrand.

Marked contracyclical increases in the purchase of lottery tickets from dream merchants were usually prompted by recessions. Downturns tended to set off muttering from the commercial middle classes about the mounting bad debts of miners and howls of protest from Protestant ministers upset by the 'irrational' profligacy of the working class. But a better-housed, more socially stable white working class on 'civilised' wages, benefiting from the political protection of the Pact government, helped stave off a sharp spike in the sale of lottery tickets. This meant that the usual clamour surrounding the LML of previous eras subsided as Dr Faustus set about the new delights of the decade.

Unlike speculators, who thrive on stock market turbulence, most successful businesses rely on predictability and stability for success – even those operating in the grey economy, hovering somewhere between unpopular laws and criminal sanctions. The Roaring Twenties, the age of flappers and prohibition in the United States, marked an era of unequalled prosperity for the lottery concessionaires – the brothers Naylor working from the Rand and, across the border, Padre Vicente. The fact that the concessionaires also owned the Delagoa Bay Money Agency, in a period marked by the constant devaluation in the purchasing power of the escudo, provided the partners with additional profits that the seedy BNU gladly shared in.

After Rufe's hurried, pre-flight reconstruction of the company, in 1919, direction of the lottery fell under the control of the Naylor brothers and their bankrupt old faithful, Seccombe, who was rehabilitated two years later.[30] In 1921, George welcomed the oldest brother, Peter Charles, newly arrived from India, and the youngest, 29-year-old Harry, from Australia, to Johannesburg. The three, working on a full-time basis from Rufe Naylor's Building, on Eloff Street, were particularly active setting up new lottery agents in the year leading up to the 1922 mineworkers' revolt, and in the months immediately thereafter that bore some of the financial scars of the strike.

The Witwatersrand police were noticeably more active in their attempts to contain, but not to eradicate, the LML in the months before the June 1924 election of the Pact government than they were in the years that followed. August 1921 saw another raid on an inner-city Johannesburg printer who had just completed a batch of some 40 000 tickets, which, if all sold, would have brought in about £20 000 for the month (close on £11 million sterling today). But, usually, the police were content to make the occasional arrest of a ticket-seller in the hope of demonstrating to church and state that they were being vigilant and dealing with the 'evil'.[31]

None of this deterred the Naylors. The brothers never thought of moving their head office – complete with its Chicago-style desk featuring secret compartments and recesses – from the city centre, where the police, some of whom were on the Naylor payroll, never found anything too incriminating.[32] But, as in all functioning corrupt systems, the higher-ups had sometimes to be seen to be holding to account the 'masterminds' behind schemes the public subscribed to. Peter Charles and George were both prosecuted in their earliest days in the business, but it was the two marginals, Seccombe and young Harry, who were either pushed to the fore or who drew most of the police fire before 1925.[33]

Harry Naylor, for example, was prosecuted three times over a 36-month period, on the last occasion being handed the maximum sentence of £100 or six months.[34] But therein, too, lay a tale. The magistrates, caught by a dated and roundly disliked archaic law, were unwilling to impose prison sentences without the option of a fine. For the three Naylor brothers, who dealt in thousands of pounds each month, £100 was a trifling amount – all in a day's work.

Rufe's departure and the sale of his shares heralded some reorganisation by the family of the business nationally, and especially in

Durban. Initially, van der Linden made the expensive, time-consuming monthly round trip – by rail – via Johannesburg to Lourenço Marques, collecting lottery tickets embossed with the Delagoa Bay Money Agency logo. But after the police had twice searched but not arrested him, at Park Station, Johannesburg, they came up with a new scheme to expand the Natal market. Van der Linden purchased a guaranteed block of tickets each month that was held in trust for him, in Lourenço Marques, in Peter Charles's name. In return, as a regional manager, van der Linden was paid 12 per cent commission on all tickets sold, rather than the customary ten per cent. More importantly, he was provided with duplicate tickets, in Durban, thereby reducing costs and avoiding most problems with the police.[35]

In the larger cities, regional managers included a few trusted women with the necessary accounting skills. They were supported by 'accredited agents', men who directed sales drives into selected inner-city retail operations and the larger working-class base. In Johannesburg, many 'high class' firms bought blocks of tickets, which they passed on to members of makeshift 'associations' that were offered a discount on the purchase price. Elsewhere, many factories allowed lottery agents easy access to their premises. In the retail sector for lottery sales, which almost never saw prosecutions, class alone provided agents and purchasers of tickets with protection from the police.[36]

In the wholesale market, where the risks of being confronted by a paid informer and of police entrapment were higher, there were no women in sight, even if they bought tickets in significant numbers. Accredited agents employed an army of males – barmen, small shopkeepers, travelling salesmen and waiters – who would either sell tickets directly to the public or, when in doubt, refer them back to the agent for vetting. Barbers, some of them recent Catholic or Greek Orthodox immigrants from the Mediterranean, were among the favoured vendors along the Witwatersrand. They disposed of lottery tickets much as they sold another under-the-counter item considered to be potentially morally polluting in a repressive, middle-class Protestant society – condoms. By mid-1922, detectives claimed that lottery tickets 'were being sold in practically every town in the Union' – without the help of any marginal foreign hairdressers.[37]

The secret behind the lottery's success, however, lay elsewhere.

Van der Linden once explained its appeal to a curious judge. The lottery took root so quickly and became so popular among the working class not only because the first prize of £2 000 was so substantial but because even the lesser prizes were paid out instantly, in cash, without demur.[38] But all that, in turn, was possible only because of an efficient and reliable national and international communications system provided by the Post Office and its telegram service.

South African undercover detectives, without seeking prior approval from their Mozambican counterparts, regularly slipped into Lourenço Marques to monitor lottery operations. The police, searching for evidence of possible contraventions, wanted to be certain that the monthly draws – overseen by Portuguese authorities and Naylor Express visitors – were honest, transparent and public. The draw always was – without exception.[39]

Within two hours of drawing the winning numbers in Lourenço Marques, clerks in the Naylor Building, in Johannesburg, fired off telegrams to the regional managers, accredited agents and runners for distribution across the country. Winners knew about their success within a day or two and were paid – in notes – by agents who collected winnings from the post office in registered letters. As with the Ponzi scheme in the United States, it was infrastructure provided, and subsidised, by the state – the Post Office, telegrams and railways – that underpinned the profitability of the grey economy.[40]

The state, however, hindered the expansion of the lottery almost as much as it helped it. The grey economy – of indeterminate status and beyond easy reach of law enforcement agencies – meant that entrepreneurs such as the Naylors inhabited a liminal world without formal police protection. Grey businesses were vulnerable to opportunistic predation by criminals of lesser distinction. 'Gangsters' had no legitimate call on police protection from 'criminals', which is why lottery bosses were sometimes forced to resort to bribery, blackmail and threats of violence. But that, too, led to complications. On the one hand, gangsters heightened the propensity to violence, but, on the other, their lack of access to the state encouraged the settlement of disputes within supposedly 'criminal' organisations. The lottery bosses frequently intervened in disputes to enforce codes of conduct, thereby reducing the risk of violence. All of these elements were on display, albeit in embryonic form, in or around the LML operations throughout the turbulent 1920s.

For the Naylors, the never-ending stream of fake lottery tickets sold by confidence men, underwritten by unscrupulous printing firms, was a major problem. The social anonymity preferred by most Lourenço Marques agents made it easy for peripatetic petty criminals to present themselves as LML agents. Their most ambitious scams centred on forged copies of the Delagoa Bay Money Agency/LML ten-shilling tickets, which were themselves only 'authorised' duplicates of what was legitimately issued in Mozambique.[41]

As with *matryoshka* dolls, those who bought lottery tickets were often left visually unpacking a ticket within a ticket, hoping that, at the heart of the assemblage, they would come across the fine print that pointed to authenticity. Genuine 'Calcutta' or 'Duggan's of Dublin' sweepstake tickets, for horse races run in England or Ireland, were sold on by the Naylors at 2/6 each and, by the mid-1920s, could be 'bought all over the Union'. The problem was that these, too, could be forged. In Johannesburg, the Naylors sought to limit the damage by issuing warnings in the press about any sudden rash of fake tickets in the face of a less than enthusiastic response from the police.[42]

There was little the Naylors could do when dealing with outside competition. What they could deal with more effectively were difficulties arising from within their own organisation – acts of commission or omission by regional managers, authorised agents and other ticket vendors. Predictably, the more egregious problems were reported in the press. Many others, coming from the lower end of a supply chain served by social marginals and unemployed whites acting as agents or ticket vendors, may not have been reported on. Some nogoodniks stole the cash destined for winners, some of whom were reluctant to disclose their good fortune in public. Other runners came up with self-imposed 'commission' charges or handed over only part of the winnings. Shady businesses often attracted equally shady characters.[43]

What sanctions LML line managers used in instances that did not end up in court is not clear. What is striking, however, is how often, in cases involving those lower down the social order, men and women were unwilling to accept indemnity from prosecution in return for giving evidence against the lottery owners, or they refused to answer questions.[44] It was in the courts that popular, quasi-legal lottery sales intersected with policing initiatives and the underworld. It was an ethical and political swamp and left magistrates – piggy in the middle – squirming in the state's dirt. Magistrate JC Juta found the use of police informers and traps who received a percentage of the fines imposed on lottery offenders distasteful: 'The idea of people going about and asking other people for tickets does not appear right to me. This witness has been here several times with similar stories, and I hear that he gets a share of the fines. I don't think that it is right.'[45] White informers played a significant role in a socially repressive system.[46]

Two cases that did end in the courts illustrate how the Naylors sought to navigate the vexed question of internal discipline and ensure that the reputation of the lottery remained unblemished among their poorer clients. Not all such attempts could be resolved to the full satisfaction of ticket buyers.

For a time after Rufe's flight, growth in the Natal market exceeded that in the Transvaal, with about 18 000 duplicate tickets being printed in the province monthly – about a quarter of all the tickets issued in Lourenço Marques.[47] In the Durban area, monthly sales of around £9 000 left the concessionaires with a profit of around £3 000 (about £175 000 today).[48] In recognition of this, van der Linden's discount on tickets was raised to 20 per cent and the bankrupt Seccombe, along with his daughter (the first of the next generation of the family to go into the lottery business), was sent to assist the east coast operation. The path to Seccombe's eventual rehabilitation was further cleared when he, too, was belatedly granted a five per cent share in the Lourenço Marques concession.[49]

On a visit to Natal, in March 1922, Peter Charles heard complaints about clients being 'paid short'. One of van der Linden's agents, Morris, and an associate, Lindolent, had sold a book of tickets to John Durno, a sugar mill worker at Mount Edgecombe, who did not have the cash to settle his debt immediately. Soon thereafter Durno did, but Lindolent had not yet paid Morris for the booklet. Things got complicated when a ticket allocated to Durno, who, in effect was – and subsequently formally became – a sub-agent, won the first prize of £2 000. Since Lindolent, but not Morris, had not been paid, Morris refused to hand over the prize to Durno, claiming that, technically, the ticket was his. Van der Linden was called in to settle the dispute and, in his words:

> I introduced Mr. Morris to Mr. Durno and told them that was no affair of mine, but that I always desired to see a dispute of this sort settled amicably so as to avoid litigation, therefore they must come to some arrangement. I also told Durno that he had the ticket and so long as he held it I would not pay Morris. Morris and Durno then left me and went into the mill. They remained away from me for nearly two hours, and when they returned they informed me that they had decided to share the prize.[50]

Peter Charles was having none of it. He felt that mistakes had been made and that Durno was entitled to the full amount. He consulted with the other partners and decided that van der Linden 'would have to pay Durno £500 to finish the matter, otherwise they would discontinue selling [van der Linden] tickets in Delagoa Bay. I felt very annoyed.'[51] Van der Linden settled with the unfortunate mill worker, who received £1 200 of the £2 000 cash prize.[52]

Shortly thereafter, the Natal Attorney General, J Barclay Lloyd KC, led a vigorous attempt to shut down a lottery that he considered to be endemic. Peter Charles Naylor, Seccombe, van der Linden, Selig Morris and Barney Moseley, along with FJ Gill, a printer, were all charged with a 'conspiracy to commit fraud and contravening Law No. 3 of 1902' for conducting a lottery. The charge was part of an overly ambitious attempt by the state to demonstrate that the Natal lottery was really an independent operation that had nothing – other than the printing of duplicate tickets – to do with the Lourenço Marques Lottery. It was possibly the weakest line of attack, and even before the trial commenced, Gill was discharged. That game was not worth the candle.[53]

In August 1922, the remaining five accused appeared before the sanctimonious Justice FS Tatham – brother of Ralph Tatham, Rufe's one-time partner – and a jury in Pietermaritzburg in a trial lasting several days. It was an important public outing for the new lottery management and a sign that the family that plays together, stays together.

The senior Naylors and Seccombe were understandably keen to prove that the lottery was legal in Delagoa Bay. To that end, the defence drew on a witness not from the Mozambican administration, which would be embarrassed by the connection, or the Holy Father, who risked being an embarrassment of a different kind, but from the charitable wing of the company in Lourenço Marques. Senhor Feio, secretary to the Social Relief Society of Mozambique, testified to the legitimacy of the lottery and that the society benefited from the value of each draw to the tune of two per cent.[54]

Peter Charles and Seccombe, at the core of the family interest, were represented by senior counsel who readily admitted to the seemingly peripheral role that Naylor played in the day-to-day running of the lottery in Natal. Seccombe, then resident in Durban, was more directly involved. Van der Linden and the other accused had to make do with their own defence, who had a hard time in playing down their role in an extensive sales operation.

The main charge, of conspiracy to perpetrate a fraud, went by the board after Feio's testimony. The jury found Peter Charles not guilty on both charges and he was released. Seccombe, a four-time offender, was sentenced to the maximum fine of £200 but, in yet another concession to public opinion, avoided doing jail time. Van der Linden and Moseley were fined £150 each, and Morris, deemed to be marginal, had his charges withdrawn. The bosses were left almost unscathed and the lottery, in Natal as in the Transvaal, continued.

Over 48 months, attorneys general in two different provincial settings had fought and lost their battles with the lottery concessionaires. The following morning, with the case settled, Judge Tatham took time before the start of a new day's proceedings to deliver an *ex cathedra* homily about the iniquity of the lottery and how little ordinary folk stood to benefit from it.[55] Church and state were attempting, unsuccessfully, to convince the subject classes about what was in their best interests, when, in their own minds, they already knew and remained set on doing as they pleased as regarded gambling.

Back in Johannesburg, another case illustrated how the Naylors could be left exposed by authorised agents selling on tickets to sub-agents who then, in turn, sought to defraud or steal part of the cash prizes of lottery winners. As in Durban, such criminal acts prompted public prosecutors to deal with the concession owners themselves, charging them with running a lottery. In the final analysis, passing on cash to winners through a chain of agents, rather than through bank accounts, always pointed upwards, towards the brothers Naylor.

In June 1922, Peter Charles and a Carlton Hotel waiter, Albert Siebert, were found guilty of running a lottery and sentenced to fines of £25 – or two months' imprisonment with hard labour.[56] But, upon payment of the fines, Siebert was immediately rearrested on a charge of theft. It heralded more bad publicity.

Marguerite Jeeves, a widow, had bought two tickets from a friend, who had got them from Siebert, who had got them from an authorised dealer, Antonio dos Santos. When the widow won the first prize of £2 850, Siebert offered to collect her winnings at the Naylor Building, saying that he was owed £200 'commission' to be shared with dos Santos. Siebert collected the cash from Peter Naylor, who called on Mrs Jeeves to celebrate her success and subsequently attempted to minimise any personal and professional damage.

Siebert refused to hand all the winnings to the widow, giving her only £1 400 before walking away with the other £1 450, believing that, because the lottery was illegal, he could not be prosecuted for theft. But he had reckoned without Mrs Jeeves. She sued him, successfully, for the balance of her winnings.[57]

The Durno and Jeeves cases revealed in public what was privately becoming increasingly evident – the financial success of the lottery and the Naylor brothers. The South African economy may not have grown spectacularly as in the supposedly Roaring Twenties else-where, but in the gambling, entertainment and recreation sectors it was indeed a touch closer to the United States and other economies. Indeed, it was Rufe Naylor's earliest ventures in cinema, horse racing, theatres and the lottery that first alerted other entrepreneurs to the extent of the hidden, marginal, disposable income of white workers on the Witwatersrand, and how it could be unlocked and fed into dreams of home ownership or living the good life. It was the success of the Naylors, in the early 1920s, that tempted IW Schlesinger into thinking about opening a casino in Lourenço Marques – the 'Monte Carlo of South Africa' – and that persuaded a few mining magnates to build the luxurious Polana Hotel.[58]

Rufe Naylor had an obsessive desire to turn any stream of income into venture capital for the start-up of the next enterprise, which often did not turn out well. It led him to conducting Ponzi-like schemes and moving repeatedly between rags and riches within a matter of months. His successors, the brothers Peter Charles, George and Harry, suffered fewer such compulsions and enjoyed the benefits of steadier accumulation, even if they lacked Rufe's dynamism and daring. With income tax rates that only rose later in the decade, the growing wealth of the brothers could be tracked through their lifestyles.

Of the older Naylor brothers, George appears to have been the more conservative investor, the better financially organised and the less given to gambling recklessly on his own account. After the Durno case he was also much closer to *consigliere* van der Linden than was Peter Charles, and he and van der Linden often worked together. Unlike Rufe and others who banked with the notoriously cavalier Standard Bank, George banked with Barclays, in Pritchard Street, a branch that was always well disposed to him:

> Account opened with us since 1922, which has always been satisfactorily conducted. We have no information regarding his exact financial standing but the account in our books shows a large turnover and usually reflects 4/5 figure creditor balances. In addition, we hold on to his account, good gold mining shares showing substantial value and a Johannesburg residential property ... most conservatively valued at £5 600.[59]

That house, in Lower Houghton, was close to another owned by Peter Charles. It was not George's only property. He and four others owned shares in the BVB Ranch, near Gravelotte in the northeastern Transvaal, which had a small emerald mine on it. The BVB Ranch may have been an outgrowth of Rufe's one-time interest in the potential of property in that part of the province. George also had a share in a family house at Winkelspruit, close to Durban.[60]

But it was not by chance that Rufe had gone to India, in 1921, and chosen Peter Charles, over George, to take charge of his shares in the lottery. Peter Charles was no Rufe, but in terms of decisiveness, extroversion, gambling, risk-taking and love of modern technology and style, he was much closer to Rufe than was George. To settle pressing gambling debts, Peter Charles was once forced to sell some his family's furniture and lost a cattle farm for unknown related reasons. But, as the money rolled in over the decade, he, too, moved out of the Schlesinger-owned suburb of Orange Grove and bought a more extensive property, in fashionable Lower Houghton, off Munro Drive.[61]

Peter Charles's property at 66 Houghton Drive, spread over 2.5 acres, boasted a swimming pool, tennis court and five-car garage. Like Rufe, who owned three vehicles in Johannesburg at a time when most people could not afford one, Peter Charles found expensive cars irresistible. He eventually owned three stylish, state-of-the-art Alvis sedans manufactured in Coventry. These were so prestigious and thin on the ground that, each year, he paid for a specially trained mechanic to visit South Africa and service them.[62]

At the Mozambique end of the lottery, Padre Vicente was possibly closest of all to Rufe in character. Awkward personality traits, including ambition, argumentativeness, elastic ethics and impatience, ensured that the fireworks of his changed lifestyle crackled loudly above the coastal community. So close to Naylor in mode was the holy one that an Italian resident once suggested that he should have been properly baptised 'Padre Vicente Rufe do Sacramento Naylor'. Either way, there would have been some symmetry since both men had, in any case, earlier adopted names of their own making.[63] Both were discontents, wanting to be reborn into lives wholly of their own making.

There were other parallels between the Padre and his financial mentor. Vicente had a passion for daring new investments and projects that did not always work out. Like Naylor, who had acquired *Life, Sport and Drama*, Vicente bought a newspaper, *O Africano*, to advance his views and burnish his reputation locally as a fervent Portuguese nationalist. But, like *Life, Sport and Drama*, *O Africano* was not a success, and when it in turn closed, it did so at a cost of 'hundreds of pounds' to the priest.[64] That may have been an underestimate.

Padre Vicente got caught up in the brief post-war fever when Lourenço Marques was being touted as the next Monte Carlo. He served on the important tourist board, the Conselho de Turismo, and he and others were drawn into founding the Delagoa Bay Turf Club. Unlike his earlier efforts to raise capital to purchase the lottery concession, this time prominent local financiers and their well-connected kin fell over one another to get involved in the project. Among those notables were R d'Aguiar, JJP Mendes Gil, J Santos Rufino and another friend of the owners of the lottery concession, Dr AAC Casqueira. But, like Rufe Naylor's Krugersdorp racecourse, the Delagoa Bay Turf Club was a total failure and so Sacramento lost 'more than fifteen thousand pounds'.[65]

Some of these ill-fated projects had to be viewed from afar because, shortly after the reconstruction of the lottery company, the Padre retreated to Portugal and bought an expensive home in upmarket Estoril, where he chose to live during the early 1920s. It matched a second home, the Casal de Sacramento Vicente, built in Lourenço Marques at a cost of more than £10000, that upon his death became the property of the Catholic Church. Picking up on the Naylor template, he also built three smaller houses in the city that he let at modest rentals at a time when his wealth showed signs of evaporating completely. In addition, he poured thousands more into improvements to Quinta da Boa Sorte, the farm at Mailana, seen purely as an investment. While yet another spectacularly expensive failure, the farm did give him some joy as a hobby.[66]

In Estoril, Vicente's financial problems were compounded when he lent money to friends who either could not or would not reimburse the loans. But for an effectively defrocked priest, the Holy Grail was papal forgiveness for his past transgressions in Mozambique. The purchase of indulgences had been abandoned by the Catholic Church after the Council of Trent, in the 16th century, so direct payments in cash no longer offered a route to absolution. However, as Vicente knew, the back door to the Vatican was never securely bolted. Supplicants could navigate secret passageways leading to forgiveness by engaging in private and public acts of charity, and he did so. His private actions remain largely unknown, but the public ones were so conspicuous that Pope Pius XI would clearly have been briefed about them.

In 1923, Vicente bought the Monastery of Cucujães for £15000 (about £1 million sterling today). Covering the political and theological bases, he offered it to the government of Portugal as a seminary for the training of secular priests – as he himself had undergone in Cernache – through the Sociedade Missionária das Missões Ultramarinas.

Accompanied by Lisbon's Bishop of Augusta, D Rafael da Assuncão, he then embarked on a pilgrimage through a few European capitals that culminated in a visit to Rome. The objective was unchanged – getting pardoned and reinstated as a priest in good standing.[67]

There were reasons to be hopeful. Pius XI was known as a pragmatist. Indeed, he later signed, and then regretted having done so, the Reichskonkordat with Nazi Germany. But a troublesome priest who had defied bishops and lived a scandalous life, and whose political reach was not unconnected to the fact that he had become a millionaire by running a lottery, was a test of tolerance that many a pope might have failed. Moreover, Pius XI may have had some complementary misgivings. He later reissued Leo XIII's encyclical *Rerum Novarum*, expressing reservations about capitalism and financial greed. The sources of Vicente's wealth and charitable acts were clearly problematic. Whatever the reason, the pilgrimage appears to have been a failure and thereafter the Padre's relationship with Bishop Assuncão deteriorated swiftly.

The unravelling of Vicente's relationship with his papal intermediary centred on a complaint that Assuncão and the Church had adopted a disdainful and marginalising attitude towards missionaries – secular priests – in the colonies. This personalised line of argument, drawing on Vicente's own history, was compounded by distance when Assuncão was made prelate of Mozambique and sent to Lourenço Marques. A bitter war of letters spread through the most senior ranks of the Church, first in Lisbon and then in the Vatican.

In late 1925, Bishop Assuncão wrote to the papal nuncio in Lisbon, from Lourenço Marques, suggesting that Vicente's record proved that he should on no account be allowed to return to Mozambique. But the prelate could not have chosen a worse moment to try and exclude the vexatious secular priest from his former domain. Portugal was in a period of even greater political instability than usual, culminating in a coup d'état in late May 1926. The change of government heralded a strengthening of the state and the slide into the Salazar dictatorship that followed. Amid all these uncertainties, Vicente, whose finances were already becoming strained, had the additional worry that the lottery concession, granted for a ten-year period, was set to lapse in 1927.

It was not a moment to be confined to the delights of Estoril.

As a fervent patriot skilled in negotiating the currents and counter-currents of Church politics, Vicente got permission from the nuncio, in Lisbon, to return to Mozambique even before the Lisbon coup took place. Indeed, days after the coup Vicente, 'his maid and a niece' disembarked in Delagoa Bay, where the prolonged economic and social uncertainties had stoked yet another surge in settler national-ism. Assuncão and the Church were on the back foot and the unfor-tunate bishop was about to experience all the torments of purgatory.

In the two years that followed, Vicente used his influence and money to become the polarising figure around which missionaries up and down the coast organised in order to voice their unhappiness with Bishop Assuncão and the Church establishment in Mozambique. A personalised campaign was conducted in private, and then in public through articles in the press, to mobilise the secular priests and chip away at the credibility and standing of Assuncão to the point where even the nuncio in Lisbon, Effrem Forni, sensed that it had been a mistake to allow Vicente to return. Within six months of the arrival in Lourenço Marques of the little party from Estoril, news of the priest's powers of disruption and disorganisation were echoing in the inner-most sanctums of the Vatican.

In December 1926, Assuncão was granted an audience with Pius XI. But even before he got the chance to raise the problem of Vicente, the Pope 'told me about this priest and the need not to leave him in this prelature'. But a Pope's wishes are not a papal decree. Hostilities between the prelate and the priest raged on for three more years while Vicente manoeuvred his way up and down the Church hierarchy until he was forced to return to Portugal in 1930.[68]

The arrival of Vicente in Mozambique coincided with the passage of Legislative Decree No. 104 in Lisbon – where the priest was polit-ically well-connected – which curtailed some administrative and reli-gious freedoms in the colony. Assuncão saw these developments as having been instigated by secular priests, alumni of the same college of missionaries, at Cernache, as the troublesome one. The decree, in his view, privileged secular missionaries over the Vatican's priesthood, stoking discontent in the lower ranks of the Church. As the bishop put it in a letter to the nuncio:

> I did not conceal the grief that the publication of the decree occa-
> sioned me because it was an attack on the church's freedoms, an
> abusive invasion of civil power and personally detrimental to the
> Prelate of Mozambique ... The news of the promulgation of the
> decree and the coincidence of its publication in Mozambique with
> the arrival of Father José Vicente, the chief paladin in the Ministry
> of Colonies that he favours, further enlivened a feast of content-
> ment among the secular priests.[69]

Vicente, who occupied terrain halfway between church and state,
was a man for all seasons, a past master at playing the one off against
the other.

By the time Assuncão met Pius XI face to face later that same year,
Vicente had already given the bishop another painful nip in the behind
for reasons both commendable and opportunistic. Some months earlier, the 'Bishop and officials endorsed the institution of a "European
College" to be maintained with public funds, but from which all non-
Whites were excluded'. Vicente, with strong ties to the *mestiço* intelli-
gentsia via his earlier commitment to *O Africano* and his experience with
black miners on the Witwatersrand, saw in this another opportunity to
mix high principle with low personal interest. A struggle followed, and
'[i]n protest, the general population – Blacks, Mulattoes and Indian
Christians – stopped making financial contributions at masses and
instead started slotting into the offering collection boxes letters of criticism against such moves [segregated education facilities]'.[70] It was yet
another example of Vicente's ability to position himself strategically.

But, in Mozambique as in Portugal, and especially in the 1920s, it
was never a simple choice between church and state. Populist settler
politics, driven by economic uncertainty flowing from a financial
meltdown, made for additional complexities. It was not as if the settlers constituted a homogeneous grouping. A distinction was drawn
between *naturais da colónia*, 'natural colonials' born in the colony or of
long standing, and recent settlers. That, and the success of the original
Naylor-Vicente joint venture, along with the priest's wealth, meant that
bidding for the renewal of the lottery concession, in 1926, was likely
to be more fraught and vigorous than it had been back in 1917. Local
interests would weigh more heavily than any South African interests.[71]

In Johannesburg, the Naylors, realising that the concession was about to lapse, and that it might be difficult to hold on to their existing shares in the company, made hay while the sun shone. A flood of British football pool coupons entered South Africa through the mails in 1925, prompting an immediate response. The brothers raised the first prize in the lottery by a third, from two to three thousand pounds.[72] While the Natal market for lottery tickets remained sound, renewed emphasis was placed on the Rand outlets. It seems that a larger number of booklets than usual were smuggled into the country via the Naylor Express and other rail services. Regular agents and runners were paid the handsome salary of £60 a month.[73]

The ongoing success of the lottery in South Africa, combined with settler discontent in Mozambique, ensured that tensions around the renewal of the concession escalated during late 1926. The perennial complaint that the company never paid the charity arm of the operation its full, or a sufficient, share of the proceeds took pride of place in the tendering process. George Naylor, in an echo of the Pietermaritzburg court case, was wrongly accused of selling 'fake', that is, duplicate, tickets, which meant that Peter Charles led the tendering process for the Naylor brothers. It also fell to Peter Charles to defend the company and Vicente when they were attacked in the columns of O Radical. The established partnership between the Naylors and a priest who no longer enjoyed access to a relatively secure political base could not hold.[74]

The concession was won by a consortium of local entrepreneurs and the Naylor brothers, who then cut van der Linden, but not Seccombe, into the deal. The lottery was given the neutral name of 'Lourenço Marques Lotteries Ltd', a political concession, one suspects, that would have provided the Naylors with a bit more legal cover in Johannesburg and one that fell easily on settler ears, avoiding the name of a foreign-based entrepreneur. In 1930, amid yet more colonial political turbulence, there was an unsuccessful settler appeal to the government in Lisbon to reverse the decision to grant the concession to the Sociedade Mercantil de Moçambique for a decade.[75]

The new concession provided for a better-constructed and more generous dispensation for the city's central charities board in a difficult decade. There was an almost immediate dividend when, over the 1927–1928 cycle, the benevolent society was handed £17000 by the lottery company. In 1929, the charity board mutated into the Sociedade Carvoeria Limitada.[76]

Interestingly, there was little sign within the new coastal grouping of either the leading local capitalists who had earlier been burnt in the ill-fated Delagoa Bay Turf Club or of Padre Vicente. It is true that Vicente's income declined substantially after 1926, yet his influence had not yet been fully eclipsed. His old friend and notable from *O Africano* days, José dos Santos Rufino, was appointed manager of the Sociedade Mercantil, which managed the lottery on a day-to-day basis. There may have been more continuities than changes in the lottery for the Naylors after 1926, but the Padre's acts of charity, poor investment choices and personal loans left him without sufficient returns, and in less than a decade his wealth was reduced to a few hundred pounds.[77]

The Great Depression and the Lourenço Marques Lottery: Pillow Fighting in an Ideological Fog, 1929–1933

'It was', Dickens famously wrote, 'the best of times and it was the worst of times.' And, depending on where you found yourself in the hierarchy of capital, class and colour in South Africa, so it surely was for most people during the Great Depression. The problem of resorting to the wisdom of opposites, however, is that it lacks suppleness, the capacity to apply it meaningfully to the political economy of gambling since, as already noted in the case of lotteries, it is the bad times for the majority that often make for the good times for the few. The sharp drop in economic temperature in bad times is often offset by an incoming wave of political hot air, producing a confusing, lingering ideological fog.

The centrality of gold to the economy ensured that South Africa, unlike many other better developed countries, or those with exceedingly feeble economies, such as Mozambique, did not suffer deep, sustained damage through the Depression. South Africa's saving grace was that, in December 1932, it and other countries abandoned the gold standard and pegged its currency to the pound sterling. But not even that wise decision, one of hindsight, can conceal the full extent and trauma of the 1929–1932 downturn, which did much to usher in the lingering end of the Pact government.

Per capita growth in South Africa remained steady over most of the 1920s, and the decade saw no structurally significant increase in the wages of the white working class. A steady drift from the countryside to the towns saw the country's rural white population fall from about 41 to 37 per cent between 1921 and 1931. The tempo and volume of that movement, comprised largely of Afrikaans speakers, increased, however, when a significant drought coincided with the Depression, and thereafter it accelerated well into the 1930s. On average, urbanised Afrikaners earned about two-thirds of what their English-speaking counterparts did. It was estimated that, by 1932, there were over 300 000 'poor whites' countrywide, and by the following year many qualified for direct financial assistance, while 'perhaps one in every twelve white male workers was employed on a public or subsidised works programme'.[78]

Profound hardship placed hope, as well as the means of purchasing lottery tickets, beyond the reach of a significant number of whites, let alone people of colour in an increasingly unequal, racially ordered society. The growing numbers of those economically vulnerable in the cities and towns, along with those who had already slumped into crime, encouraged yet more predatory behaviour across a wide front, including in the sector devoted to gambling.

Confusion around the changes in the names of what, up to 1928, had been known as 'Rufe Naylor's Lottery' and the owners of the holding company provided a favourable context for those intent on deceit and theft, creating the micro-climate necessary for the sale of fake lottery tickets. By December 1929, confusion around the authenticity of the LML was so great that the Naylors were forced into a publicity stunt that even their absent brother would have been proud of. The LML, as we shall see, was by then also coming under renewed pressure from two long-standing rivals – the Calcutta and the Irish sweepstakes. Anecdotal evidence suggests that, throughout the Depression, white workers shopped around among lotteries and sweepstakes in search of the best possible return by way of prizes for what were modest investments.[79]

The Naylors' Depression publicity stunt, although devoid of

threats of the sort that characterised Capone's reign of terror in Chicago during the 1920s, shared some elements with organised crime in prohibition-era America when it came to moral ambiguity, politics, police complicity, the press and style. Like Rufe, Peter Charles and George Naylor were adept at finding and utilising the pivotal point of public opinion in a society always jammed up by church and state.

On a Friday morning in mid-December 1929, by prior arrangement, David Louw, a reporter on the *Rand Daily Mail*, was picked by three men in a car 'at a certain street corner at 7.30 am'. 'The moment I stepped into the car', wrote Louw, 'it was made known to me that I was expected not to divulge the names of anybody present at the draw, or the place where it took place.' The car set off and Louw 'had not the faintest idea where we were going', or so he said. It eventually drew up at the rear entrance of a hotel that was not more 'than a thousand yards away from one of the biggest [police] stations' on the Rand.

Only a fool would have bet against the three 'big men' present in a large reception area, replete with tables loaded with 'sandwiches and several bottles of whisky', being the Naylors and van der Linden, or the hotel being in an East Rand mining town. The lesser names were those of the lottery company's regional managers, drawn from 'various centres of the Union such as Bloemfontein, Durban, Maritzburg, Port Elizabeth, Cape Town, Johannesburg, Pretoria and so on', along with 20 regular 'agents'. It could have come out of a Dashiell Hammett crime novel.[80]

Louw and an unnamed MP, almost certainly from the Labour Party, along with a few other 'public men' – probably from the Transvaal Provincial Council – were invited to check the drums containing about 40 000 numbered lottery tickets. The party witnessed the drawing of winnings ranging from a first prize of £20 000 to a third prize of £2 000 and all the way down to £2. The Naylors were fighting to hold on to their share of the market in the face of growing competition from the Calcutta and Irish sweepstakes, and Peter Charles was frequently in and out of Lourenço Marques.[81] The story made for great reading over coffee in the Christmas season but did not appeal to the Minister of Justice or the Commissioner of Police.

To show that they could respond to public humiliation, detectives staged a series of raids on 6 January 1930. Twenty-four lottery agents were picked up across Johannesburg, including many of the usual suspects – a barman, a couple of commercial travellers, two hairdressers, a porter, a storekeeper, and so on. The raids were an attempt by the police to demonstrate to the public, and to their superior officers, that they were actively involved in suppressing lottery-law violations, but in truth few were fooled. It was little more than a sardines-as-sharks showpiece, an appetiser of sorts before the main course.[82]

The real sequel came shortly after New Year when the police, responding to embarrassment felt at the highest level, arrested Louw and John P Cope, a fellow journalist of liberal views, in the hope of getting them to reveal the names of those behind the grand hotel draw. It was a classic case of killing the messenger, and the reporters were swept off into a preliminary hearing. But the reporters, hand-picked to witness the draw, were as adept at reading public opinion and the weakness of the state as were the Naylor brothers.

The initial probe degenerated into a farce. The preliminary examination revealed just how thick was the ideological fog that had settled over the cities when it came to lotteries. The journalists, true to their code of professional ethics, refused to disclose the names of their informants, or to reveal any other information about their hosts at the hotel draw. Even so, their testimony dropped a few clues so revealing that only the hard of hearing could have missed which company directors and lottery they were referring to. The lottery, they said, had been operating for 12 years, and in Mozambique, where it was legal, the Sociedade Mercantil was the principal concessionaire.

But deafness was not the only affliction handicapping the court. Major RS Mitchell believed that only Louw, and Louw alone, could bring some clarity to the events at the hotel. Despite their best efforts, Mitchell and the detectives had seen or heard nothing that threw additional light on the lottery. Asked whether he knew the names of any persons connected to the lottery, Mitchell replied, 'I didn't then and I don't now.' 'Have you heard the name Naylor mentioned in connection with the lottery?' the Major was asked. His answer was unequivocal. "There is a Naylor supposed to be connected to it. But I want to make it clear that I have no evidence to that effect.' 'The lotteries', he continued, 'are conducted by clever businessmen who do it with great secrecy' and 'he had examined several people regarding this lottery draw without securing any information.' 'The public is all against us in the matter of lotteries', he added.[83] Church and state were operating on distant planets.

A fractured wrist cannot sustain a balled fist. Lacking strong evidence from the police, the prosecutor, Glanville Shawe, was left with little to brandish before Magistrate JH Britten, who was equally discomfited by the proceedings. Unlike Mitchell, who had fallen back on the old three-monkeys trick, the prosecutor became almost apologetic in tone. The state, if not the church, was effectively running up the white flag for the first time since it had first engaged seriously in battle with the Naylors, back in 1917. Shawe admitted:

> It has been said, too, that everybody is contravening the Lottery Law. To a large extent I am afraid that is so. Nevertheless, there is a very large number of people in the Union who consider it a serious offence to contravene the Lottery Law – a fact which is proved by the penalties laid down by legislation. And for that reason, we cannot look upon it as slightly was we would on a card party, for instance. And I am compelled to look on the matter in that light in doing my duty to the State.[84]

Compulsion, duty and penalties had, however, never been of a piece in the magistrates' courts when it came to flouting the venerable lottery law, as Shawe must have known only too well. As we have observed, it was difficult to think of a single case in which those infringing the law had been given a custodial sentence, and those running the lottery had, almost without exception, not only come up with any fine imposed by the court but had then frequently gone on to repeat the offence.

The journalists' unwillingness to cooperate in the matter went to the very heart of the ambivalence around lotteries in the country. Here, too, Shawe was reluctant to balance conflicting impulses when it came to compulsion, duty and sentencing: 'Since Louw and Cope have declined to give the information, I ask for the enforcement of the penalty laid down in the relevant section of the Act. I ask that they be committed for the rest of the day, that is until four or five o'clock.' The men from the hotel had reason to be optimistic.

Like Shawe, the magistrate was aware that his afternoon constitutional would entail walking on eggshells, and he wanted to commiserate with Mitchell, who had been made to appear foolish. 'The police, in view of the divergence of public opinion', Britten said, 'appear to have exercised a wise discretion in the past in not harassing those persons who have contravened the law in an unobtrusive manner.' It was yet another white flag from the state, but when it came to sentencing, Britten hoped to show that he was made of sterner stuff than the public prosecutor. He dismissed a relieved Cope, but sentenced Louw to 'eight days imprisonment suspended for seven days pending appeal'.[85]

Not wanting to be outdone by the magistrate's plaintive solo, Shawe rose to lead the choir in a hymn for peace: 'On behalf of myself and the police I would like to say that relations between the police and the Press have always been most cordial and, notwithstanding what has now taken place, I hope these cordial relations will continue.'[86] It had been a tough day at the office for the state, and Major Mitchell had yet to talk to the Commissioner of Police, and the Commissioner of Police, no doubt, had yet to speak to the Minister of Justice, who spoke only to the church and God. A leader in the *Cape Argus* captured the nature of the choking fog enveloping most of the country:

> The Chief of Police cannot expect the public to believe that the promoters of lotteries are so amazingly cunning that nothing short of heavy expenditure [on professional informers and traps] or the imprisonment of a journalist or two can lead to their suppression. The proceedings must greatly damage the prestige of the police and bring the law into ridicule.[87]

The police and the press may have felt that the show was over, but, as we will note in due course, the Minister of Justice, Oswald Pirow, was far from satisfied with the response from the state. He had good reasons for remaining sceptical, and more especially so during a depression, when lotteries expanded.

First, noise from the Louw case flushed one or two political birds from the parliamentary undergrowth, revealing feathers perhaps best kept from public view. The less said openly about the undocumented church-state alliance around lotteries, the better for all. Admittedly, it was not all bad news. Within hours of the case, the liberal JH Hofmeyr, a Balliol man and a staunch Christian, came out against the lottery, not on ethical or scriptural grounds but for economic reasons. Lotteries, he said, contributed to financial instability in the state, and even though winnings might contribute to sound commercial investments, they were offset by the net outflow of funds through gambling.[88]

Muttering from within the ruling National Party was more upsetting and potentially damaging than that coming from Hofmeyr and the SAP opposition. Dominees, in droves, were happy enough to walk through the sunshine of hypocrisy provided their heads were covered by laws honoured more in the breach than in the observance, and if they were accompanied, at a suitably respectful distance, by their equally befuddled politician brothers.

A meeting of the Pretoria Central branch of the National Party calling for a national lottery illustrated how an unguarded microphone could amplify the dangers of loose talk, further confusing a people already standing at the crossroads of church and state, of a Calvinist heaven and a gambling hell. The branch secretary, Ben van der Walt, said that 'in spite of the fact that the church opposed lotteries, ministers of religion bought lottery tickets'. Another senior branch member, Mr G van Rensburg, let the side down even more badly. He had, he said, 'sold over a hundred lottery tickets to Members of Parliament during the course of two afternoons'. By a 'large majority' the meeting resolved to set up a committee and extend an invitation to David Louw to help produce 'propaganda' for a state lottery. The proletarianisation and secularisation of urban Afrikaner society was on display for all to see.[89]

The second reason for the Minister of Justice to be concerned was better hidden from the public. The Louw case had sent a clear message to those operating in the quasi-legal grey economy – the Naylors, their regional managers and the lottery agents. The state was just not up for a serious fight with them; if they remained relatively discreet and respectful of church and state sensitivities, the lottery could continue to operate as 'normal'. But there was another signal – one probably more alarming for the Naylors than it was for the police. If the brothers continued to operate in the grey economy with impunity, black-market criminals could as easily ride in on their coattails.

As the Depression deepened in 1930–1932, so the sale of fake Delagoa

George Naylor and Paul van der Linden at Le Bourget Airport, in Paris, 1930, after a round of lottery lobbying in Lisbon.

Bay lottery tickets by small-time hustlers escalated in the larger cities of the Transvaal and Natal.[90] A confidence man, pretending to be a detective, intercepted a lottery agent and relieved him of all his tickets.[91] Opportunistic fraud and theft were overshadowed by organised crime, some of it on the Naylor Express itself or, as the switch to motor cars became increasingly affordable and popular, in small towns on the route to Mozambique such as Bethal and Carolina.[92] At the border itself, police intercepted a courier ferrying more than £12000 in lottery prize money from Lourenço Marques to Johannesburg. It was the cue for train robbers to track lottery funds and tickets moving up and down the eastern main line.[93] In 36 months at least four mail bags containing cash, lottery tickets and other registered items were stolen from trains running between the East Rand junction and the border at Komatipoort.[94]

By 1930, the situation had deteriorated to the point where George Naylor and Paul van der Linden felt that they had to go to Europe to reassure the Portuguese authorities that the lottery was in good hands and still viable. Little is known about the visit, but they were photographed standing beside the new Blériot 'Golden Ray' aircraft transporting them from Paris to London.[95]

The last Minister of Justice in the Pact government (1929–1933) was ambitious, opportunistic and treacherous in equal measure. He found crimes around lottery operations reprehensible, but they did not dismay him nearly as much as did the lottery itself. He was the son of German immigrants, a staunch Lutheran and, unlike his predecessors, not one to turn a blind eye to the 'problem' of gambling. Indeed, some of his attitude may have stemmed from having seen it all close up. In 1917, he had been a member of the Transvaal Provincial Council trying to come to terms with the issues of racecourse bribery and corruption that revolved largely around Rufe Naylor. For Oswald Pirow, crimes up and down the east coast corridor, such as the train robberies, only reinforced the view that the real evil – the lottery – was flourishing yet. A Middle Temple lawyer, an athletic man with strong views who, as the 1930s unfolded, went on to meet Hitler and Mussolini before setting up his own Nazi-like 'New Order' movement, Pirow was bent on a campaign to combat gambling and lotteries of all kinds, starting in 1930.[96]

On Pirow's watch, the Johannesburg Central Post Office was more active than usual in checking on the boxes of agents, intercepting mail containing money destined for foreign lotteries and sweeps, and reporting to the police. 'We must confiscate hundreds of pounds each month', a postal official said. 'Of course, we can't lay our hands on every agent, but we unearth many of the bigger men.'[97] But it was wishful thinking. For reasons that can only be speculated on, the dragnet snared small-scale operators but almost never LML agents, who, when they did appear in court, were invariably well defended by attorneys.[98]

Pirow and his Commissioner of Police, IP de Villiers, presided over two large-scale raids aimed, or so it was claimed, at disrupting the principal lottery. Neither was a triumph and neither ended particularly well.

The first, in November 1931, under the command of the unfortunate Major Mitchell and two detectives, was hailed as 'unusually successful'. But, in truth, like the bald gentleman raising his fedora to a passing beauty, it was more in hope than anticipation: 'More lottery promoters have been arrested and successfully prosecuted in a month than were formerly prosecuted in a year.'

Quite so. But it went nowhere. There was little sign of enthusiasm from magistrates moored between a steady stream of public hostility and the jetty of a Kruger law. The 20 men successfully prosecuted yielded a total of £390 and ten shillings in fines. Of the Naylor operation there was no sign; perhaps the police were again showing 'discretion' or earning a little on the side. They were pillow fighting in an ideological fog. When forced to choose, magistrates sometimes headed off the path of common sense, as when an unemployed 75-year-old was fined £5 for selling lottery tickets.[99]

The second raid, in February 1931, was, like the 'one hundred yards' dash for people with no sense of direction', simply embarrassing, leaving the police and the press at odds. The police, encamped around Carolina, at a base within easy reach of the point where the Mozambican, Swaziland and South African borders converged, insisted that the operation was focused on intercepting lottery agents and that it ended satisfactorily. The press insisted that the raid was originally focused on Lourenço Marques-based opium smugglers and that the arrest of two Portuguese lottery agents was a serendipitous coincidence.[100]

Whatever the truth, the action led to a bit of diplomatic rumbling – the only instance of the lottery being the subject, in passing, of an official exchange between the Mozambican administration and the South African government. If the church-and-state pact around lotteries was silent within South Africa, then so, too, was the pact between Lourenço Marques and Pretoria. Neither government wanted to jeopardise the flow of black mine labour to the Rand.

Governor General JRP Cabral was, however, sufficiently peeved about the arrest of two Portuguese nationals to raise the matter with the Lisbon government. D Steyn, the South African consul general in Lourenço Marques, rushed to reassure Cabral that press reports 'were not based on fact at all' and 'grossly exaggerated'. He – Steyn – regretted that the report, 'the product of [the] very vivid imagination of our South African journalist should have been the cause of trouble and worry to Your Excellency'. And there the awkwardness rested.[101]

In Pretoria, the Minister of Justice remained intent on suppressing the lottery, but the unintended consequence of his actions only gave the press the chance to highlight the weakness of the state and the structured hypocrisy that pervaded every level of society when it came to gambling. If Pirow had been as serious about the issue as he was about pursuing his own career, he would have proposed new legislation with penalties that went well beyond the provisions of Law No. 7 of 1890. But he could not and knew only too well that he could not.

Coming out publicly against a deeply entrenched part of English-speaking, and an emerging section of Afrikaner, working-class culture, in a government built around a 'pact' between the Labour and National parties, was to invite trouble. Indeed, insofar as the unity of the government stood or fell on introducing a state lottery to replace the Lourenço Marques and other lotteries – and it most certainly did not – the Labour-nationalist alliance was clearly not only already in disarray but increasingly so. In public, this policy hesitancy came across as confusion at best, as weakness at worst. Pirow's aggression and the police blunders invited lottery lovers to push back at the existing 'policy' as it related to gambling. The underlying issue had been festering ever since the hotel draw.

Political activists in National Party strongholds in Pretoria and Vrededorp had already come out publicly for a state lottery, and in 1931 there was another sign of working-class discontent in Roodepoort, on the West Rand. Mayor MJ du Plessis called a meeting to discuss the pros and cons of a state lottery and threw out 'a challenge to any parson to debate the matter on any platform in the country'.[102] The dominees and their English-speaking counterparts had to come and publicly defend their partnership with the government about lotteries. The challenge carried the potential for yet more tension, and nowhere more so than for Protestant ministers on the East Rand, where a love of gambling and lotteries ran deeply in English-speaking white working-class communities that were also strong Labour Party supporters. Lotteries threatened to put distance between the churches and Brits and Boers alike.

The Labour Party leader, Walter Madeley, a graduate of India's Bombay Cathedral High School and MP for Benoni, backed the idea of a state lottery but had given up trying to persuade his Pact partners to ignore the church. 'The majority of the present Cabinet is against sweepstakes in any shape or form', he argued 'and the country might as well give up hope of having a state lottery.'[103] The party might have given up hope for a state lottery in public, but in private it had taken matters into its own hands and was moving in the opposite direction. Against government policy and Pirow's wishes, and in contravention of the law, the Labour Party was conducting a lottery in a professional manner for the benefit of its supporters. One arm of the Pact government was attempting to suppress lotteries while the other was, simultaneously, promoting them. White working-class culture was in robust health not only in South Africa but across the border, in Rhodesia, where white workers were much less hamstrung by the power of the Protestant churches.

In 1929, Jack Keller of the Rhodesian Railway Workers' Union organised the 'Unity Stakes' to assist the unemployed as the Depression bit. The state thanked him by prosecuting and fining him.[104] But the idea of a lottery was born, and in 1934 a referendum endorsed the state-driven venture, launched the following year. In South Africa, Madeley and the Labour Party followed developments closely and compared notes with their counterparts.[105]

The Labour Party had a long-standing interest in the 'Royal Calcutta Turf Club's Derby Sweepstake', dating back to at least the formation of the Union. Based on the result of the English Derby, the Calcutta Sweepstakes had a large international and South African following.[106] The Johannesburg police, too, followed it, but prosecutions were few since it was not clear which Kruger-era laws it violated. In 1921, 'a lad' who had sold a ten-shilling ticket to a man in a 'public lavatory' in Turffontein was prosecuted and placed on probation. Rumour had it that the Labour Party was the moving force behind sales, and the early 1920s saw the Calcutta mired in a few ticket-selling 'scandals' in England, which Scotland Yard was supposedly taking a keen interest in.[107]

But it was in the mid-1920s, after the Pact government took office, that the sweep – possibly benefiting from a Labour presence in the cabinet and police reluctance to move against it – began to enjoy a boom among South African punters. White workers, reaping the rewards of the 1922 miners' revolt, were undeterred by an annual outlay of 10 to 15 shillings on a ten-rupee ticket because, although the odds against drawing the name of a horse in the Derby were great, the potential reward lay in the realm of the inconceivable. The organisers of the sweep ploughed 40 per cent of the takings into the first prize, 20 per cent into the second and 10 per cent into the third. The remaining 20 per cent was split between those who had drawn the name of a horse that completed the race, which was held in May of each year.[108]

So, while churches along the Witwatersrand peddled hope for the next world, white workers invested in the Calcutta in the hope of improving their lot in the here and now. By 1927, with globalised capitalist economies purring along at unprecedented rates, the sweep attracted a stake of £420 000, with the winner taking £168 000.[109] In the late 1920s, the first prize regularly topped £60 000 and the second £40 000 (respectively, about £3.8 million and £2.5 million today).

The onset of the Great Depression, in 1929, turned up South African interest in the Calcutta and the Irish sweeps to fever pitch, which lasted throughout the downturn. It reached a point where the Pact government could no longer turn a blind eye. Even entrenched structured hypocrisy needs to be indulged in with a measure of discretion, or else it lends itself to agitation by the clergy and mockery by the faithful, which can become a handicap during a general election.

In that same year, 1929, it was reported that white South Africans had won the first and second prizes in the Calcutta.[110] It was claimed that, since its inception, South Africans had won no less than £260 000 in prizes in the sweep (about £16.5 million today).[111] Winnings on the Irish Sweepstakes went unreported, suggesting that it had less of a following. Eighteen months later, in 1931, South Africans drew 15 of the 27 runners in the Calcutta, and, since tickets were often shared among syndicate members, it was claimed that 56 people stood to win 'at least £30 000 each'.[112]

If the Labour Party was informally involved in the sale of sweepstake tickets, as had been rumoured a decade earlier, then the response of the government and the workers during the Depression further emboldened it in its effort to turn the Calcutta into an informal national lottery by stealth. But the party may have been a touch too sanguine about how any covert moves by it might be received.

In 1930, shortly after the East Rand hotel draw, the general secretary of the Labour Party, William Wanless, embarked for a four-month stay in India, where he become a 'grandstand member of the Calcutta Turf Club' – a necessary step to be able to acquire and sell tickets. At the request of 'party members' he chose not to name, he 'investigated the conditions of the running of the Calcutta Sweep'. The call for that inquiry almost certainly emanated from within the most senior ranks of the Labour Party. Wanless, a Cornish name meaning 'hopeless' or 'luckless', might not have been the wisest choice for the mission. A second party member went to Dublin to study the newly established Irish Sweep.[113]

On the Rand, a Labour Party 'sub-committee', under Wanless, set up the infrastructure for a mail-based lottery. Day-to-day operations were then put in the hands of the party's capable national organiser, Charles Henderson, who until only months earlier had been Walter Madeley's parliamentary private secretary at the Ministry of Posts and Telegraphs.[114] A no-questions-asked printer produced Labour Party-headed notepaper and numbered tickets and Henderson supervised the issuing of thousands of letters soliciting entries for the Calcutta and Irish sweeps. The ambitious scheme was brought to a halt only when paid informers and Post Office collaborators tipped off the police.[115]

The sequel played out in October 1930 when Henderson was fined £80 and CL Lowe £100, or 12 months with hard labour, for running a lottery. It is unclear to what extent this was the seminal moment in a reported decline in the popularity of the Calcutta Sweep, which then gave way to the Dublin/Irish sweep, in which the Labour Party retained a significant interest.[116] Either way, it was a remarkable moment in which the dominant party in the Pact – the Calvinist National Party – was pushing for the prosecution of senior members of its partner in government, the Labour Party. Officially, the left hand did not know what the right was doing and both parties went into a three-monkeys routine.

As before, Pirow and the National Party, the party of church and state, failed to tighten the existing legislation or to introduce new laws. When it came down to governance, retaining political power almost always trumped prayer. 'Nothing is more revealing of an age', the historian James Laver once wrote, 'than its hypocrisies'[117] – and all that without ever having visited South Africa.

Pirow, however, never wanted for friends or support in his campaign against gambling and his refusal to come out openly against a state lottery. He could afford to keep relatively quiet because, just when the confusion around the lotteries was greatest and the ideological fog thickest, those who claimed the best eyesight of all and those with the shrillest of voices moved in among the benighted working classes, urging them to concentrate harder and see the light. And, as ever, the darkest places of all lay between the East Rand towns of Germiston, Benoni, Boksburg, Brakpan and Springs. Satan loved those places.

The Church Champion

As the heartland of South Africa's emerging mining economy, boasting a significant number of skilled and semi-skilled workers drawn from the United Kingdom, the East Rand had a few of its deepest theological roots buried in the 19th-century English industrial revolution. While the bringers-of-light were drawn from the larger Protestant denominations – the Dutch Reformed churches, Lutherans and Presbyterians – it was those churches with origins more directly linked to the social traumas of the industrial revolution – the Methodists and Wesleyans – whose visions and voices were dated and detached from reality when addressing the emerging East Rand working class.

At the risk of simplifying to the point of senselessness, early-20th-century Methodists in South Africa were predominantly Wesleyans. But among them lay a smaller branch of the great movement, the Primitive Methodists, known also as 'Ranters'. Primitive Methodists, keen to return to the evangelical roots of John Wesley, had branched out from the Wesleyans proper around the mills and potteries of Staffordshire in the early 19th century.[118] After the Anglo-Boer War, in the imperial era, they, like their Wesleyan brothers and sisters, stressing the virtues of 'industry and obedience', took a greater interest in South Africa, reaching out to black migrant workers through missionaries. As EP Thompson put it, 'Primitive Method[ism] was a religion *of* the poor' and orthodox Wesleyanism was 'a religion *for* the poor'.[119] The United Methodist Church of South Africa only emerged as a statutory entity in the country after all Methodists, Wesleyan and Primitive, joined forces during the Great Depression and were recognised as a single entity via a Private Act in 1932.[120]

Before that, the Primitive Methodists, embodying a reasonably close and direct evangelical link between the social turbulence of the English industrial revolution and southern Africa, had a presence in the rural eastern Cape that went back to the 1820 Settlers and well into the mid-19th century.[121] Their presence predated the mineral discoveries, but the mining revolution on the Highveld provided them with a renewed sense of purpose as they witnessed an exodus of black migrant workers to the emerging inland industrial centres, along with

The Reverend Archibald Kidwell, Primitive Methodist, and interwar lobbyist of note against dog racing, lotteries and pinball machines on the Witwatersrand.

the attendant social problems. The Primitives' acceptance and encouragement of male and female preachers extended their social reach.

Archibald A Kidwell (1884–1954), the grandson of an 1820 Settler, was raised in Jamestown, in the eastern Cape. His father was a devout Primitive Methodist lay preacher, and the family, infused with British and English patriotism of a type providing a much-needed sense of security in a frontier setting, were convinced imperialists bent on advancing the civilising mission of church and state, with a special calling to bring the word of God to Africans. Archibald, who served as a missionary on the Zambezi for some time, starting in 1899, embodied all their beliefs and values.

After a long tour of duty among Primitive Methodist communities in various parts of England, Kidwell returned to an increasingly turbulent South Africa in 1913. In 1920, in the wake of the Great War, the descendants of the 1820 Settlers commemorated their centenary, establishing a countrywide association to underscore their British identity. The fully ordained Reverend Kidwell was willing to answer a new calling. Setting aside churchly duties for an agreed period of 15 months, Kidwell became the organising secretary to the 1820 Settlers' Association in the Transvaal and adjacent regions. The new setting provided him with first-hand insights into the lives that Africans led in the mine compounds on the rapidly urbanising Witwatersrand. It was a setting made for a Primitive Methodist. Although opposed to the social segregation of blacks, and to the Native (Urban Areas) Act 21 of 1923, which restricted Africans to certain areas, Kidwell was nevertheless willing to accept the emerging repressive dispensation.[122]

For the year and a half that he was based in Johannesburg, Kidwell was indefatigable in his efforts to place the 1820 Settlers' Association on the map. His duties put him within easy reach of the rich and famous, providing him with a notable social profile even before he became a more controversial figure among white workers on the East Rand. His appearance on a platform with Sir Lionel Phillips gave him an entrée into mining circles.

The mine owners provided Kidwell and his missionary wife with access to the mine properties, where their paths would have crossed that of HW Baker of the South African Compounds and Interior Mission. Indeed, small as Primitive Methodism was, it was extremely active on mine properties along the Witwatersrand.[123] When the Governor General, Prince Arthur of Connaught, bestowed his patronage on the new settlers' association, in Port Elizabeth, in April 1921, Archibald Kidwell was on hand. And where royalty went, Jan Smuts was never far behind.[124] But Kidwell's network did not end there.

The Sons of England, a benevolent, male, patriotic and Protestant society that had first taken root in the eastern Cape and was on good terms with the more secretive Freemasons, saw in the Reverend a kindred spirit.[125] Kidwell understood the imperial project perfectly and reassured his brethren: 'The magnanimous spirit of the British people [has] often been stigmatised as weakness, but upon the pages of history it [will] be described as one of the mightiest uplifting agencies in the development and progress of the world.'[126]

Kidwell became 'Grand Chaplain' to the Sons of England. His family's scarring during the industrial revolution, along with the inheritance of a radical Protestant tradition, made for a rough but reasonable fit with the social revolution taking place along the Witwatersrand.

Kidwell's standing underpinned efforts to develop and expand the urban African mission. As superintendent of the small Primitive Methodist Africa Missionary Society and chairman of the Germiston Methodist Circuit, his previously stuttering efforts to raise funds were rapidly transformed. With the generous financial support of the directors of the City Deep Mine and others, the society opened a new

Primitive Methodist church for African worshippers on the corner of Main and Maritzburg roads, in inner Johannesburg, in 1923.[127]

In 1924, in a decade critical to the history of African segregation and urbanisation, Kidwell set out on a self-funded tour of Canada and the United States to examine the 'conditions of American Negroes'. Predictably, his travels took him on the obligatory pilgrimage to Booker T Washington's Tuskegee Institute, whose socially conservative philosophy appealed to a Methodist operating in a colonial situation. The flip side of that was his dismissal of the radical Marcus Garvey, about to be imprisoned for two years for mail fraud. Kidwell 'described Garvey's famous slogan of "Africa for the Africans" as a bubble that would soon be pricked', which earned him a rebuke from the National Association for the Advancement of Colored People.[128]

Kidwell's US travels coincided with the mid-term of America's flawed attempt to impose prohibition. The ban on alcohol resonated with deep-seated Primitive Methodist beliefs and made Kidwell a minor authority on the subject when he returned to South Africa, and he became chairman of the South African Temperance Alliance.[129] In addition to public lectures and sermons, over the next three decades Kidwell became one of the three most prolific writers of letters to the editor of the *Rand Daily Mail* and was widely known for his especially tough stance not only on alcohol but on gambling. He was, for example, 'the first to rant against dog racing in Johannesburg'.[130]

But, like others aspiring to wield influence in a society undergoing rapid change, Kidwell found his left and right feet on opposite sides of a widening social crack. It pulled his legs so far apart that it threatened to split him down the middle. Constituency and country, idealism and practicalities, along with the vexed questions of race and class, all conspired to limit his ability to influence those whom he sincerely hoped to be able to serve, and to shape.

Primitive Methodism, child of the English industrial revolution, was, as we have said above (quoting EP Thompson), a religion *of* the poor while Wesleyanism was a religion *for* the poor. Kidwell's problem was that in interwar South Africa, the composition of 'the poor' was itself undergoing constant, significant, structured change. To whom exactly, then, were the Primitive Methodists and their cousins in Christ, the Wesleyans, addressing themselves during a mining revolution in which class and colour were being redefined in new ways? While there were a large and growing number of enfranchised 'poor whites' in cities and towns, a racially enforced imposed migrant labour system was manufacturing an even larger number of poor blacks.

The future of Primitive Methodism lay with black workers, the future of mainstream Methodism with white workers. After 1922, urban whites, pushed into supervisory roles and the lower middle class, were no longer all that poor, nor were they only manual workers. This meant that while Primitive Methodists-turned-Methodists, such as the Reverend Kidwell, found themselves preaching social doctrines drawn from the English industrial revolution that might have had some appeal for black workers, the same doctrines chimed less and less with the aspirations, class positions, consciousness and lived experiences of economically and socially upwardly mobile whites along the Witwatersrand.

As the 20th century unfolded, Kidwell ranted away about social ills that had once bedevilled a working class that, in the English industrial revolution, was comparatively culturally and ethnically homogeneous. But in South Africa he was preaching to a racially divided working class. On the Witwatersrand, white miners were increasingly privileged, while to be a 'worker' was to be black. And white workers were unwilling to be bullied by Protestant ministers.

Kidwell emerged as a controversial public figure during the Great Depression, and his presence was felt in church circles throughout the 1930s.[131] His and his colleagues' socially repressive policies were aimed at the heartland of a white working class that displayed little enthusiasm for Christian militancy. If the prescripts of Methodist ministers – led by Kidwell – were strictly followed, then on Sundays, congregants would not visit parks and recreational facilities, play sport, go shopping or attend theatrical performances that charged admission fees, and would avoid 'unnecessary travelling'. So widespread were these 'evils' that some churches had already been forced to change their hours of worship to accommodate those straying from the path of righteousness. Weekdays were just as hazardous. Bars and dog racing were clearly to be avoided, and the number of licences for them strictly controlled by the state. Women should think twice before either dancing or smoking. Alcohol was not to be served at weddings, and marriages were supposed to be indissoluble. What joys these strictures left some 100 000 white and 700 000 black Methodists, many of them shift workers, to enjoy outside of Sunday church services was unstated.[132] Kruger's old platteland Doppers would have both approved and understood.

No one could accuse Kidwell of having a bee in his bonnet. Somewhere down there nested an entire swarm of precepts, not all of them Bible-based. But there is no clear-cut biblical injunction against gambling. In the late 16th century, Calvinist ministers in German towns, seeking to shake loose the noose of their Lutheran regional rulers, encouraged congregants to partake in lotteries as a way of raising funds to replenish military supplies.[133] While Methodists had long been opposed to 'gaming', John Wesley himself had said, in the 18th century, 'I never bought a lottery ticket myself, but I blame not those who do.' Along with the demon drink, lotteries provoked especially 'strong utterances' from a radical preacher lost on the frontier of a fast-evolving mining society.

Lotteries and racing of all types were singled out as dangerous threats to the moral well-being of Kidwell's white flock. Predictably, it was Kidwell, a fluent Afrikaans speaker himself, and a colleague, the Dutch Reformed Church dominee RA Theron, who took up the challenge of the mayor of Roodepoort, MJ du Plessis, and East Rand MP J van den Bergh to debate the virtues of a state lottery publicly. Adding lyrics to mine-owner music, Kidwell was confident in his claim that gambling ruined a man's character, impoverished his family and led to a 'loss of industrial efficiency'. As the Depression lifted and better times returned, Kidwell claimed that gambling had become a more serious problem than drunkenness in what must have been a close contest.

Some years later, Kidwell also had an explanation for why the Allies had been caught napping during the early phases of World War II: 'If in England the time, energy and brains put into football pools and horse and dog racing had been devoted to studying the needs of the country, Germany could never have gained her advantage.' Clearly, the Lutheran Minister of Justice, Pirow, did not have to rely on Afrikaner Protestants for his Depression-era drive against lotteries; some Methodists and Presbyterians were not far behind the pack.[134]

It was the supposedly profligate working classes – black and white

– who bore the brunt of the attack on gambling in good and bad times alike. No clergyman ever set himself so single-mindedly, so whole-heartedly, against the rich who devoted themselves to owning and breeding horses, or to exclusive race meetings held across the country, than did Kidwell in his campaign against lotteries. Instead, it was dog racing that attracted lightning from forked tongues during the interwar years.[135] Class had a dynamic of its own within the confines of a white society ever more intent on cutting itself off from the African majority.

Kidwell was, of course, not the only clergyman in a working-class constituency to fear that the country was coming adrift from its spir-itual moorings by the late 1920s. In 1930, the Reverend PJS de Klerk, of Germiston, was sufficiently alarmed to call on the newly elected chairman of the Afrikaner Broederbond, LJ du Plessis – a fellow alum-nus and theologian from the University College of Potchefstroom – to establish a 'Calvinist Bond'. The brotherhood, they said, was 'not a political movement' and might include 'even the Calvinistic English churches'. The stated aim was to 'reinstate the principles of Calvinism in our national life' that had largely been lost sight of 'for the past three centuries'. But, for whatever reason, the bond was stillborn and no more was heard of the movement over the years that followed.[136]

During the worst of the Great Depression, white workers had renewed reason for slipping back into the dreamworld of chance and financial windfall that presented itself through lotteries – as they had done previously, in 1906–1908 and during World War I. Their objec-tive may no longer have been the acquisition of a house or property, but the desire to be transported from immediate economic hardship to a safer and more secure future. What the Naylors made of the 1929–1933 ideological onslaught of the churches, government and state is unknown, but it did little to curb their enterprise, even if the period was marked by some volatility in working-class preferences around sweepstakes.[137]

On the contrary, the agents and regional managers drawn from across the country at the 1929 hotel draw bore testimony to how strongly the lottery had taken root throughout the Union. The pri-mary focus undoubtedly remained in areas where the white work-ing class was strongly represented, in Natal and the Transvaal. But, during the Depression van der Linden had been transferred from the east coast to Cape Town, testifying to the existence of new markets away from the northern industrial core. In the early 1920s, the lottery was bringing in about £6000 each month, but by 1930 more than 300 booklets, each containing 40 tickets, were being printed in Johannesburg, and national receipts were estimated at £12000 (about three-quarters of a million pounds today).[138] The lottery had become a popular, illegal, countrywide phenomenon from Durban in the east to Doringbaai in the west, and from Muizenberg to Messina.

Lotteries, Pinball Machines and the Moral Panic of 1933–1939

Whenever an economy's tail gets caught in the door of acute financial stress, as happens in a depression or recession, it sets off discordant howls of anguish about the ills of gambling that are heard right across society. Churches and governments, charities and welfare agencies, industrialists and law enforcers, the press and the police, trade unions and the unemployed – all cry out in the dark, each hoping to come up with a 'solution' to the difficulties that come with lotteries, and to address their own needs in ways that might also benefit the wider society. Such baying for remedial action at times of cash scarcity, often class- and race-bound, was evident during 1929–1930.

By the same token, however, gambling and lotteries give rise to less muttering and noise when purses are putting on weight. Cats sleep deepest when the fire has died down and the embers give off a comforting glow. When the Great Depression lifted, in 1933, it heralded a boom that lasted throughout the remainder of the decade and beyond, to the end of World War II. Driven by gold, plentiful foreign exchange and an unprecedented capacity to settle foreign debt, gross domestic product per capita almost doubled in real terms (that is, after being adjusted for inflation) and the Wage Board – intent on protecting white wages in the 1920s – could turn its attention to less skilled workers.[139]

If lottery tickets, in the first two decades of the 20th century, were often bought out of a yearning to acquire a house and property that might serve as a base for the assembling and shaping of a white working-class family, by the 1930s and 1940s they appear to have been more frequently acquired in the hope of obtaining a few of the better things in life, not just its necessities. In the absence of data, there is no way of proving this hypothesis, but there are other – suggestive – reasons that might help account for what, on the surface of things, looks like a change in motivation for the purchase of lottery tickets.

Industrial conflict on the Witwatersrand centred around the white working class was made manifest in the strikes of 1907, 1913 and 1922 as a society dominated by single immigrant miners gradually made way for married workers permanently resident in the country.[140] The decades that followed are noteworthy for the absence of intense violent confrontations on the same scale.

It was the 'civilised labour' policies of the Pact government, which provided white workers with structured security in the workplace, that came at the expense of black workers. It was the state that plucked the sting out of workplace resentment among whites, and it was the state that went on to apply the balm of a welfare programme that, by the 1930s, made for increasing social and economic security at home.[141] As the flames of earlier decades died down, to be replaced by coals of contentment, the cat was ever more inclined to curl up, and the state more reluctant to rouse it from its slumbers. Issues of colour tended to trump issues of class in the white electorate, and an uneasy modus vivendi emerged between the government and the white working class.

A good deal – but certainly not all – of the drop in temperature in the white body politic can be traced through the composition of the makeshift 'Fusion' government, formed in 1934, which replaced the Pact government, in which the Labour Party had a considerable say. The white working class was far from politically dead, but it was struggling as issues of colour and class increasingly took precedence over those of class and colour.

This shift in state policy came in two stages, heralded by South Africa coming off the gold standard late in 1932. That was followed by a short-lived coalition between JBM Hertzog's National Party and Smuts's South African Party in the lead-up to the general election of 1933, in which the pair of political newlyweds saw off a challenge from DF Malan's 'Purified National Party', but hardly comfortably so in terms of the number of votes cast. The honeymoon over, the two parties merged formally, giving birth to the United Party (UP). The Fusion government was led by Prime Minister Hertzog, with Smuts as Deputy Prime Minister and Minister of Justice; both generals were the products of an anti-imperial war and, in Smut's case, of a rebellion in 1914 and a working-class revolt in 1922.[142] Age, vast experience in civil administration and first-hand knowledge of the horrors of war made for a canny blend of common sense and pragmatism that was frequently more evident in 'Slim Jannie' than it was in Hertzog. Both traits infused law enforcement in the interwar years.

Some of the Fusion government's deftness of touch and political footwork was on public display when JH Hofmeyr, Smuts's liberal right-hand man, addressed a public meeting on the role of church and state in combating 'social evils'. The broader topic, its eventually narrowed focus and the venue all hinted at what was really a silent debate between Hofmeyr and Kidwell. The meeting, under the auspices of the Temperance and Social Welfare Committee of the Methodist Church, took place in the Central Methodist Hall, Johannesburg. Hofmeyr argued that when it came to excessive alcohol consumption, Sunday sport and lotteries, the citizenry could not be rendered moral by an Act of parliament. But the state, he readily conceded, should not encourage its citizens to indulge in activities detrimental to society.

The audience followed Hofmeyr's eyes and listened carefully to his words as the question-begging sleight of hand took place right under their noses:

> The State regarded gambling as an evil and that, fortunately, had been the view of every South African Government.
>
> 'The State wants to extirpate [all] these evils, but the State can only go part of the way. The larger part, the more difficult part, lies with the Church. It is only by co-operation between Church and State that these social evils can effectively be tackled, and I hope the Church will have the strength and power to play its part.'[143]

When it came to gambling, the alliance between church and state was not one between partners of equal standing. 'The larger part, the more difficult part' of the struggle against the lotteries lay not with the lawmakers, or the law enforcers, but had to be shouldered by those brandishing the Bible and the cross. Dogma and dog collars were more important than Hansard and handcuffs. Minister of Justice Smuts concurred: judges, magistrates, the police and public prosecutors had, at best, a watching brief over the lotteries and, as before, continued to make use of informers when considered necessary.

But the state had never boasted a perfectly symmetrical structure, and when it did move, it often did so in an awkward, slightly disjointed fashion. Unlike a millipede, feet moving effortlessly in unison, the state struggled to coordinate its limbs, and never more so than when negotiating the thick undergrowth of industrial society. Creaking joints, such as those of the Labour Party and Transvaal Provincial Council, made marching in step with the government difficult. Late in 1933, weeks before the new coalition was announced, the Provincial Council, building on the economic uncertainties that helped make political realignment a possibility, yet again passed a motion – this time carried by 41 votes to 11 – asking the government for a referendum to determine support for a provincial or state lottery to underwrite welfare projects. It was suggested that, by then, only the United States was spending more on lottery tickets and sweeps based outside its national borders – overwhelmingly in England and Ireland – than was South Africa. At the height of the Depression, South Africa was exporting more than half a million pounds sterling annually to cover its gambling bills. The Labour Party's support for a lottery was unwavering and it continued to push for an accommodation well into World War II.[144]

In Johannesburg, notably on the East Rand but all along the Witwatersrand, the older generation's stubborn attachment to dog racing, horse racing and lotteries, not to mention its love of the thirst-quenching propensities in white working-class culture, continually frustrated Protestant crusaders and temperance advocates. With the Depression behind them and the economy sailing into calmer waters, the cries from the crow's nests by Protestants and temperance advocates about social hazards grew desperate and shrill. From on high they spied the approaching shoals of Satan, while below their captains failed to acknowledge the existing dangers or to change course. And by the time war threatened, the noise had become deafening and a sense of fear palpable.

The new four-legged gambling horror, pinball machines, raised moral problems that, in white middle-class minds, both paralleled and needed to be coupled to lotteries. As with horse racing and lotteries in 1906–1908 and during World War I, the glitzy, glass-topped tables triggered a full-scale moral panic across the Witwatersrand. And, as before, it drew together so many leading elements from the church, civil society and organised commerce that even Smuts and the pragmatic Fusion government were forced to engage in a little ineffectual counterpunching before the bell sounded for the May 1938 general election.

The devil, it is said, makes work for idle hands. If so, then it is unsurprising that the coin-gobbling pinball machine slid out of Lucifer's workshop during the Great Depression. The unemployed – on an unprecedented scale – were in search of cheaper amusements and small-scale cash returns as the economy languished and 'leisure' time expanded. The first coin-operated machines appeared in the United States in 1931.

In its early form, pinball involved propelling a metal ball into play on a slanted table via a spring-loaded lever. The ball was guided into a series of strategically placed holes by 'flippers', earning the player points that could be converted into cash prizes paid out by the proprietor of the establishment. After an electronic version, replete with a backdrop of dazzling flashing lights, accompanied by distinctive sounds, appeared two years later, pinball became an urban craze. By the mid-1930s, scores of manufacturers in Illinois were turning out thousands of machines.

In search of post-Depression markets for their expanded production, it took American pinball manufacturers less than 12 months to discover a new outlet in South Africa, happily locked into a period of unprecedented economic prosperity. Leading companies in Chicago, such as Automatic Industries and D Gottlieb & Co, exported the latest versions of their pinball machines to Johannesburg, where they were hired out, on a 50 per cent commission basis, to proprietors of amusement arcades and hundreds of small businesses in white working-class towns across the Witwatersrand. By mid-decade, corner cafés, downmarket tea rooms and smaller retail outlets, many of them owned by recent Mediterranean immigrants – Greek, Italian, Lebanese and Portuguese, unencumbered by Calvinist reflexes – boasted pinball machines and 'claw cranes' that came their way via the same suppliers.

It was claimed that each machine, on average, earned the proprietor £15 per month.[145]

In industrialising Benoni, Boksburg, Germiston and Springs, the chambers of commerce, dominated by Protestants seeking to safeguard their share of the retail trade, claimed that there were, on average, 50 pinball tables to be found in each of the East Rand mining towns. Proprietors of small establishments found it convenient to weld their financial interests to religious zealotry to advance the 'public good'. Comments by the president of the Benoni Chamber of Commerce, at the height of the panic, captured some of their concerns:

> From a purely commercial point of view, one must bear in mind that these so-called games are not manufactured in South Africa and hence give no employment to South Africans. They require no attendants and therefore provide no employment in the towns where their use is permitted. They are attracting persons who can ill afford to waste money and, I have no doubt, are causing young men to become unnecessarily indebted in other directions.[146]

As to hidden prejudiced ethnic thinking, Mr R Goddard said that he felt indignant, but that 'the law of libel prevents me from expressing myself more clearly'.

As with lotteries a decade earlier, pinball machines flourished on the East Rand in the protective shade of legal uncertainties. In the case of the lottery, a game of chance, some of the complications could be traced to the lottery being legal in Mozambique but with tickets sold, illegally, in South Africa. But the lottery trade was usually winked at, on both sides of the border, because of other economic considerations pertaining to the flow of African mine labour.

Pinball machines were different. Playing pinball was not only a matter of chance; it incorporated an element of skill that helped determine the outcome of the game and the winner's eligibility for a prize in cash or goods. The initial thrust that brought the metal ball into play could be influenced by the spring-loaded release mechanism. Once in play, on a slanted table, the ball could be trapped and released via the flippers and directed to various point-scoring opportunities – 'bumpers', or recesses – spread right across the board. The outcomes of pinball games were determined by an unequal mix of chance and skill, making it difficult for frustrated prosecutors to gain convictions on the grounds that the machines were gambling accoutrements, pure and simple.

As early as November 1934, in a case referred to the Supreme Court, the state conceded that there was an element of skill in pinball. Justice Tindall ruled that a proprietor could not be prosecuted for having pinball machines in his establishment. Playing them, he opined, was not like betting or buying a ticket in a lottery, but was more akin to a fairground booth hosting shooting or ring-tossing games.[147] Tindall's ruling made magistrates reluctant to convict proprietors like Peter Vasilos, owner of the Savoy Café in Boksburg. In 1937, Vasilos's defence team brought a pinball table into the magistrate's court, to demonstrate anew the element of skill in the game. Fifteen years later, in 1952, the same scene again played itself out in a Johannesburg court when an attorney, a detective and the prosecutor all played a game of pinball to demonstrate to a bemused magistrate how skill and the propulsion of metal balls had to battle chance and gravity on an inclined surface to score points.[148]

Protestant churches across the Reef, and more especially along the East Rand, did not take kindly to legal difficulties preventing the state from clamping down on the latest 'evil'. Pinball tables were added to a list of objections about perceived state laxity relating to excessive alcohol consumption, dog racing, football pools, lotteries and contraventions of the Sunday Observance Act. All the listed items were forms of recreation well-entrenched in a white working-class culture that was already two or three generations deep. The churches, like the mine and factory owners, and the small shopkeepers, all wanted the disposable incomes of white workers to fit more neatly into their view of a disciplined and ordered industrialising universe controlled by themselves.

But the East Rand was not 19th-century England. For the most part, the Wesleyans and others were howling into a Witwatersrand wilderness. The church's mission was rendered more dispiriting by working-class indifference, facilitated by the relative prosperity of the interwar years. Financial gloom and war might drive up church attendance in dark days, but a buoyant economy seldom lit the way to chapel or cathedral – sales took precedence over souls. Many Protestant clergymen, in the

1930s, thought that evangelical Christianity and organised religion had reached a turning point in mining towns. They feared that the golden calf was attracting far more followers than was the cross.

The Reverend William Meara, who came to head the United Methodist Church, felt that believers were surrounded by 'nominal Christians'. 'The story of the Church within recent years', he lamented, 'has been one of a tragic drift from evangelical religion.' He was hardly on his own in taking so gloomy a view. The Methodist Dean of Johannesburg, the Reverend WA Palmer, believed that the city was largely 'pagan'. There had been, it was said by some, an alarming decrease in the number of churchgoers, and 'with certain glorious exceptions', opined another minister, it was a generation with 'little love of the church'.[149]

Often as combative as they could occasionally be upbeat, the Methodists' sense of foreboding was shared, to a greater or lesser extent, by most Protestant churches in the key industrial centres. As the return of the good times dawned, in 1934, about 500 devout Christians, 'led by representatives of all the Protestant Churches in Johannesburg', joined a 'Procession of Witness' that marched from the Central Methodist Hall to the City Hall in a call to 'people who had lost touch with their churches'. There they were joined by others singing hymns, and together they 'held their right hands aloft as a profession of faith and an avowal of allegiance to the Church'. Five years later, as political tensions among white English and Afrikaans speakers resurfaced, blending into fears about the coming of another world war, the Mayor of Johannesburg, J Page, led another hopeful 'Back to Church Programme' across the city.[150]

Clerical anxieties about an ethical and spiritual vacuum developing amid the material prosperity of white communities extended to beyond their elderly or middle-aged congregants. It included schoolboys, adolescents and first-time wage earners. The quickening pace of industrialisation and urbanisation after World War I gave rise to increased employment opportunities for young white males, which, in turn, created a new source of disposable income for a few competing gambling enterprises. Whereas older, better-paid workers continued to patronise the lotteries, paying ten shillings for a ticket in the hope of getting a cash windfall, youngsters in search of modern entertainment that tested their hand-eye coordination and offered the prospect of a modest cash reward at threepence a time, found pinball machines almost irresistible. For those propagating old-style evangelical religion, such as the Reverend Kidwell, it meant that the church was fighting, but slowly losing, its battle against cafés.

A one hundred per cent increase in the cost of playing a game of pinball, from threepence – a 'tickey' – in the early 1930s to sixpence by mid-decade, was absorbed effortlessly by youthful devotees of the new, flashing electronic gods. When a couple of determined burglars smashed their way into an inner-city Johannesburg café housing two pinball tables, in 1938, they made off with £80 (about £5 500 today) in sixpences.[151]

The two-decades-old National Thrift Movement, which focused on East Rand schoolchildren and did its best to encourage them to become habitual savers, appears not to have enjoyed much success along the Reef or more widely.[152] In 1936, Dr Emil Baumann, the MP for working-class Rosettenville, and a man with an interest in, and knowledge of, 'child welfare', 'regretted the lack of support given to the National Thrift Movement' and claimed that 'South Africa had the unenviable reputation of being the least thrifty country in the world'.[153]

It was not as if the office bearers of the National Thrift Movement did not care about pinball machines and the youth. *Au contraire*, they tracked the craze conscientiously, to the point of obsession. They interviewed the Minister of Justice, chief magistrates, senior police officers and public prosecutors to remain abreast of the 'chance and skill' complexities and monitor what they saw as a tardy response by the state to discourage 'the habit of gambling'.[154]

On the East Rand, at the height of the moral panic, in 1937, those fearful of the future – including a city councillor and Rotarian who had set up a Boys' Club – were, as ever, deeply concerned about the future of 'the youth'. 'The youth', of course, was a hobby-horse first corralled by Noah and then allowed to populate all places through all times. Social workers, often women recruited and trained by those least critical of the excesses of capitalist societies, joined activists chanting slogans about pinball machines threatening the 'moral fibre', 'self-control' and 'welfare' of young men. In Benoni, a schoolmaster, having told his pupils to avoid the new electronic games, was puzzled. 'Where they get the money to play those games', he lamented, 'I do not know.'[155]

Had Mr Chips – who had just made his appearance in popular fiction – asked around, he would have stumbled across an answer soon enough. Among schoolboys, money for pinball games had, allegedly, either been given to the lads by, or stolen from, their distraught mothers (which itself hinted at another new source of disposable income). The 'chief patrons' of the machines, however, were said to be between 'the ages of 15 and 22', and prominent among them on the East Rand were teenage apprentices and first-time workers earning 'small wages' that they could 'ill-afford to squander'.[156]

The unarticulated part of these complaints, one suspects, was that – as with patriarchs and lotteries – a source of marginal disposable income controlled by men was being directed outwards, into gambling outlets, rather than back into the working-class family budget. The National Thrift Movement saw a financially sound domestic unit as helping to shape an evolving white South African identity. 'Thrifty homes', ran one of the movement's campaign slogans, 'make wealthy states.'[157] The Reverend Kidwell called out the dangers. Gambling, he said, led to 'the impoverishment of homes, the deterioration of character, prevalence of fraudulent practices, loss of industrial efficiency and the breaking of laws'.[158] In short, in poorer working-class families, lotteries and pinball machines had the potential to undermine financial and social cohesion. The suspicion grows when we note how the guardian of family life, the National Council of Women, used its 1936 annual conference to decry 'the use of pinball machines in cafés by people under the age of 18'.[159]

Family-centred concerns about gambling were nothing new to Methodists, either Primitive or Wesleyan. They and others had been making similar arguments about lotteries for more than a decade. The churches had led the way. In the economically propitious 1930s, militant Christians were joined by others in society – civic leaders and middle-class women – in coupling and equating lotteries and pinball machines as a 'social evil' when, in truth, the two were only distantly related. It mattered not; the underlying consensus was sufficiently strong to put a spring back in the steps of clergymen in whose veins the evangelical tradition coursed. And the tune was catchy enough to spread to other parts of the country. The Natal Methodist Church

Synod believed strongly that lotteries and pinball machines were a 'serious menace to the moral and spiritual well-being of the youth of the country'. The Durban Ministers' Association linked the Protestant ethic to industrial progress in a way that would have enjoyed the support of almost all employers. Lotteries, they argued, were 'subversive of honest toil'. 'South Africa needs work and business efficiency, and lotteries strike at the root of these things.'[160]

But, by the mid-1930s, daytime rustling in the electoral undergrowth about lotteries and pinball was often drowned out by the nocturnal roaring of political lions intent on hunting down and killing off what was left of the emaciated African franchise in the Cape Province. Smuts's Department of Justice had long shied away from unnecessarily direct confrontations with the Naylors that might trigger cross-border tensions with Portugal. The interwar period appears to have seen very few prosecutions for lottery offences that could be traced back to the operators of the Lourenço Marques Lottery or their many agents.

By the mid-1930s, the Ministry of Labour and Social Welfare – a coupling of portfolios that spoke, in part, to the needs of white working-class families in urban areas – was overseen by the largely ineffectual AP Fourie. If Smuts was hamstrung in his actions against lotteries by the international parameters within which he had to work, then he and Fourie were handicapped at home by Justice Tindall's pronouncements about the chance and skill components of pinball games. 'The Department of Justice', a 1935 communiqué ran, 'has been for a long time considering the question of whether it is possible to take action against the owners or other people connected with the [pinball] machines.'[161] At best, Smuts, one of the finest legal minds in the country, had only ever managed a standoff when it came to complex gambling issues. With an election due in 1938, it was a problem of some interest because the substrata of the white electorate were being carefully realigned.

The 1930s, more than any other decade since the Anglo-Boer War, saw the conscious, systematic and successful raising of Afrikaner political consciousness. The efforts of nationalists expanded and strengthened links between church, economy, party and state in ways that facilitated the eventual emergence of an ethnically dominated, racially segregated republic of the type apartheid South Africa became after 1948. Among the nightmares of DF Malan's Purified National Party, which had parted ways with its nationalist predecessors in 1934, was that the continuing urbanisation of Afrikaners would see working-class consciousness and culture, including gambling, erode the God-ordained unity of a homogeneous white 'volk'.[162]

In the governing UP, Smuts and Hofmeyr knew that the Protestant churches – Afrikaans and Anglophone – were constructing a foundation of sorts through their common opposition to lotteries and pinball machines. But so poor was the bespectacled couple's eyesight that while they could see the wall, they were unable to read what was written on it. It is true that, as the May 1938 election approached, they sensed that something was happening, but Smuts, who could see distant international politics clearly, was often a trifle short-sighted when it came to reading domestic politics in his backyard.

Smuts's hesitancy on gambling issues had little, if anything, to do with the outcome of an election that saw the governing UP lose more than 20 seats. But it did not help, and may have contributed to the confusion and prevarication in the lead-up to the election. Like the breeze that combs the long Highveld grass first in one direction and then the other, Smuts bent back and forth as he sought protection from the electoral winds swirling around him.

In politics, timing is often the best litmus test when it comes to revealing motivation and sincerity of purpose. In April, weeks before the election and after Smuts had been considering the 'chance and skill' dilemma for a 'long time', the Department of Justice, the police and the proprietors of establishments housing pinball machines suddenly reached agreement about the future of Satan's toys. All machines would be withdrawn from operation by 10 May – eight days before the election – or the authorities would be forced to take, some unspecified, action. In a telling simile that whispered ethnic prejudice, a morning newspaper reported that the machines 'had been condemned to be exported like "undesirable immigrants"', and at midnight on 10 May, a few diehards staged a mock burial for a pinball machine in an ice-cream parlour.[163]

But, as café frequenters suspected, and the proprietors and Smuts must surely have known, the demise of pinball machines was not imminent. It was part of an electoral Punch and Judy show, a seasonal entertainment that would need to be placed on a far firmer legal footing. The chance-skill bifurcation had long confounded legal advisers in the Department of Justice, and so, a month after the election, Smuts proposed to amend the gambling law to provide him with arbitrary, sweeping powers to deal with the gambling problem whenever the winds of populism picked up. The amended bill would 'give the Minister wide powers to define as lotteries schemes, games or contrivances which cannot readily be defined as lotteries under the existing law, and its provisions can be applied, if the Minister so desires, to football pools and pin-table'.[164]

In the case of football pools and pinball machines, any differences between chance and skill were to be obliterated at the stroke of a ministerial pen. There was no sober or intelligent person in the world who would confuse a lottery ticket with a pinball machine, but, given Protestant spectacles and enough to drink, a pinball machine could, with a bit of help, assume the shape of a lottery ticket.

Unlike lottery tickets, which were sold covertly from under the counter, pinball machines, like prostitutes on a downtown street corner, flashed their electronic invitations brazenly, from the recesses of suburban corner cafés. The rich could gamble comfortably and without harassment from the grandstand at the racecourse of their choice, but the gambling culture of the white working class had to be concealed, to be hidden from ideologically active middle-class Protestants. Class-based hypocrisy, as with colour-based hypocrisy, was becoming steadily more acceptable to a lily-white South African electorate.

For all that, it took the better part of a year before the Minister of Justice was ready to submit the Gambling Amendment Bill of 1939 to parliament. In introducing the bill, in February that year, Smuts said that he had hoped to present it earlier but 'was approached by certain financial interests who pleaded that some time be given to them'. He had acceded to their request, but the time had come to deal with the ambivalence of the courts when balancing chance and skill components in gambling. 'Whenever there was an element of skill in a game', he grumbled, the 'courts were inclined to give the benefit of the doubt to the persons charged.' It was frustrating, and the best way of dealing with it was to give the judges no choice. 'Unless some power was given to the Minister to declare what was a lottery or a game of chance', Smuts said, 'it would be difficult to enforce the law and gambling would develop more and more'. A bill that enjoyed the support of the churches made for a very pleasant day at the office and MPs engaged in 'a number of Sunday School speeches on the evils of gambling'. The House approved the bill. And for one glorious, happy, sunny afternoon, church and state walked arm in arm.[165]

Malan's Purified Nationalists were willing to stuff themselves with any hors d'oeuvres offered by Smuts but made it clear that they would only be satisfied with an entrée that included a ban on all bookmakers and dog racing.[166] For patriotic Afrikaners, alien forms of gambling not only prioritised white working-class awareness and conscious-ness over organic forms of ethnic and national consciousness but were frequently underpinned by foreign elements, at a time of grow-ing anti-immigrant and antisemitic sentiments within the ranks of Calvin's chosen and those striving for purity.[167]

Those believing in the onward march of progress were cheered by the sight of General Smuts having run up a flag calling the faithful to yet another battle with gambling, but to squint-eyed cynics look-ing on from afar, it seemed like just any other old white flag. The news passed down from the church towers and police barracks to true believers was also not entirely reassuring. The 'financial interests', proprietors housing pinball machines and white working-class youths had not taken fright instantly, and were not about to head for the hills. The general was going to have to make some adjustments to his plan.

Part of the problem was that legislation passed to control the perceived indiscipline and moral weakness of the Rand's white working-class youth was slow to take root in other, more commer-cial urban centres. For hard mining men in the north, the only Big Smoke ever seen in Cape Town might as well have come from the odd snoek-processing plant. Two months after the passage of the new Act, socially irresponsible elements in the sleepy southern city were reportedly still playing away merrily on the devil's devices. Law enforcement authorities had neither the enthusiasm nor the resources to eradicate machines that had to be treated as if they were lotteries, which, in any case, they had largely ignored. 'The police authorities are giving the proprietors of these machines a few days' respite. From July 1, however, the regulations will be gradually enforced, and the authorities will begin to bring offenders to heel.'[168]

But the companies owning the machines, the most important of which had strong American ties, along with the café proprietors – almost certainly the unnamed 'financial interests' that had ensured the delay in the introduction of the Act in 1938 – were not ready to be brought to heel. Two months later, in November 1939, the Minister of Justice had to eat a slice of humble pie. The rest of the pie was wrapped in pages torn from the *Government Gazette*. The new wisdom was:

> [I]f by the operation of any pin table it was not possible to obtain any prize or benefit, or if the only benefit it was possible to obtain was the return of the money paid for the use of the pin table, or the right to use it again without payment, or both, the pin table would *not* fall under the prohibition of the Act.[169]

A compromise had been reached between the general, the captains of industry and the café proprietors that the church and white working-class youth could probably buy into. Pinball machines would dispense prizes only in kind – a refund or more games – but not regurgitate coins. 'Free' games won on the machine did not qualify as 'prizes' but as something else, although what exactly that was no one knew. Like the lottery, pinball machines were left to lurk in history's waiting room, in a liminal world patrolled by a church and state that lived together openly, always content to tell the electorate how much they longed to get together and consummate a fully legal union in God's eyes.

PART V

NAUSEA

*The theologians, taking one with another, are adept
logicians, but every now and then they have to resort
to sophistries so obvious that their whole case takes
on an air of the ridiculous.*
HL MENCKEN, *MINORITY REPORT: HL MENCKEN'S
NOTEBOOKS* (1956)

Nelson's Eye on Mozambique in
World War II, 1939—1945

With the momentum of a decade's prosperity behind it, the
South African economy, freed from territorial conflict
by its distance from the major theatres of war and protected from global competition, breezed into World War II with a
following wind. Significant growth in manufacturing capacity, aided
by price and wage regulation, saw a sustained surge in gross domestic
product and an increase in taxes, all of which contributed to sound
annual budget surpluses.[1]

The ship of state was, however, being hurried along by an underlying political current as well as by the favourable trade winds. It was
not long before the unpredictable political current was causing more
turbulence than was the steady economic wind. The outbreak of war
came in the wake of a decade's dedicated cultural labour by Afrikaner
activists. It culminated in the emotional outpourings of the 1938 Great
Trek centenary celebrations, which, in turn, helped reignite and fire up
a narrower ethnic nationalist consciousness. The war also pried open
old imperial-republican antagonisms, signalling the end of the Fusion
government. Collectively, these forces opened the way for a seminal
realignment in Afrikaner politics, heralding an era in which church and
state, driven by conservative Afrikaner neo-Calvinists, could move

closer, paving the way for the ever-grander apartheid thinking that was to follow.[2]

In the first week of September 1939, Prime Minister Hertzog called a cabinet meeting proposing to his UP colleagues that South Africa adopt a stance of qualified neutrality in the war. Smuts, Hertzog's deputy, wanting to align the country more fully behind the British effort, demurred and won the hour by a vote of seven to six, but the matter was then referred to the House of Assembly. Two days later, Hertzog's motion was defeated in the House, and he promptly resigned. Smuts became wartime prime minister and the Hertzog and Malan factions joined forces in the Herenigde – reunited – National Party, early in 1940. As the leading historian of the coming of Afrikaner hegemony has suggested, 'Without the political polarization brought about by the war, which from the war vote of 1939 was increasingly drawn on language lines, Malan's NP would have been unlikely to come to power in 1948.'[3]

With Smuts preoccupied by matters military abroad, JH Hofmeyr became deputy prime minister and, in effect, the guiding hand behind most matters domestic, including the old chestnuts of gambling policies and state action/inaction. Hofmeyr, as we have seen, felt that the church rather than the state should lead the charge when it came to amending or proposing gambling legislation. His UP colleagues in parliament, however, and more especially those in working-class constituencies on the Witwatersrand, where the Labour Party's push for a provincial or state lottery enjoyed considerable support, were less keen to take a back seat on gambling legislation. Pushed from the left by the Labour Party to approve a state lottery, and from the right by Afrikaans and English Protestant churches to eliminate dog racing and suppress the Lourenço Marques Lottery, the ruling UP members began to shift their weight uneasily from one foot to the other. That shuffle of uncertainty – a jig, one fit only for a wake – increasingly defined the party.

In the Transvaal Provincial Council, the socialist Labour Party, losing electoral traction despite a surge in the industrialising wartime economy, pleaded continually for a state-sanctioned lottery that might cater for its English-speaking constituents in its working-class strongholds.[4] The 1930s had seen an unprecedented period of growth in the profits from dog racing and, it seems, the LML. On the East Rand, those who bought shares in the Union Greyhound Racing

Association for £10, in 1932, would have seen them rise in value to £180 per share by 1942. As with pinball machines, much of the dog and other racing business was serviced by unloved Mediterranean café owners, or Chinese and other storekeepers who formed part of a seedy bucket shop trade that functioned openly without major hindrance.[5]

The East Rand continued to be seen by some as a sprawling gambling hell dominated by the white working class in which dog racing, pinball machines and the lottery – frequently seen as linked by their middle-class adversaries – continued to hold sway while the state, wisely, stayed away. But where the police hesitated to tread, Protestant clergymen from both language groups rushed in – as during World War I, when wartime gambling increased rather than decreased.[6] Social anxiety and moral panics were friends rather than the foes of true believers hoping to spread the faith among their benighted brethren.

Having 'won' the pinball war – a pyrrhic victory – Anglophone East Rand ministers resumed their struggle against the ascendant 'evil' of dog racing, coupling it, as before, to lotteries and knowing that they enjoyed increasing support from their Afrikaans-speaking, counterparts.[7] When it came to racial segregation, Afrikaans and English Protestants might slowly be moving apart, but when it came to gambling, they remained within touching distance. Afrikaner Calvinists wanted to wean poor urban whites from the threat posed by a predominantly working-class consciousness into a cultural fold – in keeping with an exclusively ethnic nationalist future – while English-speaking Protestants, looking back, like the 19th-century Wesleyans, wanted to shape their congregants into a disciplined, sober and thrifty English working class without the social 'evils' that had scarred the first industrial revolution.

As ever, the East Rand remained the nursery of white working-class resistance to exploitative practices in the workplace and to cultural objections by a shaky church-state alliance hoping to restrict all forms of gambling, other than elite horse racing, in the dusty mining towns. And, as before, it was Kidwell of Germiston, supported by another Methodist, the Reverend HG Leverton of Springs, who led the charge against the supposedly twinned evils of dog racing and lotteries. As the air thickened with anxieties about the coming of war, Kidwell and Leverton sent up flares about the threat that gambling was said to pose domestically. In August 1939, Kidwell got the Methodist Synod, sitting at Benoni, to support the government in its efforts to deny the oxygen of legality to any notion of a provincial lottery.[8] Leverton led a long and ultimately successful campaign to keep Springs dog-racing-free, by launching a strong sensationalist attack against the sport's two governing associations.[9]

So egregious was Leverton's attack on dog racing that the African Greyhound Racing Association felt compelled to reply. The association readily conceded that the illegal bucket shop trade was widespread but, from inside knowledge, suggested that it was about to be brought under control by the state. It denied Leverton's assertion that the industry had an annual turnover of £3.5 million and countered with what, it implied, were carefully researched facts. The average weekly attendance at three racetracks was of the order of 12 000, it stated, that is, about two per cent of the Rand's European population, and 'the average sum spent at various tracks weekly does not exceed 8s 6d per person'.[10]

With the unresolved moral panic over pinball still fresh in their minds, a new round of Protestant pyrotechnics threatening and white women newly enfranchised, mutterings about 'social evils' that threat-ened the working-class family set the teeth of Witwatersrand MPs on edge. This was particularly evident on the East Rand, where nervous United Party MPs had to pick their way carefully between familiar old Labour Party and new National Party ideologies as they clucked their way towards what, they hoped, were a few safe electoral nests.

On 1 March 1940, as the real war began rumbling in earnest, the UP caucus, alarmed 'by the serious growth of gambling in the Union and its detrimental effect on national welfare' requested the government to consider the appointment of a commission of inquiry to report on the matter. Hofmeyr, who organised the House of Assembly's busi-ness, and whose Baptist and Presbyterian background left him with no liking for gambling, set aside an afternoon for the debate.[11] All forms of gambling were to be probed, but given ruling-class interests, the MPs managed to avoid the sport of kings, which was conveniently ignored. The motion was proposed by FB Allen (UP Roodepoort, a West Rand mining town), seconded by no less than BJ Schoeman (NP Fordsburg, a working-class stronghold of white railway work-ers) and strongly supported by almost all the East Rand MPs.

Whereas in pre-World War I debates it was the disposable incomes

JH Hofmeyr (LEFT) and Colin Steyn (RIGHT), United Party cabinet members unwilling to endorse, or to oppose, a South African national lottery.

of single males, many of them immigrant miners, that were the primary target of those intent on eradicating 'social evils', by the 1940s it was the well-being of the white working-class family, replete with previously unenfranchised wives, that became the focal point of concern. Allen believed that gambling would 'cause misery to [workers]' and more especially so 'when dog-racing night fell on pay day'. Shopkeepers agreed: 'On the Witwatersrand gambling was becoming an obsession and the gambling instincts of the people were encouraging private enterprise to extend still further the existing gambling facilities.' Leslie Blackwell (UP Kensington, later Judge Blackwell) felt that 'South Africa was one of the most gambling-ridden countries in the world'. The Labour Party MP for Durban North, the Reverend CFM Cadman, far from any East Rand crucible, was adrift from his party. Schools should teach 'every boy and girl that it is dishonest to take money that has not been earned'.[12]

Stranded in no-man's land, between the preferences of the incoming tide of Calvinist ideology from right-wing platteland churches and the outgoing tide of left-leaning organised labour in urban constituencies, the UP danced its way into electoral confusion, reverting to bluster and the shuffle of uncertainty. With Hofmeyr nowhere to be seen, it fell to the party's Minister of Justice to shut down the blast of hot air. Colin Steyn, the minister, had felt the heat but did not know where to position himself: 'He [Steyn] did not want to commit himself for or against any of the arguments but he would remind members that moral persuasion was more effective than legal persuasion, although legal persuasion could not be dispensed with.'[13] It was a stale old Hofmeyr cigarette butt passed around as if it were a Havana cigar.

And, as if that were not sufficient, the minister drew on another favourite old white South African saw, one usually reserved for arguments about the advancement of African political rights – the theory of unripe time. In principle, the idea of a commission was admirable, but the timing was unfortunate. It would not be possible to appoint a commission at the present time, said Steyn, since '[a] number of [other] important commissions' had already 'been postponed'. It was a magnificent outcome to the debate, as pleasing to the governing UP as it was to the National Party opposition – a political miracle that promised everything and nothing simultaneously. The House loved it. The motion was adopted unanimously.[14]

Hot air generated during the debate condensed, giving rise to yet more uncertainty around the issues. While Steyn, head in the clouds, was content to live with a promise of rain in a country crying out for a few drops of common sense, the police, tasked with enforcing Kruger-era laws, were not. It used to be that public prosecutors, urged on by their superiors, would push the police to act against gambling establishments, but in the age of the shuffle it was the police that now pressed the minister for badly needed updated legislation.

By 1941, the police could wait no longer. The Deputy Commissioner of Police drafted the clauses of what a new bill governing gambling might contain. He passed the potato to the Commissioner of Police, who passed it to the Secretary for Justice, who passed it to the Minister of Justice, who, alas, had no one left to pass it to. The thing was too hot to handle. How would battle-hardened returning soldiers take to being told by a nanny state that they were not to play with nasty dogs or buy lottery tickets? Only a more overtly religious regime, one in which church and state were far closer to one another than they were under the Smuts government, could do that. It was, Hofmeyr had argued, the church that had to lead the fight against 'social evils'. Troops who had seen Cairo by night might have had different ideas about what constituted an 'evil'.

And so there the thing lay, in the minister's in-tray, throughout the war. In 1941, the Secretary for Justice told the Commissioner of Police that the draft bill was 'receiving consideration'. In 1942, he again wrote to him, stating that 'little hope can be held out of legislation on [gambling] being introduced during the present session of parliament'. In 1943, 'a heavy legislative programme' meant that it 'would not be possible' to amend Kruger-era legislation. So it went on, year after year, until Smuts and Hofmeyr introduced a clever sidestep into the shuffle. The issues would be disaggregated in such a way as to demonstrate a willingness to deal with the dog racing that bedevilled the East Rand working class, but again to ignore the more vexed question of lotteries.[15]

In June 1947, the UP-dominated Transvaal Provincial Council passed legislation abolishing dog racing but, with an eye on the upcoming general election, in 1948, granted proprietors of racetracks a two-year grace period to wind down their businesses.[16] The police were happy enough to grab a bone thrown their way, but the measure did little to satisfy their need for substantial integrated national, rather than provincial, legislation to deal with the private gambling clubs that had flourished during the war. But the problem around lotteries remained unresolved and so the police returned to the fray via the Minister of Justice.[17] Neither Smuts, nor Hofmeyr, the liberal man of principle, had reservations about restricting gambling, but they were about to fight for their political lives in an election and, predictably, nothing happened.

Somewhere along the line, possibly as a result of the loosening of social bonds during the war, highly visible dog racing on the Witwatersrand had become uncoupled from the national trade in lottery tickets in the minds of legislators.[18] MPs were slowly groping their way towards an overarching policy on gambling that might, simultaneously, satisfy religious and secular, as well as urban and rural, constituencies. But how might a committee of white democrats fashion a cricket ball from a hen's egg?

Away from these political goings-on, in Johannesburg, the Naylor brothers found the trajectory of the debate on dog racing unsettling.

As ever, there were important forces ranged against popular support for the lottery. Coupled with new wartime restrictions on the movement of men and money in and out of the country, these all pointed to the need for an urgent review of the managerial arrangements governing the LML.

The review came at the worst possible moment. Ten years had elapsed since the lottery concession had been renewed, and in 1939 it was again up for renewal. Portugal's neutrality in the war was a mixed blessing. It had the virtue of reminding the Salazar government how welcome the swelling income from casino gambling was becoming. Lisbon, unexpectedly elevated to a promising locale for an influx of secret agents and spies, 'had the last great gambling house in wartime Europe, located along its coastline at Estoril'. Among the British agents whose imaginations were fired by this exotic, seductive setting was Ian Fleming, whose fictional James Bond became a major success story.[19]

But wartime neutrality brought with it destitute and deprived refugees, some Catholics, seeking additional relief measures from church and state.[20] The Salazar administration insisted that the Lourenço Marques Lottery be administratively anchored in Lisbon, and that there would be an increase in the charitable dimension that would be directed into the local Misericordia to provide more assistance to the indigent.[21] The Naylors thus had to renegotiate the concession without the help of the enigmatic Padre Vicente, who had died in Portugal in 1933. It was a severely challenging time.

In Mozambique, the lottery manager, José dos Santos Rufino, and the lawyers did the legal and political legwork for a new deal. Santos Rufino persuaded Manuel Sampaio, a respected metropolitan financier in Lisbon, to open doors in the Salazar administration, and he became the 'managing partner' in the new company, the Empreza Commercial de Lotarias Ltda. Sampaio's share in the business was nominal and the financial fuel for the refit came from the Naylor brothers and their southern African partners. Between them, George and Peter Charles Naylor, along with Albert Adamson in Durban and Paul van der Linden in Cape Town, owned no less than 88 per cent of the shares. The remaining portion went to Santos Rufino, who handled the lottery logistics.[22]

At the best of times the lottery demanded considerable managerial acumen to function successfully. A transnational business, legal in one country, whose 'products' were sold illegally in a neighbouring domain, came with embedded problems. Cross-border flows of different currencies, professionally crafted tickets and attractive prizes required a formal legal organisation on the one hand and an informal, illegal, parallel structure on the other. In peacetime, under 'normal' circumstances, the Mozambican and the South African authorities, both heavily reliant on the Rand mining industry for their economic well-being, tolerated the lottery, provided that the business was conducted discreetly, on a nudge-and-a-wink basis. But when one country was drawn into a costly, far-off world war as a belligerent, and the other, the poorer, remained neutral, borders and cash flows came under far greater scrutiny from a nervous military intent on countering spies, and from a fiscus that was stretched.

The Naylors had, as best possible, avoided South Africa's catch-all border and fiscal nets by opening bank accounts in various countries under real or fictitious names. In Lisbon and Lourenço Marques, accounts for Sampaio and Santos, Portuguese nationals, posed few problems. An old friend of the lottery, Dr Antonio Casqueira, provided additional flexibility via the Swiss family that he hailed from. In near-bankrupt Mozambique, the Banco Nacional Ultramarino, the de facto central bank, opened accounts for nearly anyone.[23]

It was just as well that the opening of accounts by foreign nationals posed few difficulties since the fictious names assumed by account holders pointed to imaginations that had not been stretched unduly. The bank of choice for the leading shareholders in the Empreza Commercial de Lotarias, the Naylors, remained the Standard. Since World War I, it had serviced the needs of bucket shop owners, lottery agents and racecourse crooks with discretion of the sort greatly admired in banking circles. And if the Standard would not help, Barclays would.[24]

On trips to Delagoa Bay, George Sylvester Naylor, well known in the city under his own name, was welcome at the BNU under the name 'Mr White' – 'Mr Black' presumably being a less promising option in a colonial society. Naylor did better with his cover occupation, claiming to be a director of the now difficult-to-trace Central Timber Company – a plausible choice of 'occupation' in the city that forwarded the most lumber of all to Rand mines.[25]

Paul van der Linden, in effect the travelling national general manager of the lottery, found it even harder to come up with plausible
fictitious names. In 1930, he had run an account for the lottery under
the name Paul J Nednil – 'Linden' spelt backwards, schoolboy fashion.
By World War II he was still struggling, often merely combining his
name with those of the Naylors. Barclays was content to do business
with him in Cape Town, Durban, East London, Johannesburg and
Pretoria under the name 'Paul Sylvester'. Neither that, nor the name
'Peter Charles', supposedly 'retired' in Winkelspruit, were names that
would have puzzled Criminology 101 students unduly.[26]

As the lottery business gained wartime momentum, bar a few exceptional months during the worst phases of the conflict, two unnamed
'companies' went on the offensive, using petitions to pressure the government into legalising a national lottery. Young women were paid £1 a
day to collect signatures in Cape Town and Johannesburg – both Naylor
strongholds. Both these company initiatives were brought directly to
the notice of the Minister of Justice. But Steyn, who had learnt all he
needed to know at the feet of the masters, Smuts and Hofmeyr, knew
exactly what to do, and the third monkey covered its eyes.[27]

The assertiveness of the lottery operators and the surge in confidence of the Naylor brothers derived, in part, from the exceptional wartime conditions. Existing prohibitions on gambling 'were unofficially
lifted during the war years' as civic groupings scrambled to find ways
of providing financial support for the Governor General's National
War Fund.[28] In Johannesburg, all forms of private and public gambling
thrived without official contestation. God, it seemed, was unwilling to
tolerate gambling in peacetime, since it so clearly was a 'social evil', but
apparently minded less during a time of mass slaughter.

By early 1940, the underground part of the new lottery concession
was back up and, as before, operating reasonably smoothly in South
Africa. According to George Naylor, who came under investigation in
1940–1941 and had reason to understate rather than overstate the business, £8 000 worth of tickets were printed in Lourenço Marques each
month and an additional £12 000 in South Africa (about £1.3 million
today). Santos Rufino had a private post box in Johannesburg and, on
his frequent visits there to collect huge sums in cash, usually stayed at
the luxurious Carlton Hotel, as did van der Linden on his own visits

north. Some of the couriering of cash, tickets and prizes, however, was said to be left in the hands of two railway employees, who moved thrice weekly between Johannesburg and Lourenço Marques: a certain Calçado Bastos and a young electrician, Machado do Cruz, who tended the air conditioning on the train once known as the Naylor Express.[29]

By World War II the lottery was the largest nominally 'illegal' business in the country, and there could not have been a man in the country, from barber to banker, from miner to minister, did not either know it or suspect it. It was a situation filled with other tragic, ethical and political ironies. On the one hand, the governing classes were pushing and pulling the white working-class electorate into an ever more formalised, institutionalised and legalised racist dispensation. On the other, they claimed they were safeguarding the moral well-being of the same white workers but denying them the right to gamble. Constructing a racist society was moral; buying a lottery ticket clearly was not.

And so the national pastime of (dis)organised hypocrisy continued apace. As the author of an unsigned memorandum in the Treasury put it, 'Naylor is engaged upon a business that is contrary to our laws, but which appears to be winked at by the police'; in the margin, encouraging yet more winking, he wrote, 'words after "laws" deleted in copies of memo sent to the Reserve Bank'.[30] Bankers, policemen, ministers and politicians – all in on the game. Capitalism sometimes plays havoc with the eyesight, causing blindness.

By then, however, a new problem began to surface. Under 'normal' circumstances all the authorities of a peacetime state were ready to turn Nelson's eye to Mozambique when it came to the lottery. But South Africa was at war. The war brought into play new, relatively independent institutions that had no institutional memory of deceit and international relations. The military, now manning and scanning the borders, were a law unto themselves.

Trouble arose when Dr Casqueira needed £1 728, in Johannesburg, to pay for medical supplies that, simultaneously, required settlement in Switzerland. This was at a time when the lottery had experienced a £8 000 loss over two months during the closing quarter of 1940. Santos Rufino, who had personally conveyed £20 000 in lottery receipts over the border shortly before, asked George Naylor to place the funds into Casqueira's Johannesburg account. 'Mr White' would then be reimbursed in Lourenço Marques even though the lottery company was experiencing a short-term cash flow problem. Rufino wrote to Naylor, on 30 September 1940, but the letter was intercepted by the Controller of Censorship, who forwarded it to the Director of Intelligence.[31]

The director, Colonel Thwaites, outcomes-driven in matters where the last thing the state needed was a clear-cut response, passed the parcel to the Director of Customs and Excise, who had no use for it. Even then, the letter might have been conveniently lost in one of the state's warehouses of studied neglect had it not been for the Controller of Censorship, who had developed a growing interest in illegal Lourenço Marques–Johannesburg transactions.

Not content with having opened the Rufino–Naylor correspondence, he and Thwaites followed up on it in the manner expected of the army. The controller uncovered yet more correspondence about lottery cheques and, late in November, received a tip-off that Rufino, then staying briefly at the Carlton Hotel, was about to return to Lourenço Marques 'with a large sum of money on him'. But Rufino was back on the coast before the police reacted. The envelope in the warehouse peeled open, and the contents slowly spilled out.[32]

The extent and nature of the illegal transnational connections was exposed, but unsurprisingly it took six months before the embarrassing disclosures were resealed and sent back to the warehouse of state neglect. Lottery transfers, facilitated by the banks on either side of the border since 1919, and the couriering of cash by Rufino and others – 'undetected' by border officials or the police upcountry since at least 1929 – became part of interdepartmental correspondence about Casqueira, George Naylor and van der Linden's contraventions of the Emergency Finance Regulations and the Lourenço Marques Lottery. The state artillery was put on display but not used.[33]

Between late 1941 and mid-1942 official correspondence about the Rufino–Naylor exchange crossed the desks of the Commissioner of Immigration, the Commissioner of Police and his deputy, the Chief Cashier and Deputy Cashier of the Reserve Bank, the Director of Customs and Excise, the Director of Intelligence, the Censor, the Union consul in Lourenço Marques, and the Secretary for Finance, whose minister, JH Hofmeyr, was finding funds for the war effort. It was another case of unwritten civil service rule number 505 – that is, the more desks a letter crosses, the less likely it is to lead to meaningful action. Senior officials in Barclays and Standard banks were instructed to report. George Naylor was summoned, and put his cards on the table. His past contraventions of the archaic lottery law were dug up, and his attorneys, Dumat, Pitts & Blaine, briefed about pending action. Naylor was left to sweat.

The issue cooled off to the point where none of the administrators or law enforcement officers, beyond those in the Treasury, appeared to have an active interest in the matter. Death by neglect suited the government, but not George Naylor, who activated an insurance policy that may or may not have worked. In mid-February, van der Linden, a man with nationalist credentials dating back to the 1914 rebellion, called in at the Cape Town office of an old friend, JH Grobler, the cunning, anti-Asian, racist United Party MP for Brits.[34]

Van der Linden wanted an introduction to the Secretary for Finance, Dr HS Steyn, whom he wished to talk to about the Lourenço Marques Lottery. Grobler, however, was cute enough to pretend that he did not know what any subsequent discussions between van der Linden and the Secretary might be about. Grobler wrote Steyn a note, which he then conveniently failed to hand over in time for van der Linden to take north with him to Pretoria.

In the interim, smart as a jackal eyeing a chicken-run door, Grobler wrote directly to Steyn, telling him to expect a visit from van der Linden, and enclosing the letter of introduction for handing over personally. Grobler informed Steyn that he did not know what van der Linden wanted to speak to him about but felt sure that Steyn was unlikely to be able to be of assistance. The Secretary for Finance, who may or may not have got to speak to van der Linden, nevertheless kept both letters, which he filed without adding an explanation.[35]

What van der Linden told Naylor about his visit to Steyn is unknown, but by April 1941 George Naylor could take the uncertainty no longer. He instructed his lawyers to write to Steyn asking him to confirm that 'the Treasury does not intend taking any action against him under the regulations and that he may consider the matter closed'. But it was rule 505. The Secretary for Finance was not yet ready to play his final card. He told Naylor that the matter was 'still under consideration', and so the issue rested until the middle of June.[36]

We will never know if van der Linden's intervention with Steyn was decisive, but by then Treasury officials were ready to retrieve the warehouse package and dispose of it entirely. In a 'confidential' handwritten internal memo, one official noted that the 'Standard Bank would appear to be the chief offender in that they accepted deposits to non-resident accounts, and I suggest that we drop the matter and inform Dumat, Pitts & Blaine accordingly'. Ah, yes, chimed in a second, but George Naylor should be 'warned that any further contravention of the emergency regulations would be viewed in a serious light'. It was hilarious, a bit like the Herman Charles Bosman joke that if men on death row did not stop making a noise they would get into 'serious trouble'.

A third official, less frivolous of disposition, advised that the banks should be instructed 'to keep a close check on accounts opened under fictitious names', adding, 'P.S. Secretary [Steyn] agrees that no steps should be taken regarding contravention of the lottery laws.' Monkey business as usual. The Secretary for Finance never formally, personally, signed off on the lottery breach. A few days later, Steyn received a further written confidence-booster when the Reserve Bank's Deputy Chief Cashier informed him that it was 'most unlikely that the banks would knowingly permit the conduct of accounts under fictitious names'. Quite so, even though Steyn and many others had information that pointed to the contrary over a period of at least 20 years. Little wonder, then, that the file on Naylor was subsequently marked 'secret'.[37]

The army and the war had forced a reluctant state bureaucracy to range its artillery power against its supposed financial enemies – Naylor, Rufino and Casqueira. All the King's howitzers and all the King's men, however, refused to engage the lottery or its multinational proprietors meaningfully. The order to fire never came, and the LML, having survived two world wars, was ready to continue the fight through its familiar peacetime guerrilla operations.

But the rules of engagement for gambling proprietors and the state were on the threshold of a profound change, and more especially so when it came to the electoral terrain on which the conflict would be decided. Whereas before and during World War II skirmishes around the legitimacy of dog racing, lotteries and pinball machines were confined largely to white working-class English neighbourhoods along the Witwatersrand, after the war, as the electoral bite of organised labour weakened, the contest shifted progressively towards more affluent middle-class suburbs across the country. As successive Afrikaner nationalist governments discovered, fending off the hopes that stemmed from a shrinking white working-class culture was less problematic than fending off the increasingly sullen resistance of an expanding, economically empowered white middle class, even if the state enjoyed increasing support from neo-Calvinists. A 'national' policy on race that separated people by colour was easier to sell to the electorate than were class resentments among the whites.

The Stalemate Prolonged, circa 1943–1948

For most white South Africans, there were noteworthy differences in the national economy that took shape after Union, in 1910, and then developed until the founding of the republic, in 1961, and into the decades beyond. From 1910 to 1945, an economic depression and a few recessions, between longer periods of prosperity, made for a bumpy, uncertain journey on the long haul to increasing material comfort. By comparison, in the years after World War II, once the safety belts of segregation, apartheid and cheap black labour had been installed and more tightly secured, the journey became much less turbulent. The destination, entrenched white economic privilege, was in sight.

From World War II and into the early 1970s, 'the economy grew rapidly and steadily, with real GDP almost tripling between 1948 and 1970'. The distribution of income was, as so often is the case, uneven, with the share in value of profits over labour 'rising from 38% in 1945 to 47% by 1950'. Even then, despite the occasional dip, per capita income increased by two per cent per annum between the outbreak of the war and the mid-1960s. The National Thrift Movement was hardly a notable success, but the Post Office Savings Bank – about as close as possible to a people's bank – nevertheless reported an increase of about £7.5 million in savings in 1942. Greater disposable income and savings may have helped white workers cope with a brief period of post-war inflation and shortages of certain foods occasioned by exports to more lucrative markets.[38]

Seen only in terms of the policies of major political parties on lotteries – a thoroughly misleading exercise, since there were other, far more important developments crystallising around race issues in the country – the 1943 election results were ominous and revealing. The National Party, the party hoping to usher in a new dispensation in which church and state might be as inseparable as Siamese twins, polled 300 000 votes – more than it had ever achieved. Its leader, the Reverend DF Malan, perhaps realising that urban Afrikaner voters were, as we have seen, far from averse to dog racing and lotteries, was smart enough to maintain a public silence about the 'evil' of gambling. But one did not need to be a true believer to decipher the code built into his parliamentary language. In 1943, Malan had pointedly asked for the 'elimination of all parasitic activities from our economic life'.[39]

In terms of the actual number of seats won, however, Smuts and the ruling UP had increased their share from 72 to 89. It was a false dawn. His party was always uncertain on just how closely church and state should be permitted to dance. The spurious debate in the House on gambling, sanctioned by Hofmeyr, in 1940 had signalled that the kings of shuffle were aware of the need to be seen to do something. But, since they did not have a clue about what to do, they then did what they did best – nothing. The government and senior civil servants were content for Nelson to keep his telescope glued firmly to his right eye while urban constituencies on the East Rand, mostly UP strongholds, were happy enough to gamble on dogs, pin-balls and lotteries.

The Labour Party, older but perhaps no wiser, and with less easy access to the energetic Nationalist lasses it had courted in Pact times, was another largely fooled by the 1943 election results. It increased its number of seats from four to nine and, having learnt a few of the important sidesteps in the shuffle, was occasionally willing to dance into the false dawn with elderly UP members.

Of all those invited to the House party, Labour was the saddest when it came to lotteries. Since the party's inception, almost a half-century earlier, it had argued openly and consistently for a provincial or state lottery. It had sent its senior office bearers on reconnaissance missions to see how lotteries were conducted in India and Ireland and had, for a time, organised and run its own illegal sweepstakes. As the 'socialist' party, it was also the one most ideologically inclined to attempt to keep the churches and the state as separate as possible.

But the Labour Party was terminally ill. The old craft-based white working-class culture, grounded largely in the mining industry, was giving way, at glacial pace, to a more modern, often less skilled, but slightly better-paid dispensation in manufacturing. Its members were becoming available for co-option into a racially segregated middle class, and to confirm their changing status by voting for the UP or the nationalists. And as the country gradually eased away from class- to colour-based electoral issues, the Labour Party was reduced to the remnants of stubborn white working-class redoubts.

In 1915, still very much in the ascendant at a time when Rufe Naylor was assiduously cultivating political links with the party, Labour secured ten per cent of the national vote and had four seats in the House of Assembly. After the failed revolution of 1922, and approaching the zenith of its political arc, the party garnered 15 per cent of the national vote in 1924 and, with 18 seats, entered a pact with the nationalists that lasted until 1933. It was an era when Paul van der Linden's long-standing nationalist credentials stood the vibrant LML in good stead.

By 1938, however, the Labour Party was well into its long walk into the electoral wasteland of white politics. Van der Linden was forced to use a back door in the UP to try and safeguard the lottery's wartime cross-border financial transactions. By then, Labour's percentage of the national vote had fallen to six per cent. In 1943, about five per cent of the national vote earned it nine seats, while that number fell to three per cent in 1948. And there sat the Labour Party, waiting in the undertaker's parlour, a crumpled lottery ticket protruding from the breast pocket of a frayed suit. In 1958, the bell finally tolled: with 0.23 per cent of the white vote, the party failed to win a seat.

It is misleading to suggest that the fortunes of the LML offer a perfect parallel to the decline of the Labour Party and rise of the white middle classes. Nevertheless, even without clear-cut definitions and hard data, it would be interesting to plot those trajectories on the same sheet. But, in the absence of readily identifiable axes and supporting statistics, the best that can be done is to interrogate the silences, track spending patterns on various other forms of gambling and pick up on a few fragments of the Naylor family's history.

World War II ushered in a shift in management roles of the renewed LML concession that Rufe Naylor's ageing brothers, Peter Charles and George Sylvester, acquired at the start of the war. The brothers, both in their sixties, were preparing to pass the baton to a second generation of Naylors, to those sons who had not necessarily acquired professional qualifications but become successful, solidly middle-class citizens, or better. George, the younger of the two, pinned his hopes on his son, Norman, who took care of his interest in the lottery but during the war left for New South Wales, where he died in 1943.

Peter Charles, an inveterate gambler, was always interested in dog and horse racing, and would bet on most things, sometimes incurring huge losses. At one point in the 1930s, he was forced to sell the family furniture to meet gambling debts, and at the start of the war lost a cattle farm to his passion but then gained another, in the Magaliesberg, by calling in debts. He claimed to be a 'director' of a timber company but, in truth, there is nothing to suggest that he had any full-time occupation other than gambling. By the time the Naylor family ran into trouble with the Reserve Bank, in 1941, he was ready to pass on his share of the concession to his son, Stanley – 'Stan' – and then duly did so.[40]

Under new stewardship, and profiting from the government's willingness to rely on the three monkeys as guardians of the state's interests, the lottery did reasonably well. A cultivated ignorance in government circles over the 1943–1948 electoral cycle was of considerable help. Stan Naylor took over the luxury home, in Houghton, and retained the downtown office, along with the desk with secret compartments and the names of those willing to provide advance warning about impending police raids. He later became involved with Master Products and the Atlas Screw Company, which may have signalled a scaling-back of his own interests in the lottery. But, if dog racing and football pools were anything to go by, the gambling industry remained in fine fettle. For the first time ever, a decade passed without a Naylor lottery prosecution.

Profiting from the changes in class composition that saw some whites spilling over the old working-class weirs of the East Rand, new dog-racing tracks were built in more affluent and accessible downstream locations. Racing at the Wanderers and Wembley stadia, in Johannesburg, provided Afrikaner municipal, railway and other workers in Booysens, Braamfontein, Mayfair and Vrededorp with ready access to new outlets. Like the pinball horror of the 1930s, the popularity and spread of dog racing upset cultural warriors and Afrikaner nationalist ideologues.

HF Verwoerd, then a newspaper editor, warned that accelerated proletarianisation and urbanisation meant that poor Afrikaners were in
danger not only of losing their old nationalist cultural consciousness
but of becoming deracinated working-class internationalists.[41]

Many post-war priests and politicians, sensing that the cultivation
of white nationalism was bearing electoral fruit, hoped to further narrow the gap between church and state. A close alignment between the
two would provide a strong foundation for a more authoritarian and
focused regime, one that could deal firmly with the 'native problem'.
But, in truth, it was not so much a black problem the country was
facing as a white one – how to come up with a simple ideological
'solution' that catered for the racism of the enfranchised.

God and gambling offered one useful, if indirect, way of cultivating white religious-political unity. A few influential Afrikaner dominees, some University of Potchefstroom-trained, found that adding a
zealous Anglophone minister or two helped strengthen the Calvinist
cement needed to construct a more robust Protestant bridge across
the river of dog-racing evil that swirled beneath them. One of them
was Archibald Kidwell. Old Faithful erupted regularly into a shower
of letters to the editor on the subject, even though he no longer resided
among the workers of the East Rand. His new house was in Parkview,
home of the chattering middle classes, nestled securely below the mine
owners' mansions looking out from their perches on the Parktown
and Westcliff koppies.[42] Led by the reverends William Nicol and
AA Meiring, the united Protestants assembled an anti-racing coalition
that, in addition to the churches, boasted the support of 180 welfare
bodies and three-score youth organisations – with over 18 000 members – as well as 100 school principals and the welfare department of
the Johannesburg City Council.[43]

Even with all that middle-class muscle on display, the Christian coalition might not have been comfortable demonstrating on the East Rand, or
in working-class Braamfontein or Vrededorp. But central Johannesburg
held no terrors. In March 1946, a thousand people attended a meeting
in the City Hall and unanimously adopted a resolution opposing all dog
racing. Afrikaner purists, following church dogma, confronted the 'evil'
directly, but the English clergy, who along with their congregants often
thought of themselves as more educated, modern and progressive than

their Afrikaner counterparts, presented arguments that appealed more to the statists within their ranks. They were concerned that dog racing imperilled the 'stewardship of money and time'.[44] Ah, there it was – time and money! The ideological grease and spray needed for a successful economy. Marx and Weber would be forgiven a smile.

Afrikaans- and English-speaking middle-class representatives readily conceded that the stewardship of time and money was important when it came to dog racing and the profligate white working classes. Indeed, they saw it as their Christian duty to enhance the well-being of those less fortunate than themselves. But what of the lottery? Unlike a decade earlier, when the issues of lotteries and pinball machines were cast as Satanic consorts, nothing had been explicitly linked to the dog-racing 'evil' at the City Hall meeting. Had the working classes fallen out of love with the lottery? Or were even the middle classes tiring of the UP's silence and shuffle routine around the issue?

Some may indeed have been growing weary. Well, certainly in the white middle-class suburb of Craighall Park, in the parliamentary constituency of Johannesburg North, where, a few months later, Hofmeyr was preparing for what was destined to be the election of the epoch. A few influential constituents had very different ideas from Hofmeyr, a Baptist-Presbyterian militant when it came to civic duty and lotteries. His election committee, with an eye on the 1948 election, wanted him to come out in favour of a state lottery. It would dry up the flow of funds, not only to Lourenço Marques but also to other increasingly competitive and popular sweepstakes based in Malta, Southern Rhodesia and Ireland. Such monies, they argued, were best retained within the country and redirected into supporting local hospitals and needy charities. But Hofmeyr was having none of it. When they persisted, he did as he so often did and threatened to resign on principle. That settled their little 'tussle'.[45]

The UP was not alone in experiencing difficulties when it came to determining how deeply dog racing, lotteries, pinball machines and sweepstakes were rooted in the various classes, or how more explicit policies might be punished through the withholding of votes. The ascending National Party was not much clearer. Calvin was an assured guide when it came to the broad issue of 'gambling' but of almost no help when it came to managing the gaming interests of the rich or the middle classes – the financial and moral backbone of church and state alike. Like the UP, the nationalists knew better than to attempt to dismantle the horse-racing industry, even if they were ready to come down harder on bookmakers, who happened to be drawn, in disproportionately large numbers, from Catholic and Jewish communities.[46]

But middle-class moralists in the National Party were more certain what to do at the other end of the spectrum, with dog races and the working classes. Fortunately for the party, it had nothing to say about dog racing before the 1948 election; the hopelessly discombobulated UP had done all the dirty work for it. The shuffle masters, having heard the middle-class music in the City Hall and worried about what it might credibly present at the hustings, decided that it would take no more nonsense from the weakening Labour Party and the white working class. In mid-1947, the UP used its majority in the Provincial Council to announce the end of dog racing on the Rand.

Despite having won the 1948 election, the National Party was not yet out of the gambling woods. Indeed, in a way, the City Hall meeting and the UP's opportunistic ban on dog racing had complicated its in-house problems with activists. In clerical garb, the National Party had provided conductors for the City Hall concert, but it had done little by way of thanking its cultural nationalists directly. It had to demonstrate that it was serious about the broader problem of gambling, but, like the shufflers that preceded it, it was uncertain about how exactly it could push ahead on the chronic lottery issue without provoking some middle-class muttering. The answer, drawing on a red herring that swam uninvited into the sea of public opinion, was inspired.

In taking on the football pools, the nationalists found a target that all Protestant ministers would approve of but that would strike hardest at the English-speaking working class, who, in any case, were mostly UP or Labour Party supporters. Under the National Party, priests and politicians could cooperate more closely. God's work and that of the party became inseparable.

Based on correctly predicting the results of league matches played by clubs spawned in the cities of imperial England during the tail end of the industrial revolution, football pools had been around in South Africa for more than two decades without arousing the ire of the meddling classes unduly. But, in 1948, the year of the nationalist triumph and a few months after the ban on dog racing came into effect, there had been a notable upsurge in working-class interest in the pools. Some of it, it seems, was directed from Anglophone Bulawayo, in Southern Rhodesia.[47] The slightest whiff of 'social evil' set the nostrils of Satan sniffers a-twitching. A new round of chasing after law and order followed. A vendor of football pools was charged with promoting games of chance. But, as had happened during the great pinball panic, magistrates and judges were forced to concede that the pools contained elements of both skill and chance. Yet again, attacks by the public prosecutors were thwarted.

With the breeze of public opinion at their backs, and encouraged by their success in having seen off the dog-racing fraternity, the united Protestant churches, women's associations, youth organisations and school principals set their sights on doing the double and getting football pools outlawed. Several deputations descended upon the office of the new Minister of Justice.[48] The minister, CR Swart, a lanky man raised with a ramrod-straight nationalist backbone, was not given to swaying before gusts of legal uncertainty, and within months introduced the Prohibition of Sports Pools Bill of 1949 to a House of Assembly that sometimes doubled as a House of God.

'Blackie' Swart – more of an 'I' than a 'we' minister – told the House that he had assured deputations that the 'evil' would be halted in its tracks. Echoing Smuts, he said, 'I will put a stop to this kind of thing if the courts could not deal with it successfully.' 'This whole system was an evil one that had a bad influence on our sport-loving people.' The new law would prohibit the circulation of sports pools coupons and prizes – defined as widely as the Kalahari Desert – regardless of whether they originated from within or beyond the country. As with lotteries, the Postmaster General was empowered to intercept cash or coupons, but the maximum penalty would be raised to a fine of £500 or two years in prison. 'Furthermore, it is provided that no newspaper or any printing works may place, publish or print any notice or advertisements for sports pools.'[49] It was the old, cold, lottery law warmed up for breakfast.

The tougher penalties hinted at the coming of a new and progressively more authoritarian and socially repressive regime. Even old UP shufflers, pretending that the Pools Bill was somehow an extension of their own efforts at eradicating the pinball menace, felt that a loyal and patriotic opposition had to commend Swart's new initiative. The UP turned chameleon, which, it felt, was better than playing possum. 'We on this side of the House', squeaked Colin Steyn, 'support the Minister in this Bill.' That was the same Colin Steyn who, as Minister of Justice, in 1939, did not want to commit himself 'one way or another' when it came to new gambling legislation. Losing the election had seen the UP sprout hair in a few places that no gentleman dared be seen scratching in public should it ever become itchy.[50]

With the UP as keen as the nationalists to be seen as matchmaker between church and state, it was left to an outsider to question the logic and wisdom of any closer relationship. Sam Kahn was a genial communist elected by Africans in the western Cape Province to represent them in a national assembly that was about to be purged of 'undesirable' political elements such as himself. He saw the bill as more common-law marriage than heaven-sanctioned union.

The situation was farcical. 'The Minister knows', Kahn said, that 'it is idle to pass laws that people will not observe.' Kahn knew what he was talking about. Back in the year of the Bolshevik Revolution, in 1917, he and a few Jewish radicals had been prosecuted for illegal gambling in Johannesburg. Following an old Ambrose Bierce dictum, Kahn reminded the House that, although not prohibited by legislation, there 'was a far more important and dangerous form of gambling carried on in the Stock Exchange'. The bill did not deal with the sport of kings, and he sensed it was a stalking horse. The nationalists' real quarry would be revealed soon enough. In a prophetic sideswipe, he suggested that 'it was going to become a criminal offence in the future for anybody to buy a ticket in the Irish Sweep or the Rhodesian Sweep' – the lotteries.[51]

The bill, Kahn argued, was a class-targeted 'puritanical measure' pressing hardest on the working man who saw 'nothing wrong in a harmless flutter for 3 or 6d', or who was 'looking for some form of escape from his financial problems under capitalism'. 'This is kill-joy legislation', he added, and the 'Bill should be called not a Sports Pool Bill, but a Spoil Sports Bill.'[52] The House loved the bill and it passed into law by a substantial majority. The nationalists already knew that the days of 'communist' views were numbered.

The Rise of the South African Police State: Neo-Fascists and the Massacre of the Mails, circa 1950–1965

Viewing their part of the world only through the racist monocle that white voters increasingly preferred between 1949 and the mid-1960s – the economy – South Africa was a runaway success. There were good reasons for seeing it that way. The kickstart that came when the gold standard was abandoned in the 1930s provided momentum that was augmented by devaluation, in 1949, and by the opening of the new Free State goldfields in the 1950s. Mining, along with agriculture and manufacturing, all benefited as gross domestic product almost tripled and per capita income nearly doubled. When set against other indicators, however, 'the South African economy grew less rapidly than most other similar countries' in what was a 'golden age of capitalist development globally'. 'Inflated earnings and living standards for white South Africans', however, belied an economy that was far 'less competitive internationally'.[53]

Accelerating economic development drove white South Africans towards ever better times, as manifested in an emerging consumer culture, even as black South Africans, deprived of the most basic rights of citizenship, fell ever further behind in their pursuit of socio-economic security. By the mid-1970s, car ownership among whites in South Africa was exceeded only by that in the United States. Enhanced material prosperity induced social changes that, in turn, informed party politics where, as we will note, it posed difficult questions of Calvinists intent on restricting gambling amid growing white affluence.[54]

Led by General White Fear, eyes blinkered, kitbags stuffed and rifles at the ready, and with military bands playing patriotic medleys, the South African electorate struck out bravely on the long march it had chosen into the woods of apartheid, authoritarianism and international isolation. At each enforced election stop – in 1953, 1955, 1961 and 1966 – voters welcomed yet more smug nationalists into their ranks – apparatchiks, cheerleaders, lieutenants, racists and neo-fascists with serious misgivings about democracy and democratic institutions.

The National Party gained 15, 9, 2 and then 21 seats in four apartheid elections spanning barely a decade. The UP lost seats as fast as the nationalists gained them – 8, 4, 4 and then 10. The Labour Party, pulling aside its blinkers, got a glimpse of a signpost suggesting that citizens' rights might come in colours other than white and was lined up before the firing squad. In 1953, it lost a seat, and then lost five in 1958 and then, in 1961, was put out of its electoral misery when it failed to win a seat. Given hard choices, colour usually trumped class.

The police force, which had been purged of extremist paramilitary right-wing elements by the Smuts government during World War II, was put through the wringer for a second time – this time to rid the unfolding order of stained UP undergarments. Once that cycle was complete, the thinking of many senior uniformed officers was, as a popular radio jingle had it, 'whiter than white'. Army, navy and police personnel loved the new unwritten rules. Political repression spawned resistance and the need for bigger budgets and yet more force to contain it. Undemocratic regimes open 'peace-time' political spaces in which the armed and secret forces can play more important roles. A slew of politically repressive laws, such as the Suppression of Communism Act of 1950 and the Criminal Law Amendment Act and Public Safety Act, both of 1953, gave new purpose to the security division of the South African Police.

Proactive legislation by a new no-nonsense government lifted spirits in the uniformed division of the police and raised hopes of its being given new tools to work on old problems. The police, unlike most military personnel, lived within the cities and suburbs where they, along with the politicians and priests, were expected to discourage the breeding and spread of the 'social evils' that upset some in the urban middle classes. The uniforms had reason to enter the 1950s more hopefully than they had the previous decade since the state had already gifted them legislation for the suppression of pinballs and football pools in 1939 and 1949. The problem was that not all forms of gambling lay within the confines of the working class or, as with horse racing, were exempted from scrutiny because of roots among the more privileged. Card games for gain and the lotteries, for example, had an elasticity of appeal that often stretched well into the reaches of the middle and upper classes.

The 1950s saw the launching of the first atomic submarine and the first orbital satellite. In South Africa, the police were tasked with curbing gambling and lotteries using Calvinist handcuffs forged by the Volksraad in the 19th century. Laws No. 6 of 1889, 7 of 1890 and 1 of 1892 – focused on cards and dice, gambling dens and lotteries – were not fit for purpose and were deeply resented by police officers. They seldom hesitated to bring their complaints to the attention of their superiors, who were almost as quick to pass them on to the fiery Minister of Justice, CR Swart.

From the moment the National Party assumed office, in 1948, the police complained about how they were fighting gambling and lottery-running with their hands tied behind their backs.[55] It could not have helped that the uniforms remained handicapped at a time when besuited security types were being granted arbitrary powers that circumvented the courts. Why should the repression of 'social evil' lag behind political oppression when the Afrikaner churches and the state were moving closer together and justifying a manifestly unethical regime? Could it be that the National Party, once in power, for all its talk, could do the shuffle just as well as its languid UP predecessors? Surely, old working-class grievances could not possibly hold the new order at bay when the power of organised white labour was all but lost to parliament?

The shift in the thinking of the law enforcement authorities could be traced back to 1949, when the police drafted a bill for dealing with 'gambling dens', which, unlike lotteries, centred on middle-class Catholic and Jewish immigrants rather than white workers, who were largely Protestant. Law No. 6 of 1899 specified that only premises that allowed unrestricted access could be deemed 'gambling dens' capable of undermining public morality. Enforcing so antiquated a law required many hours of expensive police surveillance of facilities that were often surrounded by African guards who provided early warnings of police spying or raids.[56] Moreover, those running the dens would claim – and it was difficult to distinguish or prove otherwise – that they were engaged in private games of chance with friends or relatives. To get around the problem, the police wanted all 'private gambling' outlawed.

The law dealing with gaming houses in the Transvaal, the Deputy Commissioner of Police protested in 1949, had 'become obsolete'. 'From a Police point of view, it is considered necessary', wrote the

Acting Commissioner, 'that all laws dealing with gambling, betting and gaming be revised.' His successor, the Commissioner, pointed out that 'as the law stands at present [it] is practically impossible to obtain a conviction', and that it gave rise to a 'feeling of frustration' in the force.[57] The police, rather than strongman Blackie Swart, the minister, were leading the charge for a change in the law.

By the end of that year, Swart was finding the pressure from his senior officers to amend the laws difficult to resist. A high-powered meeting at the Palace of Justice in the presence of the Chief Law Advisor, REG Rosenow, was held on 20 December. The police outlined their difficulties in implementing the gambling laws in Johannesburg and proposed new legislation. But Rosenow, while conceding that enforcing the existing law was practically impossible, was not convinced that new legislation giving the police more discretion would solve long-standing problems, and informed the minister accordingly.[58]

The Chief Law Advisor, perhaps a hand-me-down official in the Department of Justice from the previous UP administration, was old school – a muddle-through, pragmatic, shuffle man. Rosenow's memorandum to Swart – who, for all his fire-eating nationalism, was a lawyer by profession – was filled with a certain cautious wisdom. In his opinion, previous judgments provided adequate guidelines for those seeking to implement the law. The bill the police proposed was a classic case of 'the cure being worse than the disease'. Rosenow's suggestion was to let the matter rest on the 'principles that had been developed by the courts over the passage of time' and do nothing. When the police returned to the fray with new suggestions for a revision of the draft law, they were curtly dismissed as being 'destructive rather than constructive'.[59]

The police were miffed. The Deputy Commissioner told the Acting Commissioner that if the police bill proposed was going nowhere, 'then little if anything could be done to curtail the type of gambling taking place in the [Witwatersrand] Divisions at present'. The uniforms sulked. For three years there was not a single raid on a 'gambling den'. In truth, there was not much to deal with anyhow. By their own admission, such gatherings were usually few and unrestricted access impossible to demonstrate. The 'offenders' later included some Afrikaners and English speakers, along with men drawn from the 'medical and racing community'. But, for the most part, it was the usual suspects – bridge clubs, Jews playing their much-loved Faro and Klaberjass, Greeks drawn 'from all walks of life, and some Lebanese won't-works'.[60]

It was pathetic. But the uniformed police did not want to be left behind the Special Branch, or the electorate. Politicians and Protestants, intent on fashioning a more segregated world, sought to keep Africans as well as Catholic immigrants at arm's length, while the Immorality Act of 1957 attempted to ensure the ethnic and racial purity of a Calvinist 'nation' that might otherwise spend its time copulating with women of colour. As in nature, totalitarianism abhors a vacuum, and just as the political domain demanded cleansing from street to state level, so society's alleys and byways demanded new sanitary measures. The police watchdogs gave their minister no rest and just continued barking.

The noise from the canine unit was incessant throughout 1950. The police amended their draft bill and harried a Department of Justice intent on protecting the minister. The police were fobbed off with the reply that 'the matter was receiving the attention of the law advisors', who were in no hurry. Patience wore thin and, late in 1951, the police were told that 'the Minister has instructed Law Advisors to endeavour to draft legislation'. By mid-1952, growling gave way to some snarling. 'The matter is urgent', the Commissioner of Police informed the Secretary for Justice, 'and it will be appreciated if the proposed amendments to the Gambling Law could receive early attention'. But, in bureaucratic space, paper moves through time in ways that defy an Einstein's understanding. Urgency grew whiskers longer than Calvin's and a consensus was eventually reached in late 1954. It had taken half a decade.[61]

Even then the Minister of Justice's proposed changes to existing legislation on gambling houses were tucked into the General Law Amendment Act 62 of 1955, rather than in a new, stand-alone Act. Police powers of arrest and confiscation were extended into domestic domains and private clubs. 'I hope', the minister told the House, that 'the objection will not be raised that we are now violating the private sanctity of the home.' And then came the classic riders that frequently accompany creeping totalitarianism: 'I want to give the assurance that the police will act carefully ... People who play cards in private homes need not to worry about this.' The Commissioner of Police was equally comforting, the law was 'clear' and 'each case will be treated on its merits'. The law, it was being suggested, rested on discretionary fairness and the revamped police behaving in a considerate, socially responsible fashion.[62]

But, amid an erosion of civil liberties that started at the political core and was finding its way to the margins of white society, there was a strange silence. Card and dice games in clubs or homes, along with football pools, were going the same way as pinball machines and dog racing before them. The East Rand, home to the dwindling white working class, was being cleansed of 'social evils' and Old Nick was surely on the back foot. But what was he up to? In the past, whenever an 'evil' had been singled out for attention from the state it had, almost invariably, been shackled to a terrible succubus, the one given to seducing bachelors, husbands and most working men – the cursed lottery.

As white society assumed more of a middle- than a working-class profile, so there was less of substance for churches and activists to link lotteries to as part of the supposedly twinned evils that caused so much moral and social mayhem during the interwar years. For most of the 1950s, there was eerie silence around the question of lotteries. It was as if the lottery, like a stray cat that had taken to sleeping in the lounge, had become so familiar to the priests and politicians, let alone to the police and people, that they had given up trying to shoo it out. Perhaps they sensed that the lottery was a cat with nine lives, one the state had been trying to get rid of for more than 60 years.

The LML concession had been put out to tender for renewal in 1949, months after the nationalists assumed control in Pretoria. The Mozambican administration knew that without access to the Witwatersrand, the lottery was worthless. So, too, did the South Africans. Both parties were intent on keeping to an unwritten understanding that the transnational lottery fell beyond the purview of both. Neither government wished to jeopardise the flow of cheap black migrant labour to the Rand coal and gold mines, which, in terms of real wages, saw indentured workers earning less each year. But the prospect of feeding off white affluence was no longer confined to Lourenço Marques, and other regional players were taking a much greater interest in southern wealth.

As expected, the renewed concession accommodated a second generation of Naylor men as major partners responsible for sales in South Africa. Unlike their fathers, however, Stan and, to a lesser extent, Norman could no longer call on Paul van der Linden, whose services dated back to Rufe's time. It was a sign not only of the ravages of time individually but also that the lottery, which had once enjoyed a near-monopoly, was no longer spreading out across the Union at the rate that it had during the interwar years.

Cash-flush Stan kept the lottery office in downtown Johannesburg running, along with the inherited hardware of the trade and a few soft-touch policemen in CID headquarters. A third-generation Naylor, a grandson also named Peter, recalls visiting the office as a boy with his father in the 1950s and watching as the scramble-and-hide routine was activated when Stan received a phone call from the police warning about an impending raid. But, if the underlying integrity of the lottery security system was to remain in place, and the gambling squad not to become totally discredited through a conspicuous lack of success, not all raids could be allowed to end in failure.

Taken as a whole, the 1950s were remarkable for how few convictions there were for lottery offences. Between them, a decrepit lottery law, bribery, a lack of civilian activism in prosperous times and a lack of ministerial enthusiasm all fed into the apparent indifference of the police. The exception was in 1952, when an ambitious Deputy Commissioner of Police snapped at Blackie Swart's heels in the hope of prodding him to pass a new gambling law. As had happened so often over the years, an undercover detective was sent to Lourenço Marques to determine whether the lottery was 'straight' and, unsurprisingly, came back with the usual answer – it was.

From a police perspective it was a disappointing answer since it failed to add momentum to their push for new legislation. Sensing that he could not get at the lottery at the point of origin, the Deputy Commissioner decided instead to squeeze the operation at the Johannesburg end. Detectives had no difficulty in identifying the Naylors' inner-city agents – a rather sad grouping of elderly white males marooned in blocks of downtown poverty, hoping to supplement their incomes with Friday-night beer money. The only interesting discovery was Charlie Delwani, an African runner in the Western

Native Township. Africans, including miners, had been buying lottery tickets since World War I, but Delwani's presence hinted at the fact that, as the old white working class continued to shrink, the Naylors were hoping that some of the slack in sales would be taken up by the newer, expanding, low-paid, urban black working class.

In 1952, the police alarm never sounded in the Naylor Building and a raid yielded Stan, 31-year-old 'company director', and Norman, 33-year-old 'clerk'. The foot soldiers were picked up at various points in the city. The magistrate and prosecutor, like those before them, were not thrilled at the prospect of anchovy-snatching. What they needed was to catch, tag and release a great white. The charges against Delwani, Norman and one other were withdrawn, and a few old egg-on-tie salesmen had the cash found on them – one had £95 – returned. Stan Naylor was found guilty of 'being in charge of the lottery office' and 'fined £50 with the alternative of two months' imprisonment with hard labour'.[63] It was hardly a triumph for the state.

As had happened before, in the period leading up to the amended law on gaming houses, the police then took no further action against those operating the Lourenço Marques Lottery. Instead, the gambling squad earned its keep by conducting occasional raids on East Rand cafés, checking on pinball machines. But, as with the lottery, pinball machines were not without an allure of their own, nor were café owners beyond drawing the police into their orbit. Two senior officers became so enamoured of the light-flashing, audio-intoxicating devices that café owners clubbed together to buy them pinball machines, at £250 each, for installation at the policemen's homes. Rather unusually, the officers were charged and successfully prosecuted for bribery.[64]

Significantly, the 1950s, a decade of increasingly repressive political and social legislation, saw a rise in the number of complaints about gambling coming not from the old stalwarts – the churches and civic associations – but via anonymous letters to the police.[65] The more authoritarian, the more corrupt and the greater discretionary police power becomes, the more fearful the citizenry. And the more fearful the citizenry, the stronger the police become.

Yet, even as the police state was taking shape under the guidance of zealous nationalists, the decades-old public silence around lotteries continued. The police, ever more muscular when dealing with deviations

from white racist political norms, found it difficult to understand why
the government, supported by one or two rock-hard Protestant cabinet ministers, continued to content itself with a marshmallow-soft
approach to lotteries. The hidden link between the LML and indentured black mine labour eluded them, and, as we shall see, there were
other reasons for their neglecting to act against several new lotteries
that appeared in the 1950s. It was not as if the police had given up hope,
but, when they did point out the need for new legislation, they were
gesturing to deaf men who also clutched white sticks.

Uniformed police in the big cities were those most likely to point to
the gap between election chatter and action. In 1954, a sub-inspector
in the detective department, in Johannesburg, reminded his uniformed
superior about the inadequacies of the existing provincial ordinances
and appealed for consolidated national gambling legislation. His letter
prompted the Commissioner and senior officers across the country,
who, when asked for a written opinion, were of one mind. Gambling,
pinballs and lotteries were all out of control. The situation called for
immediate, drastic, remedial action from the Rip van Winkle legal
draftsmen who had nodded off, quite happily, back in 1890.

The high-ups in the force, reading the political climate of growing intolerance correctly, were in no mood to tolerate ambiguities.
Lotteries should be prohibited, and the mere possession of a ticket
would be construed as an offence. It was unthinkable that prizes and
results of lottery draws could be either broadcast live, over the socially
undesirable Lourenço Marques Radio, which was being beamed over
the Highveld, or published in local magazines or newspapers. What
was needed was consolidated legislation enforced by judges and magistrates who were wont to cough and splutter when asked questions
that demanded a straightforward 'yes' or 'no' answer.

So, yet again, the police drafted legislation: the 'Gambling, Betting
Houses and Lotteries Suppression Bill'. It was a title that, for those of
a frivolous disposition, might have been cut from the same cloth used
by those who had crafted the Suppression of Communism Act. But,
of course, it was not. That was a serious act; its origins lay more with
politicians than with priests. The draft was forwarded to the ministry,
where the secretary knew what to do with it. As before, the draft was
slid into Rip van Winkle's stately old oak cabinet.[66]

Suppression was the watchword of the day, but clearly not all suppressions were of equal importance. And so, the draft lay there, a snake hibernating within the folds of church and state, waiting for the season to change so that it could emerge with a new skin and go mousing. And as the winter dragged on and on, the reptile's prey multiplied. In 1959, four years after their draft bill, the police listed lotteries, old and new, that were operating freely within a country aspiring to republican status. The world was closing in on South Africa, and lotteries in Northern Rhodesia (Ndola, Kitwe, Mufulira), Southern Rhodesia (Auto-lot), Lourenço Marques, Ireland and Malta had infiltrated the affluent south.[67] What had started as a problem arising from a complex relationship with Mozambique, around World War I, had assumed a wider regional and international dimension. The difference between Calvinist electoral claptrap and the unwillingness of the state to act was there for all to see. The nationalist government talked softly but was wanting of a big stick.

The problem went deeper. The white South African electorate had long since grown accustomed to voting clean and living dirty, to wanting its cake and eating it. It bayed publicly for apartheid and increased segregation while, simultaneously, employing a growing number of African workers and servants. So, too, it supported a government that told them it would clamp down on gambling, pinballs and lotteries while knowing that, in practice, it was probably never going to happen. Having got away with the big racist lies, small ones were somehow less daunting, and the fungus of deceit thrived, since everyone, from top to bottom, knew it but pretended that it did not exist.

Double standards and working misunderstandings underwrote white quotidian life. Hypocrisy embedded itself in perverse forms of consciousness that were sometimes revealed in apparently insignificant things, not excluding the gambling laws. As a high-powered interministerial committee examining the vexed lottery problem reported a few years later:

> Participation in foreign lotteries has been consciously tolerated over many years. It must be conceded that, in this respect, state agencies have been remarkably tolerant of the associated behaviour. Indeed, it was probably indulged in to such an extent that the idea

gradually took root in the public mind that any transgressions
would be silently condoned by the state. Postal items dealing with
lotteries circulated freely – unimpeded – and this might well have
contributed to the idea of condonation by the state.[68]

What the committee would not concede was that state 'tolerance'
was not born of benign indulgence by various governments but a concession won, over half a century and more, by the Naylor family and
resistance that had its roots in the culture of the English-speaking
white working class on the East Rand.

But, just as the police were began to despair of help coming from the
government in their struggle against the lotteries, there were signs that
the season of state somnambulance was coming to an end. The snake
was stirring. It started around 1961, when the nationalists regained the
beloved republican status lost in the Anglo-Boer War. Economic progress and republican fervour boosted self-confidence and left nationalists with the sense that they were fully in control of their reactionary
racial policies and any international consequences that they might
entail. As pertinently, Prime Minister Verwoerd (in office 1958–1966)
made appointments to two key cabinet positions that were ideally
suited to mounting a counterattack on the 'parasitic' lottery invaders –
the ministries of Justice and of Posts and Telecommunications.

Dr Albert Hertzog, son of JBM, was appointed Minister of Posts
and Telecommunications in 1958. He held the post for a decade,
becoming one of the longest-serving cabinet ministers in the country's
short history. Given his implacable opposition to the introduction
of television and the insidious English 'liberalism' it might give rise
to, the nomenclature of his portfolio might best be viewed as being
partly humorous. Hertzog was a courteous and urbane conservative
even among the most stalwart of rural conservatives. A child of the
Nederduitse Gereformeerde Kerk, the Oxford and Leiden-educated
minister – who eventually left the National Party because of its failings
and went on establish an ultra-right-wing party – was anything but a
joke. The Post Office Act, dating back to the formation of Union, in
1910, along with a later (1953) amendment to the Criminal Law Act,
provided the minister and Postmaster General with the authority to
intercept items of mail, including those dealing with lotteries. The

Dr Albert Hertzog (LEFT) and John Vorster (RIGHT), the Afrikaner nationalist strong-men who, in 1964 and 1965, orchestrated the demise of all lotteries operating in South Africa.

minister, who might well have felt at home in Calvin's Geneva, was no friend of lotteries.

His partner at the Ministry of Justice was, if anything, even more daunting. Balthazar Johannes (John) Vorster was destined to become prime minister after Verwoerd's assassination, and, later still, president. An ardent nationalist since his student days, John Vorster was a law graduate of the elitist University of Stellenbosch. Stellenbosch, along with the University of Potchefstroom, provided the ideological loin-cloths used to cover apartheid policies when clever Afrikaners offered rationalisations for bare-arsed institutionalised racism. Vorster's anti-imperialist, right-wing sympathies got him interned during World War II as a 'general' in the neo-Nazi Ossewabrandwag. As Minister of Justice (1961–1966) he was midwife to the most repressive political legislation the country had ever known.[69] He was, however, not devoid of logic or a sense of humour, once describing South Africa as the 'hap-piest police state in the world'. He was only half correct; even a broken clock is right twice a day. For the outcomes-driven Vorster, lotteries were less about flouting Calvinist injunctions than about exercising total political control.

Hertzog and Vorster, unlikely twins, were uncomfortable in the modern world and grew apart politically in the latter part of the 'Swinging Sixties'. In the early years of the decade, however, they were more than ready to cooperate when it came to the suppression of lotteries. Hertzog always wanted to turn back the clock; Vorster was more interested in how the thing worked.

Ironically, the cabinet's interest in lotteries may have come from chirping emanating from the oldest white working-class thicket on the Witwatersrand. Answering a parliamentary question, in 1963, the Minister of the Interior said that he had received more than 70 petitions 'from the East Rand' pleading for the introduction of a state lottery, each signed by between 25 and 50 people.[70] Hertzog saw the petitions as the tip of an iceberg that needed more careful examination. Since January that year, using powers vested in him as minister, the Post Office had intercepted thousands of inward- and outward-bound letters suspected of being connected to the lotteries. It went back further. Indeed, between 1 December 1963 and 22 February 1964, in just three months, the Post Office intercepted 1 045 000 items sent from abroad by lottery agents to addresses within South Africa. Of those, less than 100 were found to contain correspondence not directly related to lotteries.[71]

The findings were disturbing. The lottery law, supposedly a dyke protecting public morals from what could no longer be termed a 'social evil' without raising a giggle, did not have a hole in it; the wall itself had collapsed. How could one build a solid foundation for a white 'nation' when many people, already reasonably well-off, yearned for wealth without working for it? But, coming in the wake of the republic, the breach in the dyke triggered other deep-seated concerns. How could the republic assert its independence and assume its rightful place in the world when it was sending more money out of the country through lottery purchases than it was getting in by way of prizes?

There were other problems about to become even more pressing. As part of the 'grand apartheid' vision of 'separate development', a collaborating black chiefly elite in the Transkei was about to take control of a legislative assembly as a prelude to, one day, becoming an independent state within the republic's borders. What if the Transkei chose to set up its own lottery? Would not other tribal authorities do the same once they, too, had partaken of a delusion-inducing potion? What if the godless crossed the borders and went gambling as they did in Mozambique? More worrying still, what if the 'wind of change' that Harold Macmillan had warned about, in 1960, started howling across southern Africa and the High Commission territories of Basutoland, Bechuanaland and Swaziland became independent? Would they, too, not want to set up lotteries capable of sucking the financial lifeblood out of the great white republic?[72]

The future of lotteries was surely far more complex than met the eye. The government, peering inwards, was constantly having to re-educate the white electorate and provide voters with a vocabulary tailored to new-think as it tried to prevent a collision with the future. The ox-wagon of state, unable to find a way forward, turned around to face a sun setting fast on civil liberties. On 28 November 1963, Hertzog took his idea of setting up an interministerial committee (IMC) to the cabinet, to explore ways of preventing South African citizens from participating in foreign lotteries, not excluding the High Commission territories and the Transkei.[73] Justice was blind, but there was nothing wrong with John Calvin's eyes; he saw everything. The minister might have been fretting about ethics and finance, but his colleagues were far more taken with the regional and international political dimensions of the problem.

At a time when 'strong' men in the cabinet were becoming as feared as they were revered, the political twins already stood out as nationalist notables. Vorster, bulldog-stocky and golf-playing, was physically imposing. Hertzog, by contrast, slim and trim to the point of appearing emaciated, eschewed alcohol and, strictly speaking, would not even qualify as a teetotaller. Visitors to his office would be offered coffee or tea while he confined himself to sipping whey from a flask. But, when it came to fighting lotteries, he was a man among men, a man in a hurry, and keen to show off his political biceps.

Hertzog designed the architecture and administration of the IMC to spare his cabinet colleagues time and effort. It left them in no doubt as to how determined he was about halting the invasion of the lottery mercenaries. The IMC would report to him, and *he* would submit its report to the cabinet as the basis for new consolidated legislation. All mundane logistical work would, however, fall to senior departmental officials nominated by their respective cabinet ministers. He, personally, would appoint the chairman of the working subcommittee, while ministers could choose whom to represent them on the subcommittee. It would be an unequivocally state-led process, one that Protestant churches could follow.

And, if a Christian state was going on a crusade against the foreign and the godless, the subcommittee would have to be led by a brave uniformed officer. The choice of Lieutenant General JM Keevy, Commissioner of Police, had much to commend it. Not only would it reassure the cabinet but it would also spike any objections from the Minister of Justice, since Keevy reported to Vorster – himself once a 'general' and leader of an energised jackboot squad.

Hertzog impressed the urgency of the matter on Keevy, who passed it on to Major General RJ van den Bergh, a man ostensibly destined to be his successor as Commissioner, and who came to stand in for him as chairman and convenor for most of the subcommittee proceedings. In addition to van den Bergh, the secretary of the subcommittee was drawn from the police along with the Chief Administrator from the Department of Justice, BJ Parsons. In effect, the security establishment had three representatives on a committee of just six, with the remaining positions filled by senior, sometimes the most senior, administrators from the departments of Finance, the Interior and Posts and Telecommunications. Their superiors, in turn, served on the main IMC.[74]

General van den Bergh mobilised his forces at once. The subcommittee met for the first time before Christmas 1963, within days of the cabinet go-ahead, and continued with its high-octane research and deliberations over the opening months of 1964. Delighted by the interim findings of the subcommittee, Hertzog could not wait to use the data to draw his twin further into a web well spun.

On 12 February, Hertzog wrote to Vorster, lamenting the fact that under existing legislation, the Post Office was obliged, upon request, to return any monies it had confiscated to senders or receivers, limiting its effectiveness in the drive against lotteries. Over six weeks the Post Office had intercepted over R90 000 (about US $125 000 today), at a time when the economy was booming.[75] It was not just the police and Special Branch trying to protect 'the nation'. The Post Office, too, was out on the front line, fighting the good fight.

But the amount that the Post Office pickpockets had got their hands on, in money orders, postal orders and notes, paled next to the sums leaving the country in much-sought-after rands. Intelligence provided to General van den Bergh by the Post Office revealed that hundreds of foreign-based agents were sending lottery tickets to the republic each month. A minority of agents were based in Ireland, Mozambique and Nigeria. The majority, by far, were to be found in Malta (50) and in Northern (100) and Southern (110) Rhodesia.[76] It was those lotteries closest to the fatherland that attracted the most attention.

The monthly Ndola Lottery, with a first prize of R100 000, and generous second and third prizes, as well as 25 Volkswagen cars as consolation prizes, was, by some margin, the most popular of the invaders of the white south. A few Ndola agents flew between the larger urban centres but most, provided with cars, moved freely in and out of country towns and were suspected of delivering large sums, in cash, across the border. A significant amount of those outgoing funds flowed back into South Africa as prizes or donations to local charities each month. The latter were not always without irony. In December 1963, the principal of the Dutch Reformed Church School in Oudtshoorn kept his eyes shut but his hands open when he received a cheque for £100 from the lottery.[77]

General van den Bergh and the subcommittee claimed that 'reliable sources' provided their basis of their assessment of the Ndola Lottery's parameters but acknowledged that information relating to the Southern Rhodesia State Lottery (SRSL), dating back to 1935, was not of the same order. Indeed, the subcommittee relied on the detailed reporting of an enterprising, well-connected journalist in Salisbury to provide it with a reasonable overview of the hated SRSL.[78]

As with the Ndola Lottery, the vast majority of SRSL tickets sold, as well as the prize winners, came from south of the great grey-green greasy Limpopo. According to the unnamed journalist, citing 'authorities':

> The total amount of money paid in from all tickets since the lottery began in 1935 (up to September 1963) was £27 163 040, for which £5 720 274 was paid in Southern Rhodesia and the balance of £21 543 766 was subscribed from beyond Southern Rhodesia's borders ... It is estimated that South Africans have won between £12 000 000 and £14 000 000 from the Southern Rhodesian State

Lottery in prize money since the lotteries began 29 years ago – a
little under £500 000 a year.[79]

On average, over three decades, the SRSL had paid 'more than
17 per cent of the face value of each lottery' and incurred about 20 per
cent in expenses.

By the early 1960s, the LML, which had once dominated the South
African market, was in the third rank of insurgent forces. Over 40
years it had become quite domesticated. Alone among the biggest
contenders, its tickets were issued in English as well as in Afrikaans,
and its prizes rendered only in South African currency – testimony to
how trusted it remained even as the white working class continued to
shrink. The nationalists took no joy from the fact that the lottery was
partly house-trained. Just because the pill was smaller than the other
two did not make it less bitter to swallow.

The brazenness, depth and strength of the enemy forces peddling
tickets within the borders of the fatherland shocked even hardened
whey, if not whisky, drinkers. As soon as Hertzog got the cabinet
go-ahead, he ordered the Postmaster General to engage in unrelent-
ing war on insurgent foreigners. Cardboard-box coffins, stuffed to
the hilt with postal casualties, were stacked and stored out of the sight
of civilians who had voted for discretion and not mass destruction. As
previously noted, in 12 weeks more than a million postal items and
monies related to the lotteries were intercepted, confiscated, trashed
or forwarded to a Cape Town depot to await any claims for refunding.

Amid such huge losses, the lottery insurgents were forced to retreat
from the central Post Office stronghold they had occupied over many
years. The drastic downward adjustment of prize money that followed,
along with a severe cutback in donations to South African charities, testified to the punishment meted out by the patriotic forces. The battle
of the brown envelopes, in 1963, was won by Hertzog and General van
den Bergh's forces and appears to have been decisive. The South African
archives fail to reveal if the Calvinist enforcers won a subterranean war
that may have dragged on for a few more years yet. The real outcome
of the war will become known only when historians have examined
surviving dispatches in the Harare, Lusaka and Maputo archives.

Some idea of the damage sustained by the invaders can, however, be pieced together from the archives in Pretoria. The organisational backbone of the Ndola Lottery was provided by the MOTHs (Memorable Order of Tin Hats) – military veterans of the two world wars – and, within weeks of the South African counterattack, the disruption was so great that the Ndola's January draw had to be rescheduled. On 3 February 1964, the lottery manager in Ndola, DA Foster, spelt out what was happening to one of his stalwart agents, the former Mayor of Simon's Town, Lewis C Gay:

> The interception of mails is almost 100% effective resulting in only a trickle coming through. This has necessitated combining the January, February, and March draws. Being non-profitmaking and due to the fact that we are receiving very little revenue, we had to drastically reduce expenses, necessitating making some 47 of the staff redundant and other stringent economies have had to be effected. It is our considered opinion that the South African Government intend to continue with this clamp down on lottery mail both incoming and outgoing and so as from April we will continue to operate in a small way until such time as we can implement plans from rebuilding. This is a tragedy and when one considers the good that has been done by this Lottery, we are determined to continue, even if on a much smaller scale.[80]

The good achieved by the lottery was said to be extensive. As Foster had previously informed aspirant lottery ticket vendors:

> An immense amount of goodwill exists between this Lottery and the people resident in South Africa. Our prize lists and monthly donations to charity clearly demonstrate that the funds remitted to us are by no means 'one-way traffic'. Hundreds of charities and thousands of people throughout Southern Africa are dependent upon the support of this Lottery – which has never let them down. We produce the best prize list available in the lottery business and ever-increasing donations to charity and other worthy causes.[81]

The sequel to the Post Office squeeze was predictable: 'Owing to the mails being intercepted by the South African Postal Authorities the prize list has been drastically reduced, as also donations to charity.'[82] What Calvin, who took charity and poor relief seriously, would have made of this we know not.

The SRSL, too, suffered a mauling. In 1961, benefiting from the buoyant South African economy, the first prize in the SRSL was increased fivefold, from £10 000 to a whopping £50 000. But once the totalitarian twins, Hertzog and Vorster, gained fuller control of lottery mail passing through the Central Post Office, the SRSL, like its Northern Rhodesian equivalents, had the stuffing knocked out of it. In February 1964, its managers were forced to reduce the first prize to a modest £15 000.[83]

This promising news was summarised by General van den Bergh, reduced to confidential documents and circulated with care. His preliminary findings reassured Hertzog and the Minister of the Interior, Johannes 'Jan' de Klerk – an alumnus of the rumbling Calvinist volcano that was the University of Potchefstroom and father of FW de Klerk – that van den Bergh should push on. Evidence demonstrating that the lotteries were an open financial sore on the republican body would be incorporated into the final report to the IMC.

The General lost no time; his subcommittee report was ready by March 1964. The capture of the Post Office, the invasion of people's mail and the drafting of the report had all been accomplished in three months. The cautious commercial banks had been bypassed. It had been a military-like operation, of a piece with a developing police state, not the customary foot-dragging civil service exercise. Officials at the Reserve Bank and the Treasury had, however, been sceptical from the very beginning of the inquiry. They were living through seven fat years and were not convinced that the subcommittee could come up with long-term practical solutions to the lottery problem.[84] Despite these reservations, the subcommittee had applied its mind to the basic question that had been put to it: how damaging exactly were the foreign lotteries to the national account?

It was not difficult to estimate. The incoming donations to charity and prize monies, reasonably accurately known because they were published in the host countries, had to be subtracted from the estimates of outgoing amounts spent by South Africans on acquiring lottery tickets. The net loss of capital to the republic, on the three leading lotteries, ostensibly calculated down to the last rand by the subcommittee, was said to be comprised of the following:

Ndola Lottery	R479 400
Southern Rhodesian Lottery	R515 664
Mozambican Lottery	R280 000

In total, it amounted to a little more than R1.5 million in 1964 or, rendered in contemporary values, about R135 million (US$9 million).[85]

The subcommittee's report was forwarded to Commissioner Keevy and other departmental officials, where yet another committee washed its face and trimmed its hair, before eventual presentation to the powerful IMC. The committee, overseen by Hertzog and Vorster, along with Jan de Klerk, would then decide what happened next. Keevy's groomers, armed with scissors and soap, needed to tidy up the report in such a way that it did not leave any of the ministers feeling that their reflection in the men's-room mirror left any of them looking too ambitious, too nosey, overstepping the mark or just plain stupid. Who knew who the next prime minister might be?

The Postmaster General, appreciating the nature of the emerging police state and perhaps sensing which of the strongmen might one day succeed Verwoerd as prime minister, set about the task of protecting the twins with gusto. A war against the lotteries was one thing but disclosing the body count from the great Post Office massacre was another. It would not look good. The number of mail items intercepted, and the amount of money confiscated, he argued, should be rendered only in 'general terms', avoiding disclosure of the actual statistics. No problem. Likewise, none of the Hertzog–Vorster correspondence was to be revealed. Discretion was the better part of valour. Again, no problem.[86]

The dream of extending police and Post Office control of lotteries took shape as committee members passed around the pipe of eternal hope. But, unlike the Commissioner and everyone else, Dr JH de Loor from the Department of Finance took only one puff. Even police states cost money. Funding for enhanced surveillance had to come from somewhere, so he coughed up a few reservations that were duly incorporated for further deliberation. The Treasury wanted more detail as to what the true cost of an ongoing campaign against insurgent lotteries might be and was strongly opposed to the extension of exchange control measures to the adjacent High Commission territories.[87]

But, like Rome, a totalitarian state cemented by electoral support is not built in a day, nor is it dependent on a single piece of legislation. More frequently it is the cumulative product of the attrition of civil liberties achieved by a political and law-enforcing elite over a protracted period. Despite noisy police pleas, dating back to 1960, for comprehensive new legislation to cope with lotteries, and Hertzog's muscle-flexing in 1963, the final report of the IMC was more mouse squeaking than lion roaring.

The summation in the report commenced on a giveaway tentative note – '*if* the campaign against the lotteries is to be intensified' – followed by a predictable set of recommendations. The police, it seemed, no longer required new national legislation. All they asked for was for stiffer penalties and for their Post Office friends to retain the power to invade the mails for evidence of transgressions of existing legislation and a consolidation of the provincial legislation.[88] The ministers agreed. All they could agree to do was to deliver a new bill with a series of technical interventions to repeal what remained of the 1890s laws and to consolidate the existing legislation.

Vorster introduced the bill in the House, in April 1965. He then left it to his sidekick and successor as minister, SL Muller, to push Gambling Act 51 of 1965 through the legislative process. Of the brain behind the Post Office massacre, Hertzog, there was no sign. Government spokesmen emphasised that the bill was a mere consolidation, a tidying up, of existing laws. Vorster, a leading architect of policies of total control, reminded the UP that the most draconian clause, one providing the minister with the power to circumvent the courts, came from Smuts's 1939 pinball-machine legislation. Even police states are erected, in part, on older foundations. The purging of the police, both during World War II and after 1948, testified to that.[89]

It was, as usual, a case of my repressive legislation, necessary at the time to ensure social stability, differs from yours, aimed only at centralising power. So UP members ignored old war stories dating back to Smuts, or Vorster's incarceration as a neo-Nazi. Instead, they trotted out the old rocking horse of a state lottery – a pony that they had to tether when they were in power – and hummed and hawed about elements of chance and skill being present in almost all forms of gambling. A few got closer to the mark – the diminution of democratic accountability in a system increasingly characterised by rule-by-the-minister – and noted the puzzling absence of the sinewy Albert Hertzog.

Two opposition MPs punched away at Vorster, who never flinched, swatting their objections to the bill as being 'childish from start to finish'. One warned that the minister was assuming 'despotic powers' that 'could be exercised quite arbitrarily or even capriciously' depending on who occupied the post. The other captured some of the reservations creeping into the thinking of a minority of white voters who feared the growing reach of Vorster's political police, the feared Special Branch. 'The public', he argued, 'are particularly worried about the power given to the postmaster general to intercept all mail' relating to lotteries. The bill, he argued, created a new 'suspicion branch' with the Minister of Posts and Telecommunications as 'Chief Suspector'. But Hertzog no longer appeared to be comfortable with what Vorster was proposing. They were on to something. Hertzog told the Senate that 'Ninety-nine per cent of the Bill is not something that I have been responsible for, or what I propose, or what my department is now proposing'.[90] Vorster was a heavyweight authoritarian; Hertzog, by comparison, was a flyweight conservative.

The unstated rivalry between the twins was not something the National Party forgot when Verwoerd was assassinated in the House of Assembly, in September 1966, and members looked around for a successor. Nor did Hertzog, who survived as a cabinet minister for just 36 months before being purged by Prime Minister Vorster for his leaden-footed ideological inflexibility at a time when state policies needed to become more fleet-footed.

Act 51 of 1965, of a piece with the emerging police state, officially banned all forms of gambling – bar horse racing – seemingly putting an end to participation in all externally based and illegal local lotteries. Yet, for all the state's dusting around lottery cobwebs, somewhere, perhaps in downtown Johannesburg, or out on the East Rand, a few old-timers must have been smiling. Priests and the politicians had been wielding the same old feather duster for three-quarters of a century but, somehow or other, Ole Daddy Longlegs always came back. Housework, as we are often reminded, is never done.

PART VI

RELAPSE

*Thought's a luxury. Do you think the peasant sits
and thinks of God and Democracy when he gets
inside his mud hut at night?*
GRAHAM GREENE, *THE QUIET AMERICAN* (1955)

When writing history, it is best to look the elephant in the eyes, to portray it as seen front-on. The larger distinguishing features – eyes, ears, trunk and tusks – are then readily imprinted on the mind. But, to arrive at an informed appreciation of the true proportions of the beast, and to see it in full motion, it is best viewed from a safer distance, at an angle, from side-on. It may therefore be helpful to start by briefly sketching the global context to our viewing.

It is probably an analytical and conceptual stretch to see the South African mining revolution as having all that many direct links to the industrial revolution of the 18th and 19th centuries. Distance and time alone would probably correctly make such connections seem implausible and unpersuasive, despite the expansion and reach of British imperialism in the late 19th century.

But would the flip side of that line of reasoning, that there were no continuities between the industrial revolution and the South African mining revolution during the late 19th and early 20th centuries, be equally implausible? Only a moment's reflection should be enough to suggest that it probably is not. Starting in the 1870s, the London Stock Exchange mobilised hundreds of millions of pounds, capital accumulated during the industrial revolution, for investment in the new South African diamond and gold mines. And by the late1880s, tens of thousands of British craftsmen, miners and workers, proletarian descendants of the very same revolution, were making their way to the Witwatersrand in search of new opportunities. British capital and labour were as central to the gold mines as steam power was to generating electricity.

In the struggles between capital and labour that followed in South Africa, in the early 20th century, financially well-endowed capitalists brought with them modern managerial ideologies from around the world, and a veneer of ruling-class culture derived from across Europe. Impecunious clerks, immigrant craftsmen, manual labourers and others arrived with an enduring working-class culture, including a love of gambling, that derived almost solely from the English industrial revolution and dated back to the 18th century and before.

Not all such connections can be relegated to the domain of distant abstraction. Direct, albeit wafer-thin, personal connections between a white working-class gambling culture in South Africa and the tail end of the industrial revolution are not impossible to find. Indeed, some such distant ties were embodied in a historical actor or two actively promoting, or discouraging, gambling at the heart of the mining revolution. One, a bookmaker-entrepreneur, promoted betting on the outcome of foot races between professional athletes that he shuttled between Salford – a venerable gambling centre in Lancashire – and Johannesburg, in the early 20th century. Another, a minister of religion who railed against all forms of gambling on the East Rand during the interwar years, was a direct descendant of an 1820 Settler and a militant Primitive Methodist, of a church whose origins lay in the Staffordshire Potteries. But our interest here lies with the nature of white working-class gambling in the mining revolution, and that requires us to focus more on the middle distance.

The distinguishing features of the short-lived white South African state (1910–1994) have been captured successfully, many times, front-on. Within the context of imperialism and colonialism, a vast agrarian hinterland with the richest treasure troves of diamonds and gold on the planet was appropriated and rendered profitable. International financiers, resident white capitalists and managers combined to harness a cheap, migrant and oppressed black male labour force to that end. The result, determined by a state constructed on unashamedly racist lines, determined to maintain minority privilege, and to prevent meaningful progress for the majority, proved to be an economic windfall and a political disaster.[1] When the inversion of the racial order eventually came, it heralded a short-term triumph for a new political elite, followed by another economic disaster for the long-suffering black majority.

Seen side-on, while moving in the calculated manner that characterises it, that brutal history reveals as many contradictions, para-
doxes, ironies, successes and failures as there are cracks and wrinkles
on an elephant's skin. Developing an understanding of how the South
African state evolved, how fast or slowly it moved, how clumsy or sup-
ple it could be, what the limits to its reach were, or how it approached
and circumvented obstacles, is a challenging exercise. It requires the
closest observation, careful tracking of movements and a willingness
to hand- and nose-test the freshness or staleness of the scat.

Probing the rise and largely undocumented decline of the white
working class may be one way of getting closer to an appreciation
of the state's changing capacity and limitations. In broad terms, the
history of the rise of the white working class, thus far, has focused
on its dramatic struggles against the mine owners and their local
managerial agents to secure an economically and racially privileged
position within industry and society. The strikes of 1907 and 1913
and the full-scale miners' revolt of 1922 stand out as markers. But
most such workplace-centred studies focusing on political consciousness and class struggles have, understandably, not dealt with shifts
in the quotidian culture of men moving from mine boarding houses
and married quarters into the working-class suburbs and towns of the
greater Witwatersrand.

We lack a comprehensive single-volume social history of the Witwatersrand's white working classes over the formative decades between
1890 and 1940. The cultural excesses of fortune-seeking, migrant single males based in mining camps, who were then slapped and moulded
into more familiar shape as a resident working class by employers and
the state, remain largely unexplored. It was only after a lengthy struggle that immigrant workers assumed the more reassuring profile of a
reasonably contented, ordered, permanently resident, married, well-
housed, industrial proletariat capable of reproducing itself, and willing
to do so, in what were already racially segregated cities.

Nor do we have an integrated study that readily identifies and
incorporates those distinctively Calvinist and Protestant features of
the class culture that came to characterise the South African industrial revolution. These gaps in our knowledge are as deep and wide as
the Southern Ocean. How were notions of industrial time formulated

and inculcated into the working classes? How were public holidays and time and spaces for recreation lost or won? How did religion inform social structures at work and at play? How were the ideas of thrift and savings transmitted, and by whom? How was wealth conceived of, and how did that change over time to provide some intergenerational security or mobility?

The sources that can answer these questions, from local to national level, are to be found everywhere: the National Archives, church and court records, the *Government Gazette*, Hansard, trade union publications, newspapers and magazines, school, college and university curricula, the records of licensing boards, voluntary associations and women's organisations, and more. We are not so much lacking in historical sources as in active historical imaginations.

For various reasons, large-scale, commercial, organised gambling presents itself as a useful vantage point from which to view the cultural, economic and political landscape that accompanied the making of the white working class in South Africa's turbulent industrial heartland. Handled carefully, slid gently into place, gambling, and more especially lotteries, can provide us with a small window into the heart of a class set in a history that was truly without frontiers.

Archival light from distant eras, refracted through the prism of gambling, readily splits into rays capable of highlighting the changing fortunes of the classes or individuals they happen to fall on. Some rays, direct and bright in colour, are easily followed. Others, angled and fainter of hue, are more difficult to trace. The extent to which lotteries are openly supported or repressed in various communities tells us something not only about their culture, tradition and religion but also about how the power of the state is assembled, exercised and reproduced in a multicultural and multiracial country such as South Africa.

These considerations around lotteries-as-litmus are rendered even more complex and fascinating because the industrial revolution in southern Africa took place in a wider region in which imperial Britain and Portugal once held sway. An affluent Anglophone, Protestant, industrial and urbanised core pushed up against an impoverished Lusophone, Catholic, commercial and rural periphery on its eastern flank. The effects of the mining revolution were never confined to South Africa but spread across much of central and southern Africa. Regional history will assume its rightful place when, instead of asking only how South Africa shaped the destiny of its immediate neighbours, we ask how the adjacent territories helped shape *its* economy and the wider society.

But juxtaposing South Africa and Mozambique in this way does not do justice to the depth and complexity that those foundational contrasts gave rise to. True, in practice, differences were sometimes bridged through formal treaties. But, more often, informal or unspoken agreements were intertwined in linkages that played themselves out in everyday cross-border business alongside ingrained suspicions and resentments born of ambition and gross inequality. Capital flows and currency exchange, the mass movement of indentured black labour, tariffs, taxation and rail transport all formed part of the wider cultural nexus in which other, unregulated, activities were allowed to operate so long as they did not imperil the much deeper underlying economic fundamentals bringing the two countries together. The best example of uncontested, unregulated cross-border trade, legal in Mozambique but not in South Africa, was the Lourenço Marques Lottery, floated in 1892, which subsequently went on to thrive across the region between the two world wars.

Looking back, the successful rooting of the LML on the Witwatersrand during World War I can, in part, be attributed to the wider imperial context into which it was born, and to the influence of two Indian Ocean British colonies, Australia and India. Years later, two other colonies, Northern and Southern Rhodesia, contributed to the popularity and spread of lotteries in the Protestant soils of the Union. The first Australian lottery, sired of a financial collapse in Sydney, and of indeterminate legal status, was conducted, in 1849, in a colony with a significant number of Catholics. The Australian and Tasmanian lotteries were among the first lotteries to gain a toehold in South Africa. Other British immigrants, including some with experience in India, were familiar with the Calcutta Sweep, a horse-race-based lottery that, for many decades, had a significant popular following in southern Africa. Indeed, it was to India that the British-heavy South African Labour Party looked for a model that might address the hope of white workers for a lottery in the early 1930s.

That the initially weak link between lotteries in South Africa and Australia strengthened rather than weakened as the number of immigrant miners from the island continent declined could be traced to the entrepreneurial genius of one man. He successfully partnered with a Catholic priest in Mozambique who, because of the personal and other hostilities he invoked, was, in effect, defrocked by the church. The two were liminal beings, drawn from the margins of the emerging social orders, with a taste for financial adventure and not unduly concerned with the norms of morality interpreted through pre-existing dispensations. Both were, by skill and by temperament, well suited to running a cross-border, quasi-legal lottery in South Africa's growing grey economy.

Rufe Naylor defied categorisation. At various times – often simultaneously – the Australian was a bookmaker, broker, currency dealer, cinema and theatre owner, concert impresario, commercial farmer, election and publicity agent, drama and film coach, financier, filmmaker, horse breeder, insurance agent, lobbyist, lottery and magazine owner, mining director, mineral and property speculator, municipal politician and town councillor, organiser of professional athletic meetings, racecourse owner and minor philanthropist – all of this during short intermittent stays in South Africa between 1908 and 1920. Lubricating his overlapping enterprises and entrenching his position in an increasingly competitive market, however, required mastery of several of the darker arts of metropolitan capitalism. While seldom, if ever, successfully prosecuted for any truly serious offences while based in South Africa, he was almost certainly guilty of bigamy, blackmail, bribery, forgery and tax evasion. Although now largely forgotten, he was also a folk hero in both Australia and South Africa.

Naylor's legendary success was predicated on more than just a nose for business opportunities. He had an unmatched ability to link gambling and entertainment enterprises to the underlying social changes taking place on the Witwatersrand. He 'read' and understood how working-class culture was shifting, from one built largely around immigrant miners living in single quarters to one increasingly centred on married couples with children residing in the mine villages or the emerging segregated suburbs of Johannesburg. He saw the fading of the frontier and the coming of the family.

Naylor, who had witnessed some of the same changes in the goldfields of Australia, made a point of selling his entertainment and gambling

outlets as part of healthy, honest and frequently al fresco family entertainment. Bars, bucket shops, saloons and horse races might conven-
tionally have been almost exclusively for the use of male wage-earners,
but there was nothing preventing female clerks, shop assistants, typists
and housewives from buying lottery tickets, attending a concert or a
theatre, or gambling at an outdoor dog-racing track.

Naylor's partner in the lottery business, Padre José Vicente do
Sacramento, may have been a failed missionary, but he was a 'pioneering' success in Lourenço Marques and, for a time, 'a millionaire'. He
idolised Naylor and mimicked several of his entrepreneurial efforts in
Mozambique and Portugal, albeit with conspicuously less long-term
success. Like Naylor, he refused to allow his interests to be circum-
scribed. He was actively involved in currency dealing, commercial
farming, the property and rental market, and a racecourse, and was
a minor philanthropist. He broke the implicit vows of his calling,
defied the Catholic hierarchy, entered a common-law marriage that
lasted only for as long as he was penniless, defrauded the church and
did other things known only to the Pope.

So well did the lottery do as a transnational business, from its
founding in 1917 and into the 1960s, that the enterprise saw the active
involvement of two generations of the Naylor family, despite the
venture's questionable legal status in South Africa. Much of its lon-
gevity could be attributed the tenacity of the owners of an extensive
organisation in a politically hostile climate. The Naylor brothers mas-
tered the logistics necessary for the receipt of tens of thousands of
lottery tickets at various rural and urban pick-up points, distributed
the tickets nationwide and shipped enormous sums of cash and winnings through the region's porous borders. That, in turn, was based
on an understanding of how the public infrastructure of the Empire
and colony changed over time.

Rufe Naylor and the brothers who followed him into the business were aware of how public and privately owned infrastructure,
harnessing the latest technology, could improve the efficiency and
reach of the lottery operations. In Australia, Naylor had used the
telephone and the difference in time zones across the continent to
fraudulently manipulate the odds and announce the winner of an east-
coast horse race while he was in Perth, on the west coast. In South

Africa, the family used the telephone, telegraph, railways, steamships and, above all else, the local and international postal service to expand and entrench the lottery business across the subcontinent. In a way, then, a privately owned lottery benefited from cross-subsidisation by the state.

From the 1930s, football pools and lotteries in England, Ireland and Malta used the same state-subsidised support services to penetrate the southern-hemisphere economy at a time when their own markets for postal gambling may not have been expanding at the same rate. For much the same reason, there was an all-round growth in lottery receipts across the globe after World War I. The expansion of road networks and affordable motor cars in the 1930s, and later still air links, allowed the Northern and Southern Rhodesian lotteries ever easier access to a mass market for lotteries in the white south.

The brothers Naylor were as adept at incorporating modern technology into their front-line defence and surveillance systems against a state intent on limiting or extirpating the Lourenço Marques Lottery. Bribed police officers telephoned advance warnings of impending raids to the Naylors' head office in downtown Johannesburg. As part of their counterintelligence operation, and to cross-check the fidelity of officers who had already been corrupted, the brothers employed informants in the telephone exchange to provide any additional information needed to safeguard their underground operations.

Risk and uncertainty are features universally associated with business. Both elements were prominent in the Naylors' transnational lottery enterprise. The lottery operated in an officially hostile but quasi-legal market dominated ideologically by Calvinists intent on exercising a chokehold over the main political parties when it came to working-class gambling. That gambling was more of a class-and-morality than a morality-and-class issue for the Protestants was evident from how comparatively tolerant they were of horse racing while rounding on dog racing, football pools, pinball tables and lotteries, all deeply rooted in the white working-class towns of the East Rand.

Lotteries, whether privately or state-run, are most often born amid structural financial crises in the state, in times of deprivation and economic hardship. Their origin speaks of class and class action. The poor, unemployed and working classes readily embrace the hope for a fantastical ticket-based escape from the same restrictive parameters of class, education and skills that confine, condemn and lock them into a frequently dreary and routinised proletarian existence. George Orwell captured some of the resultant desperation when laying out the response to the Ministry of Plenty's lottery in his novel *Nineteen Eighty-Four*. That lottery, with its weekly payout of enormous prizes, was the one public event to which the proles paid serious attention. It was probable that there were some millions of proles for whom the lottery was the principal, if not the only, reason for remaining alive.

The prospect of wealth acquired through a lottery rather than through work runs contrary to Protestant ethics, but it does simultaneously provide the state with some of the political sedative necessary to dull the conscience of the few with the power who determine the economic fortunes of the many they preside over. The larger a lottery's support for charity and other worthy causes, the less likely there are to be direct demands on the tax-hungry treasury to expand welfare payments to the underprivileged. The lottery acts as a pressure-release valve in society and, taken holistically, benefits the political elite and state more than the dispossessed.

Big business and its oldest ally, the state, frequently have difficulty in comprehending fully the logic informing working-class behaviour when it comes to purchasing lottery tickets during economic downturns or in failing states. Instead of conceding that the deeper the crisis, the more desperate the attempt to escape from poverty by purchasing a ticket to dream, the leaders of commerce, industry and the government caution the poor to be more frugal, to avoid gambling and to divert such little disposable income as they do have into providing life's bare necessities. Why 'waste' money when you have so little?

The apparent paradox of contracyclical expenditure, of white workers spending more rather than less on lotteries during depressions and recessions, can be tracked through much of the first half of the 20th century. Protestant churches in urban areas and the state were horrified to witness how the 1906–1908 recession, the wartime and post-war inflation-induced hardship of 1917–1922 and the Great Depression of 1929–1933 prompted a surge rather than a decline in demand for football pool coupons and lottery tickets. The hope, if not the mathematical reasoning, of workers was that while a little bread may go a long way, owning a bakery was a more attractive long-term proposition when poor or hungry.

In much the same way, the popularity and 'successes' of the lottery in post-1994 democratic South Africa speak to food insecurity and pervasive black unemployment. Seen en masse, in structural rather than personal terms, the greater and longer the economic disaster confronting a country, the more protracted and sustainable the 'successes' of a state lottery will be. The more the economy contracts, the greater the potential for growth in the lottery. The more open and successful an economy is at rewarding effort and merit as part of a programme of social mobility, the less the need for a lottery to deal with the plight of the underclasses through charity or voluntary organisations.

Lotteries are born of structural financial disaster and sustained by the financial peril of the most hard-pressed sections of society. Or, as one commentator puts it, 'The lottery, as it always has, remains a regressive tax, with a higher proportion of the total spend on the lottery coming from the poorest socio-economic groups.'[2] A perfectly functioning economy, a dream shared by hopeful capitalists and communist ideologues, would have no need of a lottery.

Seen in socio-psychological terms, it is precisely because lotteries thrive where the rivers of hope and uncertainty meet that they occasionally give rise to moral panics among the ruling class, the privileged and those most attached to the existing order. Whereas the underclasses are more inclined to indulge in gambling in hard times, signalling a measure of fear and uncertainty, the church and the state, tied to elites and political parties, are more inclined to try and eradicate any squeals hinting at 'moral' or 'social' decay. Indeed, it was often the horror of the white working-class family being financially ruined through the uncontrolled betting of its male members, along with the unstated danger of manifest social unrest, that fuelled the church and state panics that usually preceded attempts at new legislation to eliminate or restrict gambling.

It was those locked into commerce, including scores of small shopkeepers, who were responsible for the press-driven moral panic that led to the 1909 commission on gambling on the Witwatersrand. It was the store owners who complained loudest about the proximity of working-class paydays to race meetings. That panic, fed by Naylor's innovative gambling enterprises, culminated in the hurried passage of Act 37 of 1909, the Horse Racing and Betting Restriction Act. Likewise, it was the Rand's bribery and gambling scandals of 1917, coupled to wartime angst, that fuelled the passing of the Horse Racing and Betting Restriction Amendment Ordinance, No. 11 of 1917.

In the wake of the Great Depression, the installation of hundreds of flashy electronic pinball machines in cafés on the East Rand, many of them owned by Catholic or Greek Orthodox proprietors, triggered acute moral anguish in Methodist-led Protestant circles. The great fear of the late 1930s was that schoolboys and young apprentices would become addicted to the new pastime and, by diverting small disposable incomes into gambling, undermine the financial and social security of the white working-class family. As a social problem, gambling and gender go together much as Sammy Cahn, the lyricist, once hinted at love and marriage going together like a horse and carriage.

A major stumbling block for church and state, then in a relatively weak relationship but one that would strengthen over the following decade, was how to identify and isolate elements of chance and skill in pinball games. Magistrates and judges had long been hesitant to impose fines or prison sentences on popular forms of gambling, and more especially so when there clearly were elements of skill involved in the games. The courts frustrated church and state alike by refusing to apply the harshest repressive measures at their disposal. In a sign of things to come, Smuts and the Fusion government avoided a further standoff with the judiciary by passing the Gambling Amendment Act of 1939, which granted the Minister of Justice arbitrary powers to declare pinball games to be, like a lottery, a game solely of chance.

Smuts's frustration with a judiciary unwilling to hand down deterrent sentences dated back the post-bellum British occupying administration under Milner. Anchoring legislation that dated back even further, to Kruger's republican government in the early 1890s, was too outmoded and legally imprecise to cope with the social revolution that the Witwatersrand had undergone after the transition to sustained deep-level reef mining after 1895. Gambling was deeply embedded in immigrant working-class culture, and white miners were never the most pliant or law-abiding constituency in a fast-urbanising setting.

Until World War II, police, public prosecutors, magistrates and judges had a better sense of the public mood on the Rand and the shortcomings of outdated gambling legislation than did MPs in Cape Town. Political parties wanted to keep the churches onside in relation to gambling excesses, but not at the cost of losing electoral support in the Union's industrial heartland. The result was that from Union, in 1910, until well into the 1940s, unless gambling or lotteries became so intolerably brazen and law-flouting that it could no longer be kept from the public or ignored, police and prosecutors often chose to do nothing other than remind legislators that it was up to them to provide them with new legal instruments. Discretionary law enforcement was the handmaiden of police corruption. It was the state that made an uncertain, poorly defined gambling universe even more liminal than it already was. But, by World War II, moral panics, never easily separated from electoral cycles and church complaints, had assumed new proportions.

As had happened during World War I, when the drums of war conjured up fears that horse racing and lotteries might herald a social implosion on the Witwatersrand, World War II let loose the dogs to chase white moral rabbits. The provincial Dog Racing Commission began its hearings, in 1942, against the backdrop of the continued urbanisation of the rural poor and the growing influence of neo-Calvinists within the Afrikaner Protestant churches who had the ear of the ascending National Party. The seemingly distant planets of church and state were moving closer than they had been since Kruger's day. As DF Malan, the first modern prime minister and himself a minister in the Dutch Reformed Church, put it: 'It was not the state but the church who took the lead with apartheid.'[3] Likewise with gambling laws – and the clergymen giving evidence and the members of the Dog Racing Commission sensed it.

The usual suspects – the supposed dangers of acculturation, addiction and deracination, and the potentially fatal consequences of impoverishment within the cities – were paraded before the wide-eyed, shrill-of-voice panel. Satan was running amok, and the Bible, backed by legislation, was the best shield against moral implosion. The nationalists did not have to wait on the electoral triumph of 1948 to see off the gambling ghosts that menaced fathers, mothers, sons and daughters. The UP did their dirty work for them. In 1947, the UP, trembling before the threat of a change in government, used its majority in the

Provincial Council to abolish dog racing, a decision that took effect only in 1949, ironically after the National Party had swept to power.

Success whets the appetite. The English and Afrikaner churches, having polished off the hefty bone that came with the abolition of dog racing, looked to the state with watery eyes in anticipation of more rewards for barking at any hawkers still peddling prohibited pleasures to an ill-disciplined white working class. But the nationalists, already feeding apartheid titbits to the church under the kitchen table, struggled to find more meat on a scrawny chicken carcass. It nevertheless did prise out two bits of legislation to stem the whimpering.

The Prohibition of Sports Pools Act of 1949 was warmed-up legislation dealing with a problem that had been around for 20 years. So, too, was the General Law Amendment Act 62 of 1955, which, in keeping with a growing disregard of established civil liberties, allowed for the ready invasion of clubs or homes that the police suspected of being used for purposes of gambling.

The shift towards authoritarianism and government by ministerial decree was underpinned by the growing dominance of Afrikaner nationalists at the polls, as evidenced in four elections between 1953 and 1966. After the advent of the republic, in 1961, authoritarianism, dominated by strongmen with neo-fascist administrative reflexes, gave rise to what, in political terms, was a police state. Albert Hertzog, at Posts and Telecommunications, and John Vorster, in the Ministry of Justice, were both willing to endorse the vigorous repression of political opponents who were, often indiscriminately, cast as 'communists'. Both were willing to bend the knee before the Dutch Reformed churches, which never stopped fretting about the growing evil of lotteries that went unchecked.

In 1963, Hertzog showed a willingness to break a lance for those in the Protestant clergy who were not already fully occupied with finding and tilting at apartheid windmills. He persuaded Prime Minister HF Verwoerd's cabinet that he and Vorster could defeat lottery operators who were raiding the country for cash and then disappearing into the surrounding international postal bush with their booty. With the help of Vorster, who provided him with an interministerial committee fed by a subcommittee, chaired and dominated by the security establishment and Post Office officials, Hertzog began intercepting all incoming and outgoing mail suspected of being linked to lotteries. Within a few weeks, well over a million postal items and lottery funds had been seized.

For the first time since Union, the police enjoyed strong ministerial and cabinet support for anti-gambling legislation. It came at a time when apartheid policies were plunging the country into international isolation and opprobrium, and the police were more than willing to lead the charge against any forces, external or internal, hostile to the new republic. Hertzog's Post Office attacks and a 1964 report on the 'suppression of lotteries' revealed the extent of the financial haemorrhaging and dealt foreign-based lotteries a fatal blow.

The finishing touches and make-up were applied in the white electorate's mortuary of preference – parliament. Vorster's Gambling Act 51 of 1965 consolidated existing legislation, banning *all* forms of gambling throughout the country other than the sport of the class untouchables – horse racing. It had taken more than six decades since the formation of Union for a country without an officially established church to align white nationalism, Protestantism and republicanism reasonably fully. After half a century of resistance from the white working class, the government hoped that it had – yet again – rid the country of lotteries. The hope of a gambling-free future beckoned for all true believers. But new colour-sensitive nationalists and a black working class were already in the wings preparing for a future in which hope would triumph.

THE BIRTH OF THE SOUTH AFRICAN NATIONAL LOTTERY: AFRICAN NATIONALISTS AND THE ECLIPSE OF THE OLD ORDER, CIRCA 1965–1997

B roadly put, the most repressive of South Africa's anti-gambling legislation, and the often-half-hearted attempts to enforce it, tracked the same arc that marked the consolidation of white political power underwritten by steady, sometimes spectacular, economic progress between World War I and the mid-1960s. Regardless of which political party or parties were in power, the English and Afrikaner churches played different, but often leading, roles in compelling the government of the day to respect Protestant abhorrence of gambling among the white working class. Notable milestones along the muddy path to a creating a cleaner moral universe were attempts to suppress pinball machines (1939), the successful outlawing of dog racing and sports pools (1949), and the clampdown on all gambling, including lotteries (1965).

Again, stated generally and thus possibly misleadingly, church and state were bound by an unstated clause of cooperation in their version of a social contract that was bent on suppressing gambling for most of the 20th century. There was, however, never a moment in the history of the goldfields, from 1890 to 1965 and beyond, that white workers on the Witwatersrand did not resent and resist the attempts of the top-down, church-state alliance to repress what they thought of as an integral part of an authentic working-class culture.

Early formal and informal resistance to restrictive laws came via the Labour Party, which, attempted, unsuccessfully, to promote the idea of a state lottery. But after the Great Depression, with white working-class disposable incomes rising – in part at the expense of cheaper black labour – resistance became more muted and secretive, which may help account for the clustering of anti-gambling legislation in the years after World War II. This was during the same period when the ears of the anti-democratic National Party were opened to the pleas and shouts of the Calvinists, many of whom had been trained at the ultra-conservative Potchefstroom University for Christian Higher Education. Church and state grew stronger as the white working class, once protected at the point of production and at home by strong trade unions, slowly declined.

In some important respects this schematic outline of the first half of the 20th century leading up to the advent of the white republic, in 1961, contrasts with the history of gambling legislation that followed on the advent of the black republic, or, put more accurately, the first democratically elected government, in 1994. South Africa's economic decline, which had long roots, became steadily more manifest as white nationalists attempted to see off the mounting and varied challenges of black nationalists. If the church and state alliance was broadly intact before the Soweto uprisings of 1976, it became progressively more frayed thereafter. The Dutch Reformed churches began to examine the ideology of apartheid more critically and the government mobilised its citizenry for a godless, unjust war against a pressing future and the majority of the country's inhabitants, denied citizenship solely on the basis of skin colour. The old white church-state marriage, solemnised in the 1890s amid a loud exchange of anti-gambling vows, was going to end in a *sotto voce* separation.

All that might be self-evident, but it forms an important part of the background of the reversal of government policies on gambling. The state moved from a position of outright hostility to gambling prior to the transition to a democratically elected government to one more tolerant and supportive of the various modern gambling 'industries'. That, in turn, was a development informed by an underlying attempt to deal with the economics of poverty in a society marked by gross and increasing inequalities, but one in which the black working-class' trade union movement had an important say.

The structural changes to the economy imposed by apartheid policies, along with increasing industrial conflict in the decades leading up to the new political dispensation, came at a cost compounded by certain underlying factors. Economic growth slowed from five per cent in the roaring 1960s, when it assisted in heightening the walls around an increasingly isolated and repressive state, to 1.5 per cent in the 1980s.[1] Profit rates, declining for many years, continued to dip, discouraging new investment while exports decreased and imports increased.

An urban-based black working class, strongly rooted in manufacturing rather than mining, and severely repressed in all respects, was backed by a growing, militant trade union movement and the tiny, exiled leadership of the African National Congress (ANC), set on political liberation. In a small way, this dispensation mirrored, and prefigured, some of the conditions necessary for the emergence of a new working-class culture and a different attitude from the incoming elite.

The first half of the 20th century saw the rise of a white working class in a mining economy that resented a Calvinist-led, church-state alliance that sought to clamp down on a gambling culture and the populace's love of lotteries. The second half saw the expansion of an African working class, rooted in manufacturing, partly affiliated to Protestant and independent black churches, but hardly insistent on an alliance between church and state. Presented crudely as drama, the declining white working class, departed stage right, had been denied all forms of legal gambling bar horse racing by an authoritarian, racist church-state alliance. The insurgent black working class, entering stage left, helped usher in an ostensibly non-racial, democratic dispensation, untrammelled by a church-state alliance, thereby creating space for policies on gambling and lotteries that were more tolerant and relaxed.

After the mid-1970s, the South African government and the police state clung to power while simultaneously attempting to make such regional and ethnic political concessions as, they hoped, would allow them some relief and ease an eventual transition to black majority rule. When it came to gambling, however, the increasingly shaky old church-state alliance tried to hold the line along the Witwatersrand. But old Calvinist trails, marking unquestioned authority in town and countryside, vanished as soon as the borders of the nominally independent Bantustans – Transkei (1976–1994), Bophuthatswana (1977–1994), Venda (1979–1994) and Ciskei (1981–1994) – were crossed. There, whites could go drinking, gambling and whoring, just as they had once done freely in the neighbouring Catholic state of Mozambique. In colonial settings, some ideas of redemption and sin have largely unwritten spatial coordinates.

In 'white' South Africa the church-state mechanics, by then more comfortable in overalls than in dog-collars, continually adjusted, or forged, improvised parts for the anti-gambling machinery designed by Kruger back in the 1890s. But advocates, attorneys and sinners on the modern Witwatersrand and in other industrial cities never once stopped probing the weaknesses in gambling legislation, with the result that the laws demanded constant tinkering.

The Gambling Amendment Act 39 of 1988 laid down stiffer penalties for infringements to cope with the lawless in a time of inflation. Forty-eight months later, the Gambling Amendment Act 144 of 1992 sought to smash the old chestnut of chance-and-skill with one mighty swing of the legislative sledgehammer. The Act was designed to 'expressly prohibit certain games irrespective of whether or not the result thereof is determined by chance'. Twelve months later, the General Law Sixth Amendment Act 204 of 1993, going back to a conundrum first lit up by pinball machines in the 1930s, tried to deal with the problem of winnings that came by way of granting further 'free' games rather than cash.[2] And so on it went, faltering church candles lighting the past just as the first rays of weak sunlight appeared to lighten up the future.

By the early 1990s the future of the beleaguered state was becoming so apparent that even the white electorate, with eyes that had hitherto been able only to sense the differences of colour, belatedly abandoned its blurred vision, hoping that one day everyone else would marvel at a multicoloured 'rainbow'. Negotiations between the old and new colour-coded nationalists, conducted over several years, moved ahead, and in March 1992 the white electorate voted to abandon its apartheid past. Encouraged, two years later the country held its first non-racial democratic elections underpinned by a universal franchise. The glittering tinsel on a package of new freedoms would soon illuminate everything, including the longed-for right to gamble freely.

A freely elected government lost no time in signalling to the masses – black and white – that the rusted old lattice of gambling laws had collapsed and that it would soon be opening a brand-new network. The bullet train of progress, running along a high-speed track without carriages reserved exclusively for the use of men of the cloth, would dash into the future at previously unheard-of speeds. Within weeks of a new government assuming office, in August 1994, one of the chief dispatchers of legal trains into an exciting, possibly boundless future, Professor NE Wiehahn, issued an interim report on gambling.

Wiehahn, who in 1995 presented his final report to the government, drew aside the heavy drapes beloved by the old order with a flourish, and the saloon cars of state were flooded with light. The doubter, used to snuff out the last flicker of hope for legalised gambling bar horse racing, Act 51 of 1965, was no longer fit for purpose. It did not reflect 'the true moral viewpoint of the majority of South Africans and the government should legalise lotteries and ... gambling in the Republic of South Africa'. A relieved cry of 'Hallelujah!' must have gone up from millions of homes around the country. The bullet train had, in one sharp sprint, dragged South Africa clear of the late 19th century and was about to enter a short tunnel of hope debouching into the exciting 21st century.[3]

But standing up suddenly after a protracted period of being seated can induce dizziness. The breathless Wiehahn report was, perhaps understandably, short of historical and sociological insight and sensitivity. It failed to appreciate the significance of the impending shift from an unstated church-and-state dispensation to a more robustly secular order and begged many questions. When had gambling legislation in the country ever reflected the 'true moral viewpoint of the majority of South Africans'? Where and how had that ever been tested? And what moral viewpoint was it, then, that would inform the 'majority of South Africans' who have long had, and continue to have, a sorely compromised understanding of how attitudes, beliefs and values relate to institutionalised corruption, deceit and theft? Wiehahn's wishful contention had more empty compartments in it than a bent politician's wallet, and, over time, the very same problems would bedevil a new Lotteries and Gambling Board.

But, picking up speed, the train sped on through the tunnel, bursting out into the exciting new landscape on the far side of the mountain. Within 36 months of liberation, the 'new South Africa', beset by a myriad of other pressing structural economic, social, and political problems, gave birth to spanking new gambling legislation in the shape of the Lotteries Act 57 of 1997. 'The people', 'the nation', needed to dream of escaping the harsh realities of life.

Act 57's objectives revealed how heavily the past weighed on society and what the future might look like. It was intended to 'regulate and prohibit lotteries and sports pools' (ah, a touch of the bad old past there then), 'to establish a National Lotteries Board; consequentially to amend the Post Office Act, 1958' (aha, no more mail snooping) and 'the Gambling Act, 1965' (goodbye Calvinism), to repeal the State Lotteries Act, 1984 (Ciskei), and the Lotteries Decree, 1989 (Transkei) – farewell to venal black collaborators – 'and to provide for matters connected therewith'. Whew! At last, the job was properly done.

The National Lotteries Board, presiding over a state-owned but privately operated lottery, was duly appointed in 1998, to be replaced the following year by the National Lotteries Commission (NLC), which also oversaw the National Lotteries Distribution Trust Fund (NLDTF). In 2000, President Thabo Mbeki launched the National Lottery at a butcher shop in the Cape Town township of Langa. Lotteries and poverty were blood brothers. The dismembering of the golden calf and the misappropriation of the parts that followed, however, were not determined upon amid the symbolism of poverty but in the boardrooms, clubs and restaurants of a very corpulent elite.

Some of the people, those chosen by their gods, prayed and did not play lotto at all. Many more, in numbers that agnostics might argue amounted to a massive tax on the poorest, played and prayed. By the mid-2000s, around R3.5 billion was being spent on the lottery each year, with most of its income, more than one rand in every three, coming from Gauteng, the heartland of industry.[4] Lotteries can grow anywhere but usually prefer hard urban soils.

Through the NLC and the NLDTF, thousands of worthy, and a growing number of unworthy, causes were supported. The economy was shrinking and the number of charities and non-governmental organisations (NGOs) dealing with poverty proliferating. National economic failure feeds growth in sectors devoted to charity and NGO operations. But as those who commanded the *ancien régime* discovered, gambling legislation requires frequent servicing and updating as punters and profiteers discover new ways of circumventing good intentions. Parliamentary housework is never done. The Lotteries Act 57 of 1997 was amended no less than three times from 2001 to 2013.

Yet, despite all the necessary parliamentary maintenance, something was going wrong with the network. It was as if the faster the bullet train hurtled towards a brave new world of charity and good deeds, the more it appeared that the future – travelling at the same speed as the train – was receding. That could not possibly be true because, as everyone knew, if that were so, the bullet would be going nowhere. It had to be a frightening, speed-induced illusion.

The problem could not possibly lie in the system since it was widely believed that 'revolutionary' liberation and progress, driven by the most modern and sophisticated of legal technology in a constitutional democracy that was admired across the world, was near infallible. No, the problem had to lie not with the machinery, but with the cadres, with its personnel. But how was that possible? Had not the Wiehahn interim report, the timetable, pointed to the existence of a new 'true moral viewpoint of the majority of South Africans'?

The problem with 'true' moral viewpoints is that they seldom venture out into the sunlight in everyday clothing. They stride out in sunglasses, wrapped in turbans that partially conceal the alignment of their eyes. Whether they see straight, or squint, is only apparent once they have stripped down. The eye muscles of morality are linked to human frailty by tendons of attitude, belief and value. It is the sinews of culture that make the muscles of morality function optimally.

Lotteries can never be lifted clear of, or isolated from, considerations of culture, economics and politics. From early on, the African political elite, even further from an 'established' church than the Afrikaner nationalists were, found itself having to struggle with a few of the same difficulties that had confronted previous administrations during the interwar period. But, unlike earlier governing parties who presided over lotteries based outside the country, the ANC had to deal with a domestically based operation that was controlled and manned by South Africans replete with South African attitudes, beliefs and values – many of them highly problematic.

For several years, the national lottery has been plagued by a growing number of allegations of corruption, fraud, misappropriation and mismanagement in the upper echelons of the organisation. Managerial parasites, bursting with ubuntu-like public utterance, privately drew on, or were supported by, funds drawn largely from impoverished black households across the country whose male and female members were constantly having to be educated about the need to 'gamble responsibly' – a paternalistic lesson handed down by a few perpetrators of larceny on a grand scale. In 2007, the lottery was disrupted for weeks as the management of the operation underwent uncoordinated changes.

By 2013 the NLC chose to 'relaunch' an anti-fraud campaign, a startling admission. The campaign does not seem to have been a success. By 2018, the NLC was being subjected to forensic investigation by journalists devoted to examining 'corruption, maladministration and nepotism'.[5] The police force, purged for the third time since its founding, did not seem to take much, if any, interest in these matters. But then, in December 2020, offices of the NLC were raided by a special investigation unit probing allegations of corruption.

No significance can be attached to the date, but on 1 April 2021, in a 'sponsored story' that appeared in a national weekly in a country plagued by mass illiteracy, the NLC laid out how it was allaying any public misgivings or misperceptions. As is often the case, in South Africa, the NLC did not want for well-meaning encouragement and support from European sponsors who, like some who purchase lottery tickets, may be over-invested in hope.

Together with the Organisation for Economic Co-operation and Development, the OECD, the NLC staged a virtual conference, held at the Twin Rivers Estate, Pretoria, on 'Anti-corruption and Integrity'. Lottery deliberations and debates had moved from a Langa butcher shop to an 'estate'. A former Deputy Public Protector, an advocate, set the scene by noting that corruption was 'widespread' in the private and public sectors, but then, warming to the task, reassessed the viral load and declared it to be a 'pandemic'. An expert on ethics advised the NLC to 'tighten the screws on anti-corruption and gift policies' and pleaded for 'intellectual honesty', which, apparently, went beyond the usual parameters of just honesty. But the audience need not have worried too much. The NLC Secretary, another advocate, admitted that 'greed and power [were] at the core of corruption and the National Lotteries Board [was] taking charge of dealing with the scourge in the organisation.'[6]

The conference was dominated by advocates and other legal experts focused on 'anti-corruption' but apparently less so on verifiable delivery issues or integrity. Accountants, auditors, charitable bodies or frustrated recipients, supposedly benefiting from lottery funding, might have been able to shed additional light on some of the problems bedevilling the organisation. A casual observer might have come away with the idea that the problems were overwhelmingly technical, that the codification of norms and standards or a revision of codes and legislation would go a long way towards solving ills deeply rooted not only in the national lottery but throughout the society. There were elephants in the conference rooms but, or so it seemed, no one wished to confront them.

And yet, no one could accuse the conference organisers of not understanding the importance of attitudes, beliefs and values. They did. It was just that they did not want to spend too much time exploring the dark side of those attributes. If they were going to link corruption to cultural issues, then it had to be done indirectly, in celebratory rather than accusatory fashion; after all, Africa was known for its singing and dancing. And so local choirs and dance groups were brought on to entertain conference participants in acknowledgement of a job well done. 'Through song and dance, the groups celebrated the good cause of fighting corruption, sending out a message that South Africa will one day be free from the grip of corrupt officials.' And so the bureaucratic elite of a self-confessed, badly corrupted organisation belted out an anti-corruption message to a computer-bound, 'mesmerised' international audience, in an event partly paid for by willing purchasers of lottery tickets.[7]

Looking back, then, the Afrikaner nationalists tried, and largely failed, to keep the lottery out of their hoped-for Calvinistic culture. African nationalists have a different but much bigger problem – how to eradicate a secular culture of fraud, theft and lying from within the workings of the lottery organisation itself. It raises a question perhaps only legislators can answer with confidence: is it better to have a lottery based inside or outside the borders of a country? But, looking ahead, perhaps remember what the choir sang. Forget the past, buy a ticket for the present and hope to be pleasantly surprised … *One Day*.

SELECT BIBLIOGRAPHY

The extensive primary sources used in this study – some published, many more unpublished – are fully listed in the relevant notes. Likewise, dates of articles appearing in newspapers in Australia, New Zealand, Mozambique and southern Africa are to be found in the notes. The short bibliography that follows contains only those secondary sources that have been consulted most frequently. Readers are invited to explore the notes for other less-used published sources.

Articles

Arndt, E.H.D. 'Pre-Union Building Society Legislation', *South African Journal of Economics*, Vol. 9, No. 3 (1948), pp. 143–155.

Coleman, M. 'The Origins of the Irish Hospitals Sweepstake', *Irish Economic and Social History*, Vol. 29 (2002), pp. 40–55.

Darnell M., 'Attaining the Australian Dream: The Starr-Bowkett Way', *Labour History*, No. 91 (November 2006), pp. 13–30.

Davies, A. 'The Police and the People: Gambling in Salford, 1900–1939', *The Historical Journal*, Vol. 34, No. 1 (1991), pp. 87–115.

Girvin, S.D. 'The Influence of an English Background on Four Judges Appointed to the Supreme Courts of the Transvaal and Orange River Colony, 1902–1910', *Legal History Review*, Vol. 62, No. 2 (1994), pp. 152–158.

Grundlingh, A. '"Are We Afrikaners Getting Too Rich?" Cornucopia and Change in Afrikanerdom in the 1960s', *Journal of Historical Sociology*, Vol. 21, No. 2/3 (June–September 2008), pp. 143–165.

Hyslop, J. 'The Imperial Working Class Makes Itself White: White Labourism in Britain, Australia and South Africa before the First World War', *Journal of Historical Sociology*, Vol. 12, No. 4 (1999), pp. 398–421.

Hyslop, J. 'A Scottish Socialist Reads Carlyle in Johannesburg Prison, June 1900: Reflections on the Literary Culture of the Imperial Working Class', *Journal of Southern African Studies*, Vol. 29, No. 3 (September 2003), pp. 639–655.

Morier-Genoud, E. 'The Vatican vs Lisbon: The Relaunching of the

Catholic Church in Mozambique, c. 1875–1940', Working Paper 5, *Basler Afrika Bibliographien* (Basel, 2002), pp. 1–16.

Mouton, F.A. '"Fascist or Opportunist?": The Political Career of Oswald Pirow, 1915–1943', *Historia*, Vol. 63, No. 2 (November 2018), pp. 93–111.

Phimister, I.R. 'Markets, Mines and Magnates: Finance and the Coming of War in South Africa, 1894–1899', *Africa: Rivista semestrale di studi e ricerche*, II/2 (2020), pp. 5–22.

Seekings, J. '"Not a Single White Person Should be Allowed to Go Under": *Swartgevaar* and the Origins of South Africa's Welfare State, 1924–1929', *Journal of African History*, Vol. 48, No. 3 (November 2007), pp. 375–394.

Seekings, J. 'The Carnegie Commission and the Backlash Against Welfare State-Building in South Africa, 1931–1937', *Journal of Southern African Studies*, Vol. 34, No. 3 (2008), pp. 515–537.

Ticktin, D. 'The War Issue and the Collapse of the South African Labour Party, 1914–15', *South African Historical Journal*, No. 1 (November 1969), pp. 59–80.

Tothill, D. 'Early Australian–South African Connections up to the Establishment of Official Relations in 1945', *Australian Journal of International Affairs*, Vol. 54, No. 1 (2000), pp. 63–77.

Van Onselen, C. 'Who Killed Meyer Hasenfus? Organized Crime, Policing, and Informing on the Witwatersrand, 1902–8', *History Workshop Journal*, Issue 67 (2009), pp. 1–22.

Books

Atherton, M. *Gambling: A Story of Triumph and Disaster* (London, 2006).

Brain, J.R. *The Catholic Church in the Transvaal* (Johannesburg, 1991).

Clarence-Smith, G. *The Third Portuguese Empire, 1825–1975: A Study in Economic Imperialism* (Manchester, 1985).

Costa, T.M. *Cartas de Moçambique: de Tudo um Pouco* (Lisbon, 1934).

Crwys-Williams, J. *A Country at War, 1939–1945: The Mood of a Nation* (Johannesburg, 1992).

De Klerk, W. *The Puritans in Africa* (London, 1975).

Duffy, J. *Portuguese Africa* (Cambridge, Mass., 1959).

Giliomee, H. *The Afrikaners: Biography of a People* (Charlottesville, 2003).

Giliomee, H. *The Last Afrikaner Leaders: A Supreme Test of Power* (Cape Town, 2012).

Giliomee, H. *Maverick Africans: The Shaping of the Afrikaners* (Cape Town, 2020).

Gutsche, T. *The History and Social Significance of Motion Pictures in South Africa, 1895–1940* (Cape Town, 1972).

Hexham, I. *The Irony of Apartheid: The Struggle for National Independence of Afrikaner Calvinism against British Imperialism* (New York, 1981).

Katz, E.N. *A Trade Union Aristocracy: A History of White Workers in the Transvaal and the General Strike of 1913* (Johannesburg, 1976).

Katzenellenbogen, S.E. *South Africa and Southern Mozambique: Labour, Railways and Trade in the Making of a Relationship* (Manchester, 1982).

Lochery, N. *Lisbon: War in the Shadow of the City of Light, 1939–1946* (New York, 2011).

Moodie, T.D. *The Rise of Afrikanerdom: Power, Apartheid and the Afrikaner Civil Religion* (London, 1975).

Parsons, N. *Black and White Bioscope: Making Movies in Africa, 1899 to 1925* (Pretoria, 2018).

Paton, A. *Hofmeyr* (Cape Town, 1964).

Stals, E.L.P. (ed.). *Afrikaners in die Goudstad, Deel 1: 1881–1924* (Pretoria, 1978).

Thompson, E.P. *The Making of the English Working Class* (London, 1963).

Vail, L. and White, L. *Capitalism and Colonialism in Mozambique: A Study of Quelimane District* (London, 1980).

Van Jaarsveld, F.A. *Die Afrikaners se Groot Trek na die Stede* (Cape Town, 1982).

Van Onselen, C. *New Babylon, New Nineveh: Everyday Life on the Witwatersrand, 1886–1914* (Cape Town, 2001).

Van Onselen, C. *Showdown at the Red Lion: The Life and Times of Jack McLoughlin, 1859–1910* (Johannesburg, 2015).

Van Onselen, C. *The Night Trains: Moving Mozambican Miners to and from South Africa, circa 1902–1955* (Johannesburg, 2019).

Van Zyl-Hermann, D. *Privileged Precariat: White Workers and South Africa's Long Transition to Majority Rule* (Cambridge, 2021).

Chapters in books

Grundlingh, A. 'Dogs, Dominees and the Afrikaner Working Class: Cultural Politics of Greyhound Racing on the Rand, 1932–1949', in *Potent Pastimes: Sport and Leisure Practices in Modern Afrikaner History* (Pretoria, 2013), pp. 14–33.

Hobart Houghton, D. 'Economic Development, 1865–1965', in M. Wilson and L. Thompson (eds.), *The Oxford History of South Africa, Vol. II* (Oxford, 1971), pp. 1–48.

Hyslop, J. 'The British and Australian leaders of the South African Labour Movement, 1902–1914: A Group Biography', in K. Darian-Smith, P. Grimshaw and S. MacIntyre (eds.), *Britishness Abroad: Transnational Movements and Imperial Cultures* (Melbourne, 2007), pp. 90–108.

Mountford, B. 'The Pacific Gold Rushes and the Struggle for Order', in B. Mountford and S. Tuffnell (eds.), *A Global History of Gold Rushes* (Oakland, 2018), pp. 88–108.

Nattrass, N. and Seekings, J. 'The Economy and Poverty in the Twentieth Century', in R. Ross, A. Mager and B. Nasson (eds.), *The Cambridge History of South Africa*, Vol. 2 (Cambridge, 2011), pp. 518–572.

ACKNOWLEDGEMENTS

I aspire to writing a book on my own, but remain enmeshed in a network of colleagues, correspondents, friends, family and relatives who, having my interests at heart, are reluctant to allow me to go my own merry way. They constantly encourage and inform me, and protect me from my ignorance and ill-discipline. But not even they can save me or this book from any remaining blemishes. The remaining errors of fact and interpretation are mine and those whose names are listed below should be exempted from criticism even though they move in dangerous circles.

Missing from that list are the names of two valued colleagues who, sadly, passed away before this work appeared and who require special mention. The archival research and ordering of the findings for this book would never have been possible had it not been for the assistance and remarkable professionalism of two valued colleagues – Cecilia Bailie, in Pretoria, and Tozio Mugabe, in Maputo. I thank them and salute them still.

For more than two decades now, I have profited from how colleagues in the Centre for the Advancement of Scholarship, the Department of Historical and Heritage Studies and the University of Pretoria have enthusiastically cheered on and underwritten my research and writing. Nothing has changed and I am deeply thankful, since I know, from personal experience, that confidence, trust and insight are not necessarily the hallmarks of university administrations. How lucky, then, am I to have benefited from the endorsement and unwavering support of Professors Karen Harris, Alois Mlambo, James Ogude and Tawana Kupe – colleagues who I am delighted to say are also my friends?

A book in the hand is worth two in the bush that is commercial publishing. Only alcohol and fine fare, in prodigious quantities, prompt publishers to believe the tales spun to them by hopeful authors. I love the puff of optimism that drifts across the table at publishers' lunches; it's the whiff of realism that comes from those who try to sell the books that I cannot stand. For very many years now the late Jonathan Ball and his exceptionally ardent successors, Eugene Ashton, Jeremy Boraine and Annie Olivier, have indulged my ideas with an enthusiasm that is belied only by the sales figures that follow. I would also like to thank the indefatigable, meticulous and thoughtful Alfred LeMaitre, who has had to edit not only this book but two others. Leaving friends out of pocket at lunch is vaguely tolerable; depriving them of a decent profit margin in a country that struggles to tell a reader from a reindeer is unforgivable. It is hard to know whether it is better to have friends who never learn and cannot see through you, or ones who learn very slowly. Either way, I owe both my sincere thanks. Now, it's over to the booksellers ...

The limited authoritative sources for a study of this type on the grey economy – where popular and supposedly 'criminal' transactions intersect with everyday street realities – render this work especially reliant on newspaper reports to help track the intensity and periodicity of long-term trends. This project would have been simply impossible were it not for the University of Pretoria holdings of digital back copies of the newspapers cited, and, in addition, for the valuable and unfailingly generous professional assistance of Michelle Leon at NewsBank Inc.

A historian who abandons the highway and heads off into the woods of ignorance in the hope of emerging at the other end with some – any – understanding of some of the more arcane areas of research would be well advised to try and keep up with specialist guides who know the way. True, I may well have lagged far behind, but at least I know those who know far more than I do. Let me point them out to you. You never know when you might need their counsel. I am indebted to Father Diamanto Antunes, Joel Cabrita, James Campbell, Johan Fourie, Hermann Giliomee, Albert Grundlingh, Jon Hyslop, Neil Parsons, Jeremy Seekings, Shane White and especially Jeanne Penvenne, who has, over many years, been unfailingly generous in offering her advice and guidance as I sneak over the border into historical Mozambique. Their expertise is to be admired; their patience exemplary. I am as indebted to Peter Naylor and his relatives for their willingness to share information.

Closer to home – sometimes literally – or easily accessible in other ways, I gladly recall all those who have had to endure endless 'lottery' static-distorting emails, digitised messages or phone calls that once held out the hope of becoming vaguely interesting. Sorry about that. Among those who have suffered most are Barbara Groeblinghoff,

Paul la Hausse, Deborah James, Bill Johnson, Rob Kaplan, Patrick Pearson, Stan Kahn, Jeremy Seekings, Milton Shain, Richard Steyn and June Sinclair. I cannot recall for how many decades I have been the beneficiary of Ian Phimister's friendship and remarkable professionalism, but I remain deeply in his debt as well as that of all the others mentioned. My thanks, too, to Phil Stickler for the maps, and to Cecilia Kruger for help in sourcing photographs. If I have inadvertently forgotten to thank someone, then all I can do now is apologise and thank them. A book boasts the name of the author but, in truth, that is almost always an outrageous lie. All of you have contributed to this one in ways that not even you may recognise, and I thank you.

Engaging the historical imagination and thinking about how to solve problems is always great fun, researching a pure joy, ordering material tedious and writing extremely demanding. What starts out as art-in-the-mind often ends up simply as so much arthritis-of-the-soul. The whole process of seeing a book through from start to finish demands the ongoing care, love and support of the author as he or she contorts into an unrecognisable shape waiting for that one big fix, the release that comes when the date for publishing materialises. This book has been one short of its familiar quota of nurses and that has made for very hard going. It would never have been completed were it not for other members of the Bozzoli family, my sister, Cherie, and more especially my wonderful children Gareth, Jessica and Matthew. I thank you all for seeing me through the fever and the panics.

Charles van Onselen

NOTES

Introduction

1 See B. Mountford, 'The Pacific Gold Rushes and the Struggle for Order', in B. Mountford and S. Tuffnell, *A Global History of Gold Rushes* (Oakland, 2018), pp. 88–108 [hereafter Mountford and Tuffnell, *Gold Rushes*]. My thanks to Ian Phimister for drawing this and other secondary sources to my attention. The Witwatersrand, of course, differed in that it was not a transient 'rush' but the start of a unique long-term mining economy.

2 There are notable exceptions. Among the best is A. Grundlingh, 'Dogs, Dominees and the Afrikaner Working Class: Cultural Politics of Greyhound Racing on the Rand, 1932–1949', in his collection titled *Potent Pastimes: Sport and Leisure Practices in Modern Afrikaner History* (Pretoria, 2013), pp. 14–33 [hereafter Grundlingh, 'Dogs, Dominees and the Afrikaner Working Class'].

3 Calvinists, their changing ethnic and racial beliefs, and the political expressions of Calvinism in South Africa in the 19th and 20th centuries demand a far more refined understanding than is presented in this work on the history of gambling. Biblical scholars and church historians will need to look elsewhere for the precision they rightly seek. I have used the word 'Calvinist' (the self-description most often used by the historical actors themselves) to refer broadly to Protestant churches following Calvinist doctrines in relation to gambling, thrift, leisure and recreation in the 20th century. I have used the term neo-Calvinism to refer more specifically to that self-selected ethnic and racial elite that arose after 1857 and which, in the interwar years of the 20th century, drove not only social oppression generally but segregation and apartheid policies. For some of the complexities and ironies that these considerations involve, see, for example, John W. de Gruchy, 'Calvin(ism) and Apartheid in South African in the Twentieth-Century: The Making and Unmaking of a Racial Identity' (unpublished paper).

4 Nor did these vulnerabilities disappear in the latter part of the 20th century. For the historiographical context of this ongoing reality, see D. van Zyl-Hermann, *Privileged Precariat: White Workers and South Africa's Long Transition to Majority Rule* (Cambridge, 2021), pp. 1–20.

Part I

1 See M. Atherton, *Gambling: A Story of Triumph and Disaster* (London, 2006), pp. 6–10 [hereafter Atherton, *Gambling*].

2 See I. Hexham, *The Irony of Apartheid: The Struggle for National Independence of Afrikaner Calvinism against British Imperialism* (New York, 1981), p. 61 [hereafter Hexham, *Afrikaner Calvinism*]. The date of the founding of the Dopper church, in 1859, may not be entirely fortuitous; for the significance of

the year 1857 in the history of the Reformed churches and the broader context, see H. Giliomee, *Maverick Africans: The Shaping of the Afrikaners* (Cape Town, 2020), pp. 134–172 [hereafter Giliomee, *Maverick Africans*].

3 Hexham, *Afrikaner Calvinism*, p. 67.

4 See C. van Onselen, *Showdown at the Red Lion: The Life and Times of Jack McLoughlin, 1859—1910* (Johannesburg, 2015), p. 217 [hereafter van Onselen, *Showdown*].

5 For a comprehensive list of all anti-lottery laws in southern Africa prior to the formation of Union, in 1910, see Republic of South Africa (RSA), National Archives of South Africa (NASA), Pretoria, SAB, Ref. L/18/31, Vol. 2, 'Dobbelry – Johannesburg', 1951–1963, P.J. Wessels to Commissioner of Police, Pretoria, 10 April 1959 [hereafter volumes one and two are referred to as RSA, NASA, SAB, Ref. L/18/31, Vol. 1 and Vol. 2 respectively].

6 Van Onselen, *Showdown*, p. 218.

7 This paragraph is based on 'Tailings' and 'the Turf', *The Star*, 22 August and 14 November 1893; *Rand Daily Mail*, 20 and 22 May 1912; G. Clarence-Smith, *The Third Portuguese Empire, 1825—1975: A Study in Economic Imperialism* (Manchester, 1985), p. 99; and L. Rousseau, *The Dark Stream: The Story of Eugéne Marais* (Johannesburg, 1982), p. 109. On the desire to siphon off some of the Rand's haul of sweepstakes into Mozambique, see also *Diplomatic and Consular Reports, Portugal 1897, Trade and Commerce of Lourenço Marques and District*, Annual Series No. 2162 (London, 1898), p. 7, and Mozambique (MOZ), Maputo, Arquivo Histórico de Mocambique (AHM), Fundo: Administração Civil: Caixa – 1502, Lotaria Provincial, Rufe Naylor 1, Santos Rufino to Governador Geral da Colonia de Mocambique, 16 September 1930 [hereafter Caixa 1502].

8 See Mountford and Tuffnell, *Gold Rushes*.

9 The best work on an Anglophone international proletariat has been done by Jonathan Hyslop. See, among other works, his 'The Imperial Working Class Makes Itself White: White Labourism in Britain, Australia and South Africa before the First World War', *Journal of Historical Sociology*, Vol. 12, No. 4 (1999), pp. 398–421 [hereafter Hyslop, 'White Labourism']; and 'The British and Australian Leaders of the South African Labour Movement, 1902–1914: A Group Biography', in K. Darian-Smith, P. Grimshaw and S. MacIntyre (eds.) *Britishness Abroad: Transnational Movements and Imperial Cultures* (Melbourne 2007), pp. 90–108.

10 See D. Tothill, 'Early Australian–South African Connections up to the Establishment of Official Relations in 1945' *Australian Journal of International Affairs*, Vol. 54, No. 1 (2000), pp. 63–77. I.R. Phimister's 'Markets, Mines and Magnates: Finance and the Coming of War in South Africa, 1894–1899', *Africa: Rivista semestrale di studi e ricerche*, II/2 (2020), pp. 5–22, is essential reading on the 1895 boom.

11 See van Onselen, *Showdown*, pp. 221–222.

12 See 'Randlords and Rotgut, 1886–1903' and 'Prostitutes and Proletarians, 1886–1914', in C. van Onselen, *New Babylon, New Nineveh; Everyday Life on the Witwatersrand, 1886—1914* (Cape Town, 2001), pp. 47–108 and 109–164 [hereafter van Onselen, *New Babylon, New Nineveh*].

13   For the resulting confusion, see *Sunday Times*, 12 July 1914.

14   See van Onselen, *New Babylon, New Nineveh*, pp. 32–36, and 40–41.

15   See *Rand Daily Mail*, 30 October 1923, for an illustrated example.

16   On moneylenders, see *Rand Daily Mail*, 8 May 1909.

17   *Rand Daily Mail*, 8 May 1909.

18   On the Cape conviction, see RSA, NASA, Pretoria, TAB, Ref. 196/19, Illiquid Case Payment W.T. Seccombe vs R.H. Tatham, Judgment, 8 July 1919.

19   M. Darnell, 'Attaining the Australian Dream: The Starr-Bowkett Way', *Labour History*, No. 91 (November 2006), pp. 13–30. Before 1910 Johannesburg had at least two Starr-Bowkett schemes – a further sign of early Australian influence on the Witwatersrand. See E.H.D. Arndt, 'Pre-Union Building Society Legislation', *South African Journal of Economics*, Vol. 9, No. 3 (1948), pp. 143–155.

20   See *Rand Daily Mail*, 20 February 1908, and RSA, NASA, Pretoria, K 23, Vol. 14, K. Vachell, Deputy Commissioner of Police, Transvaal Division, South African Police, Memo on Rand Sporting Club, 20 October 1917 [hereafter Vachell, 'Rand Sporting Club, 20 October 1917'].

21   On the disorganisation of the provincial lottery in Mozambique at the time, see correspondence in MOZ, AHM, Maputo, 'Lotarias, L. Cohen, 1897–1910'. For illegal lotteries on the Rand incurring only a suspended sentence, see, for example, *Rand Daily Mail*, 19 January 1911.

22   See *Rand Daily Mail*, 6 May 1909.

23   See 'The Gambling Commission', *Rand Daily Mail*, 6 and 8 May 1909.

24   See also RSA, NASA, Pretoria, TAB, LD, Vol. 96, Ref. AG5720/04, First South African Starr-Bowkett Building Society, 1908–09.

25   See *Rand Daily Mail*, 1 December 1909, 1 December 1910, 1 December 1911 and 7 December 1912.

26   On Naylor's early life, see *The Star* (Johannesburg), 12 April 1927, which draws heavily on an article that first appeared in the *Daily Guardian* (Australia) of an unknown date.

27   *The Star*, 12 April 1927.

28   See, among other sources, *Kalgoorlie Miner*, 21 November 1905 for the previous year, and *Wanganui Herald*, 27 December 1906, and *Kalgoorlie Western Argus*, 30 January 1906.

29   *Wanganui Herald*, 22 December 1906.

30   *Norseman Times* (Western Australia), 4 May 1906.

31   Paragraph based on information contained in *The Star* (Christchurch) 17 May 1907; *Rand Daily Mail*, 14 September 1908; and A. Macdonald, 'Colonial Trespassers in the Making of South Africa's International Borders, 1900 to c. 1950', PhD thesis, St John's College, Cambridge, April 2012, p. 184, f/n 73.

32   See especially *Rand Daily Mail*, 28 January 1911.

33   On Naylor and athletics, see, among many other sources, *Rand Daily Mail*, 22 February 1909, 11 and 12 March 1909; on cycle races, 16 June 1909, 6 and 26 August 1910; on sculling, 7 October 1910; and on whippets, 21 January 1911, 'Dog-Owner to Sporting Editor' 28 January 1911 and 9 October 1911.

34   *Townsville Daily Bulletin* (Australia), 27 September 1939.

35   On warning signs, see, for example, *Rand Daily Mail*, 21 August 1909.

36   An excellent account of this early period in Naylor's career and his interest in professional athletics is to be found in D.M. Pitchford's, 'Making the Transition: Empire, Amateurism and Reggie Walker, the "Little Natalian" Sprinter', MA thesis, Department of History, Manchester Metropolitan University, September 2013.

37   Some of the Stadium's early history can be traced in *Rand Daily Mail*, 22 February, 22 April and 21 August 1909.

38   *Rand Daily Mail*, 22 April 1909.

39   Among many other items, see *Rand Daily Mail*, 24 June 1909, 4 October 1909 and 26 August 1910.

40   See van Onselen, *New Babylon, New Nineveh*, pp. 342–343.

41   RSA, NASA, Pretoria, K23, Vol. 14, West Rand Racing Club, The Petition of the West Rand Consolidated Mines, Limited 27 July 1910 [hereafter RSA, NASA, Pretoria, K23, Vol. 14].

42   *Sunday Times*, 26 April 1908

43   See B. Rostron, 'The Personal and Political Ghosts that Haunt Cape Town', *South Africa News*, 11 June 2017 and L. Davies, F.R. Karl and O. Knowles (eds.), *The Collected Letters of Joseph Conrad*, Vol. 6 (Cambridge, 2002), p. 403, Conrad to L.R. MacLeod, 5 April 1919.

44   See 'The Racing Craze' and, for a response from a church, see, for example, F.W. Collyer, 'The Gambling Craze', in the *Sunday Times* of 10 January and 13 June 1909.

45   On the Attorney General, see *Sunday Times*, 14 June 1908; and for Naylor and Seccombe's evidence, 22 April 1909.

46   See *Sunday Times*, 20 June 1909, and, for a fine overview of the issue and the newspaper's changed position, *Rand Daily Mail*, 13 January 1910.

47   See the review carried in *Rand Daily Mail*, 1 March 1910. On Bernberg's career, see *Voice of Labour*, 5 August 1910, and, more especially, *Rand Daily Mail*, 21 June 1913.

48   See *The Star*, 14 February 1919. Although not mentioned by name, Naylor was almost certainly the unscrupulous entrepreneur alluded to in M. Levenson (ed.), *South African Odyssey: The Autobiography of Bertha Goudvis* (Johannesburg, 2011), pp. 144–146.

49   See, for example, *Rand Daily Mail*, 11 March 1912.

50   See *Rand Daily Mail*, 23 and 25 November 1909, 21 January and 24 October 1910, and N. Parsons, *Black and White Bioscope: Making Movies in Africa*, 1899 to 1925 (Pretoria, 2018), pp. 15–16 [hereafter Parsons, *Bioscope*]. See also T. Gutsche, *The History and Social Significance of Motion Pictures in South Africa*, 1895–1940 (Cape Town, 1972), p. 99 [hereafter Gutsche, *Motion Pictures*].

51   When Seccombe staged 'The Hero of Jerusalem' and fell foul of the by-laws – as he and Naylor did periodically – it was the rabbi who gave evidence in Seccombe's defence; see *Rand Daily Mail*, 27 October 1909.

52   On Friedman, see *Rand Daily Mail*, 15 February 1910; and on Naylor and Friedman, 2 July 1912.

53   *Rand Daily Mail*, 24 October 1910.

54   RSA, NASA, Pretoria, TAB, WLD, Vol. 5/202, Ref. 639/1912, *Ex Parte*

Application, R.T. Naylor and M. Prechner.

55 See, for example, *Rand Daily Mail*, 22 February 1909.

56 *Rand Daily Mail*, 8 November 1911, 8 May 1912 and 17 May 1917.

57 *Rand Daily Mail*, 17 October 1910, 25 March and 31 May 1912. Naylor offered open-air film shows at the Stadium, which avoided some of the problems associated with safety, insanitary conditions and overcrowding; see Gutsche, *Motion Pictures*, p. 100.

58 See, among other sources, *Rand Daily Mail*, 12 March, 29 May, 21 August and 4 October 1909.

59 *Rand Daily Mail*, 3 November 1910.

60 See Gutsche, *Motion Pictures*, p. 103, note 22.

61 Gutsche, *Motion Pictures*, p. 104.

62 For the business background to the departure, see Parsons, *Bioscope*, p. 26, and for the dinner, *Rand Daily Mail*, 20 July 1912.

63 See Parsons, *Bioscope*, pp. 14 and 29.

64 *Rand Daily Mail*, 21 May 1913.

65 *Rand Daily Mail*, 23 and 31 May 1913.

66 See Parsons, *Bioscope*, p. 29.

67 RSA, NASA, Pretoria, TAB, WLD, Vol. 5/230, Ref. 776/1913, Opposed Application: H.J. Retief vs R.T. Naylor.

68 Parsons, *Bioscope*, p. 29.

69 *Rand Daily Mail*, 6 February and 3 May 1915, and 2 December 1916. See also RSA, NASA, Pretoria, TAB, WLD, Vol. 5, File 310, Ref 366, Opposed Application George Naylor vs R.C. Mackay, 1917 [hereafter G. Naylor vs R.C. Mackay, 1917], Affidavit, W.T. Seccombe, 29 August 1917; and Union of South Africa, *Report of the Commissioner Appointed to Inquire into Allegations of Bribery and Corruption in Relation to Members of the Transvaal Provincial Council and Town Councillors in the Transvaal*, U.G. No. 48-1918 (Government Printing and Stationery Office, Pretoria, 1918), Minutes of Evidence, Johannesburg Town Hall, 15 January 1919, pp. 571–572 [hereafter *Bribery Commission*, UG 48-1918].

70 On Seccombe and the Labour Party, see *Rand Daily Mail*, 2 February 1915 and 21 May 1917.

71 See *Rand Daily Mail*, 5 December 1906 and 6 April 1907. In 1907, Tatham, who had been heavily invested in a printing firm, attempted to buy the African newspaper *Ilanga lase Natal*, and was also successfully sued by his African clerk for his failure to pay the wages due to his assistant. See *Rand Daily Mail*, 6 July 1907.

72 *Rand Daily Mail*, 13 June and 20 August 1913.

73 *Rand Daily Mail*, 15 January 1913.

74 See, especially, Tatham's letter to the *Cape Times*, as reported in *Rand Daily Mail*, 11 April 1913. For some of the strands in post-rebellion and pro-republican thinking among rural Afrikaners, see A.M. Grundlingh, *Fighting Their Own War: Black People and the First World War*, 1914–1918 (Johannesburg, 1987), pp. 26–29.

75 See *Rand Daily Mail*, 1 May and 11 July 1913.

76   *Rand Daily Mail*, 18 October 1913. For the wider context of this reading of radicals, see J. Hyslop, 'A Scottish Socialist Reads Carlyle in Johannesburg Prison, June 1900: Reflections on the Literary Culture of the Imperial Working Class', *Journal of Southern African Studies*, Vol. 29, No. 3 (September 2003), pp. 639–655.

77   *Rand Daily Mail*, 20 and 29 August 1913.

78   *Rand Daily Mail*, 10 February 1919.

79   In 1896, Tatham had spent £800 in an unsuccessful attempt to become a Member of the Legislative Assembly in Natal, and a republican meeting in Heilbron with General de Wet, much later, cost him more than £100 – see Naylor's evidence in RSA, NASA, Pretoria, TAB, TPD, Rex vs R.T Naylor, 1919 [hereafter Rex vs Naylor, 1919].

80   See D. Ticktin, 'The War Issue and the Collapse of the South African Labour Party, 1914–15', *South African Historical Journal*, No. 1 (November 1969), p. 66 [hereafter Ticktin, 'The War Issue'].

81   *Rand Daily Mail*, 9 August and 28 September 1923.

82   Tatham's troubled legal career is recounted, in part, in *Rand Daily Mail*, 9 August 1923.

83   See *Rand Daily Mail*, 11 October 1915, and Parsons, *Bioscope*, pp. 30 and 35.

84   See especially G. Naylor vs R.C. Mackay, 1917.

85   See N. Nattrass and J. Seekings, 'The Economy and Poverty in the Twentieth Century', in R. Ross, A. Mager and B. Nasson (eds.), *The Cambridge History of South Africa*, Vol. 2 (Cambridge, 2011), p. 523 [hereafter Nattrass and Seekings, 'The Economy and Poverty'].

86   See RSA, NASA, Pretoria, TAB, WLD, Vol. 5/327, Ref. 19/1919, Opposed Application, R.T. Naylor vs R.H. Tatham, 7–14 January 1919 [hereafter Naylor vs Tatham, 1919].

87   *Rand Daily Mail*, 12 June 1916.

88   RSA, NASA, Pretoria, K23, Vol. 14, handwritten 'Memo' on 'Rand Sporting Club – Newclare', probably drafted by the Acting Provincial Secretary, Transvaal, and an accompanying but largely irrelevant letter from the Deputy Commissioner of Police, Pretoria, to the District Commandant, South African Police, Krugersdorp, dated 24 August 1917.

89   RSA, NASA, Pretoria, K23, Vol. 14, K. Vachell, Deputy Commissioner, C.I.D., Transvaal Division, 'Re: Rand Sporting Club', 20 October 1917.

90   The anxious visit to Johannesburg is recalled in T.M. Costa, *Cartas de Moçambique: de Tudo um Pouco* (Lisbon, 1934), pp. 212 [hereafter Costa, *Cartas*].

Part II

1   As with Naylor, it is surprising that there is no biography of José Vicente do Sacramento, although the sketch in Costa's *Cartas* provides a useful start. Sacramento and Rufe Naylor also make fleeting appearances in J.P.B. Coelho's

novel *O Olho de Hertzog* (Lisbon, 2010) [hereafter Coelho, *Olho de Hertzog*].

2   See E. Morier-Genoud's seminal essay, 'The Vatican vs Lisbon: The Relaunching of the Catholic Church in Mozambique, c. 1875–1940', *Basler Afrika Bibliographien, Working Papers* (Basel), 2002, pp. 1–16 [hereafter Morier-Genoud, 'The Vatican vs Lisbon'].

3   Morier-Genoud, 'The Vatican vs Lisbon', p. 9.

4   All information on Vicente's early career in the Church – but not his transgressions – is taken from a biographical entry on José Vicente do Sacramento in D.G. Antunes's forthcoming *Dicionário da Igreja Católica em Moçambique* [hereafter Antunes, 'Sacramento', *Dicionário da Igreja*]. I am in Father Diamanto Antunes's debt for the assistance that he so generously provided.

5   Arquivo Histórico Ultramarino (AHU), Lisbon, Missionaries: S4 1329-30, Padre José Vicente do Sacramento, Secretary of State of the Navy and Overseas Affairs, General Overseas Direction, Memo dated 24 April 1899, which notes Sacramento's emoluments and tax status [hereafter AHU, Lisbon, S4 1329-30].

6   AHU, Lisbon, S4 1329-30, Direcção Geral do Ultramar letter to unknown recipient dated 14 November 1905, and Bishop F.F de Silva to Conselheiro Director Geral do Ministério da Marinha e Ultramar, 17 June 1910.

7   AHU, Lisbon, S4 1329-30, Direcção Geral do Ultramar letter to unknown recipient dated 14 November 1905, and Bishop F.F de Silva to Conselheiro Director Geral do Ministério da Marinha e Ultramar, 17 June 1910.

8   AHU, Lisbon, S4 1329-30, Direcção Geral do Ultramar letter to unknown recipient dated 14 November 1905, and Bishop F.F de Silva to Conselheiro Director Geral do Ministério da Marinha e Ultramar, 17 June 1910; and undated letter, Bishop [de Silva] to the Minister da Marinha e Ultramar.

9   AHU, Lisbon, S4 1329-30, Direcção Geral do Ultramar letter to unknown recipient dated 14 November 1905, and Bishop F.F de Silva to Conselheiro Director Geral do Ministério da Marinha e Ultramar, 17 June 1910.

10   AHU, Lisbon, S4 1329-30, Direcção Geral do Ultramar letter to unknown recipient dated 14 November 1905. See also Costa, *Cartas*, p. 211.

11   AHU, Lisbon, S4 1329-30, Series 1910, Prelature of Mozambique, N. 148 – 111, unsigned memorandum.

12   AHU, Lisbon, S4 1329-301908, Bishop [de Silva] to Conselheiro Director Geral do Ministério da Marinha e Ultramar, 17 June 1910.

13   See Antunes, 'Sacramento', *Dicionário da Igreja*.

14   AHU, Lisbon, S4 1329-30, Bishop [F.F. de Silva] to Conselheiro Director Geral do Ministério da Marinha e Ultramar, 17 June 1910. On the conjoined *prazos*, see L. Vail and L. White, *Capitalism and Colonialism in Mozambique: A Study of Quelimane District* (London, 1980), pp. 115–116 [hereafter Vail and White, *Capitalism and Colonialism*].

15   AHU, Lisbon, S4 1329-30, Unsigned memorandum, dated 4 August 1910, at Lourenço Marques.

16   See Costa, *Cartas*, p. 221. In Coelho's novel *O Olho de Hertzog*, p. 90, Sacramento is portrayed as having become the 'cultivator' of the widow's land in all senses of that word.

17   See, for example, how he is portrayed in Costa, *Cartas*, p. 221.

18 The financial and political context of the Church in which Vicente served on the Rand is outlined in J.R. Brain, *The Catholic Church in the Transvaal* (Johannesburg, 1991), pp. 116–126.

19 See Costa, *Cartas*, p. 209.

20 See Antunes, 'Sacramento', *Dicionário da Igreja*; Costa, *Cartas*, p. 210; and A. Hohlfeldt and F. Grabauska, 'Pioneers of the Press in Mozambique: João Albisini and his Brother', *Brazilian Journalism Research*, Vol. 6, No. 1 (2010), p. 193 [hereafter Hohlfeldt and Grabauska, 'Pioneers of the Press']. Sacramento's articles also appeared at a time when there was a heated debate about the 'denationalisation' of black migrant workers in *Diário Popular* in Lisbon; see R.J. Williams, 'Creating a Healthy Colonial State in Mozambique, 1885–1915', PhD thesis, Department of History, University of Chicago, 2013, p. 117.

21 Costa, *Cartas*, p. 210.

22 RSA, NASA, Pretoria, NTS, Vol. 201, Ref. 7565/1911/F473, Acting Secretary for Native Affairs to the Director of Native Labour, 6 October 1911: '[The Minister] considers that 15% is a disgraceful proportion of remittances to reach their destination, and that surely the Witwatersrand Native Labour Association should be able to secure a better result than this.'

23 See Antunes, 'Sacramento', *Dicionário da Igreja*.

24 See RSA, NASA, Pretoria, SAB/GG/Vol. 1012, Ref. 20/6, Gladstone to the Earl of Crewe, 16 June 1910; and Antunes, 'Sacramento', *Dicionário da Igreja*.

25 AHU, Lisbon, S4 1329-30, Unsigned memorandum, dated 4 August 1910, Lourenço Marques.

26 Morier-Genoud, 'The Vatican vs Lisbon', p. 11.

27 See Costa, *Cartas*, p. 210.

28 MOZ, Maputo, AHM, Governo Geral, Caixa 224, Processa No. 39 A, Memorandum, Sacramento, Director Geral, 11 July 1914.

29 Antunes, 'Sacramento', *Dicionário da Igreja*.

30 Antunes, 'Sacramento', *Dicionário da Igreja*.

31 Costa, *Cartas*, p. 211.

32 MOZ, Maputo, AHM, SNI, File 3-408/292, February 1920, for forced labour provided to Padre Vicente's farm at Mailana. My thanks to Jeanne Penvenne for pointing me to this and other sources relating to the holy man.

33 See, for example, Hohlfeldt and Grabauska, 'Pioneers of the Press', p. 193. Interestingly, T.M. Costa, whose book appeared a year after Vicente's death, chose to say nothing about his domestic arrangements although they are made quite explicit in Coelho's novel.

34 *Stage and Cinema*, 11 November 1916, p. 3. My thanks to Neil Parsons for this and several other important references to the wartime career of Naylor.

35 See Nattrass and Seekings, 'The Economy and Poverty', pp. 519–529.

36 See F.A. van Jaarsveld, *Die Afrikaners se Groot Trek na die Stede* (Cape Town, 1982), pp. 167–175 [herafter van Jaarsveld, *Die Afrikaners se Groot Trek*].

37 Nattrass and Seekings, 'The Economy and Poverty', p. 524.

38 F. Wilson, *Labour in the South African Gold Mines, 1911–1969* (Cambridge, 1972), p. 9.

39 For an idea of the prevailing mood on the Rand, see the 'Don't get Panicky' leader in *Rand Daily Mail*, 13 March 1921.

40 The South African National Thrift Movement appears not to have attracted the attention of either economic or social historians that it probably deserves. For a pointer as to where such a study might lead, see, for example, C. Summers, 'Patriotic Thrift: Savings Campaigns in the British World during W.W. II' – draft conference presentation, Stellenbosch Institute for Advanced Studies, September 2019.

41 On Dan Dingwall as trade unionist, see, among others, E.N. Katz, *A Trade Union Aristocracy: A History of White Workers in the Transvaal and the General Strike of 1913* (Johannesburg, 1976), pp. 125 and 387 [hereafter Katz, *A Trade Union Aristocracy*]; and, on the Dingwall couple on the Johannesburg Town Council, Union of South Africa, *Report of the Commissioner Appointed to Inquire into Allegations of Bribery and Corruption in Relation to Members of the Transvaal Provincial Council and Town Councillors in the Transvaal, Part II, the Report of the Inquiry into Alleged Municipal Corruption in Johannesburg* (U.G. 30-19), among many other references, pp. 7 and 16 [hereafter referred to as *Bribery Commission, Part I* (U.G. 48-1918) and *Part II*].

42 See RSA, NASA, Pretoria, K23, Vol. 14, West Rand Racing Club, File marked 'Naylor', 17 September 1918, Affidavit of C.T.Z. van Veyeren, 13 September 1918 [hereafter RSA, NASA, Pretoria, K23, Vol. 14]. On Mrs Dingwall's prominence in Johannesburg affairs, see, for example, *Rand Daily Mail*, 1 December and 2 December 1915, and 2 May 1916.

43 As from October 1917, Tatham, by his own admission, was retained by Naylor at a fee of £23 per week – see *Rand Daily Mail*, 18 February 1919.

44 See *Rand Daily Mail*, 2 January 1917, and Hyslop, 'White Labourism', p. 5.

45 For unsubstantiated allegations about Schlesinger's willingness to bribe politicians see RSA, NASA, Pretoria, K23, Vol. 14, West Rand Racing Club, Anonymous letter to the Minister of Justice by 'One of his Victims', 17 September 1918. What is beyond dispute is that, towards the closing years of World War I, Schlesinger frequently interacted with a few members of the Johannesburg underworld, including Naylor, Seccombe and L.S. Schmulian. See, for example, Minutes of Evidence before the *Bribery Commission, Part I*, evidence of Coetzee, 12 September 1918, p. 572; and Schmulian, 14 January 1919, p. 752.

46 For the impatient reader, it was the Standard Bank. More will be revealed, in due course, lower down.

47 See RSA, NASA, Pretoria, K23, Vol. 14, West Rand Racing Club, File marked 'Naylor', 17 September 1918, Affidavit of C.T.Z. van Veyeren, 13 September 1918

48 For one example, among dozens of others, of a Furze meeting being disrupted by white workers, see *Rand Daily Mail*, 7 March 1914.

49 *Rand Daily Mail*, 28 February 1916.

50 *Rand Daily Mail*, 18 January 1917.

51 *Rand Daily Mail*, 14 August 1918.

52 See *Bribery Commission, Part I*, p. 11, para. 15.

53   See evidence led before the *Bribery Commission, Part II*, pp. 1173–1184.

54   Minutes, *Bribery Commission*, 1919, evidence of J.A. Clark led at the
      Johannesburg Town Hall, 19 February 1919, p. 1933. On Clark, see also Katz,
      A Trade Union Aristocracy, pp. 265 and 457, note 49.

55   *Rand Daily Mail*, 12 January 1917.

56   See especially, RSA, NASA, Pretoria, K 23, Vol. 14, Vachell, 'Rand Sporting
      Club, 20 October 1917'.

57   See Costa, *Cartas*, pp. 212–213.

58   *Rand Daily Mail*, 16 February 1917.

59   RSA, NASA, Pretoria, TAB, TPD, 150A/1919, Criminal Case: Rex vs Rufus
      Theodore Naylor, evidence of R.H. Tatham, p. 20 [hereafter, RSA, NASA,
      Pretoria, Rex vs R.T. Naylor, April 1919].

60   For an outline of the legal history of the Rand Sporting Club, see police and
      other correspondence in RSA, NASA, Pretoria, K 23, Vol. 14, File marked
      'Newclare'.

61   RSA, NASA, Pretoria, Supreme Court of South Africa, WLD, *Ex Parte*
      Application, R.T. Naylor vs Rand Sporting Club, 5 March 1917, 'Extract of
      Minutes of Meeting of the Rand Sporting Club, held on 18th January 1917'
      [hereafter RSA, NASA, Pretoria, Naylor vs RSC 1917].

62   RSA, NASA, Pretoria, Naylor vs RSC 1917. See also *Rand Daily Mail*, 8 and
      9 March 1917.

63   *Rand Daily Mail*, 18 April 1917.

64   *Rand Daily Mail*, 25 April 1917.

65   *Rand Daily Mail*, 17 May 1917.

66   *Rand Daily Mail*, 17 May 1917.

67   *O Africano*, 6 August 1917.

68   The template for the Dividend Cigarette Company may have originated
      with another decade-old cigarette-lottery endeavour, the United Tobacco
      Companies (North) Limited – see *Sunday Times*, 5 July 1914, for the police
      notice prohibiting the scheme, and 26 July, for the results of the final draw
      based on forecasting the Rand's gold output for the month.

69   On customs duties see, S.E. Katzenellenbogen, *South Africa and Southern
      Mozambique: Labour, Railways and Trade in the Making of a Relationship*
      (Manchester, 1982), p. 85 [hereafter Katzenellenbogen, *South Africa and
      Southern Mozambique*].

70   RSA, NASA, Pretoria, TAB, Vol. 8/277, Ref. 692/1918, Opposed Application,
      Commissioner for Inland Revenue vs the Delagoa Bay Cigarette Co. Ltd,
      Affidavit, The Commissioner of Inland Revenue, 14 September 1918 [hereafter
      RSA, NASA, Pretoria, TAB, Vol. 8/277, Delagoa Bay Cigarette Co.].

71   As quoted from court proceedings, as reported in *Rand Daily Mail*, 27 July
      1917.

72   RSA, NASA, Pretoria, TAB, Vol. 8/277, Replying Affidavit of Walter Mortimer
      Southward, 20 September 1918.

73   See, especially, RSA, NASA, Pretoria, K23, Vol. 14, K. Vachell, Deputy
      Commissioner, C.I.D., Transvaal Division to Deputy Commissioner I/C, 20
      October 1917.

74   RSA, NASA, Pretoria, K23, Vol. 14, K. Vachell, Deputy Commissioner, C.I.D., Transvaal Division to Deputy Commissioner I/C, 20 October 1917.

75   On the suspension of the lottery, see *O Africano*, 6 August 1917.

76   RSA, NASA, Pretoria, TAB, Vol. 8/277, and *Rand Daily Mail*, 13 December 1918.

77   *Rand Daily Mail*, 29 May 1917.

78   The 'farm', it seems, ran at a loss despite benefiting from forced labour provided by the Portuguese administration; see Costa, *Cartas*, pp. 215–216. I am indebted to Jeanne Penvenne for helping me to decode the meaning hidden within the name of the property.

79   Letter to the author from P.B. Naylor, 2 May 1918.

80   Van der Linden is difficult to track in the official records, but traces of his presence can be found in Caixa 1502, Files 1–3, 'Rufe Naylor'; and in RSA, NASA, Pretoria, Treasury, File CR 4010, marked 'Secret' 'Contravention of the Emergency Finance Regulations: Santos Rufino, George Naylor and Dr A.A.C. Casquerio', 1941. He can, however, be traced relatively easily in the *Rand Daily Mail* in the 1920s and 1930s, and more especially in the editions of 25 February, 6 and 12 April 1922, and 10, 15 and 18 August 1922.

81   Letter to the author from P.B. Naylor, 24 May 2018. The real pioneers of criminal counterintelligence and in-house electronic security on the Witwatersrand were those immigrant Russian Jewish syndicates that dominated the illicit liquor trade during the late 1890s; see van Onselen, *New Babylon, New Nineveh*, p. 86.

82   RSA, NASA, Pretoria, K23, Vol. 14, Affidavit of C.T.Z. van Veyeren, 13 September 1918.

83   Paragraph based on, among several other sources, RSA, NASA, Pretoria, WLD, Vol. 5/327, Ref. 9/1919, Opposed Application, R.T. Naylor vs R.H. Tatham, January 1919, Affidavit of R.T. Tatham, 6 January 1919; RSA, NASA, Pretoria, TAB, Vol. 8/277, Ref. 692/1918, The Commissioner of Inland Revenue (applicant) and the Delagoa Bay Cigarette Company Limited, 19 September 1918; and, especially, *Rand Daily Mail*, 31 August 1922.

84   RSA, NASA, Pretoria, TAB, Vol. 8/277, Ref. 692/1918, Affidavit of C.D. McLoughlin, Commissioner of Inland Revenue, 14 September 1918.

85   See, for example, *Rand Daily Mail*, 8 August 1917. There is a useful legal discussion of the Post Office Act as applied to lotteries in the *Sunday Times* of 6 December 1914 and 21 December 1919.

86   *Rand Daily Mail*, 27 July 1917.

87   *Rand Daily Mail*, 27 July 1917.

88   See E.L.P. Stals (ed.), *Afrikaners in die Goudstad, Deel 1: 1881–1924* (Pretoria, 1978), pp. 149–150.

89   See *Life, Sport and Drama*, 28 September and 18 December 1918.

90   On church objections at the time, see, for example, 'The Naylor Case', *The Star*, 10 February 1919.

91   See, especially, RSA, NASA, Pretoria, TAB, TPD, 150/1919, Part 1 and 150A/1919, Criminal Case, Rex vs Rufus Theodore Naylor, Preparatory Examination, 14 December 1918, Affidavit of Daniel Dingwall.

92   See Ticktin, 'The War Issue'.

93   See RSA, NASA, Pretoria, K23, Vol. 14, K. Vachell, Deputy Commissioner, C.I.D., Transvaal Division, to Deputy Commissioner I/C, 20 October 1917.

94   *The Star*, 14 February 1919.

95   *Rand Daily Mail*, 29 June 1917.

96   See, for example, 'Our Comic Council' in the *Sunday Times*, 16 September 1917.

97   *The Star*, 10 February 1919.

98   *The Star*, 8 February 1919.

99   *The Star*, 8 February 1919. In 1917, a member of the Provincial Council was paid a derisory £120 a year and a member of the Executive a further £380; see RSA, NASA, Pretoria, Rex vs R.T. Naylor, 1919, Evidence of D. Dingwall [hereafter Dingwall evidence], 12 December 1918, p. 5.

100 *The Star*, 14 February 1919.

101 See Katz, *A Trade Union Aristocracy*, p. 199, and H.J. and R.E. Simons, *Class and Colour in South Africa, 1850–1950* (Harmondsworth, 1969), p. 107.

102 *Bribery Commission, Part II*, p. 6.

103 See RSA, NASA, Pretoria, K23, Vol. 14, handwritten police notes on 'Newclare'.

104 *Rand Daily Mail*, 26 July 1917.

105 Tatham evidence, 12 December 1918, p. 19.

106 See Dingwall evidence, 12 December 1918, p. 5.

107 Dingwall evidence, 12 December 1918, p. 6.

108 Tatham evidence, 12 December 1918, p. 26.

109 The Colonel, for whatever reasons, proved to be forgiving, and later he alone was willing to give evidence on Naylor's behalf at the criminal trial that followed; see *The Star*, 13 February 1919. The growing success of the Lourenço Marques Lottery during the intervening two years may have contributed to Furze's change of heart.

110 *The Star*, 10 February 1919.

111 See *The Star*, 13 February 1913.

112 On Hills, see, for example, *Sunday Times*, 6 February 1917.

113 See *Sunday Times*, 28 September 1917.

114 Hills's persistent and pointed questioning – of van Veyeren in particular – can be tracked in the extracts from the Minutes of the Provincial Council over the period; see, RSA, NASA, Pretoria, K23, Vol. 14.

115 'During the passage of the bill Naylor [accompanied by Tatham] was constantly in the lobbies, gallery and tea rooms. The lobbying was dreadful.' See Dingwall evidence, pp. 3 and 8.

116 See *Bribery Commission, Part I*, p. 7, para. 9 (111).

117 See Dingwall evidence, p. 7, and van Veyeren evidence, pp. 10–11.

118 On the refusal, see evidence of the clerk to the Provincial Council, G.H.C. Hannau, pp. 2–3.

119 RSA, NASA, Pretoria, K23, Vol. 14, K. Vachell, Deputy Commissioner, C.I.D., Transvaal Division to Deputy Commissioner I/C, 20 October 1917.

120 The letter accompanying the application, it would appear, dated back to 5 November 1917; see RSA, NASA, Pretoria, K23, undated typed Memorandum on WRRC, marked Exhibit 'E', A.6/7432.

121 See RSA, NASA, Pretoria, K23, for printed, hand-dated extracts from the minutes of the proceedings of the Transvaal Provincial Council, 14 November 1917, and *Sunday Times*, 15 November 1917.

122 See RSA, NASA, Pretoria, K23, undated typed Memorandum on 'Rand Sporting Club' recording the most important dates of official transactions relating to the R.S.C.

123 See RSA, NASA, Pretoria, K23, for printed, hand-dated extracts from the minutes of the proceedings of the Transvaal Provincial Council, 4 December 1917.

124 Dingwall evidence, 12 December 1918, p. 8.

125 Union of South Africa, The Provincial Council of Transvaal, *Votes and Proceedings* (No. 52-1917-1918), First Session (1917), Third Council, Wednesday 14 May 1918, motions [hereafter *Votes and Proceedings*, 1918].

126 *Votes and Proceedings*, 8 May 1918.

127 *Bribery Commission, Part I*, p. 1, 30 September 1918.

Part III

1 *Sunday Times*, 9 December 1917.

2 *Sunday Times*, 25 August 1918.

3 *Sunday Times*, 3 February 1918.

4 *Sunday Times*, 3 June 1917.

5 Paragraph based on material drawn from the following editions of the *Sunday Times*: 3 June 1917, and 3 February, 23 June, 28 August and 27 October 1918. Deep confusions around sweepstake law dated back to at least 1914, when the police issued instructions that sweepstakes be discontinued, amid great legal uncertainties; see *Sunday Times*, 12 July 1914.

6 See *Sunday Times*, 25 August and 27 October 1918.

7 *Sunday Times*, 23 June and 4 July 1918.

8 *The Star*, 31 August 1922.

9 On the spread of the lottery from Johannesburg to other major centres in South Africa, see *Sunday Times*, 4 May 1918.

10 *The Star*, 15 August 1922.

11 RSA, NASA, Pretoria, K23, Vol. 14, K. Vachell, Deputy Commissioner, C.I.D., Transvaal Division to Deputy Commissioner I/C, 20 October 1917.

12 *Life, Sport and Drama*, 22 November 1918.

13 *The Star*, 11 and 14 February 1918.

14 *Sunday Times*, 14 October 1917.

15 *Sunday Times*, 30 June 1918. For earlier lotteries run for white miners on the Rand, see, for example, *Sunday Times*, 9 December 1917.

16 *Sunday Times*, 12 January 1919.

17 This is neatly captured for the modern computerised age in 'The Opium of the Masses', in Atherton, *Gambling*, pp. 1–22.

18 *Sunday Times*, 9 December 1917, 3 February and 14 October 1918.

19 *Sunday Times*, 9 December 1917.

20   *Sunday Times*, 3 February 1918.

21   See *Sunday Times*, 25 August and 27 October 1918.

22   *Rand Daily Mail*, 25 June 1919.

23   RSA, NASA, Pretoria, TAB, Vol. 8/277, Delagoa Bay Cigarette Co., affidavit of the Commissioner of Inland Revenue, 14 September 1918.

24   See Naylor vs Tatham, 1919, p. 74, and *The Star*, 14 February 1919.

25   In August 1919, Naylor's disclosed liabilities stood at £16 000, most of which was a growing bank overdraft that he was struggling to reduce; see especially 'Bank and Rufe Naylor', *Rand Daily Mail*, 4 March 1919. It was strange, given that his monthly income from the LML was said to be around £6 500.

26   On Naylor's foundational role in the Prudential, see Naylor vs Tatham, 1919, p. 73; and for the fate of the short-lived company, A. van Niekerk, 'The Use of White Female Labour by the Zebediela Citrus Estate, 1926–1953', MA thesis, Department of History, University of the Witwatersrand, 1988, p. 16 [hereafter van Niekerk, 'Zebediela'].

27   *Sunday Times*, 9 December 1917, 25 August 1918 and 27 October 1918.

28   *Sunday Times*, 3 February 1918.

29   *Sunday Times*, 3 February 1918.

30   *Sunday Times*, 27 October 1918.

31   *Sunday Times*, 22 September 1918.

32   Nor was the implied class distinction/discrimination lost on readers at the time. See, for example, the humorous tail to the *Sunday Times* editorial, 22 September 1918.

33   See *Sunday Times*, 2 December 1917, 30 June 1918, 27 October 1918 and 3 November 1918.

34   *Sunday Times*, 30 June 1918.

35   *Sunday Times*, 7 December 1917, and 30 June and 27 October 1918.

36   *Sunday Times*, 2 December 1917, and 23 June and 3 November 1918.

37   *Sunday Times*, 3 November 1918.

38   For the ongoing opposition to a lottery because it weakened 'the habits of industry', see the objection of the Witwatersrand Council of Churches as reported in the *Sunday Times*, 10 May 1918.

39   *Sunday Times*, 18 September 1918.

40   See *Sunday Times*, 17 February 1917 and, more importantly, 25 June 1919.

41   *Life Sport and Drama*, 28 September, 28 October, 8 November, 18 November and 18 December 1918.

42   *Life, Sport and Drama*, 6, 22 and 30 November, 1 December 1918 and 1 February 1919.

43   See Parsons, *Bioscope*, p. 40. The telling phrase 'satirical shadow' was pickpocketed, by me, from Neil Parsons. Thanking him will only add insult to injury.

44   For Naylor's holdings in ATT, see *Rand Daily Mail*, 4 March 1919.

45   See RSA, NASA, Pretoria, K23, Bartrop, Mafeking to Police, Krugersdorp, 3 August 1917. Schlesinger was subsequently found to have behaved entirely legally in relation to his application for a non-proprietary licence although, at the time, he was working closely with Naylor, who, in turn, was dealing with the Provincial Council in his own way. See *Bribery Commission, Part I* (U.G.

30-19), p. 14, para. 20, 30 September 1918.

46   Van Niekerk, 'Zebediela', p. 16.

47   See, especially, *Life, Sport and Drama* of 12 and 19 October 1918.

48   On the envisaged £260 000 – a record claim in South Africa for libel damages – by Schlesinger and associates, see *Life, Sport and Drama*, 26 October 1918. There appears to have been no sequel to the initial issuing of summonses against Naylor and the magazine's printer.

49   *Sunday Times*, 17 February 1918.

50   *Bribery Commission, Part I*, p. 1, 19 October 1918.

51   See RSA, NASA, Pretoria, K23, Annexure marked 'A'.

52   See Naylor vs Tatham, 1919, Exhibit 'B', Memorandum of Association, The Modder West Gold Mining Company for the additional names of George Naylor, Alfred Joseph Ogden, David Miller and A. Rosen.

53   Naylor vs Tatham, 1919, Exhibit 'B' 'Prospectus, The Modder West Gold Mining Company Limited', p. 1. On Meyers as a possible Labour Party candidate for the Provincial Council, see *Sunday Times*, 17 February 1917.

54   RSA, NASA, Pretoria, K23, Vol. 14, van Veyeren Affidavit, 13 September 1918.

55   See Rex vs Naylor, 1919.

56   RSA, NASA, Pretoria, TAB, TPD, Vol. 8/227, 'Opposed Application, Commissioner of Inland Revenue vs the Delagoa Bay Cigarette Company Limited, 1918' [hereafter Commissioner of Inland Revenue vs Delagoa Bay Cigarette Company], Commissioner of Inland Revenue to W.M. Southward, Public Officer, Delagoa Bay Cigarette Co. Ltd., 11 September 1918. The Dividend case was the first brought to the courts after the passage of the Income Tax Act of 1914 and consolidated in 1917. For commercial and tax implications of the case, see P.G. Surtees, 'An Historical Perspective of Income Tax Legislation, 1910–1925', MA thesis, Faculty of Commerce, Rhodes University, 1985, pp. 135–138.

57   Commissioner of Inland Revenue vs Delagoa Bay Cigarette Company, 1918.

58   Commissioner of Inland Revenue vs Delagoa Bay Cigarette Company, 1918.

59   See RSA, NASA, Pretoria, TAB, WLD, Vol. 530/1918, Opposed Application, *Life, Sport and Drama* vs K. Vachell and Detective J.W. Peck, 26 October 1918 [hereafter, Opposed Application, *Life, Sport and Drama* vs Vachell and Peck, 1918]; and TAB, WLD, Vol. 532/1918, 26 October 1918, Opposed Application, United Printing & Publishing Co. Ltd vs K. Vachell and Detective F.J. Henley [hereafter Opposed Application, United Printing vs Vachell and Henley].

60   Opposed Application, *Life, Sport and Drama* vs Vachell and Peck, 1918.

61   See Naylor vs Tatham, 1919, Affidavit by R.H. Tatham, 6 January 1919, pp. 4–5.

62   Naylor vs Tatham, 1919, Affidavit by R.H. Tatham, 6 January 1919, p. 5.

63   Naylor vs Tatham, 1919, Affidavit by R.H. Tatham, 6 January 1919, p. 10.

64   Rex vs Naylor, 1919, evidence of R.H. Tatham, p. 25.

65   *The Star*, 11 February 1919.

66   See *Rand Daily Mail*, 10 February 1915.

67   Jan Carel Juta was the son of a Dutch sea captain but a man with a far more interesting background. He was a scion of the publishing firm of the same name and a nephew of Louise Marx, who, in turn was the sister of Karl Marx.

She had emigrated earlier to the Cape Colony and married the founder of the Juta business.

68   The three letters are to be found in Rex vs Naylor, 1919.

69   Rex vs Naylor, 1919, evidence of R.H. Tatham, p. 25.

70   Naylor vs Tatham, 1919, Affidavit by R.T. Naylor, 6 January 1919, p. 8.

71   Naylor vs Tatham, 1919, Affidavit by R.H. Tatham, 6 January 1919, pp. 7–8.

72   Naylor vs Tatham, 1919, Affidavit by R.H. Tatham, 6 January 1919, p. 14 and appendices.

73   Naylor vs Tatham, 1919.

74   See C. van Onselen, *The Night Trains: Moving Mozambican Miners to and from South Africa, circa 1902—1955* (Johannesburg, 2019), p. 32.

75   On the 'Naylor Express', see, for example, RSA, NASA, Pretoria, Vol. 955, File 1/840/26/1, A. Trigger, C.I.D. to the Deputy Commissioner, South African Police, Witwatersrand Division, 21 January 1927; *Rand Daily Mail*, 26 July 1927; and E. Rosenthal, *Southern African Dictionary of National Biography* (London, 1966), pp. 267–268.

76   Naylor vs Tatham, 1919.

77   For the background to Krause's career, see C. van Onselen, 'The Modernisation of the Zuid-Afrikaansche Republiek: F.E.T. Krause, J.C. Smuts, and the Contest for Control of the Johannesburg Public Prosecutor's Office, 1898– 1899', *Law and History Review*, Vol. 21, No. 3 (Fall 2003), pp. 483–525.

78   *The Star*, 13 February 1919.

79   *The Star*, 15 February 1919.

80   *The Star*, 15 February 1919.

81   *Life, Sport and Drama*, 1 February 1919.

82   *The Star*, 14 February 1919.

83   See also note 9 (Part IV) below.

84   The most important of Naylor's second-tier, young male loyalists seems to have been David Miller (aged 19). Miller was one of those convicted on lottery charges in 1917 and then again in 1919; see *Rand Daily Mail*, 12 April 1917, and 13 December 1919. Miller went on to study law and was admitted as an attorney in the Transvaal; see RSA, NASA, Pretoria, TAB, TPD, Vol. 8/536, Ref. 676/1928, *Ex Parte* Application, Hyman Miller.

85   See *Sunday Times*, 15 October 1915, and *Rand Daily Mail*, 20 and 23 April, and 9 July 1919.

86   See RSA, NASA, Pretoria, K23, Vol. 14, K. Vachell, Deputy Commissioner of Police, Transvaal Division, South African Police, Memo on Rand Sporting Club, 20 October 1917, and *Kalgoorlie Miner*, 22 December 1919.

87   See, especially, the excellent account 'Persecution not Prosecution' in *Rand Daily Mail*, 11 March 1919.

88   Naylor vs Tatham, 1919, Affidavit of R.H. Tatham, 14 March 1919, and *Life, Sport and Drama*, 14 March 1919.

89   See the explicit discussion of this issue, in court, in *Rand Daily Mail*, 11 March 1919.

90   See Naylor vs Tatham, 1919, and *The Star*, 20 March 1919.

91   RSA, NASA, Pretoria, Rex vs R.T. Naylor, April 1919, and *Rand Daily Mail*,

17 May 1919.

92   See RSA, NASA, Pretoria, Rex vs R.T. Naylor, April 1919; and *Rand Daily Mail*, 21 July 1909, and 27 April and 13 May 1919.

93   See RSA, NASA, Pretoria, Rex vs R.T. Naylor, April 1919; and *Rand Daily Mail*, 17 May 1919.

94   See RSA, NASA, Pretoria, Rex vs R.T. Naylor, April 1919; and *Rand Daily Mail*, 17 May 1919.

95   See RSA, NASA, Pretoria, Rex vs R.T. Naylor, April 1919.

96   See *Rand Daily Mail*, 24 April 1919.

97   Van Onselen, *New Babylon, New Nineveh*, pp. 115–146, and C. van Onselen, *The Fox and the Flies* (London 2008), pp. 145–190, and *The Cowboy Capitalist: John Hays Hammond, the American West, and the Jameson Raid* (Johannesburg, 2017).

98   *Rand Daily Mail*, 24 April 1919.

99   *Rand Daily Mail*, 25 April 1919.

100   *Rand Daily Mail*, 21 May 1919.

101   *Bribery Commission, Part II*, Minutes of Evidence taken at the Town Hall, Johannesburg, Wednesday 26 February 1919, Evidence of Morris Kentridge, pp. 2160 and 2172.

102   See *Rand Daily Mail*, 27 April 1919.

103   See *Rand Daily Mail*, 22 May and 25 June 1919.

104   For the shift from urban to rural sales of lottery tickets, see *Sunday Times*, 4 May 1919, and *Rand Daily Mail*, 31 August 1919.

105   *Rand Daily Mail*, 18 June 1919.

106   RSA, NASA, Pretoria, TAB, WLD, Vol. 196/1919, W.T. Seccombe, plaintiff, R.H. Tatham, defendant, June 1919; see also *Rand Daily Mail*, 9 July 1919.

107   See Katzenellenbogen, *South Africa and Southern Mozambique*, p. 124; Vail and White, *Capitalism and Colonialism*, p. 204; and *O Africano*, 10 December 1919.

Part IV

1   Naylor's assets are best seen in the statement presented to a court, in early 1919; see 'Bank and Rufe Naylor', *Rand Daily Mail*, 4 March 1919.

2   On the suspension of the lottery, see *Rand Daily Mail*, 11 July 1919 and 31 August 1922.

3   See Costa, *Cartas*, p. 213 and footnote.

4   Costa, *Cartas*, p. 214.

5   *O Africano*, 10 December 1919.

6   *Rand Daily Mail*, 21 June 1919.

7   Letters to the author from P.B. Naylor, grandson of Peter Charles Naylor, 10 and 12 February 2018.

8   See Parsons, *Bioscope*, p. 30.

9   Caixa 1502, Lotaria Provincial, 'Rufe Naylor', Currie & Wood (Attorneys, Sydney) to Manager, Rufe Naylor's Lotteries Ltd., 25 October 1925; see also *Rand Daily Mail*, 15 August 1922.

10   See *Rand Daily Mail*, 21 February, 8 March and 11 July 1919.

11   RSA, Pretoria, NASA, NAB, RSC, Vol. 1/5/311, Ref. 61/1918, Illiquid Case: Rufus Theodore Naylor vs Charlie Henwood, 22 August 1919.

12   *Rand Daily Mail*, 20 August 1919.

13   See RSA, Pretoria, NASA, TAB, TPD, Vol. 8/289, Ref. 510/1921, *Ex Parte* Application, W.T. Seccombe.

14   On Bristowe's legal career, see S.D. Girvin, 'The Influence of an English Background on Four Judges Appointed to the Supreme Courts of the Transvaal and Orange River Colony, 1902–1910', *Legal History Review*, Vol. 62, No. 2 (1994), pp. 152–158.

15   See RSA, Pretoria, NASA, TAB, WLD, Vol. 3/274, Ref. 386/1919, Illiquid Case Payment: John Stephan Krige vs Rufus Theodore Naylor, 10 October 1919 [hereafter Krige vs Naylor, 1919]; see also *Rand Daily Mail*, 14 August 1919.

16   On Naylor's fingerprints having been taken, see RSA, Pretoria, NASA, TAB, WLD, System 01, Ref. 1093/1931, Opposed Application: 'Truth and Sportsman Limited' vs Rufus Theodore Naylor, November 1931, Annexure 'A', 'Schedule of Witnesses Required' [hereafter 'Truth and Sportsman vs Naylor, 1931'].

17   See van Onselen, *Showdown*.

18   Krige vs Naylor, 1919.

19   *Kalgoorlie Miner*, 22 December 1919.

20   *Rand Daily Mail*, 13 December 1919.

21   On Rufe Naylor as a health 'crank', which may, in part, account for his interest in male – and, to a much lesser extent, female – athletic prowess, see *Sydney Sportsman*, 25 September 1939.

22   These two paragraphs based on reports in *The Sunday Times* (Perth), 14 and 21 December 1919, the *West Australian Sportsman*, 19 December 1919, and *Kalgoorlie Miner*, 22 December 1919.

23   Caixa 1502, Lotaria Provincial, 'Rufe Naylor', Currie & Wood (Attorneys, Sydney) to Manager, Rufe Naylor's Lotteries Ltd., 25 October 1925.

24   J. Duffy, *Portuguese Africa* (Cambridge, Mass., 1959), p. 114.

25   See *Rand Daily Mail*, 17 December 1924, 12 April and 4 May 1927, 25 October and 27 November 1929, 8 October 1931, 13 January and 13 June 1933, and 1 February 1935.

26   For the suggestion that Naylor's demise was a direct consequence of his manic lifestyle, see 'Cestus' on Rufe Naylor in the *Townsville Daily Bulletin*, 27 September 1939.

27   J. O'Hara, 'Naylor, Rupert Theodore (Rufus)', *Australian Dictionary of Biography* (Manchester, 1986), Vol. 10.

28   See Nattrass and Seekings, 'The Economy and Poverty', pp. 525–529; Katzenellenbogen, *South Africa and Southern Mozambique*, pp. 130–135; and Vail and White, *Capitalism and Colonialism*, pp. 205–208.

29   *Rand Daily Mail*, 4 February 1927.

30   RSA, Pretoria, NASA, TAB, TPD, Vol. 8/289, Ref. 510/1921, *Ex Parte* Application, William Thorne Seccombe, 13 July 1921.

31   See *Rand Daily Mail*, 19 March, 13 May and 11 August 1921, and 7 June, 4 July and 8 and 15 September 1922. For a successful police raid on Rufe Naylor's

Building – also known as Albert Buildings (after Albert Adamson, who put up some of the initial capital) – see *Rand Daily Mail*, 25 April 1925.

32　For police suspected of being on the Naylor payroll, see reports in the *Rand Daily Mail*, 15 August 1922 and 2 November 1923. Significantly, after the early 1920s, once the Pact government was in power, there appears to have been less need for bribing police, who were in any case less inclined to act against lottery agents – a trend that only accelerated in the early 1930s.

33　For prosecutions of Peter Charles and George Sylvester Naylor, see *Rand Daily Mail*, 7 June and 31 August 1922.

34　See *Rand Daily Mail*, 7 June 1922, and 27 January and 23 April 1925.

35　*Rand Daily Mail*, 31 August 1922.

36　For examples, see *Rand Daily Mail*, 8 March 1920 and 2 November 1923.

37　See, among other sources, *Rand Daily Mail*, 25 February and 19 August 1923. For a list of vendors that reaches caricature proportions, see *Rand Daily Mail*, 7 January 1930.

38　*Rand Daily Mail*, 31 August 1922.

39　Undercover South African Police monitoring of the draw in Lourenço Marques happened continuously between 1922 and 1952, if not beyond. See *Rand Daily Mail*, 17 January 1922, 27 June 1925 (three visits) and 26 June 1952. The government's Calvinist brief ran beyond the national borders into the regional economy.

40　See *Rand Daily Mail*, 8 July 1922, 10 August 1923 and 27 January 1925.

41　See, for examples, *Rand Daily Mail*, 8 July 1922, 2 November 1923 and 17 December 1929.

42　*Rand Daily Mail*, 24 February and 9 July 1927, and 7 and 18 July 1927. On R.J. Duggan, a bookmaker – whose career showed certain similarities to that of Rufe Naylor – see M. Coleman, 'The Origins of the Irish Hospitals Sweepstake', *Irish Economic and Social History*, Vol. 29 (2002), pp. 40–55. In Ireland, as in South Africa, the growing popularity of lotteries after World War I and into the 1920s was marked and is worthy of further examination within a globalised context.

43　See *Rand Daily Mail*, 3 and 7 July 1922.

44　See, for example, *Rand Daily Mail*, 13 May 1921.

45　*Rand Daily Mail*, 18 October 1922.

46　See also C. van Onselen, 'Who Killed Meyer Hasenfus? Organized Crime, Policing, and Informing on the Witwatersrand, 1902–8', *History Workshop Journal*, Issue 67 (2009), pp. 1–22.

47　*Natal Advertiser*, 14 August 1922

48　For the vibrancy of the market in Pietermaritzburg, see, for example, *Natal Mercury*, 11 August 1922.

49　See *Natal Mercury*, 15 August 1922, and *Natal Advertiser*, 18 August 1922.

50　*Rand Daily Mail*, 31 August 1922.

51　*Rand Daily Mail*, 31 August 1922.

52　*Natal Mercury*, 10 August 1922. There were other problems with van der Linden, who also operated as a moneylender and got embroiled in a legal vendetta; see *Rand Daily Mail*, 25 February 1902, and 29 November 1922.

53　*Natal Advertiser*, 1 August 1922.

54　*Natal Mercury*, 10 August 1922.

55   See *Natal Mercury*, 18 August 1922, and for Tatham's homily, *Natal Advertiser*, 18 August 1922.

56   *Rand Daily Mail*, 7 June 1922.

57   On the Siebert case, which settled an important point of law, see *Rand Daily Mail*, 7 June, 4 July and 8 and 15 September 1922.

58   See also Katzenellenbogen, *South Africa and Southern Mozambique*, p. 138.

59   RSA, Pretoria, NASA, Treasury, CR 4010, 'Contravention of the Emergency Finance Regulations – Santos Rufino, Mr. George Naylor and Dr A.A.C. Casqueiro', 1941, 'Secret and Confidential', Barclays Bank, to The Chief Cashier, South African Reserve Bank, 14 February 1941, [hereafter Contravention of the Emergency Finance Regulations, 1941].

60   Letter to the author from P.B. Naylor, 13 February 2013.

61   Letter to the author from P.B. Naylor, 2 November 2018.

62   Letter to the author from P.B. Naylor, 20 February 2018.

63   Costa, *Cartas*, p. 213, and footnote.

64   See Hohlfeldt and Grabauska, 'Pioneers of the Press', pp. 193 and 201, note 11.

65   Caixa 1502, Lotaria Provincial, Delagoa Bay Turf and Sporting Club; Costa, *Cartas*, p. 216.

66   Costa, *Cartas*, p. 215.

67   Costa, *Cartas*, p. 214.

68   See Antunes, 'Sacramento', *Dicionário da Igreja*.

69   Antunes, 'Sacramento', *Dicionário da Igreja* (author's translation).

70   See V. Zamparoni, 'Colonialism and the Creation of Racial Identities in Lourenço Marques, Mozambique', in B. Barry, E. Soumonni and L. Sansone (eds.), *Africa, Brazil, and the Construction of Trans Atlantic Black Identities* (Trenton, 2008), p. 35 [hereafter Zamparoni, 'Racial Identities'].

71   See Vail and White, *Capitalism and Colonialism*, p. 207 and pp. 233–235; and Zamparoni, 'Racial Identities', p. 36.

72   On football pools, see, for example, *Rand Daily Mail*, 28 February 1925.

73   RSA, Pretoria, NASA, SAB, JUS, Vol. 955, Ref. 1/840/26/1, Det/Serg. J.J. Coetzee to Divisional C.I.D., Pretoria, 24 September 1926.

74   See correspondence in Caixa 1502, Files marked Rufe Naylor 1, 11 and 111, Fundo, Administração Civil.

75   See *Rand Daily Mail*, 10 May 1930; Caixa 1502, Files marked Rufe Naylor 1, 11 and 111, Fundo, Administração Civil, 1926–1929, Lotaria Provincial (1926–1930), Santos Rufino, Sociedade Mercantil de Moçambique Ltda, to the Governor-General, Colony of Moçambique, 17 July 1930.

76   *Rand Daily Mail*, 15 November 1929.

77   See Costa, *Cartas*, p. 216, and Caixa 1502, Files marked Rufe Naylor 1, 11 and 111, Fundo, Administração Civil, 1926–1929.

78   The data in this paragraph has been plundered from several sources, most notably from Nattrass and Seekings, 'The Economy and Poverty', but also from W. de Klerk, *The Puritans in Africa* (London, 1975), p. 112 [hereafter de Klerk, *Puritans*]; T.D. Moodie, *The Rise of Afrikanerdom: Power, Apartheid and the Afrikaner Civil Religion* (London, 1975), pp. 46–48, 203–205 [hereafter Moodie, *The Rise of Afrikanerdom*]; van Jaarsveld, *Die Afrikaners se Groot Trek*, p. 172.

79   See, especially, the switch from the Calcutta to the Dublin/Irish sweepstake as recorded in the *Sunday Times*, 22 March 1931. The leading newspapers also provided increased coverage of sweepstake winnings, which outpaced the Lourenço Marques Lottery in terms of prizes, throughout the Depression. See, for example, the case of Major F.A. Tooth, as reported in *Rand Daily Mail*, 25 July 1930.

80   *Rand Daily Mail*, 17 December 1929.

81   See, for example, his rail journey to Lourenço Marques as reported in the *Rand Daily Mail*, 28 March 1931.

82   *Rand Daily Mail*, 7 January 1930.

83   *Rand Daily Mail*, 9 January 1930.

84   *Rand Daily Mail*, 9 January 1930.

85   *Rand Daily Mail*, 9 January 1930.

86   *Rand Daily Mail*, 9 January 1930.

87   As reported in *Rand Daily Mail*, 10 January 1930.

88   *Rand Daily Mail*, 15 January 1930.

89   As reported in *Rand Daily Mail*, 15 January 1930. For more divisions within the National Party caucus on the lottery issue, especially as seen from the perspective of an Afrikaans working-class constituency such as bellwether Vrededorp, see *Rand Daily Mail*, 5 June 1931. Frans Pretorius, MP for Vrededorp, felt that he enjoyed sufficient support for a state lottery to 'work with all my power to this end again'. Some, if not many, church-going urban Afrikaners were clearly at odds with Calvinist ministers.

90   *Rand Daily Mail*, 17 December 1929, 7 January 1930 and 7 June 1930.

91   See *Rand Daily Mail*, 7 June 1930 and, for an earlier case, 17 January 1930.

92   See, especially, *Rand Daily Mail*, 26 February 1931 and 23 March 1931.

93   *Rand Daily Mail*, 23 March 1931. For a case of post office theft of winnings, see, for example, the case of Robert Maxwell, *Rand Daily Mail*, 14 February 1931.

94   *Rand Daily Mail*, 23 March 1931, 30 January 1933 and 3 August 1933.

95   A copy of the photograph, with the names and date, kindly provided by the Naylor family, is in the possession of the author.

96   See F.A. Mouton, '"Fascist or Opportunist?": The Political Career of Oswald Pirow, 1915–1943', *Historia*, Vol. 63, No. 2 (November 2018), pp. 93–111. On Pirow's 1930–1931 campaign, see, for example, *Rand Daily Mail*, 12 January 1931.

97   *Rand Daily Mail*, 15 January 1930.

98   For examples of small-scale independent lottery operators, see *Rand Daily Mail*, 7 February 1931.

99   See 'War on Lottery Promoters', *Rand Daily Mail*, 7 February 1931, and 9 August 1930.

100 See *Rand Daily Mail*, 25 February, 28 February and 27 March 1931. For the view of the *Guardian*, as reported from Lourenço Marques and criticising the truthfulness of police statements, see *Rand Daily Mail*, 5 March 1931.

101 AHM, Maputo, Arquivo da Repartição do Gabinete, Pasta B/1, 'Contrabando de opio, suposta apreensão pela policia da Africa do Sul', Consul General South

Africa, Lourenço Marques, to His Excellency, the Governor General, 30 March 1931, and Governor General, Lourenço Marques, to the Minister of Colonies, Lisbon, 3 April 1931.

102 *Rand Daily Mail*, 15 October 1931.

103 *Rand Daily Mail*, 5 June 1931.

104 On Keller, see J. Lunn, *Capital and Labour on the Rhodesian Railway System 1888–1947* (Basingstoke, 1997), pp. 93–99.

105 *Rand Daily Mail*, 14 January 1931, 4 and 5 February 1931. See also L.H. Gann, *A History of Southern Rhodesia* (London, 1965), p. 310.

106 See, for example, *Rand Daily Mail*, 7 July 1911 and 29 January 1913.

107 See *Rand Daily Mail*, 21 and 25 October 1921. On the problems around the sweep in the early 1920s, see *Rand Daily Mail*, 27 December 1922, 2 February 1923 and 17 February 1923.

108 On the organisation of the sweep, see *Rand Daily Mail*, 7 July 1911 and 28 May 1927.

109 *Rand Daily Mail*, 28 May 1927.

110 *Sunday Times*, 9 June 1929.

111 *The Recorder* (Perth), 11 June 1929.

112 *Rand Daily Mail*, 3 June 1931.

113 *Rand Daily Mail*, 5 February 1931.

114 The South African electorate has – supposedly – always made serious demands of candidates when it comes to matters of probity, with the labour movement sometimes leading the way. Despite his convictions for lottery offences, Henderson went on to become a Senator in the Union, and his career can be traced in RSA, Bloemfontein, University of the Free State, Archive for Political Affairs, Ref. PV 11. See also *Rand Daily Mail*, 5 February 1931.

115 *Rand Daily Mail*, 14 January 1931, 4 and 5 February 1931.

116 See *Rand Daily Mail*, 30 October 1930, and *Sunday Times*, 22 March 1931.

117 J. Laver, 'Fashion: A Detective Story', *Vogue*, 1 January 1959.

118 See H.B. Kendall, *The Origin and History of the Primitive Methodist Church* (London, c. 1919).

119 E.P. Thompson, *The Making of the English Working Class* (London, 1963), p. 41 [hereafter Thompson, *The English Working Class*].

120 On the unification of the Methodist Church, see *Rand Daily Mail*, 3 January 1931.

121 For a link to South Africa, see Thompson, *The English Working Class*, p. 602.

122 For Kidwell's views on the practicalities of social segregation and the Native (Urban Areas) Act, see *Rand Daily Mail*, 14 September 1925.

123 See D.L. Gaitskell, 'Female Mission Initiatives: Black and White Women in Three Witwatersrand Churches', DPhil thesis, School of Oriental and African Studies, University of London, September 1981, pp. 150–151, 162 and 186.

124 See, for example, *Rand Daily Mail*, 5 January and 11 February 1921, *Eastern Province Herald*, 11 April 1921, and *Sunday Times*, 17 April 1921.

125 See, for example, *The Mafeking Mail and Protectorate Guardian*, 5 January 1921.

126 *Rand Daily Mail*, 10 September 1923.

127 *Rand Daily Mail*, 9 July 1923.

128   *Rand Daily Mail*, 25 September 1924. See also R.A. Hill (ed.), *The Marcus Garvey and Universal Negro Improvement Association Papers*, Vol. X, (Oakland, 2006), p. 267.

129   See Rand *Daily Mail*, 11 March and 1 October 1925.

130   See P. Lamb to the Editor, *Rand Daily Mail*, 21 February 1959.

131   On Kidwell's Depression-era stance against lotteries and sweepstakes, see *Rand Daily Mail*, 30 October 1930.

132   These prescripts can be traced in *Rand Daily Mail*, 17 and 24 March 1930, 27 and 28 January 1931, 23 April 1932 and 12 August and 25 October 1937.

133   See, for example, T. Fehler on 'Sixteenth Century Studies Conference, 2003, Session 4: Urban Calvinism', as reviewed in H-Net Reviews in the Humanities and Social Sciences. For cultural shifts in attitudes towards the lottery in the Netherlands and surrounds, see also S. Raux, *Lotteries, Art Markets, and Visual Culture in the Low Countries, 15th–17th Centuries* (Leiden, 2018).

134   On Kidwell's pronouncements see, among other sources, *Rand Daily Mail*, 20 May 1932, 16 and 23 January 1934. For cooperation between the Dutch Reformed Churches and the Methodists, see, for example, 3 December 1937.

135   For Kidwell's leading role in the abolition of dog racing, see, for example, P. Lamb to the Editor, *Rand Daily Mail*, 21 February 1959, and, more generally, Grundlingh, 'Dogs, Dominees and the Afrikaner Working Class'.

136   *Rand Daily Mail*, 16 August 1930. L.G. du Plessis was sufficiently free-thinking to attempt to link his Calvinist thinking to Marxism and, perhaps unsurprisingly, was later expelled from the National Party by H.F. Verwoerd.

137   See, especially, *Sunday Times*, 22 March 1931.

138   See RSA, Pretoria, NASA, RSA, Treasury, File CR 4010, marked 'Secret', Major, Controller of Censorship, to Commissioner of South African Police, 26 October 1940, and *Rand Daily Mail*, 24 December 1930.

139   Nattrass and Seekings, 'The Economy and Poverty', pp. 536–538.

140   Van Onselen, *New Babylon, New Nineveh*, pp. 31–36.

141   This paragraph is based on insights taken from several works of Jeremy Seekings, but more especially on '"Not a Single White Person Should be Allowed to Go Under": *Swartgevaar* and the Origins of South Africa's Welfare State, 1924–1929', *Journal of African History*, Vol. 48, No. 3 (November 2007), pp. 375–394, and 'The Carnegie Commission and the Backlash Against Welfare State-Building in South Africa, 1931–1937', *Journal of Southern African Studies*, Vol. 34, No. 3 (2008), pp. 515–537.

142   For a succinct summary of how this development fitted into Smuts's extraordinary career, see, for example, R. Steyn, *Jan Smuts: Unafraid of Greatness* (Cape Town, 2015), pp. 121–126 [hereafter Steyn, *Jan Smuts*].

143   *Rand Daily Mail*, 24 November 1937.

144   See *Rand Daily Mail*, 25 August 1933, 18 February 1939 and 23 May 1940.

145   Paragraph based on data drawn from *Rand Daily Mail*, 17 and 20 July, and 18 and 22 September 1937.

146   *Rand Daily Mail*, 20 July 1937.

147   See, especially, *Rand Daily Mail*, 21 July 1937.

148   *Rand Daily Mail*, 22 September and 25 November 1937, and 30 October 1953.

149   These observations taken, with little respect for the finer chronology, from *Rand Daily Mail*, 11 January 1933, 20 November 1934, 27 July 1936 and 19 October 1937.

150   *Rand Daily Mail*, 12 May 1934, and 22 February 1939.

151   *Rand Daily Mail*, 3 February 1938.

152   See, for example, *Rand Daily Mail*, 31 December 1932, 26 February and 23 March 1936, and 26 October 1939.

153   *Rand Daily Mail*, 28 March 1935.

154   RSA, NASA, Pretoria, Personal Papers of Dr G.W. Eybers and, among other sources, minutes of meetings of National Thrift Movement – Spaarkomitee (Pretoria) 15 August 1937, Transvaal Thrift Committee (Pretoria), 23 November 1937 and 22 February 1938, National Thrift Committee (Port Elizabeth 17 March 1938) [hereafter 'Eybers Collection']

155   *Rand Daily Mail*, 22 July, 20 and 26 August 1937. For the Department of Labour and Social Welfare's view of pinball tables as an inhibitor of the habit of thrift at school level and a precursor to social delinquency, see, for example, the report carried in *Rand Daily Mail*, 15 October 1935.

156   See *Rand Daily Mail*, 15 and 17 July 1937.

157   *Rand Daily Mail*, 30 August 1934.

158   *Rand Daily Mail*, 23 January 1934.

159   *Rand Daily Mail*, 30 April and 14 July 1936, and E. Laubscher (ed.) *Interfering Women: National Council of Women of South Africa, 1909–1999* (Johannesburg, 2000) p. 118.

160   *Rand Daily Mail*, 18 August 1938, and, more importantly, 'Eybers Collection', Minutes of the Transvaal Thrift Committee, Pretoria, 26 July 1938.

161   *Rand Daily Mail*, 10 October 1935.

162   See Moodie, *The Rise of Afrikanerdom*, pp. 197–205, and, for an East Rand focus, A. Grundlingh '"Gone to the Dogs": The Cultural Politics of Gambling – The Rise and Fall of British Greyhound Racing on the Witwatersrand, 1932–1939', *South African Historical Journal*, Vol. 48 (May 2003), pp. 181–186 [hereafter Grundlingh, 'Gone to the Dogs'].

163   *Rand Daily Mail*, 9 and 11 May 1938.

164   *Rand Daily Mail*, 21 July 1938.

165   See, especially, *Rand Daily Mail*, 16 and 18 February 1939.

166   *Rand Daily Mail*, 18 February 1939.

167   See M. Shain's seminal *A Perfect Storm: Antisemitism in South Africa, 1930–1948* (Cape Town, 2015) pp. 212–232.

168   *Rand Daily Mail*, 27 June 1939.

169   *Rand Daily Mail*, 6 November 1939 – emphasis added.

Part V

1   Nattrass and Seekings, 'The Economy and Poverty', pp. 536–538.

2   See H. Giliomee's indispensable *The Afrikaners: Biography of a People* (Charlottesville, 2003), pp. 403–446 [hereafter Giliomee, *The Afrikaners*], and

Giliomee, *Maverick Africans*, pp. 134–172. But in this context see also A. du Toit, 'The Myth of the Calvinist Origins of Afrikaner Nationalism and Racial Identity', *American Historical Review*, Vol. 88, No. 4 (1983), pp. 920–950, and I. Hexham, 'Dutch Calvinism and the Development of Afrikaner Nationalism', *African Affairs*, Vol. 79, No. 315 (1980), pp. 195–208.

3   Giliomee, *The Afrikaners*, p. 440, and Steyn, *Jan Smuts*, pp. 129–130.

4   See, for example, *Rand Daily Mail*, 18 February 1939, and 23 May 1940.

5   Grundlingh, 'Gone to the Dogs', pp. 176–177. An excellent article on the financing of dog racing, and more especially the African Greyhound Racing Association (AGRA), is to be found in the *Rand Daily Mail*, 8 February 1940. This despite new provincial legislation outlawing bucket shops the previous year.

6   The increase in wartime gambling is attested to in RSA, Pretoria, NASA, SAB, URU, Vol. 207, Commissioner of Police to the Sec. for Justice, 24 August 1941, and Deputy Commissioner of Police to Commissioner of Police, 19 October 1945.

7   For fraternal cooperation between Afrikaans and English Protestant churches, see, for example, reports in *Rand Daily Mail*, 17 April 1940 (Presbyterians and the Dutch Reformed Church) or 11 May 1940 (Methodists and the Dutch Reformed Church).

8   *Rand Daily Mail*, 17 August 1939; see also *Rand Daily Mail*, 11 May and 20 November 1940.

9   *Rand Daily Mail*, 3 February 1940.

10   *Rand Daily Mail*, 8 February 1940. These amounts were subsequently revised upwards by the AGRA, including the weekly spend, which was estimated to be around 14s 6d; see *Rand Daily Mail*, 2 March 1940.

11   See A. Paton, *Hofmeyr* (Cape Town, 1964), pp. 129 and 328, and, on lotteries in particular, p. 478 [hereafter Paton, *Hofmeyr*].

12   See *Debates of the House of Assembly*, 1 March 1940 [hereafter Hansard], and *Rand Daily Mail*, 2 March 1940.

13   Hansard, 1 March 1940, and *Rand Daily Mail*, 2 March 1940.

14   *Rand Daily Mail*, 2 March 1940.

15   RSA, Pretoria, NASA, SAB, URU, Vol. 207, Sec. for Justice to Commissioner of Police, 31 Octobrt 1941 and Sec. of Justice to Commissioner of Police, 12 February 1942.

16   Grundlingh, 'Gone to the Dogs', p. 188.

17   RSA, Pretoria, NASA, SAB, URU, Vol. 207, Commissioner of Police to the Private Secretary to the Minister of Justice, 1 July 1947.

18   J. Crwys-Williams, *A Country at War, 1939–1945: The Mood of a Nation* (Johannesburg 1992), p. 129 [hereafter Crwys-Williams, *A Country at War*].

19   N. Lochery, *Lisbon: War in the Shadow of the City of Light, 1939–1946* (New York, 2011), pp. 1–2 and pp. 126–127 [hereafter Lochery, *Lisbon*].

20   See Lochery, *Lisbon*, pp. 42–48.

21   This reconstruction was also in line with a modified lottery in Macau; see Caixa 1502, 1926–1940, Lotaria Provincial, undated, unsigned memorandum to Ministro das Colónias; also *Rand Daily Mail*, 24 October 1940.

22   See RSA, Pretoria, NASA, Treasury, C.R. 4010, File marked 'Secret' – 'Contravention of the Emergency Finance Regulations, 1940–41', Sec. Dept of Commerce and Industries to Sec. for Finance, 21 July 1941, and unsigned and undated [1941] 'Memorandum' [hereafter NASA, 'Secret', Treasury C.R. 4010].

23   NASA, 'Secret', Treasury C.R. 4010, *passim*.

24   NASA, 'Secret', Treasury C.R. 4010, *passim*.

25   NASA, 'Secret', Treasury C.R. 4010, *passim*.

26   NASA, 'Secret', Treasury C.R. 4010, *passim*.

27   *Rand Daily Mail*, 2 March 1940.

28   Crwys-Williams, *A Country at War*, p. 129.

29   NASA, 'Secret', Treasury C.R. 4010, *passim*.

30   NASA, 'Secret', Treasury C.R. 4010, Memorandum 1941.

31   NASA, 'Secret', Treasury C.R. 4010, Santos Rufino to George Naylor, 30 September 1940.

32   NASA, 'Secret', Treasury C.R. 4010. H.J. Lenton to the Commissioner of Immigration, 20 November 1929.

33   NASA, 'Secret', Treasury C.R. 4010, *passim*.

34   See Paton, *Hofmeyr*, pp. 228–229 and *passim*.

35   NASA, 'Secret', Treasury C.R. 4010, 'Geagte Oom Paul' from 'Jou Vriend, Jan', 27 February 1941, and J.H. Grobler, MP, to Dr D.H. Steyn, Department of Finance, Pretoria, 26 February 1941.

36   NASA, 'Secret', Treasury C.R. 4010; Dumat, Pitts & Blain to The Secretary for Finance, 30 April 1941, and Secretary of Finance to Dumat, Pitts & Blaine, 5 May 1941.

37   NASA, 'Secret', Treasury C.R. 4010, *passim*.

38   This paragraph derives from D. Hobart Houghton, 'Economic Development, 1865–1965' in M. Wilson and L. Thompson (eds.), *The Oxford History of South Africa, Vol. II* (Oxford, 1971), pp. 36–37; Nattrass and Seekings, 'The Economy and Poverty', pp. 540–541; and Paton, *Hofmeyr*, p. 359.

39   Paton, *Hofmeyr*, p. 359.

40   Information on P.C. and G.S. Naylor provided in letters from P.B. Naylor dated 12 and 20 February, 2 May and 24 and 5 June 2018.

41   See Grundlingh, 'Gone to the Dogs', pp. 176–184.

42   Kidwell's 'comfortable family home' was situated on the corner of Wicklow Avenue and Lurgan Road. Parkview was a much-favoured retreat for the chattering classes and the Randlords' subalterns. See Kidwell's estate as reported in *Rand Daily Mail*, 7 August 1954.

43   Grundlingh, 'Gone to the Dogs', pp. 186–187.

44   Grundlingh, 'Gone to the Dogs', pp. 187.

45   Paton, *Hofmeyr*, p. 478.

46   See, especially, the unusually restrained speech of Eric Louw as recorded in Hansard, 17 February 1939, columns 482–484.

47   See *Rand Daily Mail*, 24 September 1948.

48   For the Methodist and Dutch Reformed churches' push, see *Rand Daily Mail*, 12 and 19 August 1948, and 9 September 1948.

49   Hansard, 7 June 1949, cols. 7299 and 7300.

50 Hansard, 7 June 1949, col. 7302.

51 Hansard, 7 June 1949, col. 7303.

52 Hansard, 7 June 1949, cols. 7229 and 7300.

53 Nattrass and Seekings, 'The Economy and Poverty', pp. 541–542.

54 See A. Grundlingh's important '"Are We Afrikaners Getting Too Rich?" Cornucopia and Change in Afrikanerdom in the 1960s', *Journal of Historical Sociology*, Vol. 21, No. 2/3 (June–September 2008), p. 150, and de Klerk, *Puritans*, pp. 300–335.

55 RSA, Pretoria, NASA, SAB, URU, Vol. 207, 'Gambling, Johannesburg 1951–1963' [hereafter 'Gambling Johannesburg, 1951–1963'], Deputy Commissioner of Police to the Secretary for Justice, 30 October 1948.

56 Lookouts formed part of well-established historical practices in many working-class gambling communities, including England. See, for example, A. Davies, 'The Police and the People: Gambling in Salford, 1900–1939', *The Historical Journal*, Vol. 34, No. 1 (1991), pp. 89 and 102.

57 These quotes are drawn from letters in 'Gambling Johannesburg, 1951–1963'. See Acting Commissioner to the Secretary for Justice, 14 November 1949; Deputy Commissioner, Witwatersrand to the Commissioner of Police, undated, and Commissioner of Police to Attorney-General, Pretoria, 22 April 1952.

58 See 'Gambling Johannesburg, 1951–1963'; Commissioner of Police to Secretary for Justice, 20 December 1948; and R.E.G. Rosenow, Memorandum 'Insake Dobbelry', to 'Die Minister', 22 December 1948.

59 'Gambling Johannesburg, 1951–1963', R.E.G. Rosenow, 'Insake Dobbelry', to 'Die Minister', 22 December 1948, and unsigned memorandum, 1952.

60 'Gambling Johannesburg, 1951–1963', Deputy Commissioner of Police to Commissioner of Police, 30 June 1950, and Deputy Commissioner of Police to the Commissioner of Police, 24 October 1955.

61 'Gambling Johannesburg, 1951–1963' – see, among others, Commissioner of Police to Sec. of Justice and Sec. for Justice to Commissioner of Police, 30 December 1950, Sec. for Justice to Commissioner of Police, 9 October 1951, Commissioner of Police to Sec. for Justice, 25 April 1952, and Sec. for Justice to Commissioner of Police, 15 July 1952.

62 'Gambling Johannesburg, 1951–1963', The Minister as quoted by Attorney M. Silber in a letter to the Commissioner of Police, 21 April 1955, and Commissioner of Police to M. Silber, 23 July 1955.

63 *Rand Daily Mail*, 26 June 1952.

64 *Rand Daily Mail*, 16 September 1954. A rounded idea of how pinball machines and their possible listing as being 'banned' by the *Government Gazette* could feed into the corruption of senior police officers can be traced in *Rand Daily Mail*, 15 and 16 September 1954, and 9 October 1954.

65 See numerous examples in 'Gambling Johannesburg, 1951–1963'.

66 'Gambling Johannesburg, 1951–1963', Detective Division to The Officer-in-Charge, Marshall Square, Johannesburg, 2 April 1954; and various responses in April 1959 to the Commissioner of Police, Pretoria from Assistant Commissioners based in the various provinces. The title of the proposed bill is to be found on p. 13 of the draft bill in the same file.

67   See 'Gambling Johannesburg, 1951–1963', Divisional Officer, C.I.D., Johannesburg, to Commissioner of Police, 18 April 1959.

68   RSA, Pretoria, NASA, SAB, Vol. 5651, Ref. 339, 'Inwerkingtreding van die Wet op Dobbelary, 1965' [hereafter 'Inwerkingtreding']. The relevant passage has been translated by the author.

69   On Vorster, see, among others, H. Giliomee, *The Last Afrikaner Leaders: A Supreme Test of Power* (Cape Town, 2012), pp. 89–115.

70   See 'Gambling Johannesburg, 1951–1963', copy of question put to the Minister of the Interior, 7 February 1964, together with answer.

71   See Inwerkingtreding, SAP.1/164/41, 'Verslag van die Subkomitee wat benoem is om ondersoek in te stel na Staatsloterye', 1964, p. 6 [hereafter 'Verslag van die Subkomitee'].

72   See, for example, the threat later posed by the 'Swazipot Lottery' in 1963, *The Star*, 5 April 1963.

73   Inwerkingtreding, Confidential, 'Final Report of the Inter-ministerial Committee', undated, 1963 (original in Afrikaans) [hereafter 'Final Report'].

74   Inwerkingtreding, Secretary of the Interior to Lieut.-Gen. J.M. Keevy, 29 November 1963 and J.M. Keevy to R.J. van den Bergh, 14 February 1964.

75   Inwerkingtreding, A. Hertzog to the Hon. B.J. Vorster, Minister of Justice, 12 February 1964 (original in Afrikaans).

76   See Inwerkingtreding, Unsigned Memorandum, 22 February 1964, 'List of Lottery and Sport Pool Agents' (original in Afrikaans).

77   See Inwerkingtreding, Letter from A. Foster, Ndola Lottery, to unknown correspondent, Pretoria, 15 December 1963, and Ndola Lottery Limited, 'Donations to Charity – December 1963'.

78   See *The Star*, 22 February 1964.

79   *The Star*, 22 February 1964.

80   Inwerkingtreding, D.A. Foster to Lewis C. Gay, Esq., 3 February 1964.

81   Inwerkingtreding, D.A. Foster to Sellers, 12 September 1961.

82   Inwerkingtreding, Notice 'Special Sellers Prizes', January 1964.

83   J. Waters, *Urban Evolution, Harare: A Photographic History* (Harare, 2015), p. 93.

84   See Inwerkingtreding, 'Vertroulik', 'Verslag van die Subkomitee', 2 March 1964, paras. 1, 3 (c) and 19. For the detailed reservations of the Treasury, see Inwerkingtreding, Draft of 'Ondersoek na Staatsloterye', 'Bylae D' of 'Final Report'.

85   Inwerkingtreding, 'Verslag van die Subkomitee', p. 10, para. 13.

86   'Gambling Johannesburg, 1951–1963', Minutes of a meeting held in the office of the Commissioner of Police in Cape Town, 13 March 1964, points 2.2 and 2.6 (original in Afrikaans) [hereafter Minutes of Meeting held on 13 March 1964].

87   'Gambling Johannesburg, 1951–1963', Minutes of Meeting held on 13 March 1964, p. 2, points 8 and 9.

88   Inwerkingtreding, Commissioner of Police, 'Confidential' to the Minister of Internal Affairs, 15 May 1964, attaching Report to Inter-ministerial Committee (original in Afrikaans).

89   See Hansard, Fourth Session, Second Parliament, 9 April 1965, cols. 4372 and 4598.

90   Paragraph based on the debate, as recorded in Hansard, 9 April 1965, cols. 4372–4382.

Part VI

1   The more telling – original – observation that 'South Africa has advanced politically by disasters and economically by windfalls' is, of course, that of C.W. de Kiewiet, *A History of South Africa: Social & Economic* (London, 1957) p. 89.
2   *Atherton*, Gambling, p. 13.
3   As cited in Giliomee, *Maverick Africans*, p. 145.

Postscript

1   See Nattrass and Seekings, 'The Economy and Poverty', pp. 542–545.
2   For a catalogue and overview of existing legislation governing gambling in the early 21st century, see, for example, S.L. Monnye, 'Towards the Regulation of Interactive Gambling: An Analysis of the Gambling Regulatory Framework in South Africa', DLitt thesis, University of South Africa, 2016.
3   As quoted in S. Nzimande et al., 'Review of the South African Gambling Industry and its Regulation', submitted to the Minister of Trade and Industry, September 2010, pp. 27–28 [hereafter 'Review of the Gambling Industry'].
4   'Review of the Gambling Industry', pp. 68–71.
5   See, especially, the award-winning, pioneering journalism of N. Geffen and R. Joseph at GroundUp, 2021.
6   *Mail & Guardian*, 1 April 2021.
7   *Mail & Guardian*, 1 April 2021.

INDEX

Note: Entries in *italics* indicate photographs.

1820 Settlers 178–180, 248
1820 Settlers' Association 179–180

A

AAT *see* African Amalgamated
  Theatres Ltd
Act 10 of 1894 116
Act 37 of 1909 (Horse Racing and
  Betting Restriction Act) 26, 39, 41,
  66–67, 114, 197, 257
Adamson, Albert 138, 208, 295
African Amalgamated Theatres Ltd
  (AAT) 43–44, 46, 138
African Films Trust (AFT) 44, 51
African National Congress (ANC)
  263, 267
African Theatres Trust (ATT) 44, 51,
  111
Afrikaner Broederbond 184
Afrikaner Rebellion (1914) 13, 67,
  187, 213
Afrikaner Protestant churches
  see Dutch Reformed churches
Afrikaners, Afrikaans 8, 13–14, 20–21,
  35, 49–50, 65, 67, 81, 84, 100, 148,
  165, 170, 174, 183–184, 195–196,
  198, 201, 203, 215–216, 218–220,
  226–227, 235, 258–259, 261, 267, 269
AFT *see* African Films Trust
Albisini, João 62
alcohol (drinking) 11, 13, 22, 26, 123,
  181–183, 187, 191, 237, 274
  see also prohibition
Allen, FB 204–205
Anglo American Corporation 67, 114
Anglo-Boer War 23, 25–26, 28, 30, 48,
  58, 178, 195, 234
apartheid 8–9, 22, 195, 201, 215, 224,
  233–234, 236, 258–260, 262, 264, 277
APRC *see* Auckland Park Racing Club

ATT *see* African Theatres Trust
Auckland Park Racing Club (APRC)
  28, 33, 47, 52–53, 69–70, 72–75, 79,
  91, 93–95
Auckland Park Trainers and Owners'
  Association 75
Australia, Australians 18, 25–27, 29,
  31–36, 38, 41, 53, 63, 66, 68, 73,
  101, 111, 123, 127–128, 137, 140,
  142–145, 149, 251–253, 270
authoritarianism 224, 259

B

'Back to Church Programme' 192
Baker, HW 180
Banco Nacional Ultramarino (BNU)
  see banking
banking 3–4, 7–9, 44, 68, 70, 76–78, 85,
  115, 119, 131, 136, 146, 156–157, 209,
  211–212, 214–215, 218, 242, 285, 290
  Bank of England 7
  Barclays 157, 209, 210, 213
  Banco Nacional Ultramarino
    (BNU) 77–78, 136–137, 146,
    148, 209
  Post Office Savings Bank 215
  South African Reserve Bank 209,
    211–212, 218, 242
  Standard Bank 115, 119, 157, 209,
    213–214, 285
Baptists 6, 204, 220
Bastos, Calçado 211
Baumann, Emil 193
Benoni Chamber of Commerce 190
Bernberg, HD 39
Betting Restriction Act, 1909
  see Act 37 of 1909
Binnie, Robert 118
Bioscope Proprietors' Association 42
Blackwell, Leslie 205

Bloemfontein 28, 82, 101, 166
BNU *see* banking, Banco Nacional
  Ultramarino
Boilermakers' Union 67, 71, 85
Bok, WE 113
Bolshevik Revolution 108, 223
bookmakers (bookies), bookmaking
  6, 20, 24–25, 28, 31–33, 35, 37, 41,
  47, 52, 55, 72, 78, 93, 96, 124, 138,
  198, 221, 248, 252
    see also dog racing, gambling,
      horse racing
'booms' 4–5, 7, 9, 48
Bophuthatswana 263
Botha, Louis 38, 48–50, 97
boxing 22, 24, 40
    see also sport
bribery 7, 10–11, 17, 70, 87, 89, 91,
  94, 97, 113, 115–117, 119–121,
  125, 127–128, 131, 133, 151, 172,
  230–231, 252, 257
bribery commission (Transvaal) 97,
  113, 115, 127, 131
Bristowe, Leonard 116–117, 140–142
British Empire 15, 19, 41, 47, 86, 100,
  141, 253
Britten, JH 168–169
Bucketshop Owners' Association 115
building societies *see* Starr-Bowkett
  societies
BVB Ranch 138, 157

C

Cabral, JRP 173
Cadman, CFM 205
California 24–25
Calvinism 3–5, 14, 16, 18, 20, 25,
  37, 66, 84, 111, 147, 170, 177,
  183–184, 189, 198, 201, 203, 205,
  215, 219–220, 224, 226, 228, 233,
  235, 237, 240, 242, 249, 254, 258,
  262–263, 266, 269, 277, 295, 299
    see also Protestantism
'Calvinist Bond' 184
Calvin, John 237, 242
Camacho, Brito 144

Cape Argus 169
Cape Colony 19, 292
Cape Town 28, 50, 97, 102, 141, 166,
  185, 198, 208, 210, 213, 240, 258, 266
capitalism 3–9, 19–20, 38–39, 48, 52,
  72–73, 102–103, 160, 164, 176, 193,
  211, 223–224, 248, 252, 256
Capone, Alphonse 81, 166
Carlota, Velha 61, 64, 72
Casqueira, Antonio 159, 209,
  211–212, 214
Cassel, Ernest 3
Catholics *see* Roman Catholic Church
censorship 212
Central Board of Charities 76
Central Timber Company 209
Cernache do Bonjardim 55, 62, 161
Chamber of Mines 20, 27, 37, 65, 71
Christianity 11, 111, 162, 170, 182,
  192, 194, 219–220, 238, 262
church and state relationship 8, 15, 17,
  25, 55–56, 58–59, 64, 149, 155, 162,
  166, 168, 170, 173, 177, 179, 187,
  198–199, 201, 206, 208, 216, 219,
  221, 223, 233, 256–258, 261–263, 265
cinema and film industry 11–12, 22,
  40–43, 46, 51, 111–112, 138, 145,
  156, 252, 281
circus(es) 22, 32
City Deep Mine 180
Clark, JA 71
Coetzee, John A 75, 88, 95, 102
Cope, John P 167–169
corruption 10–11, 17, 60, 67, 85–87,
  92, 97, 113, 115, 117, 131–132, 172,
  258, 265, 267–269
    see also bribery, bribery commis-
      sion (Transvaal)
Cramer, Archibald 117–118, 128
Criminal Law Amendment Act 225,
  234
Crocodile Valley Estates 112, 114
Curator of Indigenous Labour 62–63
Curlewis, John 128–129
Currie & Wood 144

D

da Assuncão, Rafael 160–162

d'Aguiar, R 159

Daily Mail 38

Day, BR 32–35

DBCC *see* Delagoa Bay Cigarette Company

de Andrade, Freire 62–63

De Klerk, FW 242

De Klerk, Jan 242–243

De Klerk, PJS 184

Delagoa Bay 76–77, 80, 104, 110, 123, 141, 154–155, 161, 209

Delagoa Bay Cigarette Company (DBCC) 77–79

Delagoa Bay Lottery *see* Lourenço Marques Lottery (LML)

Delagoa Bay Money Agency 78, 83, 99, 104, 108, 148, 150, 152

Delagoa Bay Trading Company 76

Delagoa Bay Turf Club 158–159, 164

De Loor, JH 243

Delwani, Charlie 230–231

De Villiers, Charles W 112–113, 117, 124–125, 127–128, 130, 132–133, 135, 139

De Villiers, IP 172

De Villiers, Jacob 39

De Wet, Christiaan 49, 282

De Wet, NJ 110

D Gottlieb & Co 189

diamond mining 24, 80, 247–248

Dingwall, Dan 67, 85–86, 88–97, 103, 113, 116, 124–125, 128, 133

Dingwall, NE 67

Dividend Cigarettes 77, 81, 86, 99, 101, 104, 115–116, 119, 122, 140

Dividend Company 78–79, 82, 89, 91, 94, 116–118

do Cruz, Machado 211

dog racing 9, 18, 33, 40, 181–184, 188, 191, 198, 202–207, 214, 216, 218–222, 229, 253–254, 258–259, 261, 301

Dog Racing Commission 258

Doppers *see* Gereformeerde Kerk

do Sacramento, José Vicente 46–47, 55–64, 72–73, 77–78, 80, 82, 126, 133–137, 148, 158–164, 253, 282, 284

dos Santos, Antonio 156

Duggan's sweepstakes, Dublin 152

Duiwelsdorp (Johannesburg) 22–23

Dumat, Pitts & Blaine 213–214

Du Plessis, LJ 184, 299

Du Plessis, MJ 174, 183

Durban 23, 28, 28, 80, 102, 138, 150, 153, 155, 157, 166, 185, 195, 205, 208, 210

Durno, John 153–154, 156–157

Dutch Reformed churches (Afrikaner Protestant churches) 6, 8–9, 14, 21, 71, 80, 84, 178, 259, 262

Dutch Reformed Church 20, 84, 183, 249, 258

E

East Rand gambling and mining 48–49, 51–52, 67, 69, 114, 118, 124, 166, 171, 178, 180, 190–191, 202–205, 207, 216, 218–219, 229, 231, 234, 236, 245, 248, 254, 257

education 15, 162, 255, 262

elections 115, 131–132, 143, 147, 149, 176, 186, 189, 195–197, 207, 216–217, 220–224, 232, 259, 264

Emergency Finance Regulations 212

Empreza Commercial de Lotarias Ltda 208–209

England 7, 19, 29, 33, 47–48, 52, 66, 138, 152, 175, 179–180, 183, 188, 191, 221, 254, 303

English Protestant churches 9, 202

Evening Chronicle 47

executive resolution No. 106, 1917 96

F

First South African Starr-Bowkett Building Society 29

football pools 9, 18, 163, 183, 191, 197, 218, 221–222, 225, 229, 254–255

Forni, Effrem 161

Forward, Loyal 32

Foster, DA 241

Foster, HS 129
Fourie, AP 195
Fraser, Fred 84
Free State 80–81, 224
Friedman, Isaac 40, 43
Friedman, Monty 43
Furze, JJ 69–70, 72–73, 79, 88–89,
  91–93, 116, 194, 285, 288
Fusion government 186–187, 189,
  201, 257

G
gambling 3–11, 14–16, 18–20, 24–26,
  28–29, 31, 33, 35, 37–39, 47, 53, 66,
  68, 71, 74–75, 81, 84–85, 88–89,
  99–101, 103, 107–110, 135, 138,
  145–148, 155–158, 164–165, 170,
  172–174, 177, 181, 183–185, 187–189,
  191–198, 202–208, 210, 214, 216–221,
  223–228, 230–233, 237, 244–245, 248,
  250, 252–266, 277, 303
    see also bookmakers, horse racing,
    lotteries, pinball machines
Gambling Amendment Act of 1939
  197–199, 229, 257
Gambling Act 51 of 1965 244–245,
  260–261, 265–266
Gambling Amendment Act 39 of 1988
  264
Gambling Amendment Act 144 of
  1992 264
'Gambling, Betting Houses and
  Lotteries Suppression Bill' 232
Gay, Lewis C 241
General Law Amendment Act 62 of
  1955 228, 259
General Law Amendment Act 204 of
  1993 264
George, Edward 7
Gereformeerde Kerk (Doppers)
  21–23, 25, 30, 37, 84, 277–278
Gil, JJP Mendes 159
Gill, FJ 154
Gladstone, Lord 49
Goddard, R 190
gold mining 11–12, 15, 18–20, 22, 24,

31, 33, 48–49, 51–52, 56, 64–65, 72,
  85, 90, 114, 138–139, 146, 148, 157,
  164, 185–186, 224, 229, 247–248,
  252, 261, 286
gold standard 164, 186, 224
Government Gazette 199, 250, 304
Graf, Hermann 120
Great Depression 16, 42, 145, 147–148,
  164–165, 170, 175–176, 178, 182–185,
  188–189, 215, 255, 257, 297
Greek Orthodox 150, 257
Gregorowski, Reinhold 117
Grobler, JH 213
Guardian 83, 298
Gympie 31, 143

H
Hadfield, AC 76
Hansard 188, 250
Harvey, William 138
Henderson, Charles 177, 298
Henwood, Charlie 139
Herenigde National Party 202
Hertzog, Albert 234–238, 240,
  242–245, 259–260
Hertzog, JBM 13, 16, 49–50, 100,
  186–187, 202, 234
Hills, George 92–93, 95–97
Hofmeyr, HJ 169–170, 187, 196, 202,
  204–207, 210, 212, 216, 220
horse racing 4–9, 22–23, 25–26, 28, 33,
  37, 39–40, 46, 52–53, 65–66, 68, 70–74,
  79–80, 84–85, 88–94, 96–97, 103,
  106–107, 110–114, 118, 130, 140–141,
  145, 147, 152, 156, 159, 172, 183,
  188–189, 197, 203, 209, 218, 221, 225,
  245, 251–254, 257–258, 260, 263, 265
    see also bookmaking, dog racing,
    gambling
Horse Racing and Betting Restriction
  Act see Act 37 of 1909
Horse Racing and Betting Restriction
  Amendment Ordinance 11, 1917
  92–96, 257
House of Assembly 48–49, 97, 186,
  202, 204, 217, 222, 245

I

Ilanga lase Natal 281
IMC *see* interministerial committee
immigrant(s) 7, 21, 24–26, 48, 147,
   150, 172, 186, 189, 196, 198, 205,
   226, 228, 248–249, 251–252, 257, 287
imperialism 20, 25, 133, 146, 179, 245,
   247–248
India 28, 52, 101, 138, 143–145, 149,
   157, 174, 176, 216–217
industrial revolution, industrialisation
   6, 14, 19, 21, 103, 178, 180–182, 192,
   203, 221, 247–250
influenza pandemic 103, 110
Inland Revenue, Commissioner of 82,
   106, 116–117
interministerial committee (IMC)
   237–238, 242–244
'Internationale, The' 86–87
International Variety and Theatrical
   Agency Limited 126
investment(s) 3–5, 7–10, 20, 53, 63,
   68, 77–78, 80, 83, 90, 108, 122, 136,
   158–159, 164–165, 170, 247, 263
Ireland 18, 152, 188, 216, 220, 233,
   239, 254, 295

J

Jameson Raid 23, 130
Jeeves, Marguerite 156
Jockey Club of South Africa 28, 37, 69
Johannesburg 6, 12–18, 20, 22, 24,
   26–28, 30–31, 33–34, 41, 44, 46–48,
   50–53, 58–64, 66–71, 73–74, 76,
   80–82, 84–87, 89, 97, 100–104, 107,
   111–112, 114–115, 117, 122, 124, 126,
   128, 130, 132, 136–137–140, 142–144,
   149–152, 155, 157–158, 163, 166–167,
   171–172, 175, 180, 185, 187–189,
   191–193, 197, 207, 210–212, 218–220,
   223, 227, 230, 232, 245, 248, 252, 254
Johannesburg Athletics Club Ltd 34
Johannesburg City Council 16–17, 219
Juta, JC 120, 132, 153, 292

K

'Kaffir Boom' 23–24
Kahn, Sam 40, 223
'Kalgoorlie Hundreds' 32, 73
Keevy, JM 238, 243
Keller, Jack 175
Kentridge, Morris 131–132
Kidwell, Archibald A 179–184, 187,
   193–194, 203, 219, 302
Kimberley 24, 80, 82, 102
Krause, FET 119, 124–125, 128, 139, 142
Krige, John 140–141
Kruger, Paul (SJP) 21–22, 26, 75, 84,
   107, 116, 132, 147, 173, 175, 183,
   206–207, 257–258, 264
Krugersdorp 22, 74, 84, 85, 90, 94,
   140–141, 159

L

Labour Party 13, 16–17, 37, 39, 42, 49,
   50, 52, 67, 69, 77, 85–86, 92, 97, 104,
   107, 109–110, 113, 115, 123, 126,
   130–133, 147, 166, 174–177, 186,
   188, 202, 204–205, 216–217, 221,
   225, 251, 261
Laver, James 9, 177
Law No. 1 of 1892 226
Law No. 3 of 1902 154
Law No. 6 of 1899 226
Law No. 7 (Lottery Law) 1890 23, 26,
   29, 75, 117, 168, 174, 226
Law No. 7, 1896 25
legal system (the law) 18, 30, 68, 76,
   78, 94, 99, 108, 121, 144, 168–169,
   174, 187, 190, 197, 226–229
Legate, JB 23
Legislative Decree No. 104 (Portugal)
   161–162
Leo XIII (pope) 160
Leo, Leslie 29–30
Leverton, HG 203–204
Life, Sport and Drama 110–112, 117,
   119, 121, 126–127, 141, 143, 158
Lindolent, lottery agent 153
Lloyd, J Barclay 154
London Stock Exchange 247

Lotteries Act 57 of 1997 9, 265–266
Lotteries and Gambling Board 265
lotteries 3–4, 9, 14, 17–19, 23, 25,
    29–30, 46, 68, 70, 72–73, 75–80,
    82–85, 87, 90–91, 94–95, 99–114,
    116–120, 122–124, 126, 129–140,
    142–160, 162–168, 170–177, 183–186,
    188, 190–191, 195, 197, 199, 202–204,
    206–214, 216–218, 220–221, 226,
    229–234, 236–237, 239–245, 251–257,
    259–261, 266–269, 275, 286, 288, 292,
    295, 297–298, 302
    see also state lotteries, sweepstakes
        and lotteries
Lourenço Marques 23, 53, 56, 58–63,
    72–73, 76–77, 80, 82–83, 102,
    104–105, 109, 111, 122–123, 126,
    131, 133, 135–137, 139, 141, 144,
    150–153, 155–156, 158–161, 166,
    171, 173, 210–212, 220, 229–230,
    233, 253, 295, 298
Lourenço Marques Lottery (LML) 18,
    30, 73, 75, 99, 101–107, 109, 115–116,
    119, 122, 126, 132, 145, 147–149, 152,
    154, 164–165, 171–172, 195, 202,
    208, 212–214, 217, 229, 231–232,
    240, 251, 254, 288, 290, 297
'Lourenço Marques Money Discount
    Agency' 99
Louw, David 166–170
Lowe, CL 177
Luk, Stephen 83, 107
Lutheran church, Lutherans 172, 178,
    183
Luxemburg, Rosa 50, 67
Lynch, Mary (Seccombe) 28

M
MacLeod, RL 38
Macmillan, Harold 237
Madeley, Walter 147, 174–175, 177
Malan, DF 8, 186, 196, 198, 202, 216,
    258
Malta 18, 220, 233, 239, 254
Marxism 50, 299
Mason, Arthur Weir 121, 124–126

Meara, William 192
Meiring, AA 219
Merriman, John X 68
Methodist churches 6, 22, 28,
    178–183, 187, 192, 194, 203, 248, 257
    see also Primitive Methodists,
        Wesleyanism
Meyers, AH 115, 119
Miller, David 292
Miller, Hyman 142
Miller, William 61
Milner, Alfred 26, 257
mineworkers' strike, 1907 13, 27, 186,
    249
mineworkers' strike, 1913 13, 49, 108,
    147, 179, 186, 249
mineworkers' strike, revolt (1922) 13,
    17, 27, 65, 109, 123, 145, 147, 149,
    175, 187, 217, 249
mining industry 5–6, 11–13, 15,
    19–20, 24, 27, 29, 31–33, 35, 37, 44,
    49, 52, 56, 62, 65, 68–69, 71, 80, 90,
    102–103, 114, 118, 121, 123–124,
    126, 130, 133, 138–139, 143, 146,
    156–157, 166, 178, 180, 182–183,
    190, 192, 198, 203–204, 209, 217,
    224, 247–250, 252, 257, 263, 277
    see also gold mining, diamond
        mining
Mitchell, RS 167–169, 172
Modder West Gold Mining Company
    (MWGM) 52–53, 68, 90, 114,
    118–119, 121–122, 124, 127,
    138–139
moneylenders 27–28
Morris, lottery agent 153–155
Morris, Selig 154–155
Moseley, Barney 154–155
Moss, David 23
Mozambique 17, 23, 46, 56, 58, 62–63,
    76–77, 80, 101, 104, 106, 109–110,
    123, 133, 135–136, 144, 146, 152,
    155, 158–164, 167, 171, 190,
    201, 208–209, 211, 233, 237, 239,
    251–253, 263, 270
Muller, SL 244

municipal governance 17, 22, 26, 53, 74, 117, 131–132, 218, 252
MWGM *see* Modder West Gold Mining Company

N
Natal 48, 80–81, 84, 87, 102, 132, 138, 144, 147, 150, 153–155, 163, 171, 184, 194, 281–282
Natal Gambling Law Amendment Act 147
Nathan, Edward 79
nationalism
    African 14, 63, 261, 269
    Afrikaner 8, 13–14, 50, 100, 215, 218–219, 259–260, 267, 269
National Assembly 16, 223
National Association for the Advancement of Colored People 181
National Council of Women 194
National Lotteries Board 266, 268
National Lotteries Commission (NLC) 9, 266, 268
National Party 8–9, 50, 85, 170, 174, 177, 186, 202, 204, 206, 216, 220–221, 224, 226, 234, 245, 258–259, 262, 297, 299
    see also Purified National Party, Herenigde National Party
National Party (of RH Tatham) 50–51
National Thrift Movement 66, 193–194, 215, 285
National War Fund 210
Naylor, Amy 28
Naylor, Catherine 32–33, 81, 144
'Naylor Express' 123, 133, 139, 147, 151, 163, 171, 211
Naylor, George (Snr) 28
Naylor, George Sylvester 41, 52, 66, 71, 80–81, 137–138, 144, 148–149, 151–153, 155–157, 163–167, 171, 184, 195, 207–214, 218, 253–254
Naylor, Henry John (Harry) 41, 137, 148–149, 151–153, 155–157, 163–167, 184, 195, 207–210, 253–254

Naylor Investments Ltd 80
Naylor, Norman 218, 230–231
Naylor, Peter (grandson of Rufe) 230–231
Naylor, Peter Charles 41, 43, 52, 66, 138, 143–144, 148–149, 151–157, 163–167, 184, 195, 207–210, 217–218, 253–254
Naylor, Rupert Theodore (Rufe) 31–35, 37–48, 51–53, 55, 63–64, 66–81, 82–95, 99, 101–108, 110–133, 135–137, 139–145, 147–151, 153–159, 161, 163–168, 170–173, 184, 195, 209–211, 217, 230, 252–253, 256, 281–282, 285, 288, 290–292, 295
Naylor, Stanley 218, 230–231
Nazi, neo-Nazi 160, 172, 235, 244
Ndola 233, 239, 241, 243
Nederduitse Gereformeerde Kerk ('Doppers') 21–22, 183, 234
Nederduitse Hervormde Kerk 21
Nednil, Paul J (pseudonym) 210
Newclare 74, 84–85, 88–90, 94–97, 107, 114, 118, 129
New Tivoli and Picture Palace (Tivoli Theatre) 40, 42, 44
Nicol, William 219
NLC *see* National Lotteries Commission

O
O Africano 62–63, 158, 162, 164
Olifants Geraamte 139
Oppenheimer, Ernest 67, 114

P
Pact government 13, 16, 65, 147–149, 165, 172, 174–177, 186–187, 189, 201, 216–217, 257, 295
Page, J 192
Palmer, WA 192
Parsons, BJ 238
Penberthy, Phyllis 126–127, 141–143, 145
Phillips, Lionel 180

Phillips, WA 23
pinball machines, tables 9, 18, 185,
    189–191, 193–199, 203, 214, 220,
    229, 231, 244, 254, 257, 261, 264,
    300, 303–304
Pirow, Oswald 169, 172–174, 177, 183
Pius XI (pope) 159–162
Plunkett, GJ 79, 91–93
Polana Hotel 156
police (law enforcement) 7, 12, 17–18,
    25–26, 29–30, 37, 68, 76, 78, 80–81,
    83, 85, 93, 95–96, 99, 101–102,
    104, 107–108, 111–118, 120,
    127, 138, 140, 144, 149, 150–153,
    166–175, 177, 185, 187–188, 193,
    196, 198, 203, 206–207, 211–213,
    218, 224–235, 238, 242–245, 254,
    256–260, 263, 268, 286, 289, 295, 304
Ponzi, Charles (Ponzi schemes) 107,
    114, 141–142, 151, 157
Postle, Arthur 32–34
Post Office 87, 101, 104, 151, 172,
    177, 215, 236, 238–244, 259–260, 266
Post Office Act of 1958 83, 234, 266,
    287
Potchefstroom University for
    Christian Higher Education 184,
    219, 235, 242, 262
poverty 9, 14, 56, 61–62, 65, 84, 92,
    230, 255, 262, 266
Powell, R 79, 91–93
Prechner, Marks 40, 43–44
predestination 5, 21
Premier Starr-Bowkett Building
    Society 31
Presbyterian churches 6, 178, 183,
    204, 220
press, newspapers, journalists 27, 32,
    35, 40–41, 43, 80, 83, 87–89, 96, 104,
    107, 109–110, 113, 126, 137, 141,
    143, 145, 148, 152, 161, 166, 169,
    173, 185, 256
Pretoria 22, 40, 49–50, 74, 85, 90, 92,
    97, 105, 108, 112–113, 124, 128, 135,
    139, 145, 166, 170, 173–174, 210,
    213, 229, 241, 268

Pretorius, Frans 297
Primitive Methodist Africa Missionary
    Society 180
Primitive Methodists ('Ranters')
    178–182, 194, 248
    see also Methodists, Wesleyanism
Printers' Union 92
'Procession of Witness' 192
Proclamation 33 of 1901 26
prohibition (USA) 8, 148, 166, 181
Prohibition of Sports Pools Act of
    1949 222–223, 259
prostitution, brothels 11, 13, 22,
    25–26, 263
protectionism 50
Protestant ethic 3, 195, 255
Protestantism 3–4, 6, 8–9, 14, 17, 38,
    61–62, 75, 100, 123–124, 133, 148,
    150, 174–175, 178, 180, 182–183,
    188, 190–192, 195–197, 202–204,
    219, 221–222, 226, 228, 232, 238,
    249–251, 254–255, 257–261, 263, 277
    see also Calvinism
Provincial Council see Transvaal
    Provincial Council
Public (Civil) Service 86, 108, 212,
    216, 242
Public Safety Act 225
Public Service and Pensions Act, No.
    29 of 1912 108
Purified National Party 186, 196, 198

Q
Quinta da Boa Sorte, Mailana
    (Property of Good Fortune) 80, 159

R
racism 5, 19, 100, 211, 213, 219, 224,
    232–233, 235, 248, 263
    see also segregation
Rand Daily Mail 38, 166, 181
Rand Sporting Club (RSC) 74–75, 84,
    94–95, 107
recession(s) 5–6, 8, 27–28, 30, 38, 44,
    60, 65–66, 148, 185, 215, 255
religion 3, 5–8, 11–12, 14, 18, 20, 55,

63–64, 76–77, 84, 90, 136, 161, 170,
178, 181, 190, 192–193, 206–207,
219, 248, 250
republicanism 49–50, 62, 67, 89, 195,
201, 215, 233–234, 236–237, 260,
262, 265
Republican Party (Portugal) 62
Rerum Novarum 160
Retief, HJ 45
Rhodesia 17, 101, 175, 220, 222–223,
233, 239, 242–243, 251, 254
    Northern 17, 233, 239, 242, 251,
    254
    Southern 17, 220, 222, 233, 239,
    243, 251, 254
risk-taking 3–4, 28, 42, 86, 90–91, 133,
138, 157, 254
Robertson, Alfred 89, 94–96, 113–114
Robinson Deep Mine 45–46, 53, 63,
130
Rokeby Villa 43–44, 46
Roman Catholic Church, Catholics
17–18, 55, 58, 61, 63, 78, 123, 134,
145, 150, 159, 189, 208, 221, 226,
228, 250–253, 257, 263
Roos, Tielman 49
Rosenow, REG 227
Royal College of Missions 55
RSC *see* Rand Sporting Club
Rufe Naylor Lotteries Ltd 75–76, 78,
84, 104, 137, 165
Rufino, José dos Santos 144, 159, 164,
208–212, 214

S
Salazar, António de Oliveira 160, 208
Sampaio, Manuel 208–209
Sampson, Harry W 86, 88, 114
Savoy Café 191
Schlesinger, IW 44–46, 51, 53, 68,
111–112, 138, 156, 158, 285, 290–291
Schmulian, Chase 86, 88, 97, 102, 132,
142
Schmulian, LS (Lazar) 86–88, 97, 102,
117, 132
Schoeman, BJ 204

Scott-Luk ruling 83–84, 99, 107
Scott, William 83, 107
Seccombe, George 28
Seccombe, William Thorne 28–31,
33, 39–42, 46–49, 51–53, 66–69,
72, 74–77, 80–81, 84, 86, 95, 102,
107, 110, 115, 117, 119–121, 126,
128–129, 131–133, 138–140, 142,
144, 149, 153–155, 163, 280
secularism 3, 6–8, 19, 55, 63–64, 84,
136, 159–162, 170, 207, 265, 269
segregation 71, 84, 162, 195, 217, 228,
249, 252
Serner, Walter 141–142
Shawe, Glanville 168–169
Siebert, Albert 156
Simmer & Jack Mine 47
'Sixth Hundreds' 32–33
slavery 20, 25, 129
Smuts, JC 133, 136, 180, 186–189,
195–198, 202, 206–207, 210, 216,
222, 225, 244, 257
socialism 38, 67, 71, 109, 202, 216
    see also Labour Party
Social Relief Society of Mozambique
155
Sociedade Carvoeria Limitada 164
Sociedade Mercantil de Moçambique
163–164, 167
Sociedade Missionária das Missões
Ultramarinas 159
Soldiers' Hostel Fund 88
Sons of England 180
South African Compounds and
Interior Mission 180
South African Non-Proprietary
Trainers and Owners' Association 75
South African Party (SAP) 49, 131,
147, 170
South African Prudential Company
106, 111, 115, 118–119
South African Temperance Alliance
181
South African Typographical Union
86–87, 114
Southern Rhodesia State Lottery

(SRSL) 239–240, 242
Southward, Walter M 77–79, 105
South West Africa 47, 101
speculation 3–5, 7–8, 20, 24, 48, 78,
    99, 108, 110, 114, 172
sport 9, 24, 28, 31, 35, 47, 51, 74, 84,
    107, 110–112, 114, 117, 119, 121,
    126–127, 141, 143, 145, 158, 182,
    187, 204, 222–223, 251, 259–261, 266
'Sports Girl, The' 51
sports pools 222, 259, 261, 266
Sporting Times 28
Springs Racing Club 69
SRSL see Southern Rhodesia State
    Lottery
Stadium Sports Ground 35–36, 38,
    40–41, 43, 84, 86, 110, 114, 140,
    280–281
Stage & Cinema 111
Starr-Bowkett societies 29–31, 77, 102
state lotteries 18, 109–110, 132, 170,
    174, 177, 183, 188, 202, 216, 220,
    236, 239, 244, 256, 261, 266, 297
    see also lotteries
State Lotteries Act of 1984 (Ciskei)
    266
Staten, OW 97
Steyn, Colin 205–206, 210, 223
Steyn, D 173
Steyn, HS 213–214
stockbrokers 6, 9
stock exchange 6, 37, 223, 247
strikes see mineworkers' strikes
suffrage (women) 50
Sul do Save 133
Sunday Observance Act 191
Sunday observation laws 23, 42, 111,
    182, 187, 191
Sunday Times 37–39, 66, 104,
    108–110, 112
Suppression of Communism Act 225,
    232
Swart, CR 222–223, 226–227, 230
Swaziland 80, 173, 237
sweepstakes and lotteries 17, 23,
    25–26, 76, 84, 87, 101, 147, 165–166,

174, 175, 176, 184, 216, 220, 289
    Australian and Tasmanian 251
    Calcutta 101, 152, 165–166,
        175–177, 251, 297
    Dublin/Irish 152, 165–166, 176,
        220, 223, 233, 297
    Lourenço Marques see Lourenço
        Marques Lottery (LML)
    Malta 220, 233
    Northern Rhodesia (Ndola,
        Kitwe, Mufulira) 233, 239, 254
    Southern Rhodesia 220, 223, 233,
        254

T
Tatham, FS 154–155
Tatham, Ralph H 48–53, 67–69,
    74–75, 77, 81, 84, 86, 89, 90, 93, 95,
    97, 106, 110–112, 114, 118–122,
    124–129, 133, 138–139, 154, 282, 285
Temperance and Social Welfare
    Committee 187
Theron, RA 183
Thompson, EP 178, 181
Thwaites, Colonel 212
Tindall, Benjamin Arthur 191, 195
Tivoli Theatre see New Tivoli and
    Picture Palace
tobacco industry 22, 77, 182
trade unions 16, 42, 123, 185, 262
Transkei 236–237, 263, 266
Transvaal 16–17, 28, 35, 37–38, 40,
    48, 67, 69, 76–77, 80–81, 85–86, 89,
    97, 109, 112–113, 124, 138, 140, 153,
    155, 157, 166, 171–172, 179, 184,
    188, 202, 207, 226
Transvaal gambling commission 35
Transvaal Provincial Council 16–17,
    48, 67, 69, 85–86, 88, 92–94, 97,
    107, 109–110, 112–113, 115–116,
    124–125, 132, 166, 172, 188, 202,
    207, 221, 259, 288, 291
Turffontein racecourse 71, 130

U

Union of South Africa 26, 38, 41, 48,
65, 75–76, 78, 80, 84, 86, 101–102,
110, 112, 139, 143, 150, 152, 166,
168, 175, 184, 204, 212, 215, 230,
234, 251, 258, 260
United Methodist Church of South
Africa 178, 192
see also Methodist churches,
Primitive Methodists,
Wesleyanism
United Party (UP) 187, 196, 202,
204–207, 213, 216–217, 220–221,
223–224, 226, 244, 258
see also Fusion government
United Printing & Publishing Co Ltd
86–87, 117
United States of America (USA) 7–8,
33, 40, 66, 114, 107, 148, 151, 156,
181, 188–189, 224
Unity Stakes 175
UP see United Party
urbanisation 14, 181, 192, 196, 219,
258

V

Vachell, K 95
Van den Bergh, J 183
Van den Bergh, RJ 238–240, 242
Van der Linden, Paulus Johannes
(Paul) 81, 102, 126, 132, 138, 144,
150–151, 153–155, 157, 163, 166,
171, 184, 208, 210, 212–214, 217,
230, 287, 296
Van der Walt, Ben 170
Van Rensburg, G 170
Van Veyeren, Christian Tiberius
Zwanepoel 67, 85–86, 88–95,
97, 113, 115–116, 120, 124–125,
128–129, 133, 288
Vasilos, Peter 191
vaudeville theatre 40–42, 44
Verwoerd, HF 219, 234–235, 243,
245, 259, 299

Vorster, BJ 235–238, 242–245,
259–260

W

Wage Board 185
Wanless, William 176–177
Ward, Justice 128
Weber, Max 3, 220
Wesleyanism 178, 181, 191, 194, 203
Wesley, John 178, 183
West Rand Racing Club (WRRC)
84–85, 88, 94–96, 102
Wiehahn, NE 265, 267
Witwatersrand 5, 14–20, 22, 25–27,
30, 42, 48–49, 52–53, 56, 58, 60–61,
65–66, 70, 73, 77–78, 80, 82–83, 89,
97, 100–103, 108, 133, 135, 137–138,
145, 148–150, 156, 162, 175, 179–180,
182, 186, 188–189, 191, 202, 204–205,
207, 214, 227, 229, 236, 247, 249,
251–252, 256–258, 261, 263–264
working classes 4–7, 13–18, 20, 23,
24–28, 29, 31, 35, 37–39, 41, 46–47,
49–50, 60, 61, 62, 65–68, 70, 75,
78–79, 84–85, 88, 91, 100, 102,
108–110, 115, 122–124, 132–133,
145, 146, 147–148, 150, 156, 165,
174–176, 180, 182–186, 187–189,
191, 193–197, 198–199, 202–205,
211, 214–215, 217–222, 226, 229,
231, 234, 236, 248–251, 252,
254–257, 259–263, 297, 303
World War I 15, 18, 47, 70, 85, 103,
122, 142, 145, 179, 184, 189, 192,
203–204, 209, 231, 233, 251, 254,
258, 261, 285, 295
World War II 15, 18, 25, 183, 185,
188, 201, 210–211, 214–215, 217,
225, 235, 244, 257–258, 262
Wyndham, Hugh 97

Z

Zuid-Afrikaansche Republiek (ZAR)
20–21, 25, 116, 257